EAP Esse

D0515103

A teacher's guide to principles and practice

Olwyn Alexander | Sue Argent | Jenifer Spencer

Published by

Garnet Publishing Ltd.
8 Southern Court, South Street
Reading RG1 4QS, UK
www.garneteducation.com

Copyright © 2008 Garnet Publishing Ltd.

The right of Olwyn Alexander, Sue Argent and
Jenifer Spencer to be identified as the authors of
this work has been asserted in accordance with
the Copyright, Design and Patents Act 1988.

All rights reserved.

No part of this publication may be reproduced,
stored in a retrieval system, or transmitted
in any form or by any means, electronic,
mechanical, photocopying, recording or
otherwise, without the prior permission of
the Publisher. Any person who does any
unauthorized act in relation to this publication
may be liable to criminal prosecution and civil
claims for damages.

First published 2008
ISBN 978-1-85964-419-5

British Cataloguing-in-Publication Data
A catalogue record for this book is available
from the British Library.

Printed and bound in Lebanon by
International Press

Production

Project management: Martin Moore
Project consultant: Fiona McGarry
Editing: Alison Walford, Carole White
Proof reading: Laura Booth
Index: Sue Lightfoot
Design: Rob Jones, Christin Helen Auth

The authors and publisher would like to thank
the following for permission to reproduce
copyright material:

Zhang, X-Y and Austin, B. (2005) Haemolysins
in Vibrio species. © Journal of Applied
Microbiology. Blackwell Publishing

Atkinson, R.L. et al., Hilgard's Introduction to
Psychology, 12th edition. © 1996 Wadsworth,
a part of Cengage Learning, Inc. Reproduced
by permission. www.cengage.com/permissions

Wright, J. V. UK Political System ©
Pulse Publications

North, R. and Hort, L. (2002) Cross-cultural
influences on employee commitment in the
hotel industry: some preliminary thoughts.
© Research and Practice in Human Resource
Management, 10 (1), 22-34.

Pinker, S. (1994) The Language Instinct: The New
Science of Language and Mind. © Reproduced
by permission of Penguin Books Ltd.

'Does Class Size Matter?' Reprinted with
permission. Copyright © 2001 by Scientific
American, Inc. All rights reserved.

© 2003 IEEE. Reprinted, with permission, from
Adaptive Real-time Particle Filters for Robot
Localization, in Robotics and Automation Vol.
2 pp.2836-2841

Nunan, D. (1993) Research Methods in Language
Learning © Cambridge University Press

Longman Dictionary of Contemporary English
(2004) © Longman

Cambridge Advanced Learner's Dictionary
(2003) © Cambridge University Press

Every effort has been made to trace copyright
holders and we apologize in advance for any
unintentional omission. We will be happy to
insert the appropriate acknowledgements in
any subsequent editions.

Acknowledgements

The principles and practices in this book have attached themselves to us over three lifetimes of teaching. Although we reference many as originating from books, journals and conferences, adopting them as indispensable parts of our thinking is largely the result of seeing them at work in teachers and students we have known. For this, we owe a great debt of gratitude to staff, students and colleagues in:

Adult Basic Education Service, Edinburgh [now part of the Scottish Executive's Adult Literacy Initiative]

British Association of Lecturers of EAP

Heriot-Watt University, Edinburgh, and Approved Learning Partners for its External Programmes in Tehran and Kuala Lumpur

Institute for Applied Language Studies, University of Edinburgh

Jiangsu Polytechnic University, Changzhou, Jiangsu Province, China

Papua New Guinea Institute (now University) of Technology, Lae, Papua New Guinea

Scottish Association for the Teaching of English as a Foreign Language

Stevenson College of Further Education, Edinburgh

University of Nottingham Ningbo Campus, Ningbo, Zhejiang Province, China

York Associates Business Trainer Training, York

Dedication

To our students, who have taught us so much

Contents

To the reader

This book is for teachers of English for Academic Purposes (EAP), who prepare students for study at university or college through the medium of English. EAP is taught worldwide in a variety of contexts, by teachers from a wide range of backgrounds (many of whom are non-native English speakers) and is very different from other kinds of English teaching. Making the transition to EAP teaching is not straightforward, and teachers need a thorough induction and on-going support if they are to teach effectively in university contexts. This book aims to provide both.

In the UK, EAP has expanded considerably with the internationalization of universities. Most further and higher education institutions have well-established teaching centres and the field now has its own institution, the British Association for Lecturers of EAP (BALEAP), with an active research base and a dedicated journal. However, there are very few teacher training courses specifically for EAP and as yet no recognized EAP teaching qualification. Most teachers have learned the craft from working alongside experienced EAP teachers, and through collaboration with subject lecturers. The gap in training is beginning to be addressed, for example, by the University of Cambridge ESOL Examinations, whose revised syllabus for the Diploma in ELT now includes an EAP option, and by BALEAP, which has specified a set of competencies desirable for effective EAP teaching. These include knowledge of the norms and practices of universities and the ability to help students to acquire the language and skills necessary to function in a higher education context. Several institutions now incorporate an EAP module in taught masters courses, and others offer short professional development courses in EAP.

Since 2002, we have regularly run a short EAP teacher development course at Heriot-Watt University for teachers who work with students preparing for or already following university courses. Our course aims to build teachers' confidence by helping them to recognize good EAP practice and to reflect on how they can adopt it in their own context. This book has been developed as a result of conversations with the many participants who have attended our course. It is intended to provide a framework for teachers to reflect on adaptations in methodology and content which may be required to meet the needs of EAP students and to feel confident about using these new approaches.

Although there is now a great deal of research in language description, language learning and language pedagogy, it is difficult for teachers to keep up to date with the many and varied research strands. There is also often a considerable time lag before principles derived from this research begin to inform practice, particularly in published teaching materials. Participants on our teacher training course sometimes report feeling daunted – at times overwhelmed – when faced with a confusing array of course books, following different approaches.

Our aim in this book is to bridge the gap between theory and classroom practice in EAP. Our principles derive from an extensive review of current literature, but they have also been tested in our classrooms in order to find out what works. We translate these principles into practical approaches and, in the accompanying CD, into actual classroom materials which exemplify these approaches.

Reflection is an important aspect of teaching because it encourages teachers to consider the effects which their beliefs about teaching have on their students. We provide awareness-raising tasks, frequently based on authentic case studies, which are designed to help you to reflect on a variety of classroom situations. You become the observer of typical problematic teaching situations, and reflect on the ways in which these could be addressed. Those case studies which deal with situations when teaching goes wrong or fail to address students' needs are often based on our own experiences and classroom difficulties over many years of development as EAP teachers.

Some of the tasks are simple, practical and brief, for example, sorting or prioritizing items. There are also tasks involving more open-ended reflection on your own experience or classroom practices. Some tasks may seem very easy while others are more challenging. However, you should never feel that you are being tested. The purpose of the tasks and case studies is to encourage thought and analysis, and often there is no single correct answer. Each task has a suggested answer either in the form of a commentary in the running text, or indicated in a later part of the chapter. You might find it helpful to look briefly at a task and then study the commentary before trying the task for yourself. Our intention is for the book to provide the same kind of support and guidance that you might gain from working alongside an experienced EAP teacher.

We expect the book to be read in a variety of ways by readers with different purposes. You can read it carefully from beginning to end to raise your awareness of current principles and practice in EAP teaching and learning, or you can dip into it for guidance on specific aspects. The chapters are free standing so that if you want to explore one particular theme, you can go straight to the relevant chapter. You can gain an impression of the contents of each chapter by reading the aims at the beginning and the conclusion at the end. You can find a sense of the approach that each chapter takes by skimming through the tasks and case studies. You can, of course, choose not to do the tasks and simply read the text. However, we believe that, for teachers as well as students, being told something is not as effective as being shown something. The tasks, case studies and classroom materials show you good practice in a way that comes close to working with an experienced colleague or teacher trainer. If you want to study a theme in greater depth, you can find a list of recommended reading at the end of each chapter. References to specific sources cited in the text and cross-references to relevant material in the other chapters are listed in the notes and bibliography at the end of the book.

Many of the chapters follow a similar format. There is an orientation to each aspect of EAP, usually through student and teacher comments. This is followed by an exploration of what happens in a university context and an indication of how you can support students in your classroom.

Chapter 1: The context of EAP explores what is meant by academic purposes and examines the expectations of the stakeholders in EAP: the academics who will interact with students, the students themselves, and the teachers. Many of the themes that will be developed later in the book are introduced here.

Chapter 2: Text analysis shows you how to analyse texts so that you can read and make sense of them even if you do not understand all the content. The ideas in this chapter are important for understanding the key terms and the approach used in the rest of the book. The chapter is a tutorial with exercises to work through to clarify the concepts being presented.

Chapter 3: Course design uses insights gained from text analysis and from understanding the context of EAP to introduce principles for course design, taking into account the constraints of a context and the needs of students in their target courses. It also considers the implementation of a syllabus through appropriate methodology, including computer-mediated learning.

Chapter 4: Reading, 5: Vocabulary and **6: Writing** show how these are strongly integrated in the academic context, and build on the concepts introduced in Chapter 2. These chapters outline the skills and strategies required by academic readers and writers and suggest how these can be developed in the EAP classroom.

Chapter 7: Listening and speaking considers the skills of listening and speaking and shows how these are different in academic and ELT contexts. In particular, it deals with the notion of authenticity, and also looks at possible cultural barriers to oral participation.

Chapter 8: Critical thinking and **9: Student autonomy** examine two important requirements for academic success: the ability to think critically and function autonomously. The chapters outline what these abilities involve in an academic context and show how they can be brought into the EAP classroom at all levels.

Chapter 10: Assessment attempts to clarify key concepts in this challenging area so that you can evaluate the suitability of tests and exams for your students and grade their work consistently.

Finally, it is important for readers to go beyond this book and beyond further reading in developing their professional practice, particularly in collaboration with other teachers, by attending workshops and conferences, by team teaching, and by sharing ideas with colleagues. We wish you all success and enjoyment in your continuing professional development as EAP teachers.

Chapter 1: The context of EAP

This chapter will examine:

- academic purposes and expectations
- the implications of these for EAP students and teachers

You will have the opportunity to:

- reflect on your expectations as an EAP teacher
- reflect on EAP students' needs
- relate these needs to the contents of the book

The first question general English teachers new to EAP are likely to ask is:

- *How different is this kind of teaching from what I already do?*

In a sense, there is no such thing as general English language teaching (ELT). Every English language teacher is operating in a specific situation and has to understand as much as possible about the context in which teaching and learning are taking place. Frequently, what is taught is dictated by one of a wide variety of examinations of general English proficiency[1], which may be international or local. Often, the aims of students have less to do with passing exams and more to do with broadly improving levels of language ability. In EAP, however, the teaching and learning context is highly specific. The following task is designed to help you to think about the key features of EAP which make it distinct.

Task 1

Check your understanding of the key features of EAP.

- Cover the right-hand column in Table 1 below.
- Try to identify what features differentiate EAP from general English, and check each suggestion.

Table 1: *The differences between general English language teaching (ELT) and EAP*

Context	General English Language Teaching	English for Academic Purposes
1 What drives the syllabus?	Level driven: the main focus is what a student can and cannot do now.	Goal driven: the main focus is where a student has to get to, often in relation to a specific academic course.
2 Time available	Relatively flexible: a student may opt in and out of ELT at various points in adult life with different motivations.	Not flexible: time is strictly limited and an EAP course is probably a 'one-off' endeavour for a student.
3 What is at stake for the student?	For most students, the outcome is a sense of personal achievement or certification of the language level attained, not necessarily involving high stakes.	For almost all students, the only relevant outcome is entry to or successful completion of university study. Failure is costly in time, money and career prospects.
People		
4 Student motivation	Motives are varied and general. Students often learn general English out of interest in the language and associated cultures or a wish to become part of a global community.	Motives are specific. A high proportion of EAP students learn English as a means to entering a course at an English-medium university or in order to access a particular academic community
5 Teachers	Attracts predominantly graduates in the humanities, e.g., English (usually literature), linguistics or European languages.	Attracts a significant number of graduates in evidence-based academic disciplines, such as science, social science, business studies.

6	Teacher–student roles	Unequal: teachers are seen as language experts and students as language novices.	Teachers and students are more equal: both are learning about the academic community.

Teaching and learning content

7	Language content (grammar and vocabulary)	Potentially, the totality of the English language is possible content. Usually, students need to be equipped for a wide range of communicative situations.	Content is limited to academic discourse, e.g., emphasis on academic style: academic vocabulary and associated grammar and discourse features.
8	Language-skills balance	Speaking and listening are usually given more importance than reading and writing. Exams or students may determine the weighting given.	The main emphasis is on reading and writing. Some EAP students have a specific need, such as academic reading or writing for publication.
9	Materials	Texts and tasks are often chosen for self-expression and are usually short and quickly covered; personal response and creativity are valued.	Texts and tasks are drawn from degree study. They are for communicating information and are inherently long and dense. Clarity and objectivity are valued in student writing.
10	Text choice	Texts are often chosen from entertaining, easily accessible genres. Traditionally, there has been an emphasis on sentence grammar, with topic driving text choice.	Text choice is based on academic genres: students learn about audience, purpose and organization as well as rhetorical functions and information structure.[2]

11	Text exploitation	Variety and pace of activities are important in delivery, leading to a tendency to move quickly from text to text to maintain interest, each text having a different topic and learning focus.	Texts require more time for full exploitation. Each text may have a range of learning focuses. Texts may be linked thematically.
12	Other skills content	There is little emphasis on study skills, or these focus on language learning only. Cognitive skills are not explicitly included.	Study skills are emphasized and made explicit, particularly learner independence and cognitive skills, especially critical thinking.

A later section of this chapter, *The distinctive features of teaching and learning in EAP*, discusses the contents of Table 1 more fully.

The process of adjustment from general English to EAP teaching can involve some major shifts in approach. However, this does not mean abandoning good teaching practice. When the important differences between general English and EAP are over-emphasized, teachers sometimes begin to feel insecure and leave their most valuable skills at the EAP classroom door. EAP and other kinds of English teaching share an underlying core of methodology: all require teachers to have a sound grasp of how to promote language learning and manage all aspects of the classroom. However, a teacher wishing to adapt to the EAP context first has to explore that context in detail.

Academic discourse communities and academic expectations: joining the tribe

The internationalization of higher education has brought students from all over the world into English-medium universities, but this is not a new phenomenon. The original concept of a university was not an educational facility for local young people but a focal point where groups of international scholars sought permission to settle from the city authorities.[3] As early as the 12th century, students from a range of cultural and linguistic backgrounds crossed the Alps or sailed across the Mediterranean to study Italian thinking on law, the Greek philosophy of Aristotle or to gain access to translations of the great Arabic writers on science, medicine and mathematics. Similarly, scholars journeyed across Asia to share philosophical and religious ideas. In recent decades, modern university campuses have become more aligned to this original concept.

Greek, Latin and Arabic have all been academic lingua francas in their time. More recently, a variety of languages, including German, French and Russian, have fulfilled that role in different disciplines. At present, domination by English-speaking academic discourse communities means that thousands of international scholars are studying, researching and teaching in English-medium universities. They are today's travelling scholars and they include EAP students, who use English as the lingua franca for their academic purposes.

An academic discourse community is a group of academic practitioners (teachers, researchers and students) who share a particular discourse or way of representing, thinking and talking about the world. The members of each academic community share a culture which may differ considerably from the cultures of other academic communities. For example, the Engineering and History departments in a university are very different in terms of the way they pursue and communicate knowledge and the way their members acquire status and interact with the real world. The differences are driven by what is being studied and have profound effects on how the communities operate. However, these are human communities with all the characteristics that the word *human* implies, including rituals and taboos. It may seem surprising to think of anything labelled *academic* as susceptible to such beliefs, but they are an inevitable feature of all human groups. Becher used the metaphor of the *tribe* in his study of academic discourse communities to highlight their important social features, for example, their customs, language and hierarchical structure.[4]

Classroom materials 1.1 *Welcome to academia* introduces students to the idea of an academic community. New recruits to the tribe need to go through a period of induction (or even initiation) before they can become experts. They have to learn the specific culture of the tribe – its particular tasks, values, assumptions, history and aspirations – and its language. As well as highlighting this specificity, the metaphor of a *tribe* also puts into perspective the essentially relative values of academic discourse communities: there is nothing intrinsically better about one community than another – for example, engineers compared with historians, or the English-speaking academic community as a whole compared with that of any other language community; they are simply different.

Whether the territory is engineering or economics, estate management or ecology, teaching and learning in different academic disciplines share many features. The main methods of teaching and learning at university have been summarized by Laurillard:

- *acquisition* – lectures and reading
- *practice* – exercises and problems
- *discussion* – tutorials and seminars
- *discovery* – fieldtrips and practicals[5]

Task 2

- To what extent do you think that EAP teachers need to prepare students for these methods of teaching and learning?
- To what extent do EAP teachers use these methods themselves?

EAP teachers try to prepare students as fully as possible to benefit from the methods of teaching and learning they will meet at university. A major part of this preparation is the acquisition of the academic language that will be used in the lectures, reading materials, discussions and seminars in Laurillard's list. In addition, students need to develop attitudes, approaches and strategies that make the best use of the teaching and learning they will encounter. Rather than simply telling students about these aspects of academic study, teachers need to ensure that students experience them.[6] This means that EAP teachers should themselves adopt methods aligned with those used at university. EAP is best taught through discussion and discovery, using a problem-solving approach, practical tasks and fieldtrips into academic territory, for example, to analyse features of authentic texts and to research authentic practices. The EAP classroom is a context for research. Both teachers and students in EAP are learning about the target academic community and this requires the teacher–student roles to be more equal than in most general English classes. EAP teachers bring to the classroom linguistic expertise and knowledge of teaching methodology. Students may bring expertise in their subject disciplines, which teachers need to call on to exploit authentic academic texts effectively. The dialogue between them is an important focus of teaching and learning.[7]

In many academic courses at university, it is quite common for professional bodies to have input into the course design and assessment procedures so that students are adequately prepared for the world of work following their studies. Where this happens, the courses are aligned with professional practice and may contain elements that are special to the particular community of practice. However, many elements are common to a wide range of university courses, including undergraduate programmes. Table 2 below outlines the input, skills required and assessment methods for a typical taught masters course.[8]

Table 2: *Outline of a typical taught masters course*

Input into course	Skills required during course	Assessment methods
lectures	group working	critical essay
reading	problem solving	critical reading report
group work	search methods	examination essay
case studies	computer skills	case study essay
presentations	critical reading	business report
discussions	critical analysis	presentation
role play	synthesis	site visit report
tutorial groups	evaluation	dissertation
computer labs	conceptualization	
self-assessment	application	
reflective assessments	interdisciplinary	
peer assessment	understanding	
guest lecture		
problem-based learning		
site visits		
online discussion		
virtual learning environment		

These elements would need to be clarified in much more detail to be included in an EAP course but the table gives a flavour of the range of activities and skills involved.

Task 3

- Which elements shown in Table 2 might be particularly difficult to introduce or simulate in an EAP course?

- What important aspects of university study do not appear to be represented here but also need to be included in an EAP course?

The answer to the first question in Task 3 depends to a large extent on the teaching situation and the constraints on the EAP course. Understanding of the masters course at the level of detail required by EAP teachers might not be feasible, especially for those working outside a university. An EAP course taught on a university site with good resources and good relationships with other departments could probably introduce or simulate almost all these elements in authentic detail. However, EAP teachers who cannot access such detail can still broadly simulate a university approach. Group work, role play, presentations and discussions are fairly standard in any English language class. EAP teachers can add to these the use of authentic lectures and reading texts as input and require written and spoken outputs broadly in line with academic courses. Case studies and problem solving activities are rich resources for both language and academic skills. Promoting autonomy through self, peer and reflective assessment can also be an important feature of EAP practice, together with search methods in academic reading and critical approaches in a range of course elements. The following chapters explore these possibilities in detail. Some elements may well differ from one academic discipline or level of study to another, for example, a business report for an undergraduate Business Studies course may not be the same as one for a postgraduate course in Civil Engineering. However, generally all elements should be considered for inclusion in an EAP course, if only at a rudimentary level. Even site visits are possible, for example, to a university open day or a university website.

At the same time as helping students to become familiar with the methods of university study and to acquire appropriate skills and approaches, it is essential to remember that an EAP course is first and foremost a language course. The most important component in an EAP course is academic English, particularly the strategies to continue learning it beyond the duration of the EAP course.

The hidden curriculum

Because academic discourse communities are like tribes with territories, not all their expectations of newcomers are as explicit as those in Table 2. Sharpling talks of discourse communities within universities as involving 'a game of "insiders, outsiders and power relations", in which a cultural mismatch can frequently occur, sometimes with severe consequences'. [9] A major aim of EAP practice is to help non-native English speakers to become academic 'insiders'. Inevitably, EAP practitioners are involved in the power relations of the game and may need to take a critical stance in relation to how their students are affected. A later section of the chapter will return to this issue. At the very least, they need to be aware of the potential effects of the hidden curriculum on students.

Some of the rules of the game, i.e., the academic expectations, are well known and common to all the academic communities – for example, the need to publish research. Some rules are practised completely unconsciously. This applies especially to conventions to do with relationships in the academic hierarchy. Other rules may be obscure, contradictory or even disputed within academic communities.

In English-medium academic institutions, expectations about status and access to experts are particularly well hidden. For example, the head of a university department might be dressed exactly like the students, but he is nevertheless accustomed to his status being acknowledged through subtly deferential ways of approaching him, choice of language and other aspects of behaviour.[10] International students may expect faculty deans and professors to dress smartly, according to their status, so as to be immediately recognizable. Such students may be shocked to find these members of staff seem indistinguishable from everyone else in a UK university. Student expectations about how to approach these important people can lead to serious difficulties. The English-speaking academic community likes to think of itself as egalitarian and inclusive, particularly towards students, but in reality it can appear hostile, hierarchical and exclusive to students who do not know the appropriate conventions and procedures. Relaxed and friendly lecturers who emphasize their availability can be taken at their word and find that students phone, e-mail or turn up at their offices more frequently than they would wish. In fact, teachers in China and in the Middle East[11] are likely to be more accessible to students outside the classroom than is usual in the UK.

Some expectations are rarely articulated in clear, unambiguous language by academics. For example, it is not obvious what exactly lecturers mean by *autonomy, critical thinking* or even *academic English*, yet they use these terms to describe the requirements of university study.[12] When there are differences between academics about which rules to apply, the EAP game becomes particularly difficult. In some UK university departments, non-native English speakers are encouraged to have their written texts proofread by a native English speaker before submission; in others, this practice is strictly forbidden.[13] Rules about correct referencing vary a great deal not only between disciplines but also between departments in the same discipline at different universities.

Student expectations

The rules of the academic community apply not only to students whose purpose is entry to undergraduate and postgraduate courses in English-medium universities, but increasingly to a wider group, including academics wishing to publish papers in English-medium journals and high school children trying to achieve English-medium academic qualifications. Such students need to know exactly what is meant when told, for example, to use academic language, to be more critical, to think independently and not to plagiarize. They need to know what is expected in terms of oral and written communication, how they should behave and how they will be assessed in order to be accepted into or make progress within the community. They are among the 'outsiders' mentioned earlier and if their expectations are not aligned with those of the particular academic tribe they wish to join, then there can be major difficulties for them.[14]

EAP students may be used to a completely different set of rules about referring to the work of others. In their high school, they may have learned to quote verbatim from the works of great academics without necessarily naming them.[15] To paraphrase a great writer might be seen as a transgression.[16] The Chinese academic expectation is that the reader as well as the writer is responsible for filling in the background knowledge and understanding the implications of academic texts.[17] This contrasts strongly with the directness and explicitness with which English academic texts are usually written. One student explained this to me by saying that if the model answer I had written for the class were translated into Chinese, it would be suitable for nine-year-old readers.

Cultures vary tremendously in terms of how to approach other people when you need something from them. Students often have to approach academic staff in order to get information, support or advice and, in doing so, can encounter a minefield of potential cultural clashes, as the following authentic case study shows.

Task 4

Read the case study and suggest what went wrong in the encounter.

- What would you advise the student to do?

Case study A:
Accessing academic staff

A postgraduate student found herself struggling to follow lectures and produce coursework in her first term of an engineering course at a UK university. She knew that her problem was English and discussed the issue with her supervisor in the first term exam week. He suggested she enrol on the next EAP course and gave her the name of the tutor who ran it. She went straight to the tutor's office, where she found the tutor surrounded by piles of exam scripts. She began the discussion as follows:

- *I am a student from [country]. I would like to tell you about my situation so that you can give me some advice.*

She was dismayed to find the tutor rather dismissive and abrupt. She came away from the encounter not really clear what the tutor had said or what to do next.

In the UK, particularly at busy times, e.g., during exams, academic staff can be very stressed, so this student picked the worst time for an unannounced approach. The harassed tutor interpreted the student's opening sentence very literally as a request for what could turn out to be a lengthy tutorial and advice session. The student was not sure, as she explained later, what the procedure was for joining the course and thought she might have to 'pass' a lengthy interview or series of interviews. In fact, she simply needed to find out more about the course and then complete an application form. When I suggested a better opening sentence would have been:

- *I would like to join next term's EAP class. Could you give me some details, and an application form, please?*

she was shocked at the brevity and directness of my suggestion, even more so when I suggested she made the request by e-mail. Her expectations about politeness and respectful behaviour, as well as procedure, were completely misaligned with the context in which she was trying to operate.

Native speakers of English can experience a similar mismatch in expectations when they move from high school to university or from one academic discipline to another. One EAP teacher colleague thought she had to buy all the books on the first booklist she was given and spent her entire first year undergraduate book allowance in the first week of term. Another was deeply shocked to find her first essay in a masters module had been given a low mark for being too 'undergraduate', with no feedback to explain what was wrong.[18]

Task 5

Think back to when you went to university to begin your degree studies.

- What cultural mismatches did you experience in changing from an outsider to an insider?

In a new academic context, the rules or expectations that EAP students bring from their previous educational experiences can operate at different levels, from how academic staff dress to how to incorporate the ideas of others in their own writing. Here is a constructed case study of some imaginary students who have just begun undergraduate courses in a UK university. Although none of the students is real, their perceptions and reactions are authentic and drawn from the experiences of a range of international students.[19]

Task 6

Read the case study and try to predict any problems these students are likely to face as their courses proceed.

• Think of their expectations of study generally, of language use, and of assessment methods.

Case study B:

Early in the first semester of year one of a degree, four international students are e-mailing their friends to report on the experience of studying in the UK. Here are some extracts.

Student 1

I'm really enjoying my course, the lecturers are not strict like our high school teachers were and we don't have to work as hard as we did at school – only a few classes a week. I have lots of spare time. We don't have any exams until January. I have some long essays to write (they are the same as term papers) but not until December, which is several weeks away. There's a week at the end of the semester with no classes so I've booked a cheap ticket home.

Student 2

There's a long list of books that I have to read – I don't know how I'm going to read them all. After two weeks, I'm still reading the first book on the list. I don't really understand it – but it's by my professor and he's very famous, so I don't really expect to understand.

I did one short essay this week. It was about a topic we did in school so it was quite easy. I was very disappointed with my grade but I can see my tutor about this. She wrote on it that she wanted a critical essay. She is very friendly and I'm sure when I explain how hard I worked, she will improve my grade. I have been going to her office every day to find her but she is never there, even though I leave notes saying I'm looking for her.

Student 3

The lectures are very difficult. They're about one hour long and I can't catch what the lecturers say. But there are only five every week so I've decided that I can miss them and use the time to get the information I need from the books on the book list. I can ask the lecturers about the lecture topics because they said we could go to them for help if we need to.

As well as lectures, we have to go to tutorials. There are about ten students and a lecturer in each tutorial. Some of the other students talk a lot, but I prefer just to listen. They usually talk about things that came up in the lectures so it's a chance for me to catch up.

Student 4

The other students are OK but they don't speak to me much. They seem to spend a lot of time chatting in the coffee bar. Many of them are not English, and they don't understand me when I speak so mostly I go around with two friends from home who have just started, like me. This week I am supposed to start a group project which means working with some other students. They had a meeting but I didn't go. I think I'll just do it by myself

In some countries, students expect to work extremely hard in high school, but to be able to relax and 'coast' at university. Student 1 is severely underestimating the amount of work he has to do outside lectures, particularly the sustained and independent effort expected in writing the long essays. He should have begun working on these already. The week with no classes will not be an extension to the holiday as he assumes. It may well be a reading or study week prior to exams or a week in which to write up a group project. In the latter case, his absence will be interpreted as laziness. It will affect his classmates and possibly their grades as well as his own. He will not be popular if he just disappears.

Student 2 seems to have no strategies for purposeful reading, for example, assessing the usefulness of a book for a particular piece of coursework.[20] His slowness suggests that he is reading page by page from the beginning instead of surveying the book first and reading selectively. He also probably expects to read the material only once. He is not very worried by his failure to make sense of it because this confirms his perception of himself as a non-expert. Many students have learned to revere the experts in their field but have no grasp of how to bridge the gulf in knowledge that separates them from the level of expertise embodied in the set books and other texts. His disappointment over his first submitted piece of work should have alerted him to the fact that the assessment criteria being used to assess his writing are not what he expected: the English he learned to write in school is no longer appropriate. Perhaps this will be clarified when he eventually has a meeting with his tutor. The student's relationship with his tutor is based on a number of misunderstandings. He thinks that grades can be negotiated upwards, but this is very unlikely. The tutor may say 'no' but in a friendly way that he thinks invites persistence – until the tutor becomes angry and frustrated. He thinks she can devote as much time to him as his high school teachers may have done but she has very little time outside her teaching duties. She will have many administrative and other tasks as well as pressure to publish her own research. He needs to use her office hours or appointment system.

Student 3 has the idea that lectures are simply regurgitations of what is already in books. This is a widespread misunderstanding among students. Lectures have many purposes, including highlighting what is important in the subject, giving a framework for study, showing how material from sources such as textbooks fits into this, and explaining difficult aspects of the subject with relevant examples.[21] It is essential that student 3 attend his lectures. Fortunately, he has realized the importance of tutorials (in some universities, these are called *seminars*) for clarifying lectures, but if he misses the lectures he will fall behind.

Student 4 is failing to interact with the other students on his course. Their coffee bar chats might be reviews of the lecture they have just attended or they might be informal study group[22] meetings, both of which would benefit his understanding of the subject enormously, as well as giving him an opportunity to develop his language skills. His communication difficulties with other international students in part result from his own language skills, not just theirs. While his preference for the company of his compatriots is understandable, it will not help him to become a truly international academic or professional practitioner with good communication skills for a global context. He is in danger of becoming an 'academic tourist', someone who never truly integrates with the academic community he is studying in.[23]

To put some of these difficulties into perspective, here are some authentic comments from UK students which voice similar concerns:

- *I wish I had known how much hard work would be involved in my course.*
- *The level of the work is a lot greater than the level we were studying at school.*
- *Tutorials make such a difference to my understanding of the coursework. They help to keep me structured and on course.*
- *I struggled in the first year ... I was only aware of how to write creatively. I had no understanding of how to write critically, yet I felt the university assumed all students were capable of this.*
- *The necessity to plan ahead is vital. At work I cannot just turn around and demand shifts based around university hours.[24]*

Stereotyping international students is dangerous: every student in an EAP class is an individual with individual expectations and individual needs. Moreover, education in many countries is currently undergoing rapid reform, making generalizations about EAP students' earlier learning experiences inherently unreliable. Even students with the initial misconceptions outlined in Case study B may well learn quickly from their experiences and, with no help from an EAP teacher, emerge among the best students in their final year. International students are well represented in the lists of first-class honours degrees students in English-medium universities.[25] One reason is that they are very good at *adaptive strategies*, at observing how the system works and trying to fit in.[26] It is important to keep these strengths in mind and try to harness them when dealing with the many expectations that EAP students are likely to have.

Teacher expectations

Both EAP teachers and degree subject lecturers sometimes forget the successful international students when they meet some of the behaviour and perceptions shown by the students in Case study B. In these circumstances, it is easy to make comments such as: *these students tend to learn by rote; they are passive; they just want to copy; they cannot work in groups; they are obsessed with assessment.*

Biggs[27] evaluates such stereotypes of students in the light of a range of studies and finds them to be unhelpful 'distortions of the real situation'. For example, he contrasts rote learning, often seen by western teachers as mindless repetition, with memorization, an important study strategy. He points out the value of verbatim recall in freeing up cognitive capacity for processing and thinking – mnemonics are an example of this. His view of the students' preoccupation with assessment is that such a focus is pragmatic on the part of the students and advises us to 'make sure the method of assessment contains the content you want them to learn'.[28]

The stereotype of the copying or plagiarizing student also fails to stand up to scrutiny. Native English-speaking students too have problems with plagiarism and all students need to be taught how to operate within this particular set of academic rules.[29] It is also not true that international students are passive and will not work in groups. Outside the classroom, in other contexts, these students are active, aware and collaborative. The task of the EAP teacher is to activate these traits in a learning context.[30] Biggs identifies this as the key approach in his model of development in teaching international students.

The stereotypes of international students outlined above are often a reaction by university lecturers to difficulties encountered when first teaching such students. At this stage, teachers may believe that there is only one right way to be academic – our way – and they initially tend to blame the students for not being 'like us'. This is a deficit view of international students[31] and is based on the false premise that the students' thought processes are wrong and have to be changed. EAP teachers may sometimes take this view as well. For example, an EAP teacher may feel that the students cannot think critically and that they have to be taught how to do this.

With more experience, teachers may shift their focus away from the students and assume that the students' culture is causing the problem. For example, they might believe that the students' culture does not foster critical thinking. They feel they need to know how to teach it to this particular culture. This new perspective identifies their own techniques as inappropriate and at this stage they often report feeling de-skilled.[32] They may feel there is one right way to teach these students if only it can be found. This is still a deficit view, but of the teacher rather than the student. The exclusive focus on what the teacher does is unhelpful.

Instead of worrying about teaching techniques for specific cultures, teachers need to analyse what students actually do. At a deep level, all people share a common core of learning and thinking processes,[33] but how they use them is context dependent. For example, everyone knows how to think critically, but will not choose to use this faculty in every context: I might evaluate curtain fabric very critically in a department store, but not in my friend's house. The importance of context is well illustrated by Hitchcock's observation of third-year students from China, studying in the UK.[34] He found that, while these students' contributions to discussion were reluctant and relatively impoverished in class, their contributions to online discussion were rich, varied and showed considerable depth of analysis and critical reflection.

Classroom materials 1.2 *Rich Aunty – an introduction to writer's stance* shows writer's stance in a context that is accessible to students – persuading a family member to help with a financial problem – and explores persuasive language for taking a stance.
EAP students naturally use reflective critical thinking in many contexts but do not necessarily express it in the classroom, where they may feel reluctant to challenge group harmony.[35] The task for the teacher is to discover a context in which students are familiar or comfortable with analysing and thinking critically and to devise ways to bring this thinking, along with the appropriate language, into the academic context. This has to be an inclusive endeavour with teacher and students bringing together their perspectives to illuminate, through dialogue,[36] the deeper processes of learning that are shared by all, regardless of culture.

This contextual approach is not only essential for student autonomy, through reflecting on learning processes, but is also an important application of critical thinking, through making connections between contexts.[37] An understanding is required not so much of *cultural* difference but rather of *contextual* difference. Hitchcock contrasts the notion of the *Chinese student* (cultural perspective) with the *student from China* (contextual perspective). It is important to think of students as retaining their culture but changing their context, for example, in moving from high school to university, and in moving from an undergraduate course to a postgraduate course. To encourage learning beyond formal institutions and throughout life, different aspects of learning need to be consciously activated in new contexts, particularly in changes such as the move from school to university.

Teaching and learning in EAP

Teachers themselves experience context change if they move from general English into EAP teaching. How effective they are will depend on whether they recognize the special features that make EAP different and can meet the challenges these present.

The distinctive features of teaching and learning in EAP

The context in which EAP students will eventually study is the main source of the differences from general English teaching and learning that were summarized in Table 1 at the beginning of the chapter, and it is the most important influence on what happens in an EAP classroom. An EAP course is needs driven rather than level driven.[38] Its main focus is what the student is trying to do in the future – join the tribe – rather than what the student can do now. Often, language level is less important than a student's maturity and expertise in the subject discipline. The stakes for the student are high and the time is limited. Therefore, every minute of teaching and learning has to count, and the rationale for every activity has to be clear. A teaching approach which is seen as enabling rather than gate-keeping is essential.

The English in EAP is the language of academic discourse and focuses specifically on the vocabulary, grammar and discourse features found in academic communication, both spoken and written. Academic genres are used so that audience, purpose and organization can be examined, together with appropriate rhetorical functions and information structure.[39] These considerations mean that whole-text grammar rather than sentence grammar is the focus of study.

In university courses, information is conveyed and students are assessed mainly through written texts. In consequence, EAP students work predominantly on reading and writing while listening and speaking are restricted to lectures, discussion and seminar skills. EAP texts are inherently long and dense and it is necessary to spend time on each text to exploit it fully. However, the same EAP text will have a range of learning focuses and may be used at different points in a course for different purposes. There is little scope for self-expression, personal response and creative writing. Instead, clarity and objectivity are valued in EAP student writing. This does not mean that academic writing is neutral. Students have to learn how to recognize a writer's stance or position with respect to the ideas under discussion, and how to make and support their position persuasively in their own writing – always tempered by caution because they understand that their position can be challenged.

In preparing students for university study, EAP teachers have to ensure that students can meet all the requirements of studying in the new context. In EAP, there is explicit development of student autonomy and critical thinking at the same time as the language is learned. The word *purpose* is key in EAP. Language is always acquired for and through an academic purpose, for example, to solve a problem, to reflect on learning or to evaluate ideas.

Meeting the teaching and learning challenges

It is important to see the process of adapting to EAP teaching and learning as adding to, rather than changing, a repertoire of expertise so that EAP teachers hold on to sound teaching principles which are useful in all contexts. Good teaching in any context is teaching that works. Teachers trained in a general English teaching tradition have a set of general strategies, but may not know which are appropriate in the EAP context and consequently can feel unconfident and de-skilled.

Task 7

- If you are a practising EAP teacher, what have been the main challenges for you?

- If you have not yet taught EAP, what do you think will be your main challenges?

   Keep your list by you as you read on. What follows in this book will help you to reflect more deeply on, and possibly resolve, some of these issues.

Research on the challenges that EAP teachers perceive is rare.[40] However, it is clear that practising EAP teachers frequently report lack of confidence in understanding the complex interaction of institution and student expectations, and in meeting their needs. Some of these challenges have already been outlined in this chapter. An earlier section showed the importance of aligning EAP with teaching and learning at university, for example, through case studies, problem solving and a research-based approach to academic language.

Identifying specific knowledge or materials relating to students' disciplines is often cited as a major problem for teachers, along with incorporating this specific detail into general EAP classes composed of students from a range of different disciplines. Additional areas of concern are time constraints coupled with the need to help students with relatively low levels of language to deal with difficult authentic materials.[41]

Some general English teachers are used to having freedom to be creative in selecting and adapting interesting materials, and they report that authentic academic materials tend to be dull in comparison. However, students need appropriate materials and these are not intrinsically dull if the topics are related to the area of study that the students wish to follow – perhaps they only seem dull to a teacher with little knowledge or interest in the subject. If the teacher is bored, the lessons will be correspondingly dull and stilted,[42] but the problem is not solved by avoiding relevant academic texts. Authentic materials are essential in EAP and are intrinsically motivating for students. A pre-sessional student completed a project comparing education for accounting in China and the UK and reflected, 'I had fun doing this project … It brought out the creative side in me and it was the outside of the box thinking that I needed'. His choice of topic would not be interesting for many teachers, but his comments about what he learned show how highly motivating it was for him. Teachers need to make the effort to become more familiar with the students' subject areas by reading, by talking to lecturers in the relevant departments, and by getting students themselves to talk about their subjects.

One type of course which incorporates authentic materials for language learning is Content Based Instruction (CBI). Two models of CBI are becoming increasingly important in EAP: sheltered and adjunct.[43] The sheltered EAP model simulates an academic course by teaching content as well as language. For example, students on a foundation programme for a degree in International Business and Communications follow a syllabus in which they learn about global issues from authentic texts such as sixth-form course books that are written for native speakers of English about to enter higher education.[44] The students are assessed by exams and coursework tasks that resemble as far as possible the assessment procedures of their target degree courses. This includes assessment of content as well as language. Another example of the sheltered model is a corpus-based syllabus which uses a corpus of first-year reading texts from a Business Studies degree to generate texts, tasks and activities as well as formative assessments and summative exams.[45] The material is thus very closely aligned with the degree course and the students concentrate on the most frequent and useful vocabulary and discourse features they are likely to meet in this context. This syllabus ensures familiarity with the register and, to some extent, content of the target academic course.

In the adjunct EAP model, EAP sessions are timetabled to prepare for or follow up the academic input of the degree course. The language focus, tasks and activities in the EAP classes are based on the academic course, and assessment may be jointly carried out by both subject and language specialists. There may also be team teaching. This model is demanding in terms of materials preparation and liaison time between EAP teachers and subject lecturers. The main limitation of a content-based syllabus is the requirement that all students in the EAP class are studying the same or broadly similar subjects.

Classroom materials 1.3
Chocolate in the classroom introduces the concepts that underpin academic referencing. Students invent crazy ideas which the teacher then attempts to plagiarize.

Part of the answer to the challenge posed by academic materials also lies in the way that students engage with texts. Because academic texts are principally about communicating ideas, there is plenty of scope for teachers' communicative creativity when designing tasks for the texts. Problem solving, information gaps, games, competitions and other communicative tasks can fully engage students so that they are absorbed in learning activities. This not only lifts the atmosphere of a lesson but also enhances learning. Sometimes authenticity of task can be allowed to override authenticity of content,[46] as in the *Rich Aunty* classroom materials mentioned earlier, where a non-academic context is used to activate academic stance. Later chapters will present more ways of engaging students, particularly by enabling them to become researchers into language and learning processes.

Some teachers naturally have a more charismatic, entertaining style of teaching than others. Fun and jokes are what make classes pleasant for them and for their students. This style can also be appropriate in an EAP classroom. As long as sound EAP input is delivered, lessons can still be imaginative and enjoyable to teach. The most rewarding aspect of teaching EAP is, however, seeing students becoming increasingly competent at academic tasks.

The inherent difficulty of academic texts is a separate issue. It is related to the reader's prior knowledge, not only of content but also of other features of the text. Students can develop strategies for working out the message in relevant academic texts, especially when they are, as is often the case with postgraduates, experts in their fields. Lack of language ability in English should never be confused with lack of academic ability. Lack of English should also not be an excuse to remove students from EAP provision, whether by relegation to remedial grammar classes or into lower intermediate general English classes.[47] This is particularly important for students who have already studied English for several years in their school system. These students need to work with grammar and vocabulary in an academic context, using academic (possibly constructed) texts and tasks. They need their English to be developed for and through academic purposes.

Teachers sometimes avoid difficult texts through insecurity. Teachers as well as students find it hard to tolerate incomplete comprehension, yet this happens often to native speakers who are reading an academic text. Students need to experience this without panic and with some attack strategies.[48] Teachers also need to acknowledge that they cannot control or even know everything in the classroom domain. In fact, to do so is to deny opportunities to develop student autonomy.[49] Furthermore, to deny students the opportunity to engage with authentic texts in their subject disciplines is patronizing.

Teachers need to devote sufficient time to a text so students can use it for authentic study purposes. Academic texts are usually intellectually demanding and it takes time to work out what they mean. Often the EAP teacher is working with the students as equals in the learning process. Students need to understand whole text structure, how information flows through a text, how cohesion and coherence work, and what functions different parts of the texts have. It is essential to take time and provide support. If necessary, authenticity can be compromised and easier, constructed texts can be used to begin with. As long as students are then exposed to authentic academic texts, easier models can be useful.[50] Journalistic texts, on the other hand, cannot be substituted in the same way for academic texts. Articles from newspapers and magazines are easy to find and may sometimes be more entertaining than academic writing on a given topic. However, *journalese* is usually more linguistically and culturally demanding than academic writing.[51] This is an important consideration when choosing texts for the classroom.[52] Although some degree programmes do require students to read and comment on print media, such texts do not generally provide appropriate models for student academic writing. Subject lecturers prefer to recommend a key journal in the field as a writing style model, for example, *The Harvard Business Review* rather than *The Economist*.[53] EAP teachers need to find texts which treat an accessible topic in an academic way rather than rely on journalistic treatments of academic topics.[54]

This chapter has shown that in EAP, much more than in general English, analysis of what a student needs depends on knowing where the student is going, that is, the demands of the target academic community. Here is a case study of a student who has already joined the academic community. How well is she meeting the demands?

Task 8

Read the following authentic case study and accompanying text written by a student.

- Do you think the text fails as a piece of academic writing or are aspects of it acceptable?

- Why? Give examples.

- What do you already do in your EAP teaching that helps students to avoid these difficulties?

Case study C:

An international student is struggling with the economics module in year 2 of a BA in Actuarial Science. She had entered the degree course the previous year with a high grade for mathematics but a relatively poor IELTS score. She was advised to attend the EAP pre-sessional course but decided not to. The economics lecturer has sent some of her failing coursework to the EAP tutor and asked her to help the student. The economics lecturer's comments are in boxes on the student's text. Where appropriate, they are linked next to underlined sections in the text which the lecturer is commenting on.

Week 5 Essay Question

Using diagrams, illustrate the Slutsky decomposition of the effect of demand into a substitution and income effect. Hence justify the 'Law of Demand' which states, 'If the demand for a good increases as income increases, then demand for that good will fall as price increases.'

In the first year of Economic course, we been taught a bit of knowledge about demand. This year more details of demand are learned, which decomposed into two changes: a substitution effect and income effect. They are determined by Slutcky. However, the 'Law of Demand' also states some sort of relation among income, demand and price. What is the connection of all above? I'm going to talk about it in the essay for this week.

Let's state a equation first. $\Delta X = \Delta Xs + \Delta Xn$, in words this equation says that the total change in demand equals the substitution effect plus the income effect. This equation is called the 'Slutsky indentiy.' (Varian, page 143) Therefore, as known, the change of demand due to change of price, when the price of good changes, there are two kind of effects: the substitution effect and the income effect.

First of all, the change in demand so that the change in the rate of exchange between the two goods <u>because</u> of the substation effect.

> not 'because', it is the substn, effect!

For example, if price of good A become cheaper, people would buy more good A, and less good B. So demand of good A increase. This is the substitution effect. At the same time, if price of good A become cheaper, that is also mean even people hold the same amount of money, but the power of consummation increase in good A, people can buy a lot more <u>good A than before, so that it becomes less demand in good B</u>. That is determined by the income effect, which is the change in demand due to have more purchasing power.

> No → maybe people buy also more of B because income increases.

On the other hand, the 'diagram I' which more specifics to describe how the two effects change the demand of the goods...

Unclear! What is cause and effect?

...In conclusion, the Slutsky equation decompost that for a normal good, due to income effect if the demand of good increases when the people's income increases. <u>then the price increases in that good, due to substitution effect</u>, the demand will be reduced. That is also justify the law of demand.

It seems to me that you confuse cause and effect of the income and substitution effect. They are <u>due to</u> the price change! The link between your first part and the 'law of demand' is not clear to me.

In an essay such as this, students need to represent ideas in their own words to demonstrate understanding. The student has not fulfilled this task because understanding has not been demonstrated. The lecturer identifies the problem clearly as an inability to express cause–effect relationships. This failure to use key language for explaining cause and effect is a serious problem for study in any discipline. It is quite possible that the student also failed to understand the reading for this essay for the same reason: failure to understand causal relationships through the language used to express them. This is the most significant problem the student has and it is enough to fail the coursework assessment, despite the fact that her essay follows the academic convention of having an introduction and a conclusion.

However, there are other problems. The student is also attempting to write long complex sentences without adequate control of sentence grammar. In the third paragraph, the sentence beginning 'At the same time ...' is a good example of this. It is a long single sentence held together by *if ... that ... even ... but ... so*, with a resulting loss of the message to the reader. In addition, there is a relative pronoun, *which*, with nothing to refer to and *it* is also used with no clear reference. It is possible that, at some time, an English teacher has told this student to try to write more complex sentences – embedded clauses are often cited as evidence of a good level of English. However, academic lecturers want clarity and precision rather than 'long, complex grammatical sentences'.[55] She needs to learn how to write simply and clearly and within her competence.[56]

In addition to cause-and-effect language, the student lacks awareness of many features of academic text. Basic academic lexis is not used correctly: *determined by, among, because, substitution, demand of, consumption, power, justify, so that, on the other hand*. Less crucial but still important is her poor awareness of appropriate structure and style. She uses very informal vocabulary: *a bit of, let's*, and a direct question. She also includes inappropriate information following *we been taught* and over-uses linking devices, *first of all, on the other hand, therefore, in conclusion*, which could be a washback[57] effect from IELTS exam preparation. Finally, she has not proofread the text – an essential writing skill in academic English.

Any EAP course must enable students to use cause and effect language, and other rhetorical functions.[58] In addition, an EAP course has to teach students a clear understanding of formal style and academic conventions, how to use shorter simpler sentences and build complexity from them, how to study model answers from successful students, and how to proofread their own work.

Important issues that affect EAP practice

In addition to helping students to meet all these demands of academic study, EAP teachers have to respond to developments in the field, particularly in relation to the globalization of English-medium education. Currently, there are four contentious issues in the practice of EAP that teachers cannot ignore:

- the rise of English as an international language
- the question of whether general or only specific EAP is possible
- the extent to which EAP is the teaching of study skills
- the issue of critical pedagogy in EAP

Here, we can take only a brief look at the first three of these issues and a slightly longer look at the last. Readers who would like to reflect more deeply are referred to Hyland's recent book in which he presents thorough and balanced discussions, together with reflective questions and extracts from some of the key sources.[59]

English as an international language

It is clear that English is now predominant as an international language in fields as diverse as politics, business, technology and academia. Most conversations in English are between non-native speakers of the language and already many varieties of English can be identified from different parts of the world. Examples are Indian English, Chinese English and Malaysian English. The development of these varieties is a natural process of linguistic evolution and inevitably their grammar and vocabulary are influenced by the home languages. In addition, redundant features of English phonology, grammar and vocabulary are likely to disappear in a process of simplification driven by the overriding need to communicate clearly. Candidates for this process in academic English include:

the countable/uncountable distinction	*researches show*
third person singular s in the simple present	*the algorithm convert the signal*
non-native speaker collocation	*they made a study of, discuss about*
simplified question tags	*isn't it*

The question of who owns international English and who is responsible for maintaining its standards[60] is hotly debated. EAP teachers are at the battlefront and have to consider on a daily basis what is correct or acceptable in their students' output. In doing this, an important principle is to involve the students themselves. The teachers need to share the criteria for acceptable output and the implications of using non-native features in their English, and then decide for themselves what they want to do. EAP teachers need to become aware of the features of international varieties and also of what language usage is not acceptable, what is tolerated, and what is admired in the academic discourse communities.

General or specific EAP

Teaching students from different subject disciplines in the same EAP class requires negotiation and compromise. Some of the principles advocated in this book work particularly well when students all share the same subject area in their academic study. However, this is a luxury found mainly on in-sessional courses. Institutional constraints mean that most EAP classes, particularly pre-sessional ones, must be general because they contain a mixture of subject areas or are sorted at best into science and humanities streams. There are ways to accommodate some subject-specific EAP practice in mixed classrooms and these will be highlighted throughout the book. However, there are real advantages in teaching mixed groups.[61] EAP is principally an endeavour in which students acquire the generic tools to research the language and culture of their academic discourse community for themselves and this can be achieved in mixed and subject specific groups. Recognition that it is ultimately the students' responsibility to deal with subject specificity is a helpful perspective in developing this generic approach.

The balance of skills and language

EAP, like language teaching generally, has been prone to fashions. In the past few years, there has been an unfortunate trend towards seeing EAP mainly as *study skills*.[62] This is reflected in the tendency to divide courses into, for example, writing *skills* and reading *skills*. While there is no denying the importance of teaching the skills needed to read and write good academic English, one consequence of this focus has been a neglect of the language of academic purposes.[63] A major reason why teachers often feel de-skilled when they embark on EAP teaching, and why they mistakenly abandon their best communicative practices, is that their course books and syllabuses prioritize skills, with language as an often poorly analysed afterthought. All the chapters in this book seek to restore language to its proper place in EAP.

Critical EAP

Critical EAP is an approach that sees a role for teachers and students in challenging the academic practices which disadvantage them in their joint endeavour of accessing academic discourse communities. It is also known as critical pedagogy and is contrasted with an 'accommodationist' stance, in which teachers view their role as uncritically teaching whatever is needed to join the tribe. Benson[64] distinguishes hard and soft critical pedagogy. In the hard version, the aim is to 'challenge the power structures' of the academic community.[65] The soft version aims to help students to develop their own identity or voice in their use of Academic English.[66] The hard approach seeks to empower students as agents of change in the disciplines they choose – changing the tribe from within. Commitment to this approach, however, should not involve appropriating the students' voices, and many students may not feel ready to critique their discourse community until they are more fully integrated into it. The *soft* approach, developing a voice, is a necessary first step towards empowerment and is essential in EAP. A consequence of this is that EAP teachers have to be ready to face the challenge of critical evaluation by their own students.[67]

Challenging academic practices need not involve an aggressive stance. EAP teachers can use their linguistic expertise in particular to bring about quiet revolutions. Although lecturers who speak English as their first (and often only) language tend to be very aware of the complexities of their own disciplines, they tend to think of the features of their mother tongue as simple and obvious. This means that when lecturers try to explain their expectations about language use, the results can be useless or even counter-productive. For example, a mathematics department gave its students this advice on improving writing.

> How should you attempt to improve the quality of your writing? It is important to understand that like learning to drive it is something you have to work at. No doubt an ability to write comes more easily to some than to others, but everyone needs to put some effort into acquiring this skill, and anyone can improve if they do. Of course there are plenty of books on how to write well, but perhaps the most useful thing you can do is to read widely … and learn to observe how others write.

If *mathematics* and *do mathematics* are substituted for *writing* and *write* in this advice, its pointlessness might become clear even to the department that issued it. A lecturer in another discipline gives much more helpful advice to his students. He begins by asking them to write simply and clearly and avoid long, grammatically complex sentences.[68]

Examinations are a crucial aspect of induction into the tribe, but the language of examination questions can be particularly unclear. An academic department that was concerned about lack of consistency in its exam questions asked an EAP teacher to evaluate past examination papers. Specifically, they wanted an answer to the following question: *To what extent is the language of the examination questions consistent, clear and in line with the recommendations of our professional awards body?* The EAP teacher compared the recommendations to lecturers' questions in first year examination papers and their own model answers. She found the recommendations to be based mainly on native speaker intuitions. Several similarly subjective and rigid lists were found in use by other departments in the university. They were being used uncritically, as if they were a simple prescription for clear examination questions. In the actual examination papers, there was a lack of clarity in the use of some of the words, for example, the word *discuss*. Lecturers reported that using *discuss* in a question indicated the need for an exploration and evaluation of different views or arguments. The word seemed to feel intrinsically academic. However, *discuss* was used in questions that in fact required students simply to explain, describe or even list in their answers.[69] The outcome of the study was a set of guidelines for lecturers when setting examination questions which has been widely adopted throughout the university. Consistency in exam question terminology is important but is difficult to achieve and is not in itself enough. Lecturers need to decide for themselves, question by question, the clearest language to signal what is wanted from a successful exam candidate. A similar approach has been adopted at the University of York,[70] where there is a university policy of clarifying all language in the assessment process through a system of peer review.

Task 9

- How far do you think an EAP teacher has a role in raising language or assessment issues with other departments or subject lecturers?

- Do you have any examples of such issues that you have raised?

EAP teachers have expertise which subject lecturers generally do not have in identifying and describing authentic language use. They know that what native English speakers think they say and what they actually say can be very different. However, in demonstrating this expertise, some tact is required. When issues are handled sensitively, most subject lecturers appreciate having access to linguistic expertise, particularly when it solves a perceived problem and when it is based on good evidence, such as an empirical study or corpus analysis.[71] All students, not just non-native speakers of English, benefit from the spread of this kind of expertise throughout academic discourse communities – it is an important part of making university education more inclusive.

Conclusion

The chapter began by exploring the rules of the academic community and the expectations of EAP students attempting to enter it. Rather than cultural problems, misaligned student expectations need to be seen as differences in context. This perspective allows teachers to activate universal learning processes to help students to meet the challenges of academic study. Some of the difficulties that teachers report about EAP practice can be attributed to the adjustments that have to be made from teaching in a general English context to teaching in an EAP context. Examining the distinctive features of EAP helps to identify student needs and understand how to meet them without losing the effective approaches shared with general English teaching. The chapter ended with a brief account of the major issues currently impinging on EAP practice. In particular, EAP teachers have an important role in relating to academic communities as language experts. This can help to change practices that disadvantage EAP students. Throughout this chapter, references were made to later chapters which will examine the themes raised here in greater detail. This book identifies and justifies sound methodological principles in EAP – it is a journey to find teaching that works.

Further reading

Basturkmen, H. (2006) *Ideas and Options in English for Specific Purposes.* Mahwah, New Jersey: Lawrence Erlbaum Associates.

Biggs, J. (2003) *Teaching for Quality Learning at University: What the Student Does.* Buckingham: Open University.

Brick, J. (2006) *Academic Culture: A Student's Guide to Studying at University.* Sydney : National Centre for English Language Teaching and Research, Macquarie University.

Dudley-Evans, T. and St. John, M. (1998) *Developments in English for Specific Purposes.* Cambridge: Cambridge University Press.

Hyland, K. (2006) *English for Academic Purposes: An Advanced Resource Book.* Abingdon: Routledge.

Jordan, R. R. (1997) *English for Academic Purposes: A Guide and Resource Book for Teachers.* Cambridge: Cambridge University Press.

Chapter 2: Text analysis

This chapter will examine:

* text analysis as an aid to understanding and working with discipline-specific texts

* text analysis as a tool for prioritizing what to teach in EAP

* an accessible framework for using text analysis in the classroom

You will have the opportunity to:

* clarify key features of this framework, using example texts

* begin to see how to customize authentic texts for use with your students

Text analysis is a crucial skill in EAP because it enables teachers to work confidently with materials from a wide range of disciplines. In a recent survey,[1] teachers were asked what they considered to be most challenging about learning to teach EAP. Over 50 per cent of respondents highlighted discipline-specific materials as their main challenge. Here are some typical responses:

* *trying not to be afraid of discipline-specific materials*

* *acquiring the confidence to work with students studying subjects which are outside my scope of knowledge or interest (e.g., biomedical science, engineering)*

* *feeling comfortable with extremely able students from a range of disciplines*

* *finding/designing materials that are appropriate to students from a range of specialisms*

These teachers voiced their concerns about dealing with the content and materials of their students' future disciplines. The main purpose of this chapter is to show that an ability to analyse texts can reduce these concerns and increase confidence. Although it will never be possible to have a complete understanding of all disciplines, you may reach the position of one respondent of

* *understanding that I didn't need to understand all academic conventions of all departments but that a generalized understanding was enough.*

EAP teachers need to feel confident about working with texts from academic disciplines because their students have to deal with them constantly. At university, students are expected to read a variety of texts and understand not only what each one is telling them but also how it fits together with other texts. Often they are required to interpret what they read, e.g., by evaluating the information or the author's viewpoint. They then have to represent the information, orally or in writing, to show their knowledge and understanding. Although students are expected to include ideas from other writers, they have to write in their own words, using an appropriate academic style. Students often mention the difficulties they have with these processes:

- *There's too much to read. I have to stay up all night to do it.*
- *I can understand all the words but I can't understand the meaning.*
- *My supervisor says my writing is not like academic style.*
- *My lecturer told me 'write more logically and clearly'.*
- *What is the meaning of 'on the contrary'?*
- *How do I start a sentence?*

The purpose of EAP teaching is to support students in dealing with these problems and questions. Analysing academic texts, to understand the general vocabulary, grammar and organization which link the ideas together in meaningful ways, allows teachers to make sense of texts even if they do not understand all the words or ideas. They can then feel confident in presenting this language for students to learn and transfer to any text they read.

Test your understanding of text analysis with the following task.

Task 1

Read the authentic text below. Focus on the words you understand and answer these general questions:

- What kind of text is this?
- Why was it written?
- Where might it have appeared?

Now answer these specific questions:

- What is the thematic organization of the text; how does this match the purpose?
- What linguistic function does the word *species* have in this text?

Bacteria of the genus Vibrio are Gram-negative, straight or curved rods, motile by one or more polar flagella, that give a positive oxidase test, grow on thiosulfate citrate bile salt sucrose agar and are facultative anaerobes. Most species are sensitive to the vibriostatic agent O/129, and have both a respiratory and a fermentative type of metabolism. Sodium ions stimulate the growth of all species and are an absolute requirement for most species (Holt et al. 1994). Vibrios are normal inhabitants in aquatic environments, being very common in marine and estuarine habitats and on the surface and in the intestinal contents of marine animals (Colwell 1984; Fouz et al. 1990).[2]

Hint: Here is the text without the words you may not understand. The verbs are shown in italics and the themes are underlined. Brackets indicate where themes were omitted.

Bacteria of the ... Vibrio *are* ..., straight or curved rods, motile by one or more ..., <u>that</u> *give* a positive ... test, *grow* on ... and *are* .... <u>Most species</u> *are* sensitive to the ... agent ..., and [_____] *have* both a respiratory and a fermentative type of metabolism. ... *stimulate* the growth of all species and [_____] *are* an absolute requirement for most species (Holt et al. 1994). <u>Vibrios</u> *are* normal inhabitants in aquatic environments, *being* very common in marine ... habitats and on the surface and in the intestinal contents of marine animals (Colwell 1984; Fouz et al. 1990).

KEY

The text is a description (of bacteria named Vibrio) from the introduction to a paper published in a scientific journal. It was written to present new research.

- The descriptive function is shown by the verbs, which are all in the present tense: *are, give, grow, have, stimulate*. There are adjectives to describe the bacteria: *straight, curved, sensitive*. The text contains vocabulary normally associated with living things: *respiratory, metabolism, growth, species, inhabitants, habitats*. It has collocations which describe the conditions or agents that allow the bacteria to grow: *stimulate the growth, sensitive to, absolute requirement*.

- The text is likely to be from the introduction to the paper, which sets the research against a background of previous studies of the same bacteria: Holt *et al.* 1994; Colwell 1994; Fouz *et al.* 1990.

- The themes are underlined in the Hint and mostly refer to the bacteria being described. This is a particular feature of factual descriptions, also found in encyclopaedias.

- The word *species* is a general noun performing the function of lexical cohesion. In effect, it acts as a lexically empty substitute noun for the noun phrase *bacteria of the genus Vibrio*.

Reflection: How easy was this task for you?

If you found it reasonably straightforward and you are already using the ideas of theme and rheme or lexical cohesion using general nouns with students, you may like to skim this chapter and sample the tasks towards the end, where these ideas are put into practice. If some of the ideas in Task 1 are new to you, it is worth spending time on this chapter as it will show you how to analyse texts from a wide range of disciplines and use them with students.

The tasks in this chapter are designed to raise your awareness of a systematic approach to text analysis. Texts are not like sentences, which have well-defined grammatical structures with few exceptions. Instead, texts have varying patterns of organization and linking which are determined by authors, their purposes and audiences, and the contexts in which the texts are written or spoken. Text analysis requires interpretation and the answers to the tasks may not be obvious to you. Keys are provided for each task. You may find it useful to read the keys and then go back to the task again to help you understand the analysis.

An ability to analyse texts is important to EAP teachers:

- It helps you and your students cope with any lack of understanding of the content of texts because you feel confident of your knowledge of the framework used to present the content.
- An authentic dialogue develops between you and your students where they have knowledge of the content of texts and you have linguistic knowledge.
- Authentic academic texts are a useful source of information about the future needs of students and this helps you decide what to teach.
- It enables you to create meaningful and purposeful classroom tasks to help students identify patterns of language and organization they can learn.
- You deepen your understanding of the skills required to process oral or written texts and to represent the information they contain.
- The feedback you give on student writing becomes more detailed and useful because you understand what constitutes good academic writing.
- You can devise exams which test knowledge and skills more appropriately because you are able to explore beneath surface level comprehension of texts.

This chapter focuses on those aspects of text analysis which are most helpful when working with discipline-specific texts, and when creating classroom and test materials for students. This will not be a rigorous linguistic analysis but rather a pedagogical one. As a result, some aspects have been simplified. Many of the tasks contained in this chapter were developed for use with students and are included in the photocopiable materials. There are key questions for students at the end of each section.

Choosing texts for your classroom

Experienced language teachers often choose texts and create materials to use with their students. The choice of texts and tasks depends on the needs of the students but most teachers probably use a particular set of criteria to evaluate the usefulness of any text.

Task 2

• When choosing texts to use with your students, how do you decide on their suitability?

Look at the following text.

• What features of this text can you 'see' that might make it useful for a mixed group of EAP students preparing for undergraduate courses?

The Metropole and the Luxus Hotels

The Metropole and the Luxus are large hotels in a major British tourist and business city. The former, situated in the centre close to the famous shopping street and theatres, attracts the top end of the tourist market whereas the Luxus, on the edge of the city beside the airport, caters more for the business traveller. Both hotels have a similar number of rooms: the Luxus has 186 rooms while the Metropole has 150 rooms.

The facilities offered by each hotel reflect the market which it aims to attract. The Metropole offers a wide range of leisure facilities such as quality gift shops, a high class restaurant, a beauty salon and an outdoor heated swimming pool as well as the usual gym and sauna provided in a hotel of this class. The speciality of the Luxus is the provision of facilities to assist the business traveller such as modem points in every bedroom, fax machines and 22 conference rooms where clients can hold their own meetings.

The Luxus is part of a major international hotel chain, Luxus Hotels Inc., which owns 400 hotels in 75 countries and employs 50,000 people worldwide. The aim of this company is to produce reliable, high quality accommodation and service of a similar standard in every hotel. The group has a devolved management structure. Apart from large financial decisions, the management of each hotel is delegated to a local management team. In fact in some cases the hotels are leased or run on management contract.

In contrast, the Metropole is one of a small group of hotels owned by the millionaire Sir Marco Polo, who set up the group as an individual project after his original business empire was taken over by a larger company. He had the vision of creating a luxury hotel which would be the best in its class in each major city of the world. He also wanted each hotel to reflect the character and traditions of the city. An unusual feature of the management of these hotels is that although each hotel has its own management team for day-to-day operations, Sir Marco takes a personal part in all aspects from choosing the locations to making financial decisions.

The hotels had varying fortunes after the downturn in global travel, following the destruction of the World Trade Center in 2001. Despite its dependence on the tourist market, the Metropole has fared quite well, perhaps because Sir Marco's very individual style of management enabled it to respond more quickly to the problem. He immediately ordered modem points to be added to certain bedrooms and turned other bedrooms into conference rooms, in order to attract more business customers. The Luxus might have been expected to have fewer problems, as it catered mainly for business travellers who had to travel whether they wished to or not. However it did suffer some effects and lost the tourist part of its business. This was because people with children felt less safe staying at such a high profile hotel close to the airport. Because of its less personal management structure, the hotel was not able to respond to the crisis as quickly as the Metropole.

KEY

Here are some of the features which you might 'see' in this text:

1 **Topic** The text is about hotel management so it might be suitable for business or tourism students but it is potentially interesting and accessible to most students.

2 **Verb grammar** Paragraphs 1–3 contain mainly present tenses of verbs; paragraph 4 has past tenses; and paragraph 5 contains present perfect tenses. The voice is mostly active but there are a few verbs in the passive voice.

3 **Lexis** The text contains business terminology and collocations, e.g., *attract the top end of the market, cater for the business traveller, varying fortunes, downturn in travel*. The names of the hotels suggest that this text is not authentic but has been constructed for teaching purposes.

4 **Register** The text seems to be factual and objective and the language is neutral with no emotional overtones.

5 **Genre** The text is a case study for business studies students, intended to illustrate different management styles. Genre is not always obvious and you may need to see the text in its context (e.g., in a textbook) to be certain about genre.

6 **Rhetorical function** The text compares and contrasts the two hotels and their management styles and hence contains signpost words for comparison, e.g., *both, while, in contrast, however*. In the final paragraph it attempts to account for the varying fortunes of the hotels using the language of cause and effect, e.g., *because*.

7 **Text organization** The hotels are described individually in paragraphs 3 and 4 and compared in terms of a particular feature in paragraphs 1, 2 and 5.

8 **Paragraph organization** Paragraphs develop from general to specific ideas.

9 **Cohesion** The themes (usually the subjects) at the beginnings of sentences are the hotels or features of the hotels such as their facilities or management styles.

10 **General nouns** The text contains lexically empty nouns, e.g., *former, facilities, speciality, character, feature, aspect*, which are used to manage the development of ideas.

11 **Transfer** Business studies students could be asked to write a parallel case study comparing management styles and responses in their own contexts.

Reflection: How many of the features listed did you see in the text? Which ones do you think would be most useful for understanding complex academic texts?

When you identify features you can 'see' in a text, you are analysing the text. However, your analysis may not be very systematic. Many teachers simply look at topic, verb grammar and lexis when choosing a text. These constitute the surface level of texts and are the features which students are probably most familiar with. The remaining features mentioned in the key are not usually taught but they can explain choices of grammar and lexis in academic texts. EAP students need to know about these features so that they can access information in texts and deal with some of the problems mentioned in their comments:

- efficient reading
- understanding the overall meaning of the text and not just the words
- writing logically and clearly in an academic style
- understanding the relationships between ideas
- knowing how to start a sentence

Key features of texts

This chapter builds a systematic framework for the analysis of academic texts. The analysis is intended to lead to suggestions for EAP teaching, so it is simplified and practical. It considers the following features:

1 **Register** – the style of language used in a particular context, e.g., formal or informal

2 **Genre** – the types of texts used by groups who share communicative purposes, e.g., case study, research paper

3 **Functions** – the patterns used to achieve rhetorical purposes in texts, e.g., cause and effect

4 **Cohesion** – the ways in which text is tied together: structural, e.g., thematic progression, lexical, e.g., summarizing nouns

5 **Organization** – the development in academic texts from general to specific

These features are discussed separately in order to explain them and to show how they can be used to analyse texts. In practice, these features are not isolated aspects of text but work together to create the text. One feature might be more apparent than others in a particular text so you might use that as 'a way into the text'. What you ultimately choose to focus on with your students will depend on their needs, the syllabus and your aims for the tasks you want to create.

Register

Register refers to the use of different styles of language in different situations. Language use changes from one context to another depending on the topic under consideration (*field*), the relationship between the people involved (*tenor*), and the function of language in the event (*mode*).[3] These features relate to the overall purposes for using language:

- to communicate ideas
- to establish relationships
- to manage the communication

When you tune in to the radio, you can usually tell very quickly what type of programme you are listening to. Quite apart from the content, the way language is used in news reports is different from the way it is used in discussion or comedy programmes. Similarly, the style of academic texts is different from the style of newspapers and popular magazines. The topics may be similar but, in newspapers and magazines, the ideas are not usually discussed in depth and the relationship between the writer and the readers is very different. Register analysis helps to answer the question: What makes a text academic?

Task 3

Put the texts below in order from most academic to least academic and answer these questions:

- What features of the style of each one do you consider to be academic?
- What features of the style are definitely not academic?
- Could you use texts like these with EAP students?

Extract 1

Virtually all children go through the same sequence of motor behaviours in the same order: rolling over, sitting without support, standing while holding onto furniture, crawling, and then walking. But children go through the sequence at different rates, and developmental psychologists began very early in the history of the discipline to ask whether learning and experience play an important role in such differences.

Although early studies suggested that the answer was no (McGraw, 1935/1975; Dennis and Dennis 1940; Gesell and Thompson, 1929), more recent studies indicate that practice or extra stimulation can accelerate the appearance of motor behaviours to some extent. For example, newborn infants have a stepping reflex; if they are held in an upright position with their feet touching a solid surface, their legs will make stepping movements that are similar to walking. A group of infants who were given stepping practice for a few minutes several times a day during the first two months of life began walking five to seven weeks earlier than babies who had not had this practice (Zelazo, Zelazo and Kolb, 1972).[4]

Extract 2   Hot and Muddled

Microbes that seek extreme heat don't seem to care how their genes are organised, say scientists who have completed the second DNA sequence from such a creature. Unlike genes in most other organisms, genes that work together and even parts of the same gene can be widely separated in the genome of Aquifex Aeolicus, a bacterium that grows in hot springs at up to 95°C.

Team leader Ronald Swanson of Diversa Corporation in San Diego, California, says these microbes can tolerate such genetic chaos because they are adapted to grow under extreme but very consistent conditions. The results appear in this week's Nature (v 392, p353).[5]
© New Scientist Magazine

Extract 3

The simplest definition of democracy is 'rule by the people'. However, the word has acquired additional layers of meaning that go beyond this definition. We might begin by taking one of the most famous definitions of democracy and thinking about what it means. In 1863 Abraham Lincoln defined democracy as 'government of the people, by the people, for the people'. That has an impressive ring to it, but who are these 'people' he was talking about? What is actually involved in 'of' 'for' and 'by' the people? Can democracy be 'of' and 'for' the people without actually being 'by' them? By answering these questions we can possibly arrive at a clearer idea of democracy.[6]

Extract 4   Network Security in E-commerce and Online Banking System

As E-commerce develops quickly, network security problem is becoming much more important than before. It is reported that lots of personal information (e.g., credit card information), are divulged through Internet every day. In order to protect customers' personal information not to be misappropriated, E-commerce websites and online banks used a number of measures and their own security policy to keep them safe.

This study is designed to show people whether it is safe when they do shopping through the Internet and the reason some customers' money are stolen by illegal users from their bank account. In addition, I'm going to evaluate security degree of these policies which have been adopted by E-commerce and online bank, and tell people what they should pay attention to.

It is intended to investigate several E-commerce websites and online banks which can represent the general condition of most websites in the world, and thus find out those security measures. All these data will be analysed carefully, and these measures will be classified into different levels. Through comparing these security methods, we will see clearly whether they are effective and what we really need to worry about.[7]

KEY

Order of texts in terms of academic style

Extracts 1 and 4 are the most academic because they have academic purposes and are written for academic audiences. In contrast, extract 3 is from a textbook for secondary schools, written in an authoritative style, while extract 2 is from a popular magazine, *New Scientist*, written in a journalistic style.

Detailed analysis

Extract 1 is from a textbook used in psychology courses. Its academic features consist of specialized lexis, *motor behaviours*, and a formal and impersonal style in which questions are indirect and there are no personal pronouns. It follows conventions for citation of other texts: *more recent studies...* (Zelazo, Zelazo and Kolb, 1972). The ideas are expressed with appropriate caution: *indicate, can..., to some extent*, and are linked explicitly: by contrast, *Virtually all children..., But children*; or concession, *Although early studies..., more recent studies...* The text has fairly simple sentence structure: *children go through..., but children go through...* The main content and complexity are contained in noun phrases: *the same sequence of motor behaviours, stepping behaviours that are similar to walking*.

The text has no features which could be labelled non-academic and is the academic benchmark for the other texts. It could be used with EAP students as it has a good range of academic features to identify and the topic should be accessible to most students.

Extract 2 is a popularization of science from *New Scientist* magazine. Its academic features include specialized lexis: *DNA sequence, Aquifex Aeolicus*. Ideas are expressed with some caution: *seem to care, can be widely separated*, and linked explicitly: by contrast, *Unlike...*; or reason, *because*. The text contains some noun phrases: *the second DNA sequence from such a creature*, although the main complexity is in subordinate clauses.

The text has several non-academic features which include an informal and personal style with contractions and colloquial expressions: *don't ... care*. People are given a specific identity: *team leader Ronald Swanson of Diversa*, rather than simply being acknowledged as a cited author, and microbes have feelings: *don't ... care*. The citation is non-conventional: *this week's Nature* (v392, page 353). You would have to be careful using this with EAP students. Although the topic is academic, the structure and language are journalistic and not at all typical of academic writing. Students could use the text to extract the key information for use in an academic report.

Extract 3 is a definition from a Modern Studies textbook at secondary school level. It has several features which could be labelled academic such as specialized lexis: *democracy, the people*, and a formal style: *acquired additional layers*. However, it has a number of non-academic features. The style is personal and authoritative with personal pronouns and direct questions: *We might begin…, Who are…?, What is…?* Ideas are expressed with a high level of certainty, and questions are rhetorical as the author knows the answers to them; *we can possibly* refers to the students' understanding of the subject not the writer's uncertainty. The linking is almost too explicit, describing the process of learning: *We might begin by…, thinking about…, By answering these questions we can possibly arrive at…* The sentence structure is deliberately simple to make the definition clear for pupils at secondary level.

You would have to be careful using this text with EAP students. The style is clear and easy to read, so it would be suitable reading practice, especially for undergraduates. However, it is not suitable as a model for student writing. The use of 'we' and the question and answer format is the style used by textbook writers who are authorities in their fields. Students are expected to write in a style that is:

- 'confidently uncertain',[8] acknowledging that the writer understands some but not all of the subject

- deferential, recognizing that as junior members of their discipline they should adopt a polite, formal style

Extract 4 is a proposal for a research project written by a non-native speaker student on a pre-sessional course. It contains specialized lexis: *e-commerce, network security*, and has a formal and impersonal style with indirect questions: *this study is designed to show whether…*, and deliberate absence of the author: *it is reported, it is intended*. Ideas are linked explicitly: by purpose, *in order to…*; addition, *In addition…*; or result, *thus*, and there is an attempt to write complex noun phrases, *network security problem, customers' personal information not to be appropriated*. There are some non-academic features which are not really appropriate, e.g., contractions and personal pronouns: *I'm, we will see… what we need to worry about*. The research aims are presented with a high degree of certainty: *thus find out…, we will see clearly…* and no references are given. In spite of this, the text could be used as a model for EAP students. It is written by a student so the style is one that other students can aim for and achieve. It is appropriately formal and impersonal with explicit links between the ideas. The organization is logical and clear. There are some grammar mistakes but these do not interfere with the overall purpose, content and organization.

The purpose of most academic texts is to communicate ideas about a specific topic to an audience that the writer does not know personally. This gives rise to the following key features of academic style:

- Academic texts contain specialized vocabulary specific to the field of study.

- Academic written style tends to be formal so the vocabulary is formal and contractions such as *it's, don't, can't* are not usually used; questions are asked indirectly.

- Academic style is impersonal, so pronouns such as *I, we, us, our* seldom appear; the exceptions are reports of team research, when *we* is common, or the introductory outline of an essay or proposal or report when *I* is possible; groups of people are referred to in general ways: *researchers, psychologists, teams.*

- Authors whose work is quoted are referred to in a text using strict conventions (e.g., surname of the author with date and page number where the cited words appear).

- Ideas are expressed with caution; this requires a range of expressions for degrees of certainty such as modal verbs and adverbs of frequency and possibility.

- Connections between ideas are made explicit; as a result, linking words such as *therefore, for example, however* are common.

- People, objects, events, ideas, terms and concepts referred to are usually specified quite precisely; this requires long noun phrases.

- Sentences can be quite simple in structure, e.g., *'The advantages of (x) are (y) and (z).'* where *x, y* and *z* are long noun phrases; the main content and complexity of sentences are found in these noun phrases and not in the verbs, which tend to show relations between ideas, e.g., *be, depend on, lead to.*

Using these ideas with students

Classroom materials 2.1 *Recognizing academic style* analyses features of the style of academic texts.

It is important for EAP students to discover an appropriate academic style for their writing. Exercises similar to Task 3 can raise students' awareness of the way academic style differs from journalistic or textbook styles of writing. Texts can be chosen to suit the level of the class but should include examples of good student writing. Students can read each text and answer the following questions in order to sensitize them to register:

- How academic is this text on a scale of 1 to 10?

- Which features of the text are academic and which are not academic?

- Could I use this style in my writing? If not, why not?

Genre

Students and academic staff at university are members of an academic community with its own set of texts, for example, essays, laboratory reports or research papers. All these texts are products of communicative events aimed at specific audiences and intended to achieve particular purposes.[9] The communicative events are referred to as genres and the texts are, in effect, the records of the genres. Genres can be spoken, e.g., a lecture, or written, e.g., a field report. Genre also includes the context of the communication – the situation, the participants and their purposes – and is thus a wider label than text.[10] Analysing the contexts of academic genres and, in particular, the texts they give rise to enables EAP teachers and their students to gain insights into the ways in which academic communities share knowledge and research.

In carrying out a genre analysis, it is possible to start by examining a context to see what texts it gives rise to or by examining a set of texts to infer features of the context.[11] It is usually easier for EAP teachers to start from the texts as these are more accessible. This analysis involves determining the audience for a set of example texts and their purpose and understanding how the stages in the organization of the texts enable them to achieve that purpose.[12] The next task contains examples of more familiar genres as well as one example of an academic genre.

Task 4

- What type of publication might each of these extracts have come from?

- Why were they written and who were they written for?

- How do these features affect the way each text is organized?

Extract 1

Conveniently located in the heart of the city at the most prestigious address, the Metropole Hotel combines the noble character of a baronial home and the classic sophistication of an international hotel. The Metropole offers 188 opulent suites and stylish rooms with views towards the Castle and the Old Town, or the hotel's internal courtyard. All the bedrooms were fully refurbished in the recent £7 million refurbishment programme.

Extract 2

Shareholders were today questioning the management competence of the Luxus International Hotel chain, following the downturn in business in the wake of 9/11. How, they are asking themselves, did Sir Marco Polo's Metropole group manage to quickly shift focus from the discerning up-market city-hopper to the time-pressed business traveller.

Some might point to the slow moving devolved power-structure of Luxus international, which failed to respond quickly to a falling off in the tourist side of the business.

Extract 3

The traveller entered the small room and looked around. He sat down on the narrow bed and pulled his coat around him, shivering in the chill air. There was dirty water in the small basin and a crumpled paper bag on the floor. Like a faint mist the ghostly sadness of past inhabitants hung in the air around him.

Extract 4

An international hotel chain assesses work commitment as one of the measures in a 'balanced scorecard' of organisational performance. However the measure has been developed in the USA, on American employees. As the hotel chain expanded into the Asia Pacific region it became clear that there was a need to reassess their method of organisational performance and to test its relevance and validity in the culturally diverse Asia Pacific region. Using the cultural dimensions of Trompenaars and Hampden-Turner this paper presents a preliminary study of Australian, Malaysian and Thai employees. Surveys, focus groups, expert panels and interviews were conducted. Findings of this preliminary study show that the US dimensions for work commitment are not appropriate to the Malaysian and Thai employees who focus on relationships with co-workers, customers and their supervisors more than opportunities for personal gain or growth. Differences were also apparent between Malaysia and Thailand in relation to primary focus on remuneration in Malaysia and relationships in Thailand. A larger study will build on the current findings to explore further the drivers and outcome behaviours of work commitment in the Asia Pacific region and create an index to measure this.[13]

KEY

Detailed analysis
Extract 1 is adapted from an authentic promotional leaflet aimed at holidaymakers. Because visitors to a city usually want to stay close to places of interest, the location is the main selling point so it comes first followed by an indication of the quality and hence, by implication, the price.

Extract 2 is a constructed example which could be from a popular financial newspaper or magazine, which provides news and background on business topics. The readers are usually interested in bad news (shareholders' questioning of management) so this comes first followed by a possible explanation for it. The text also acts as a warning to any readers thinking of purchasing Luxus shares.

Extract 3 could be part of a novel set in a hotel. The writer wants to set the scene in which the action takes place but also let the reader know the mood of the traveller. She does this by describing the room as if the reader were the traveller looking at it. For this reason, the description is partly in narrative form, following the order in which the traveller might notice the features of the room.

Extract 4 is an authentic abstract from a research article. Abstracts are very brief summaries of research articles, written for members of an academic community, who use them to decide if they want to read the whole article. They are, thus, the academic equivalent of a film trailer which advertises the film in order to persuade people to pay to see it. Academic researchers gain status if their articles are read and cited so the abstract is used to emphasize the importance and relevance of the research to the discipline.

Analysing the moves in a genre

In order to achieve their overall purpose, genres proceed through a number of stages or *moves*, which each have a specific rhetorical objective. These moves express the intention of the writer at particular points in the text and do not map precisely on to sentences or paragraphs. Hyland[14] analysed research article abstracts in a variety of disciplines and suggested that the structure shown in the table below is widely used.

Move	Function
1 Introduction	Establishes the context of the paper and motivates the research.
2 Purpose	Indicates the purpose, and outlines the intention, behind the paper.
3 Method	Provides information on design, procedures, assumptions, data, etc.
4 Results	States the main findings, the argument or what was accomplished.
5 Conclusion	Interprets or extends the results, draws inferences, points to implications.

Task 5

Look back to the abstract in extract 4 of Task 4 and identify the moves, basing your analysis on Hyland's model.

KEY

The table below shows that the main moves in this abstract closely follow Hyland's model.

Move	Function
1 Introduction – establishes the context of the paper and motivates the research [by indicating the limitation of current research, signalled by *however*]	An international hotel chain assesses work commitment as one of the measures in a 'balanced scorecard' of organizational performance. However the measure has been developed in the USA, on American employees.
2 Purpose – indicates the purpose, and outlines the intention, behind the paper	As the hotel chain expanded into the Asia Pacific region, it became clear that there was a need to reassess their method of organizational performance and to test its relevance and validity in the culturally diverse Asia Pacific region.
3 Method – provides information on design, subjects in the study and data collection	Using the cultural dimensions of Trompenaars and Hampden-Turner this paper presents a preliminary study of Australian, Malaysian and Thai employees. Surveys, focus groups, expert panels and interviews were conducted.
4 Results – states the main findings and the argument [whether or not dimensions for work commitment are applicable in different contexts]	Findings of this preliminary study show that the US dimensions for work commitment are not appropriate to the Malaysian and Thai employees who focus on relationships with co-workers, customers and their supervisors more than opportunities for personal gain or growth. Differences were also apparent between Malaysia and Thailand in relation to primary focus on remuneration in Malaysia and relationships in Thailand.

| 5 Conclusion – points to implications [the need for further research to create an index to measure work commitment] | A larger study will build on the current findings to explore further the drivers and outcome behaviours of work commitment in the Asia Pacific region and create an index to measure this. |

Views of genre

Different linguistic schools formulate different interpretations of the term *genre*, ranging from descriptions based mainly on the relation of ideas in a text and the purpose of their ordering (e.g., *narrative, procedure*)[15] to definitions focused on the role of texts in their social contexts.[16] Some linguists view genres as conventional practices with relatively stable audiences and purposes. This means that the texts which record these practices also have a conventional organization, which has proved effective to date in achieving the purposes. Others view genres as a form of social action[17] in which genres are not fixed but are constantly changing through the interactions of the authors and their audiences.[18]

This chapter will regard a written genre as anything which writers think they are writing. In all areas of life, if asked what they are doing, writers will identify the genre (and therefore social purpose). People will say they are writing a shopping list, a letter to the bank manager or a research proposal, not a list of foodstuffs, an explanation of their financial position or a description of how their research will be done and why it is important. Although such genre labels are easily recognizable, the same label can apply to very different texts, e.g., a student's letter to the bank manager is likely to be different to a letter from the owner of a successful business. In EAP, genre analysis is used as a means of investigating the social and rhetorical practices of students' future discourse communities.[19] This raises students' awareness that even genres with similar names, e.g., essay and report, are specific to particular disciplines, and one instance of a genre (one text) may not contain all the typical features.

An awareness of genre is important for the following reasons:

- It highlights global aspects of text such as audience, purpose and organization.
- It encourages students to approach texts as expert readers (as they would in their own language), leading to more authentic and purposeful reading.[20]
- It leads to more authentic tasks for teaching and assessing reading and writing.[21]
- It helps students to make a connection with their future academic communities.

Using these ideas with students

When approaching a text, expert readers will first of all identify the genre and thereby the purpose and organization of that text. This makes the next step, identifying the main ideas contained in the text, easier. It is useful for students to follow this practice as well.

One of the criticisms of a genre approach is that it adheres too closely to conventional models and encourages students to produce formulaic writing which ignores the process of composing. This can be true if models are followed simplistically but most expert writers, when required to write a new genre, will automatically search for examples to get them started. Lecturers usually put copies of essays, dissertations and theses into the library so students can consult them. Teaching students to do genre analysis helps them to use these models effectively.

Exercises similar to Tasks 4 and 5 can help students to analyse texts. Texts can be chosen to suit the level of the class and tasks can be scaffolded as follows:

- Students look at short texts and match them to their genre.
- Students discover the organization of more complex texts by rearranging jumbled sections or sentences to suit the purpose of the text.
- Students use different coloured pens to highlight the organizational moves in texts such as abstracts (as shown in Task 4) or the introductions to research papers.[22]
- Instructions for writing tasks should specify a particular audience and purpose; students can speculate about what these readers already know and what they need or expect to be told.

For each text that students read, they can answer the following questions to sensitize them to genre:

- Who are the readers of this text?
- Why was this text written? What is it trying to achieve?
- What organization has been selected as most appropriate for that audience and purpose?
- What are the stages or moves through which this organization proceeds?

Functions

When writers want to show relationships between ideas, they use rhetorical functions such as comparing, defining, classifying. These functions operate at the paragraph level and inform the choice of vocabulary and sentence structures. They could be thought of as the basic building blocks of texts. They are often used by subject lecturers to give feedback to students:

- *You have not <u>defined</u> your terms.*
- *You confuse <u>cause and effect</u>.*
- *You have not explained the <u>problem</u> clearly.*
- *Your <u>argument</u> is weak in this paragraph.*

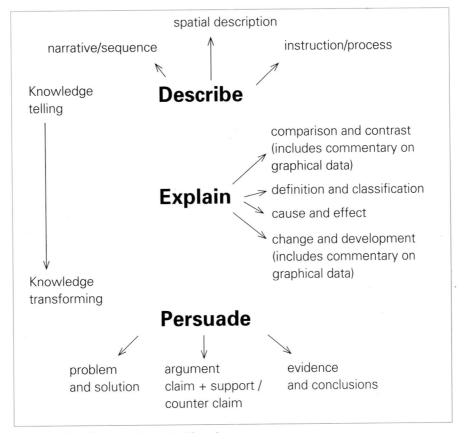

Figure 1: *Classification of rhetorical functions*

Rhetorical functions can be classified into three main macro-functions, as shown in Figure 1, depending on whether the rhetorical purpose is to describe, to explain or to persuade. Within each of these broad categories are listed the more specific functions which relate to them. There is a progression from knowledge telling, in which the writer presents information in a straightforward way, to knowledge transforming, in which the writer restructures information in order to explain or persuade a reader.[23] Observing and then describing a process is cognitively a less challenging task to achieve than deciding on a point of view and arguing for that view. Thus within the classification, there is a progression from more simple to more complex functions.

It is important to remember that texts are almost always multi-functional. Writers have different purposes, realized by different rhetorical functions, throughout their texts, so it does not make sense to talk about a 'comparison and contrast text' or a 'cause and effect text'. Some functions will cluster together, e.g., classification into categories also requires comparison of items within a category and contrast between categories; problems are usually accompanied by an explanation of their causes and effects. An analysis of the functions in texts involves looking at the *non-content* language of the text and using this to identify the main rhetorical function and any supporting functions.[24] The examples below are taken from the introduction and the final paragraph of the case study, presented in Task 2. The content words which carry the ideas have mostly been removed, leaving just the functional language (in italics) and the structure.

1. The Metropole *and* the Luxus ... *The former,* ... *whereas* the Luxus, ... *Both* ... similar...: the Luxus ... *while* the Metropole ...

This part of the text compares the two hotels: they are mentioned together in each sentence and are linked by vocabulary characteristic of comparison and contrast.

2. Despite its *dependence* on... the Metropole..., *perhaps because* ... *enabled* it... The Luxus *might* have been expected..., as... *some effects*... This was *because*... *Because of* ..., the hotel was not able...

This part of the text explains why the hotels had different experiences after 2001: the sentences are linked by vocabulary for cause and effect. There is also a degree of hedging, *perhaps, might, some,* to show that the author is speculating about the causes and is not completely certain.

Task 6

Identify the rhetorical functions contained in the following constructed text. Use the classification in Figure 1 to help you.

- Highlight the language that you used to recognize each function.
- How do these functions determine the organization of the text?

Edinburgh is one of the most beautiful cities in Europe with a city centre which has retained much of its original splendour. However, it suffers increasingly from traffic congestion. Although the population has remained relatively stable, the use of private vehicles has doubled over the last twenty years. The volume of traffic along its narrow streets is beginning to damage the foundations of some of the ancient buildings that give the city its unique character. The Council has introduced a number of measures to reduce congestion. These include a 'greenways' scheme, which gives priority to buses and 'park and ride' schemes to encourage commuters not to drive into the city centre. Critics say that because these initiatives require a voluntary change of attitude on the part of car drivers, they are not sufficient to reduce congestion. Recently, several streets have been designated one-way or closed to private vehicles altogether to keep main roads clear during rush hours. A congestion charging scheme, similar to the one operating in London, is also being considered. Until private car use becomes less convenient than public transport, because of delays and traffic jams, people will always try to use their cars.

KEY

The text is separated into sentences in the table below with the language for each rhetorical function underlined and annotated in brackets. The main rhetorical function is *problem and solution* but this is not stated explicitly. The reader interprets this through the changes that are mentioned to the city's congestion, an inherently negative concept. An increase in congestion is interpreted as a problem and a decrease as a solution. This function also determines the organization of the text. Other rhetorical functions associated with the main one are *purpose, comparison and contrast, change and development, cause and effect, reason and result.*

Organization of the text	Annotated text
Background to the problem	Edinburgh is <u>one of the most</u> [*comparison*] beautiful cities in Europe with a city centre which <u>has retained</u> much of its <u>original</u> [*development*] splendour.
Problem	However [*contrast*], it <u>suffers</u> [*problem*] <u>increasingly</u> [*change*] from traffic <u>congestion</u> [*problem*].
One cause of the problem	<u>Although</u> [*contrast*] the population has remained <u>relatively stable,</u> [*change*] the use of private vehicles <u>has doubled</u> [*change*] over the last twenty years.
One effect of the problem	The volume of traffic along its narrow streets <u>is beginning</u> [*change*] to <u>damage</u> [*problem*] the foundations of some of the ancient buildings that give the city its <u>unique</u> [*comparison*] character.

Proposed general solution to the problem	The Council has introduced a number of <u>measures</u> [*solution*] to <u>reduce</u> [*change*] congestion.
Specific solutions	These include a 'greenways' <u>scheme</u>, which <u>gives priority</u> [*solution*] to buses, and 'park and ride' <u>schemes</u> to <u>encourage</u> [*solution*] commuters not to drive into the city centre.
Evaluation of the solutions	<u>Critics</u> [*negative evaluation*] say that <u>because</u> [*reason*] these <u>initiatives</u> [*solution*] require a voluntary change of attitude on the part of car drivers, they are <u>not sufficient</u> [*negative evaluation*] to <u>reduce</u> [*change*] congestion.
Further specific solutions	Recently, several streets have been <u>designated</u> [*solution*] one-way or closed to private vehicles altogether <u>to</u> [*reason/purpose*] keep main roads clear during rush hours. A congestion charging <u>scheme</u>, [*solution*] <u>similar to</u> [*comparison*] the one operating in London, is also being <u>considered</u>. [*solution*]
Evaluation of the solutions	Until private car use becomes <u>less</u> convenient <u>than</u> [*comparison*] public transport, <u>because of</u> [*reason*] delays and traffic jams, people <u>will always</u> try to <u>use</u> their cars [*result*].

It is important for students to be aware of functions for the following reasons:

- Functions are the aspects of texts which are most transferable across academic disciplines, in contrast to genres which are discipline-specific.
- Identifying functions in texts is a way for students to recognize relationships between ideas and how these change through a text.
- Awareness of functions helps students to understand the meanings of linking expressions, e.g., *however, on the contrary, moreover,* and use them appropriately.
- An analysis of functions can generate patterns of language and organization which students can learn.
- Encouraging students to record language according to its functional meaning provides them with a useful resource for their own writing.

Rhetorical functions are a useful starting point for designing an EAP syllabus, particularly for writing.[25] Functions which are cognitively simpler can be taught first before progressing to more complex ones. Similarly, writing tasks can progress from paragraph level descriptions and definitions to multi-functional persuasive texts. This also allows functions covered earlier in the syllabus to be recycled. Functions can also be integrated with genre in a syllabus by specifying goals of authentic academic reading and writing tasks and then supporting students in the process of achieving these through smaller functional steps.

Exercises similar to Task 6 can help students to look beyond the meanings of words and understand the meaning of paragraphs and the links between ideas in texts. Texts appropriate to the level of students can be used as follows:

- Students identify the main rhetorical purpose and the effect this has on text organization, e.g., in the text about the Luxus and the Metropole in Task 2, paragraph topics are either the hotels or the particular feature used to compare them.
- Students highlight language which indicates the function of a text and then record it on a personal reference page. After analysing several texts, they will have a range of useful structures and lexis which are transferable to other reading and writing tasks.
- Students use these reference pages to write sentences, paragraphs and larger texts.
- Before submitting a piece of written work for assessment, students can be asked to highlight in their texts the functional language they have used.

Students can answer the following questions for each text they read to sensitize them to functions:

- What is the relationship between the ideas in this part of the text?
- What functional language shows this relationship?

The relationship between functions and genres

There is a great deal of variety in the terminology for analysing texts beyond sentence level and different linguistic schools draw boundaries at different places.[26] In the simplified description presented here, we will say that genres are named practices, e.g., essay, research paper, with social purposes that are discipline-specific. One genre might include several sub-genres, e.g., a research paper includes sections such as introduction, method and conclusion which can each have conventional structures. Rhetorical functions, on the other hand, operate below the level of genre to enable writers to achieve their local rhetorical purposes in texts. They are realized through general academic language which is transferable across disciplines. It is possible to analyse the same text from the perspective of either genre or function.

The text in Task 7 below is an introduction to a research paper, written by a novice researcher in the field of applied linguistics and published in a set of conference proceedings.[27] The genre moves in this introduction can be analysed using a metaphor developed by Swales,[28] which shows that researchers establish a niche for themselves within a research field in a similar fashion to an organism establishing itself in an ecological niche. Some of the moves, outlined below, are optional, depending on the research field.

Move 1: establishing a territory	by showing that the general research area is important, central, interesting, problematic, or relevant in some way	Optional
	by introducing and reviewing items of previous research in the area	Obligatory
Move 2: establishing a niche	by indicating a gap in previous research	Obligatory
	or by extending previous knowledge in some way	
Move 3: occupying the niche	by outlining purposes or stating the nature of the present research	Obligatory
	by listing research questions or hypotheses	Probable in some fields but rare in others
	by announcing principle findings	
	by stating the value of present research	
	by indicating the structure of the paper	

It is also possible to analyse this text using the function of problem and solution.

Task 7

Read the text and identify the genre moves (note that not all the moves shown above are present). Then identify the *background, problem, solution, evaluation.*

- What different information does each type of analysis contribute to understanding the text?

Research into writing as a process has brought about a transformation in the way writing is taught in both L1 and ESL classrooms. Studies of skilled and unskilled writers composing and revising their texts show these processes to be cyclical rather than linear, to occur in phases and to interact with one another (Hayes, Flower, Schriver, Stratman and Carey, 1987). Teachers now search for ways to intervene at different stages of the process, encourage the writing of multiple drafts and prompt revision through different kinds of feedback (Dheram, 1995). However, revising effectively is difficult for skilled and unskilled writers alike, the main obstacle being an inability to view the text objectively (Faigley and Witte, 1984) to see what problems it creates for its intended audience.

Teachers need to find ways to help students imagine a reader and begin to build a dialogue with that reader by way of their text (Nystrand, 1982). It is not easy to bring authentic audiences into classrooms. A promising technique, which has been evaluated for L1 writing classrooms (Schriver, 1992), is the use of think-aloud protocols, which allow writers to listen 'on line' as members of their intended audience read and attempt to understand or use their texts. The technique is similar to audiotaped feedback (Boswood and Dwyer, 1995) but with the absence of teacherly comments. The teacher stays in role as a member of the intended audience. The results of the studies with L1 writers suggest that such reader-response protocols are pedagogically useful. It is important, however, not to generalise L1 findings to ESL contexts without empirical evaluation.

The purpose of this study, therefore, was to evaluate the effectiveness of reader-response protocols as a feedback technique for a small group of ESL students as they wrote and revised their texts.

Genre moves	Text (abbreviated)	Function
Establish a territory by showing that the general research area is important and relevant [*brought about a transformation*].	Research into writing as a process has brought about a transformation in the way writing is taught in both L1 and ESL classrooms.	Background
Establish a territory by reviewing previous research.	Studies of skilled and unskilled writers composing ... interact with one another (Hayes, Flower, Schriver, Stratman and Carey, 1987).	
	Teachers now search for ways to intervene ... different kinds of feedback (Dheram, 1995).	
	However, revising effectively is difficult ...an inability to view the text objectively (Faigley and Witte, 1984) ... intended audience.	Problem
	Teachers need to find ways to help students imagine a reader ... (Nystrand, 1982).	General solution
	It is not easy to bring authentic audiences into classrooms.	Evaluation
	A promising technique... (Schriver, 1992), is the use of think-aloud protocols... read and attempt to understand or use their texts.	Specific solution
	The technique is similar to audiotaped feedback (Boswood and Dwyer, 1995) but with the absence of teacherly comments.	
	The teacher stays in role as a member of the intended audience.	
	The results of the studies with L1 writers suggest that such reader-response protocols are pedagogically useful.	Evaluation
Establish a niche by extending research to new contexts.	It is important, however, not to generalise L1 findings to ESL contexts without empirical evaluation.	
Occupying the niche by outlining the purposes of the research.	The purpose of this study, therefore, was to evaluate the effectiveness of reader response protocols as a feedback technique for a small group of ESL students ...	

The genre analysis of this text gives some insight into the context of the genre, showing the way in which a novice researcher typically creates a research space in the field of applied linguistics by extending previous research into new areas. The functional analysis, on the other hand, shows in detail the argument in the review of previous studies, which is not captured at the level of the genre analysis. Both these types of analysis contribute to a coherent picture of text organization and the logical development of ideas which is explored further in the next section.

Cohesion

'Cohesion refers to the range of possibilities that exist for linking something [in text] with what has gone before.'[29] These links, or ties, operate beyond the level of the sentence. Readers interpret them as meaningful and use them together with the context to create coherence in what they are hearing or reading. Cohesion is a property of texts whereas coherence is constructed by listeners and readers. Halliday and Hasan outline the linguistic resources available in English for creating cohesion in text.[30] You are probably already aware of many of these resources. The five main kinds of cohesive ties are shown below:

Reference

Linna told **Hossein** the secret but he kept **it** to **himself**.

The Internet is useful for finding information **which** is not available in other sources.

Substitution

Dark objects absorb more light; lighter **ones** reflect more light.

Information is linked into the program automatically if you tell the compiler to **do so**.

Ellipsis

Bacteria of the genus Vibrio are Gram-negative, [**they are**] motile by one or more polar flagella, [**they**] grow on thiosulfate citrate bile salt sucrose agar.

Vibrios are very common in marine and estuarine habitats and [**very common**] on the surface of marine animals.

Conjunction

People work harder **when** they are being observed **because** that is what they believe they are required to do.

Within the Sumerian culture the priesthood formed a quasicivil service, busying[31] itself with religion **whilst also** overseeing taxation **and** the allocation of resources.

Lexical – chains

Buckle your **seatbelt** for a **ride** on the information super**highway**.

Lexical – signalling nouns

We travelled by train to Edinburgh. The **journey** lasted four and a half hours.

An **advantage** of the factory system was that it served as a focus for the introduction of new technology.

Task 8

Find and classify the cohesive ties in the text below.

Edinburgh is one of the most beautiful cities in Europe with a city centre which has retained much of its original splendour. However, it suffers increasingly from traffic congestion. Although the population has remained relatively stable, the use of private vehicles has doubled over the last twenty years. To deal with this problem the Council would like to encourage drivers to leave their cars at home and take the bus but because of the inconvenience, many drivers do not want to do so.

> **KEY**
>
> The cohesive ties are highlighted in the text and listed below:
>
> Edinburgh is *one* of the most beautiful cities in Europe *with* a city centre *which* has retained much of *its* original splendour. *However*, *it* suffers increasingly from traffic congestion. *Although* the population [*of Edinburgh*] has remained relatively stable, the use of private vehicles [*in Edinburgh*] has doubled over the last twenty years. To deal *with this problem* the Council [*of Edinburgh*] would like to encourage drivers to leave *their* cars at home and take the bus *but because of* the inconvenience, many drivers do not want to *do so*.
>
> | reference | *one* is a determiner which refers forward to *cities in Europe*; *which, its, it* are pronouns which refer back to *city centre* or *Edinburgh*; *the* in *the population*, and in *the use of private vehicles* is a determiner which specifies that which population or where the use occurs is *Edinburgh*; *their* is a determiner which refers back to *drivers* |
> |---|---|

substitution	*do so* substitutes for *leave their cars at home and take the bus*
ellipsis	the noun phrases *the population, the use of private vehicles, the Council* have the phrases of *Edinburgh* or *in Edinburgh* missing; the fixed phrase *at home* implies at *their* homes
conjunction	*However, Although, but* indicate contrast; *and, with* [not strictly a conjunction] indicate addition; *because of* indicates a reason
lexical	there are a number of lexical chains which link the topic: *Edinburgh – cities – city centre – population – Council; beautiful – splendour; traffic congestion – private vehicles – drivers – cars – bus; stable – doubled*
signalling nouns	*this problem* refers back to information in the previous two sentences and classifies it with a general noun, *problem*; *the inconvenience* refers back to the phrase *leave their cars at home and take the bus* and evaluates it with a general noun, *inconvenience*

There is not space to discuss cohesion in detail so we will concentrate on two aspects which are not usually covered in general English courses but are particularly important for reading and writing academic texts:

- the information structure of sentences in texts – theme and rheme development
- lexical cohesion – the use of general nouns for signalling connections in texts

Information structure: theme–rheme development in texts

Information structure concerns the way a message is delivered in a clause or sentence and how writers get out of one sentence and into the next. It contributes to the smooth flow and logical development of ideas through a text and to the maintenance of topics in paragraphs. To understand this analysis it is necessary to consider clauses and sentences in terms of their function rather than their form. They should not be viewed as collections of grammatical categories: *noun, adjective, verb* and *adverb*, but as containers for ideas.

Look at the following two sentences[32] which appear to have very similar forms.

> Time flies like an arrow.

> Fruit flies like a banana.

We can ask functional questions about the ideas in these sentences.

Functional questions	Container	Grammatical function	Grammatical form
What are we talking about?	theme	subject	noun phrase (*Time/Fruit flies*)
What are we saying about it/them?	rheme	predicate	verb phrase (*flies like an arrow / like a banana*)
What are the circumstances?		adjunct[33]	prepositional phrase (*like an arrow*)

The term *theme* is used to name the first element in a clause or sentence. This element is important because it is 'the point of departure',[34] which orients readers to the message they are about to receive. It usually contains information related to the topic of the paragraph. The theme is developed within the *rheme*, which is the remainder of the sentence. The rheme is the point of the message and shows where it is heading. In simple one-clause sentences, the theme is normally the subject and the rheme the predicate, as in the examples above. In complex sentences, the theme may be the first subordinate clause, which in turn contains its own theme and rheme.

The position of ideas in theme or rheme is very important for meaning in English. This can be seen in the following sentences which have very different meanings:

theme	rheme
The teacher	destroyed the mobile phone.
The mobile phone	destroyed the teacher.

In order to maintain the topic and manage the logical flow of ideas through a text, it is sometimes necessary to change the order of ideas in a sentence from theme to rheme. English has a number of grammatical resources which can be used to do this, one of which is shown in the following task.

Task 9

Here are two paragraphs with two different topics. What is the topic of each paragraph?

In both paragraphs, sentences 3 and 4 contain the same information but it is in different places in the sentence. How has this been achieved?

A At Bettaworld we value efficiency in our workforce. We are very clear about the duties of each member of staff. The sales assistant deals with enquiries over the phone. The manager contacts clients personally. This ensures that there is no duplication of effort.

B At Bettaworld we value our clients. They make our business a success. Their enquiries are dealt with immediately by the sales assistant. Some clients are contacted personally by the manager. This ensures that they continue to do business with Bettaworld.

KEY

The topic is underlined in each paragraph below. In paragraph A, it appears first in the rheme of sentence 2; in paragraph B, it appears first in the rheme of sentence 1. The topic then reappears in the themes of sentences 3 and 4 in both paragraphs.

The verbs in sentences 3 and 4 of each text are shown in italics. They are active in text A and passive in text B. This makes it possible for the information relating to the topic of the paragraph to be placed in the themes of sentences 3 and 4.

A At Bettaworld we value efficiency in our workforce. We are very clear about the <u>duties of each member of staff</u>. <u>The sales assistant</u> *deals with* enquiries over the phone. <u>The manager</u> *contacts* clients personally. This ensures that there is no duplication of effort.

B At Bettaworld we value <u>our clients</u>. They make our business a success. <u>Their enquiries</u> *are dealt with* immediately by the sales assistant. <u>Some clients</u> *are contacted* personally by the manager. This ensures that they continue to do business with Bettaworld.

This task shows how the passive voice can be used to transfer information from rheme to theme, depending on the paragraph topic. In language classes, students are often given exercises to transform sentences from active voice to passive voice. However, transforming sentences out of their paragraph context can give students the idea that paraphrasing is an arbitrary activity not governed by any purpose. As a result, when they come to paraphrase academic texts, students tend to move information between theme and rheme without taking into account the topic of their summary.

Students need to be made aware of the reasons why information about topics should appear in theme position. They also need to be shown the grammatical resources in English for transferring information between rhemes and themes.

Classroom materials 2.5 *Topic development* gives a students' version of this task.

What to put first in a sentence

Writers make information flow logically through their paragraphs by ensuring that the topics in their themes relate to the topic of the paragraph in a systematic way. The next task uses an authentic text from an undergraduate business studies course and shows some of the choices that the writer had when starting his sentences.

Task 10

a Below are the first four sentences of a text entitled *Groups and Group Formation*. The first sentence is given but for the remaining text there is a choice of three possible sentences. All sentences are grammatically correct but only one maintains the logical flow of ideas in the paragraph. Construct the text by choosing the most appropriate sentence in each case.

Underline the theme in each sentence which shows the topic of the sentence. The first one is done for you. Indicate where the information for each theme is located in the preceding text.

Groups and Group Formation

1   <u>The group</u> is an important unit in the study of organisational behaviour.

2 a Studying groups is especially valuable when group dynamics are analysed.

  b Analysing group dynamics is especially valuable for studying groups.

  c What is especially valuable for studying groups is group dynamics.

3 a The social situation in which interactions and forces among group members occur is the concern of group dynamics.

  b Group dynamics is concerned with the interactions and forces among group members in a social situation.

  c The interactions and forces among group members in a social situation is the concern of group dynamics.

4 a The dynamics of members of formal or informal work groups and teams in an organisation are the focus when the concept of group dynamics is applied to the study of organisational behaviour.

  b When the concept of group dynamics is applied to the study of organisational behaviour, the focus is on the dynamics of members of formal or informal work groups and teams in the organisation.

  c The focus, when the concept of group dynamics is applied to the study of organisational behaviour, is on the dynamics of members of formal or informal work groups and teams in the organisation.

KEY

The first part of the text as it was originally written is shown below with the themes underlined. The information in italics in the rhemes of sentences 1 and 2 reappears in the themes of sentences 2 and 3.

Groups and Group Formation

1   The group is an important unit in the *study* of organisational behaviour.

2   a   Studying groups is especially valuable when *group dynamics* are analysed.

3   b   Group dynamics is concerned with the interactions and forces among group members in a social situation.

4   b   When *the concept* of *group dynamics* is applied to the study of organisational behaviour, the focus is on the dynamics of members of formal or informal work groups and teams in the organisation.

The themes and rhemes in the first four sentences of this text follow a simple and logical development:

Theme 1 [the group]   ⟶   Rheme 1 [study]

Theme 2 [studying groups]   ⟶   Rheme 2 [group dynamics]

Theme 3 [group dynamics]   ⟶   Rheme 3 [interactions/members]

Theme 3 [group dynamics]   ⟶   Rheme 4 [formal/informal groups]

The diagram shows how this writer has managed the information in his sentences. The first theme contains the topic, *the group*, which is known to the reader from the title. The first rheme says something about this topic which is new to the reader. However, once it has been introduced, it is familiar information and can be summarized in the theme of the next sentence. Sometimes the writer chooses to repeat a theme, *group dynamics*, so that he can say something else about it that is new to the reader. This new information is developed in more detail in the rhemes of subsequent sentences. In each sentence, the writer tries to give the reader some familiar information in the theme as a starting point for new information in the rheme. This is the way writers maintain the logical flow of ideas through their texts.

The first part of this text has a very simple information structure. However, most authentic texts are more complex than this and, indeed, this text becomes more complex as the writer develops his ideas. Nevertheless, he maintains the logical flow between given information in the themes and new information in the rhemes.

Task 10

b   Here is the rest of the text from Task 10a starting with sentence 4. Construct the remainder of the text by choosing the most appropriate sentence each time.

Underline the theme which shows the topic of each sentence. *Highlight* information in the rhemes which reappears subsequently in the text.

4 b When <u>the concept of group dynamics</u> is applied to the study of organisational behaviour, the focus is on the dynamics of members of formal or informal work groups and teams in the organisation.

5 a A group consists of two or more people interacting interdependently to achieve common goals for behavioural scientists.

   b Two or more people interacting interdependently to achieve common goals is what constitutes a group for behavioural scientists.

   c For behavioural scientists a group consists of two or more people interacting interdependently to achieve common goals.

6 a Formal work groups are established by organisations to achieve organisational goals.

   b Organisations establish formal work groups to achieve organisational goals.

   c The achievement of organisational goals is the purpose of formal work groups.

7 a The common interests of organisational members prompt informal work groups to form naturally.

   b Informal work groups form naturally in response to the common interests of organisational members.

   c In response to the common interests of organisational members, informal work groups form naturally.

8 a Even relatively simple groups are actually complex social devices that require a fair amount of negotiation and trial-and-error before individual members begin to function as a true group.

b Complex social devices that require a fair amount of negotiation and trial-and-error before individual members begin to function as a true group are what even relatively simple groups actually are.

c Before individual members begin to function as a true group, even in relatively simple groups, they require a fair amount of negotiation and trial-and-error because they are actually complex social devices.

KEY

The remainder of the text as it was originally written is shown with the themes <u>underlined</u>. The information in *italics* appears in subsequent themes or rhemes.

Notice that the themes of sentences 6a and 7b are used to contrast two different types of group. This is a very common way to handle contrast in texts.

4 b When <u>the concept of group dynamics</u> is applied to the study of *organisational behaviour*, the focus is on the dynamics of members of *formal or informal work groups* and teams in the organisation.

5 c <u>For behavioural scientists, a group</u> consists of two or more people interacting interdependently to *achieve common goals*.

6 a <u>Formal work groups</u> are established by organisations to achieve *organisational goals*.

7 b <u>Informal work groups</u> form naturally in response to the *common interests of organisational members*.

8 a Even <u>relatively simple groups</u> are actually complex social devices that require a fair amount of negotiation and trial-and-error before individual members begin to function as a true group.

The development of themes and rhemes in the final five sentences of the original text is shown in the diagram below:

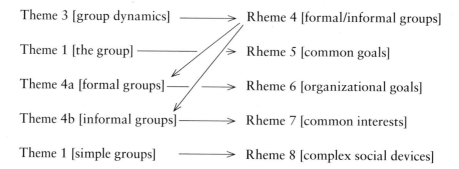

The development is now more complex with information in rheme 4 reappearing in themes 4a and 4b and information in rheme 5 being developed further in rhemes 6 and 7. The final sentence acts as a conclusion to this paragraph so it paraphrases some of the ideas which have been presented earlier, e.g., *simple groups, complex social devices*, to prepare for the next paragraph.

The information in the themes appears in summarized form because it has moved into the background. The writer expects the reader to consider it as given and only need reminding about it, e.g.,

the study of organizational behaviour ⟶ studying

However, new information in the rheme is often presented in long complex phrases and clauses because the new details require longer explanation. It is easier for readers to understand long complex phrases and clauses if they are at the end of a sentence, e.g., 8a below is easier to read and understand than 8b.

8 a Even relatively simple groups are actually complex social devices that require a fair amount of negotiation and trial-and-error before individual members begin to function as a true group.

8 b Complex social devices that require a fair amount of negotiation and trial-and-error before individual members begin to function as a true group are what even relatively simple groups actually are.

This flow of information is what university lecturers are referring to when they tell students to write clearly and logically. The key aspects of thematic development in texts are as follows:

- Readers need familiar information (usually the topic) in mind before they read something new about it.

- Familiar or given information is usually in the themes of sentences.
- Rhemes usually contain new information which is temporarily the focus of attention.
- Detailed explanations in complex phrases or clauses are easier for readers to understand if they are in rhemes.
- Information in rhemes reappears in subsequent themes in summary form because it has moved to the background.
- This movement of information from rheme to theme links the developing text to what has gone before and helps to maintain the topic.

These aspects of thematic development should be seen as tendencies rather than rules. Writers usually follow them but sometimes they have good reasons for not doing so, e.g., sometimes they want to force a marked reading of the text so they put new information into the theme and thus into the background, where it can be considered as given. On other occasions, they place old information into the rheme to emphasize it.

Information structure is a very powerful resource for creating cohesion in texts. The cohesion in the text, *Groups and Group Formation*, is managed almost entirely by its information structure. There is only one conjunction, *when*, and no substitution of pronouns for noun phrases. Academic and technical writing in particular tend to manage cohesion in this way in order to reduce any ambiguity in what is being referred to.

Working with more complex themes

The section on register showed the overall purposes for using language:
- to communicate ideas
- to establish relationships
- to manage the communication

The themes in a text help to communicate ideas because they usually contain information about the topics of clauses and sentences in order to orient readers to the ideas they are about to receive. This information might be contained in the subject of a simple sentence but, as shown in sentence four in Task 10 above, it might also be contained in a subordinate clause within a complex sentence. Themes which communicate ideas are called topical themes.

However, the theme position can also be used to establish and maintain the relationship with readers, by showing how the writer views the ideas; or it can be used to manage the communication, by preparing the reader to understand the relationships between ideas. These are called interpersonal and textual themes, in contrast to topical themes, and are illustrated below.

English teachers can be asked to work with students preparing for university study. Unfortunately, however, they are not given sufficient guidance to help them to do this.

Unfortunately is an interpersonal theme which expresses the writer's stance towards the ideas in the rheme of the second sentence. *However* is a textual theme which helps the reader to understand that ideas in the second sentence will contrast with ideas in the first. *They* is the topical theme which repeats the topical theme of the first sentence, *English teachers*, because the writer has more to say about this topic.[35]

Using these ideas with students

Exercises such as those in Tasks 9 and 10 can be used to raise students' awareness of information structure in English. When asked what should go into the first part of a sentence, students often say *'the most important information'* or *'what I want to emphasize'*. In fact, as this analysis shows, what comes first in the sentence is information which the reader already has in mind and which prepares the ground at the end of the sentence for new important information that the writer wants to emphasize.

Students can examine texts they have been working with or texts from their subject areas which can be used to create tasks similar to Task 10. Alternatively, information can be changed from theme to rheme in just one or two sentences in a text which students have to find and correct.[36]

Classroom materials 2.6 Information flow provides a students' version of Task 10.

An understanding of thematic development can also help in giving more in-depth feedback on global aspects of students' writing. Often, difficulties in students' writing lie in their choice of theme position for information which would be better placed in the rheme (or vice versa), as the following tasks show:

Task 11

A student on a pre-sessional course has been asked to write about the problem of plastic bag litter. She has suggested that one solution is to make people pay for plastic bags. Here is the part of her text which evaluates that solution.

- What could she do to her first sentence to improve the logic and clarity of her writing?

People will think over when they are going to abandon useless plastic bags stemming from economic reasons if they have to pay for them. But this policy may not be easily accepted by the retailers because they have gained large profits by offering free plastic bags to their clients.

KEY

The student could improve the logic and clarity of her writing by changing the information (underlined) from rheme to theme in the first sentence (and removing the phrase in brackets). She has already introduced the solution so it is not new information as her original sentence structure might suggest. The general noun *policy* in the theme of sentence 2 then summarizes the statement of the policy (*paying for plastic bags*) in the theme of sentence 1.

If people have to pay for plastic bags, they will think over when they are going to abandon them [stemming from economic reasons]. But this policy may not be easily accepted by the retailers because they have gained large profits by offering free plastic bags to their clients.

Task 12

A student on an undergraduate economics course has written an essay about the effects of market reforms on a centralized economy (in this case Poland). His lecturer has picked out the following sentences for comment and asked him to change them, as indicated in the comment.

- Can you make the change the lecturer is suggesting?

Liberalisation would be the second aspect of the reforms [in Poland]. This would allow market reforms to take the place of the central planner and eliminate the controls over prices, inputs and barriers to foreign trade.

- **Lecturer comment:** Make 'elimination of the controls over prices, inputs and barriers to foreign trade' the subject of your second sentence so you can clearly show cause and effect.

KEY

The rewritten text is shown below with the sentence themes underlined. The thematization requested by the lecturer shows more clearly that 'liberalisation' is seen to be the same as 'elimination of the controls over prices, inputs and barriers to foreign trade'.

> *Liberalisation* would be the second aspect of the reforms [in Poland]. *Elimination of the controls over prices, inputs and barriers to foreign trade* would allow market reforms to take the place of the central planner.

By analysing information structure in texts they are reading and writing, students can learn how to manage the topics of their paragraphs effectively and to write clearly and logically. When students start writing, they can answer the following questions to sensitize them to information structure:

- What am I talking about?
- What do I want to say about it?
- How does this link with what I've said before?

Lexical cohesion – the use of general nouns for signalling connections in texts

Topical themes in a developing text usually contain a summary of something that has gone before. This summary is often achieved by the use of general nouns to label the ideas contained in phrases, whole sentences or paragraphs.

General nouns such as *activity, approach, issue, problem, solution* are empty lexical items which rely on their context to specify what they refer to, e.g.,

> Financial <u>activities</u> include banking and insurance.

> Passive smoking is an <u>issue</u> of increasing concern.

Flowerdew[37] calls these signalling nouns and Lewis[38] describes them as 'really useful words'. They can give a very brief summary because they classify the person or thing or event or idea which has been described in more detail in previous sentences. They can also be used to specify how the writer wants the person or thing or event or idea to be considered, e.g., as a problem, a solution, an issue, an advantage. Writers can also use these general nouns to show their stance towards the information they present.

Task 13

Find the general nouns which classify in the themes of the text below. Underline the information in the rhemes which they summarize.

- How does the writer view the information?

Bettaworld is a very profitable and competitive company. Its success has led to the company creating new departments and taking on large numbers of new managers and office staff. At first this expansion led to difficulties in communication between the larger departments and their

managers. In order to solve this problem the company introduced new
ways of project based team working and improved communications
by supplying staff with individual computers and telephone lines.
The company had to borrow large amounts of capital to finance this
equipment and the staff training needed to make these changes.
However, the investment was well worth while because it resulted in
better customer service and this improvement increased the company's
profits to an even higher level.

KEY

The general nouns which classify are highlighted in bold in the themes.
The ideas they refer back to are underlined in the preceding rhemes.

Bettaworld is a <u>very profitable and competitive</u> company. Its **success**
has led to the company creating <u>new departments and taking on large</u>
<u>numbers of new managers and office staff</u>. At first this **expansion**
led to <u>difficulties in communication</u> between the larger departments
and their managers. In order to solve this **problem** the company
introduced <u>new ways of project based team working and improved</u>
<u>communications</u> by supplying staff with individual <u>computers and</u>
<u>telephone lines</u>. The company had to <u>borrow large amounts of capital</u>
to finance this **equipment** and the staff training needed to make these
changes. However, the **investment** was well worthwhile because it
resulted in <u>better customer service</u> and this **improvement** increased
the company's profits to an even higher level.

Positive general nouns:	success, investment, improvement
Neutral general nouns:	expansion, equipment, changes
Negative general nouns:	problem

General nouns are usually accompanied by *the* or other determiners, e.g.,
possessive adjectives, *its*, *their*, or by demonstrative adjectives, *this/these* or
that/those, which tell a reader that they refer to other parts of the text, e.g., *its*
success, this expansion, the investment in the text above.

It is also possible to make this reference using demonstrative pronouns, *this/*
these or *that/those*, without an associated general noun. The reference can be
to an entity larger than a noun or noun phrase, e.g., a preceding sentence or
paragraph. However, a common mistake students make is to use the pronoun *it*
rather than *this* to refer back to ideas in sentences or paragraphs. *It* can only refer
back to a noun or noun phrase, e.g., a is possible but not b in these examples:

a   Bettaworld is a very profitable company. <u>This</u> has led to expansion. ✓

b   Bettaworld is a very profitable company. <u>It</u> has led to expansion.   ✗

c   Bettaworld is a very profitable company. <u>This success</u> has led to expansion. ✓

To avoid ambiguity, student writers should be encouraged to specify the preceding information they are referring to by classifying it with a general noun as in c above.

As well as summarizing what has gone before, general nouns can advertise what is coming next, e.g.,

A computer consists of three <u>components</u>: a central processing unit, memory and input/output devices.

The <u>benefits</u> of a university degree are better jobs and increased income.

The second example is a special type of noun phrase in which a general noun, *benefits*, is linked to another noun, *degree*, using the preposition *of*. You might recognize these types of noun phrases from expressions such as a *loaf of bread, a bottle of wine, a great deal of amusing conversation*, where they refer to parts and quantities of other nouns. These double nouns are very common in academic writing, where they have a wider range of applications:

a <u>lack</u> of *skills* or *knowledge*

a key <u>element</u> of attribution *theory*

the <u>pattern</u> of *light* and *movement*

the <u>limitations</u> of integrated *circuits*

Sinclair[39] discusses their meaning in detail and points out the difference in function between the two nouns. The second noun (in italics) gives the main meaning to the phrase but the first noun (underlined) controls the grammar, e.g., a <u>lack</u> of skills or knowledge **is** a disadvantage, and also helps to focus the meaning of the second noun. Sometimes the first noun specifies a quantity or part of the second as in the first two examples above. In other instances, it tells the reader how to view the second noun, as in the last two examples.

These noun phrases can be used to tie a developing text together by advertising and summarizing information in other parts of the text. In the following example the double noun is shown in bold: the first noun of the pair advertises the sources, *your own*, *other people's*, while the second noun summarizes the phrase, *money to start a new business*:

> Raising <u>money to start a new business</u> can be a difficult and expensive task. There are two basic **sources of funding** for new businesses: <u>your own</u> money and <u>other people's</u> money.

These double nouns also play a key role in the process of nominalization, whereby ideas expressed in whole sentences are summarized as noun phrases in the topical themes of a developing text. The following constructed text demonstrates how this process works.

Task 14

a   Here is a developing text about hamburgers and the amount of fat they contain. Complete the theme of each sentence using noun phrases to summarize all the ideas up to that point in the text. The first one has been done for you.

Hamburgers contain fat.

The fat content of hamburgers is high.

_____ is dangerous for your health.

_____ should be reduced.

_____ will not be popular.

_____ should not prevent governments from putting pressure on the manufacturers to change.

Task 14

b   This results in an unnatural text. Make the text more natural by reducing it to three sentences using noun phrases and other cohesive devices.

Classroom materials 2.7 *It's in the news* shows a students' version of these tasks.

> KEY
>
> Here is the developing text about hamburgers. Each theme contains a noun phrase which summarizes the development of the ideas up to that point.
>
> Hamburgers contain fat.
>
> <u>The fat content of hamburgers</u> is high.
>
> <u>The high fat content of hamburgers</u> is dangerous for your health.
>
> <u>The dangerously high fat content of hamburgers</u> should be reduced.
>
> <u>The reduction in the [high] fat content of hamburgers</u> will not be popular.
>
> <u>The unpopularity of the reduction in the [high] fat content of hamburgers</u> should not prevent governments from putting pressure on the manufacturers to change.
>
> The following more natural version uses a double noun phrase and two general nouns (underlined) as well as other cohesive devices: *which, although.*
>
> Hamburgers contain a high level of fat, which is dangerous for your health. <u>The amount of unhealthy fat</u> should be reduced. Although this <u>reduction</u> may not be popular with manufacturers, governments should insist on the <u>change</u>.

General nouns are important for the following reasons:

- They are very frequent in academic texts and in the collocations found there.
- They are one of the main ways that academic writers link and organize ideas in their texts.
- They are applicable to a wide range of subjects and are thus useful for students to learn.
- They help student writers to summarize texts.
- If students can use general nouns, their writing begins to appear more competent and academic to subject specialists.

Classroom materials 2.1 *Recognizing academic style,* 2.2 *Controlling nouns in noun phrases,* 2.3 *Identifying general nouns,* 2.4 *The role of general nouns,* 2.7 *It's in the news* and **2.8 *Summarizing noun phrases*** help students to recognize, understand and construct noun phrases, and use them appropriately in their writing.

Using these ideas with students

You can use tasks such as 13 and 14 to raise students' awareness of the importance of noun phrases and nominalization in academic writing. These ideas are not covered in great detail in current EAP publications so you will probably have to create your own materials. Once they have worked with a text, students can be guided to identify noun phrases in the text and follow the logical development of the ideas through the noun phrases.

General to specific development of texts

Texts which explain, evaluate and persuade usually follow a general to specific development of ideas. General nouns are essential to manage this development. In the paragraph on groups and group formation in Tasks 10a and 10b, the writer creates cohesion by repeating the noun group in most of the themes of his sentences, e.g.,

groups   studying groups   group dynamics   formal groups   informal groups

As the paragraph develops these noun phrases focus on more specific aspects of the topic. They become longer as the writer specifies what he is referring to more closely, e.g.,

groups   studying groups   the concept of group dynamics

This contributes to the development of the text from general to specific ideas.

Task 15

Here is a text from an undergraduate microeconomics course about the problem of unemployment. The six sentences are not in the correct order. Number them in order from the most general (1) to the most specific (6). Look at the noun phrases containing the word *unemployment* to help you.

a _____ Unemployment benefits only pay essential living expenses.

b _____ One aspect of this increase has been the growing number of long term unemployed, those who have been unemployed for longer than one year.

c _____ Since the late 1970s the level of unemployment has been rising steadily.

d _____ They do not provide workers with the social support and sense of self worth that they can get from working.

e _____ One of the more recent problems of industrialised economies is unemployment.

f _____ Such long term unemployment can lead to serious social problems, even if those who cannot find work receive government benefits.

KEY

The correct order is shown below. The noun phrases which manage the development of the topic from general to specific ideas are underlined in the text.

1 e_____ One of the more recent problems of industrialised economies is <u>unemployment.</u>

2 c_____ Since the late 1970s <u>the level of unemployment</u> has been rising steadily.

3 b_____ One aspect of this increase has been <u>the growing number of long term unemployed</u>, those who have been unemployed for longer than one year.

4 f_____ <u>Such long term unemployment</u> can lead to serious social problems, even if those who cannot find work receive government benefits.

5 a_____ <u>Unemployment benefits</u> only pay essential living expenses.

6 d_____ They do not provide workers with the social support and sense of self worth that they can get from working.

Martin and Rose[40] describe the flow of information in text using a metaphor of waves which contain peaks of information at different levels in the text. One peak for waves at the first level is the sentence theme, often a summarizing noun phrase, which forms the point of departure for each new sentence. Overlapping this wave but with a peak of textual prominence at the end of the sentence is the new information which develops and expands ideas. As illustrated in Task 10 above, patterns of given information in themes and related new information in rhemes work together to 'package discourse as phases of information'.[41] At the next level, the peaks of the waves are the paragraph themes, the most general sentence in each paragraph which presents ideas that are developed in the rest of the paragraph. This may not necessarily be the first sentence, because that sentence may refer back to a previous paragraph in the same way that a subject noun phrase might refer back to a previous sentence. Still higher waves of information come in introductory or framing paragraphs, which might contain a thesis statement or other frame of reference to prepare the reader for the explanation or argument developed in subsequent paragraphs.

The rheme in a sentence shows where the message is heading. Rhemes are usually longer and more detailed than themes and contain new information. Similarly, the sentences in a paragraph develop the general ideas introduced at the beginning with detailed information and specific examples. Sometimes the new information in a paragraph is summarized at the end in a way which sets up the themes for the following paragraphs. In turn, each paragraph in a text develops an aspect of the main thesis or point of the text. While patterns of themes in sentences and paragraphs show the method of development of a text, in a way which relates closely to the moves of the genre, patterns of new information establish the point of a text.[42]

Using these ideas with students

You can use exercises such as Task 15 with students to sensitize them to the use of general to specific development in texts. Students can also highlight general information in introductions, paragraph themes and sentence themes. These are the containers for the main ideas or 'gist' in academic texts. These activities are particularly helpful for reading dense and complex academic texts. However, it is important not to oversimplify text organization for students. They need to understand that far from being a fixed framework into which writers pour ideas, text organization can change as writers shape their ideas to suit their purpose and audience.

An awareness of the general to specific development of texts helps students to orqanize their own writing so that their readers can follow the logic of their ideas. You can model the strategies of experienced writers by asking students to identify the points they want to make. You can then act as a sceptical reader by asking students to provide evidence or examples to support their points. This dialogue between reader and writer can be demonstrated in front of the class, using questions to elicit points and their supporting details. The responses can then be recorded to produce a paragraph with a general to specific development.

When they begin to write, students should ask themselves the following questions:

- What general point do I want to make?
- What specific details can I use to support that general point?
- How does each of my sentences link with what I've said before?

Conclusion

This chapter began by asking you what you could 'see' in a text. We hope that now you are able to look at texts from a number of different viewpoints, analysing not just the topic, verb grammar and vocabulary but also the register, genre, rhetorical functions, organization and cohesion of texts. You may like to go back to the beginning of this chapter and try Task 2 again to discover if you can 'see' more features of the text than you did before. From this analysis, we have derived a set of questions which can help students read subject-specific texts and write effectively:

Register

- How academic is this text on a scale of 1 to 10?
- Which features of the text are academic and which are not academic?
- Could I use this style in my writing? If not, why not?

Genre

- Who are the readers of this text?
- Why was this text written? What is it trying to achieve?
- What organization has been selected as most appropriate for that audience and purpose?
- What are the stages or moves through which this organization proceeds?

Rhetorical function

- What is the relationship between the ideas in this part of the text?
- What functional language shows this relationship?

Cohesion – information structure

- What am I talking about?
- What do I want to say about it?
- How does this link with what I've said before?

General – specific text development

- What general point do I want to make?
- What specific details can I use to support that general point?
- How does each of my sentences link with what I've said before?

Teachers sometimes comment that they would not want to spend a lot of time working on just one text with their students but would prefer to use a variety of texts to maintain interest. Of course it is possible to introduce the ideas we have presented to students using a range of texts. However, students get a real sense of mastering a text if they are able to work on it intensively to get as much from it as possible. As you work on aspects of this framework with your students, you can always return to texts you looked at earlier in your course to examine other features.

We will refer back to this chapter in the rest of the book as we show you how these ideas can be applied in your teaching to help students to improve their academic reading, writing, listening, speaking and study skills.

Further reading

Butt, D., Spinks, S. and Yallop, C. (2000) *Using Functional Grammar: An Explorer's Guide*. Sydney: Macquarie University.

Collins Cobuild English Grammar 2nd edn. (2005) London: HarperCollins.

Johns, A., Ed. (2002) *Genre in the Classroom: Multiple Perspectives*, Mahwah: Lawrence Erlbaum Associates.

McCarthy, M. (1991) *Discourse Analysis for Language Teachers*. Cambridge: Cambridge University Press.

Martin, J. R. and Rose, D. (2003) *Working with Discourse: Meaning Beyond the Clause*. London: Continuum.

Paltridge, B. (2001) *Genre and the Language Learning Classroom*. Ann Arbor: University of Michigan Press.

Swales, J. and Feak, C. 2nd edn. (2004) *Academic Writing for Graduate Students*. Ann Arbor: University of Michigan Press.

Vande Kopple, W. J. (1996) Using the concepts of given and new information in classes on the English language. *The Journal of TESOL France*, 3, pages 53–68. Reprinted in Tom Miller, Ed. *Functional Approaches to Written Text: Classroom Applications*. Washington, DC: United States Information Agency.

Chapter 3: Course design

This chapter will examine:

- the role of EAP courses in an academic curriculum

- the importance of course design for the EAP teacher in the classroom

- how principles of course design are implemented coherently

You will have the opportunity to:

- relate key aspects of EAP course design to your own situation

- apply principles of EAP course design when selecting and adapting materials

- relate methods of delivery to processes of learning

Designing courses is generally the remit of more senior or more experienced EAP teachers, but even those with years of teaching experience find the task challenging, as these questions[1] show.

- *I've been asked to write an EAP syllabus. Where do I start?*

- *How can I prepare a single EAP course to meet the needs of a wide range of disciplines?*

- *What kind of EAP course is suitable for low-level learners?*

- *I have no time to write special EAP materials – can I adapt our general English materials?*

- *Our students are failing because their English assessments are so different from the English syllabus we are supposed to use. What can we do?*

In addition to those who write a course, everyone in an EAP team has to be aware of its underlying principles in order to deliver it effectively, i.e., to achieve its aims.

The overall aim of an EAP course is to help students towards membership of their chosen academic community. This requires EAP course designers to gain a broad understanding of the conventions, expectations and practices of the target academic communities as well as the expectations of EAP students, as outlined in Chapter 1: *The context of EAP*. It also requires them to become familiar with the style and conventions of texts that students are likely to meet and the language they need to produce in their studies, as shown in Chapter 2: *Text analysis*. Based on this understanding, course designers can then identify the needs that the course will meet. This chapter outlines the key principles for designing and delivering EAP courses to meet these needs.

The role of the syllabus

EAP courses vary tremendously in terms of length and timing, specific aims, content, context and students. They can be as brief as two or three weeks before the start of an academic degree programme (a pre-sessional EAP course) or as long as two years, e.g., as part of a broad programme of study prior to degree level (a foundation programme). In-sessional EAP courses run concurrently with an undergraduate or postgraduate course and may be credit-bearing or simply offer support with academic writing and speaking. EAP classes can be aimed at a specific subject discipline (narrow-angled EAP or ESAP, English for specific academic purposes) or a wide range of target disciplines (wide-angled EAP or EGAP, English for general academic purposes).[2] In many countries, students are only required to read academic texts in English (EAP/FL, EAP in a foreign language context).[3] In other contexts, EAP students have a particular need for writing or speaking. Course design is a process which attempts to meet such identified needs within the constraints of the course.

Before discussing the principles underlying the design of different EAP courses, it is important to clarify the key components in an educational programme. Figure 1 shows the structure of a typical UK undergraduate foundation programme, designed to prepare students for university study. The curriculum is the whole educational programme in which students are engaged. In addition to EAP, students in this example are preparing for their future studies by following a course in IT related to the purpose of their degree. Subject-specific courses broadly linked to different degree programmes are also offered at an introductory level, e.g., an introduction to the UK business context or an introduction to social science research methods.

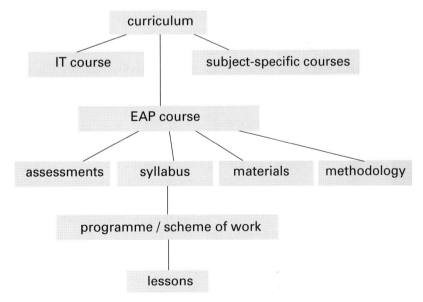

Figure 1: *A typical UK undergraduate foundation programme*

At the heart of a well-designed course is the syllabus. It is a description of what students need to learn and is usually formulated in terms of general goals or aims that the course hopes to achieve and smaller more specific learning objectives or outcomes, which outline what students should be able to understand and do by the end of a course.[4] These goals and objectives determine the choice of materials and methodology and also the types of assessment. As explained in Chapter 10: *Assessment*, the syllabus works best when the learning outcomes it specifies are closely aligned to the assessments of the course and when the materials and methodology clearly lead to the assessments.

As the discipline of EAP has developed, course designers have recognized the importance of a systematic account of what is to be learned. 'A syllabus publicly declares what the teacher regards as important to the students and so reflects a philosophy of teaching, including beliefs about language and learning.'[5] In most courses, teachers are given a syllabus to which students also have access and which links materials and tasks with individual lesson aims.

Task 1

List the reasons why it is necessary for a teacher and students to have a public description of this kind, i.e., a syllabus.

A syllabus is an account of what it is necessary to cover to achieve the aims of the course. From the syllabus, the programme or scheme of work is derived. This enables both teachers and students to see what they have covered and what they are going to cover. For teachers, the syllabus is the source for planning their teaching week and their daily lessons. It enables them to justify lesson content to students. For students, it provides a framework for them from which to make a coherent record of what they learn, providing a sense of achievement and progress. It is the basis on which to evaluate their learning and the teaching they receive. Without knowledge of the syllabus, it is difficult for students to develop autonomy and critical skills.[6]

For course directors, the syllabus is a document on which to base timetabling, the organization of resources, and guidance for a teacher taking a class for an absent colleague. The syllabus is used to induct and train new members of staff and is the means by which many teachers have learned the basics of EAP.[7] In addition, a syllabus is a prerequisite for systematic reflection, evaluation and review of learning and teaching, which is an essential process for ongoing professional development and for the continuing evolution of the syllabus itself.

A syllabus provides a basis for the accountability of the teaching department to the larger institution or to government education departments or validating bodies such as BALEAP[8] and the British Council. It shows the principles on which teaching and learning are based and how these align with other courses within a wider curriculum.

Designing a syllabus

Having established the importance of an EAP syllabus and where it fits in a curriculum, it is necessary to consider how to create one – where to start, what to include and how to organize it. Figure 2 outlines the process that will be described in this section.

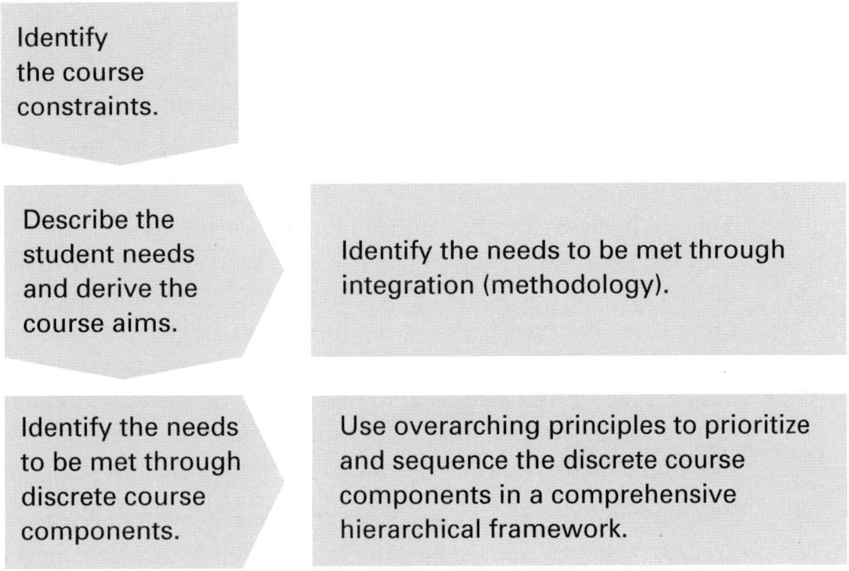

Identify
the course
constraints.

Describe the
student needs
and derive the
course aims.

Identify the needs to be met through
integration (methodology).

Identify the needs
to be met through
discrete course
components.

Use overarching principles to prioritize
and sequence the discrete course
components in a comprehensive
hierarchical framework.

Figure 2: *The process of designing a syllabus*

Identifying constraints and needs

A well-established and necessary emphasis on learner-centred approaches has led most of the literature to indicate that course design starts with needs analysis.[9] Although needs analysis is an essential step in determining course aims, objectives and content, it is not necessarily the most useful place to start designing a course. The first step is to consider the constraints of the teaching context. In practice, most experienced teachers find they have to adapt or supplement materials because of the teaching situation. Courses only work well when their design takes into account the constraints under which they will be delivered. Courses that are produced in-house for a specific target student group often build in this kind of flexibility. A course written without attention to these constraints, however carefully constructed in terms of student needs and theories of language and learning, will run into problems.

Constraints

Task 2

Think about your current teaching situation.

- What are some of the constraints you face?

- How do these constraints affect what you are able to teach?

Perhaps the most common constraint is time. Clearly, students would be expected to learn less in four weeks than in twenty weeks. Other constraints have to do with student numbers, institutional practices, availability of resources, teachers' experience and expertise, and learners' experience. The process of setting out these constraints is sometimes called a *means analysis*.[10]

Time is likely to be the constraint that has the most significant impact on course design. Either the course has too few contact hours to allow sufficient development of the students' learning or EAP components have to slot into times that are convenient for the institution rather than convenient for EAP students and teachers. Another significant constraint is class composition. EAP teachers report that dealing with mixed level or mixed discipline groups is one of their greatest difficulties[11] but student numbers rarely allow classes to be made up of learners heading towards the same academic discipline.

Although the benefits of subject-specific input into EAP courses have been well argued,[12] a course for a mixed-discipline group has to have aims that are more generic, i.e., more concerned with procedural knowledge and transferable skills and strategies.[13] The need to work with a wide range of subject specific texts provides opportunities for collaborative outcomes to tasks and a sharing of expertise. Even an apparently homogeneous group might have a need for a broad-based EAP course with generic aims because the employment opportunities beyond the university are not subject specific and employers, as stakeholders in the course, demand flexibility and a broad range of abilities.[14] In fact, course designers for homogeneous groups have to be very careful that they do not constrain the syllabus by a needs analysis which is too subject-focused.[15] The course designer, quoted at the beginning of this chapter, who was worried about meeting the needs of a wide range of disciplines might concentrate instead on the many benefits of a broad-based course.

Constraints relating to the institution within which an EAP course is delivered include lack of understanding of the language needs of either the students or the receiving subject departments. Decision makers in the institution may feel that a general English course is sufficient, especially if it is a cheaper option than employing specialist EAP teachers. On the other hand, institutional practice in some countries sees technical vocabulary as a priority and postgraduates and junior teachers from an academic department teach, by translation into English, the technical vocabulary of their discipline to undergraduates. It is sometimes very difficult to change such views.

A particularly worrying belief in some UK institutions, and one with which students and teachers sometimes too readily collude, is that students require a diet of general English to bring them to a vaguely specified proficiency level before they are ready to digest EAP. The result of this is an invisible ceiling through which students cannot pass. This is particularly demotivating for postgraduates who are already experts in their fields and who may have studied English for a number of years. These students respond very negatively to de-contextualized remedial grammar practice or an EFL course book designed for non-academic purposes.

Even when an effective EAP course has been designed and implemented, it is fragile if it depends on collaboration with or support from a single sympathetic decision maker in the institution. If this person moves to another post, the whole project has to be 'sold' to a new, probably very busy, senior post holder.[16] All institutional constraints on EAP teaching and learning need to be critically examined, particularly where they perpetuate a low-status role for the discipline of EAP, and many need to be challenged.

Constraints can relate to the teachers themselves, their experience, knowledge and preferred teaching style. Some teachers may be unwilling to adopt an EAP approach[17] and less confident teachers can feel pressure from learners to change aspects of the course, particularly if the course design encourages students to evaluate teaching and learning. For example, learners might complain that a course is not sufficiently exam focused. Even when such changes might be counter to perceived pedagogic principles, teachers sometimes comply simply to keep students happy.[18] Allowing students the freedom to express their needs requires considerable confidence on the part of teachers, and such confidence only comes with experience in a supportive teaching environment.

In course design, there is always a balance to be struck between what is needed and what is practically possible and sometimes constraints have benefits. For example, a time-constrained course can encourage course designers to promote more learner responsibility. Inevitably, degree subject courses often take priority over EAP and this also may focus course design more effectively to prioritize student needs. One answer to the question posed at the beginning of this chapter, *Where do I start?*, is to identify the course constraints, decide which should be challenged and which are acceptable and then begin to analyse student needs.

An EAP syllabus is essentially an organized description which answers the question: *What does a student need from an EAP course in order to study academic subjects through the medium of English?*

Task 3

List as many of these needs as you can for a class of EAP students that you know.

The commentary that follows should help you to begin to organize your ideas as a basis for a syllabus. Your list might include descriptions of things students need to know and things they need to be able to do, including language skills and skills for university study. This chaos of competing elements has to be sorted into a coherent, hierarchical or layered description, with unit headings and goals. An EAP syllabus somehow has to organize and describe the most important knowledge and skills that a given set of students need: from how to form the noun for the verb *produce*, to the best organization for a research report; from how to recognize critical stance to how to ask questions in a seminar. Furthermore, because the course will be limited by practical constraints such as the time and resources available, the course designer must prioritize these needs and may have to abandon some of them. Drawing up a syllabus is a complex process based on analysing constraints, institution requirements and student needs, followed by prioritizing, sequencing and integrating what has to be learned. At each step in the process, there are many possible choices and the resulting syllabus will not only be unique to you and your students but will also be constantly evolving. It is important to recognize that a syllabus is never perfect but always a work-in-progress. However, there are important principles which can help to organize the chaos into an effective syllabus.

The organizing principles for syllabus design

When creating a syllabus, the designer derives the course goals or aims from the description of the needs to be met – what is to be learned. At this point, it is useful to think of two kinds of need. There are some needs that are best met through input that is integrated into all aspects of teaching and learning, i.e., through the methodology of the course. There are other needs that determine the major units of the course. These have to be identified, prioritized and sequenced in a principled way to form the syllabus framework. Both types of need have to be specified in the course aims.

The principle of integration

Some key abilities are best developed as integral features of tasks and texts throughout the course rather than as separate lessons.[19] For example, any course preparing for academic study must help students to develop autonomy and the ability to engage critically with all aspects of learning. Coupled with this is the principle of experiential learning,[20] in which students learn from what they do and experience as well as from what they are told and shown. For example, EAP courses can simulate as far as possible the practices of academic departments in the design and implementation of assessments. Student autonomy, critical thinking and experiencing authentic academic practices are important aims in an EAP course, which are met largely through the teaching and learning approach: the methodology. This is described in the second part of this chapter and in the chapters that follow.

Overarching principles

Whatever form the description of student needs eventually takes, there are important overarching features that an EAP syllabus must have. Firstly, it must be developmental, showing how progress is made towards the main goals and the specific learning outcomes over the duration of the course. Progress can be delivered, for example, through increasingly long and conceptually complex texts or tasks, through increasingly challenging rhetorical functions, and through increasing student autonomy. A syllabus without clear development of student abilities is fundamentally flawed.

Secondly, to enable students to review and consolidate their learning, there has to be considerable recycling in the syllabus. Some recycling will be planned into the course through revision sessions and through the four skills of reading, writing, listening and speaking. Some recycling arises naturally but predictably through built-in progression, for example, the rhetorical function of problem and solution recycles cause and effect (to analyse the problem) and comparison and contrast (to evaluate solutions). Some genres also share similar features which can be recycled, e.g., a research proposal and a report may have similar introductions, both containing a short literature review. A great deal of learning recycles in a less predictable way. For example, in feedback on student writing, a teacher may point out that a student has used a collocation that was first noticed in a reading text in an earlier unit. It is important to identify and exploit these opportunities and to relate them explicitly to the syllabus.

Finally, what is learned must be transferable. Materials and activities provided to meet any given syllabus goal or learning outcome are themselves limited in scope and relevance. However, the learning resulting from them needs to extend beyond the duration of the course to contexts which are sometimes unknown or unspecifiable. This implies recycling, of course, but also requires that students are made aware of the generic nature of what they learn and are able to identify for themselves opportunities for effective transfer of learning – an important component of student autonomy. The three overarching principles of an EAP syllabus are:

- progression towards the overall course goals
- built-in, explicit recycling
- transferability across a range of contexts and disciplines

These three principles enable the course designer to build a framework for the syllabus.

Choosing where to start: building the framework

Having considered the course constraints and the principle of integration, and with the three overarching principles in mind, the course designer has to build a syllabus framework from the needs in the list from Task 3. The way designers describe needs has historically led to a confusing array of different syllabus types,[21] making it difficult for a course designer to know where to start. Syllabuses for language learning have evolved considerably over the past half-century, benefiting from new knowledge about language, its role in society and how it is learned and, in the case of EAP, a developing awareness of what is required for academic study. Because EAP syllabuses are closely related to student needs in academic disciplines, they are necessarily eclectic. This eclecticism has to be guided by a sound understanding of the underlying basis for the analysis of language and skills that gives rise to each particular description of student needs.

Task 4

The left-hand column in the table below shows a variety of ways of describing students' needs.

- For each description of needs, choose the underlying basis for the analysis from the right-hand column.

- Which kinds of analysis can most effectively provide the overarching principles of progression, recycling and transferability?

Description: Students need to	Analysis: based on
produce a literature review / give a presentation	sentence grammar
use the present perfect / use modals	vocabulary
skim and scan / proofread	
work in a group to solve a problem in a case study / work with another student to research an answer to a question	rhetorical functions
	genres and texts
use linking words such as *however* / understand affixes	
	discourse grammar
use cohesive devices / present and organize information in a paragraph	
	content and topics
describe a sequence of events / explain a cause and effect relationship / express uncertainty	
	academic skills
have an understanding of the education system they will be studying in / have background knowledge of their target academic area	tasks required at university

Sentence grammar

Grammar items such as the present perfect and modals have long been the starting point for building the framework of general English syllabuses. These items are also important in academic English. However, sentence grammar is not a good basis on which to build the syllabus framework. Analysis at the sentence level presents both teacher and learner with potentially the whole of English grammar as the syllabus – an impossibly enormous task. In addition, a focus on grammar at the sentence level ignores the specific applications that grammar items such as the present perfect and modals have in academic discourse. For example, the present perfect is important in the narrative of a literature review (an academic genre) and for indicating sequence in a description of process (a rhetorical function). Modals in academic texts are used primarily to indicate degree of certainty or possibility but their use to express permission and ability is less frequent. Sentence level grammar items become recyclable and transferable in EAP once they are associated with genres and rhetorical functions. Language analysis in EAP must look beyond the sentence level to rhetorical functions and genres to provide a framework within which grammar items that are important in academic discourse, e.g., noun phrases, can be selected and prioritized.

Although governments everywhere are trying to move school English syllabuses away from formal, sentence-based grammar to a more communicative approach,[22] most international students will have experienced grammar analysed at the sentence level and this is likely to form a strong part of their expectations of an EAP course. These expectations can only be countered by demonstrating the value of alternative approaches.

Vocabulary

EAP students need to learn vocabulary appropriate to academic contexts as well as the most frequent words in general use, but, as in the case of sentence grammar, vocabulary is not a good starting point for setting up a syllabus framework. Key vocabulary items are best learned not in isolation but in their contexts[23] and, as in the case of grammar, context is supplied by academic genres and rhetorical functions. For example, students need to be able to use correctly a wide variety of linking words, to understand how affixes affect meaning and to learn those collocations that are most frequent in academic texts. The word *however* is frequent in texts which compare and contrast (rhetorical function); prefixes are important in expressing ideas such as negativity (*un-*, *im-*), quality (*-able*, *-proof*) and scale (*micro-*). There is clear transferability to different academic disciplines of collocations such as *key factor*, *major issue* and *implement policies*, and many of these, like grammatical items, are contextualized and recycled through rhetorical functions and genres.

Rhetorical functions

Rhetorical functions, such as describing a sequence of events or explaining a cause and effect relationship, provide a linguistic analysis that is related to a text's communicative purpose rather than its form and so they are a good place to start designing a syllabus. Functions can be used, together with concepts found routinely in academic language, e.g., time, size, negativity, probability, to provide a syllabus with progression, recycling and transferable language. This type of analysis was the organizing principle of many EAP course books in the 1980s and early 1990s[24] and has considerable advantages. It combines communicative purpose with meaning-based grammar and vocabulary. Functions can generate patterns of language and organization which students can learn and which are highly transferable, e.g., all academic subjects require the description of a sequence of events and explanation of cause and effect relationships. A writing syllabus, for example, based on rhetorical functions, can be strongly developmental, progressing from paragraph level descriptions and definitions to multi-functional persuasive texts in which functions covered earlier in the syllabus are recycled.[25]

A functional analysis is not the only starting point for deciding the main syllabus units but it is particularly useful in some situations, e.g., for students with lower levels of English. Although rhetorical functions should always form an essential strand of a syllabus, they do not provide all the linguistic skills and understanding needed for students to perform competently at university so they need to be supplemented by analysis of other aspects of academic communication.

Genres and texts

Needs can be described according to the genres, or communicative events, both written and spoken, which give rise to the texts that a learner will have to understand and produce.[26] Examples are research proposals, literature reviews, e-mails to lecturers and seminar presentations. Genres can provide a particularly good starting point for drawing up a syllabus when assessments also relate to genres, e.g., where students are assessed on a literature review or a presentation. In this case, the assessments and the syllabus are closely aligned. Focus on genres brings to the fore the social nature of texts and, although genres differ enormously in language and form from one discipline to another,[27] they can be studied in such a way as to make learning transferable. By understanding how to analyse genres, identifying how purpose and audience inform the choice of content and organization, students can learn to use genres to achieve the kinds of communicative purposes for specific audiences that will be required in their degree studies.

However, academic genres specify audience and purpose rather than language, and exposure to even a wide range of genres does not directly and systematically develop language ability.[28] A syllabus based only on analysis at the level of academic genres may not provide students with enough exposure to transferable academic language, e.g., the language used to classify or to link causes and effects. In addition, authentic academic texts may be difficult to read and need considerable scaffolding. Both these difficulties can be addressed through an analysis of the rhetorical functions and discourse grammar which operate at paragraph level and support the organizational moves within the genre.

Discourse grammar

Grammatical analysis which operates at the level of the paragraph, discourse grammar, is described in Chapter 2. It equips learners to present and organize information logically and cohesively in a paragraph or longer text and to understand such texts. It is intrinsically recyclable and transferable. This is a neglected level of analysis and one which teachers sometimes find difficult to penetrate. On its own, it is not sufficiently developmental to be the basis of a syllabus. However, when combined with an understanding of rhetorical functions and genres, an awareness of discourse grammar can help students to meet audience expectations of the way texts develop, which can shift the focus of their readers away from the accuracy of the sentence level grammar.[29]

Content and topics

An analysis of student needs at the level of content has the benefit of allowing the course designer to choose motivating topics for reading, writing and discussion that are relevant to a range of academic disciplines or are related to students' experience of higher education. Such content can be valuable input into a syllabus, but on its own, cannot provide the overall aims and the unit-by-unit framework for development, recycling and transferability of language. There are also inherent dangers in a topic-focused approach. Topics that are accessible to students from a range of backgrounds can be too general, even for students who are intending to study in that field, and, without the appropriate academic genres, topics are no guarantee of academic content or language.[30] One solution to the problem of mixed discipline EAP courses has been to base content on how students learn and what life is like at university. However, there is a limit to how much time students want or need to spend talking and reading about topics such as how to study or student life. Much of this aspect of student needs can be covered first hand and experientially through the principle of integration, i.e., through the teaching approach and how the course is delivered rather than through content. For example, assessments can be designed with rubrics, deadlines and marking criteria more in line with those at university than those usually found on a general English course.[31] The syllabus can include activities such as making contact with subject departments, open day visits and, where possible, sitting in on lectures and tutorials or interviewing staff and students.[32]

When all the students are following the same academic course, an adjunct or sheltered EAP course is possible,[33] in which academic content is delivered automatically through a syllabus framework of appropriate genres and texts.

Clearly, EAP students will need particular skills to succeed in higher education. A skills analysis is often used in exam preparation courses, which have tended to dominate the EAP course book market. Often, course designers describe student needs in terms of reading, writing, listening and speaking skills. These are further broken down into sub skills, such as searching for specific information in a text and proofreading a written draft. Such skills are clearly important and need to be developed. They are recyclable and transferable and, therefore, have a place in an EAP syllabus. However, a syllabus framework constructed out of skills leads to a course that neglects language input or 'underspecifies the complexities of language issues in the academic context'.[34] Although most skills-based EAP course books have sections covering rhetorical functions, e.g., comparing and contrasting, the linguistic analysis is sometimes weak and incomplete[35] and rarely allows for the integrated development of conceptual and linguistic understanding. There is also a danger that, without a clear underlying language syllabus, transfer of language is poor across the four main skills, especially if they are taught separately. As Hyland comments: 'We have moved away from the idea of EAP as study skills, like a set of technical tools that you could just apply anywhere'.[36]

Tasks

EAP is concerned with two types of task: tasks to promote learning[37] and tasks to replicate performance in the future academic discourse community. The former is not a description of need (the basis of syllabus design) but rather an aspect of methodology. Tasks in higher education programmes require students to be able to interact to achieve specific outcomes, often of the kind required in professional practice. In both undergraduate and postgraduate courses, therefore, tasks are designed to require collaboration and some negotiation of meaning, e.g., problem solving using a case study or researching the answer to a particular question. Clearly, these types of task can make a useful contribution to any EAP course by replicating study genres and academic performance. Tasks to promote learning or to replicate academic performance can be the units of syllabus design and should be sequenced according to increasing complexity and authenticity.[38] However, it is difficult to use tasks as a starting point for syllabus design because it is not clear what makes one task more difficult than another and, hence, how they might be sequenced developmentally in terms of language. Genres and rhetorical functions provide a better starting point to allow for progression, recycling and transferability in a syllabus.

Task 5

Look at the contents map or contents page of an EAP course book or a course that you use.

- Which type(s) of analysis from the table in Task 4 are being used to organize the syllabus?

- In the same way, identify the types of analysis that underlie the list of needs you produced in Task 3.

Organizing a description of needs into a syllabus

Each type of analysis is likely to be represented in the contents, i.e., the syllabus, of a modern EAP course because each reveals a different kind of need. As Johnson points out, arguments about which type of analysis is the best basis for a syllabus

> ...are no more sensible than arguments as to whether the specifications in a construction contract should cover the foundations or the steel framework or the concrete or the glass or the interior design. The obvious answer is that all of these must be covered.[39]

All analyses discussed above are valid in EAP in that each leads to descriptions of real needs, but not all of them can provide a good starting point for organizing a syllabus. Two possibilities emerge strongly: a syllabus framework based on analysis at the level of rhetorical functions or one based on analysis at the level of genres. Both can include all three principles of progression, recycling and transferability of learning. The choice may ultimately be decided by course constraints. However, all the other needs identified for a particular group of students have to find a place within the chosen framework.

The process of syllabus design may be summarized as follows:
- identifying the constraints under which the course will operate
- identifying the needs of the students which can be realistically met within these constraints
- deciding which needs can be met through integration into texts and tasks and which should form discrete components of the syllabus
- prioritizing and sequencing the discrete course components in a comprehensive hierarchical framework which takes into account the overarching principles

The following authentic case study scenarios illustrate the process of balancing needs and constraints to produce very different syllabus solutions.

Task 6

Below are some authentic course design scenarios, described in terms of needs and constraints.

- Choose one that most nearly reflects your teaching situation.

- Suggest an outline syllabus that could meet the needs within the constraints.

Case study A:
Authentic course design scenarios

Scenario 1: *'Low level' students*[40]

Every year a small number of highly educated mature students, but 'false beginners' who had not learned English formally, applied for EAP courses at a further education college. They wished to prepare for English-medium university courses but because of their low scores on placement tests they were placed in lower level general English classes. Here, they typically made rapid progress in listening and speaking but not in their writing. Their writing was too rudimentary to cope with simple lower intermediate EFL texts, let alone academic ones. They felt frustrated and complained about being kept in general English classes when their aim was academic study, often at postgraduate level. However, there were never enough of these students at any one time to justify the cost of a special writing class.

Scenario 2: *Postgraduate students*[41]

A university engineering department asked an EAP team based at the university to provide a credit-bearing EAP course to run alongside such modules as Software Engineering and Digital Signal Processing in one of their internationally based masters courses. The students came with a high level of English but needed to improve as much as possible for future professional as well as academic purposes in a competitive field. The EAP team were already running a credit-bearing, non-specialist, postgraduate academic writing course. There was no time available to write a new course.

Scenario 3: *Foundation undergraduate students*[42]

A UK university set up an international campus in China in order to teach a range of its undergraduate and postgraduate degrees entirely in that country. The common first year of the undergraduate courses included an EAP programme with assessments that had to be passed in order to proceed. The degree programmes onto which the first cohort of students hoped to progress were International Communications Studies, International Studies and International Business. A major concern, in view of the target degrees, was the limited world knowledge and academic skills that the students may have acquired compared with the corresponding UK students embarking on the same degree programmes. Although the situation is changing rapidly, teaching and learning for most students in China is much more focused on the final high school exams[43] than in the UK, where a broader exploration of controversial issues is the norm of high school life.

Scenario 4. *In-sessional support for undergraduates*[44]

A worryingly high number of international undergraduate students in Management Studies at a UK university were achieving marks below expectations and seemed to be struggling with plagiarism. They reported language as their main problem in performing well and in integrating with other students. The Management Studies Department were willing to co-operate in providing an optional extra EAP support class and in recruiting students for it.

Scenario 1 does not require a complete EAP course or a complete writing course. It reflects a very specific need for a focus on key elements of both. A short, self-study, EAP literacy course was designed. This bridged the gap between the general English and EAP courses by taking the students from elementary to lower intermediate EAP literacy using a self-study pack. The syllabus units were rhetorical functions, starting with knowledge-telling functions such as very simple instructions (how to make a cup of tea), and progressing through eight units to describing increase and decrease (simple commentary on graphical data). The material could be covered in eight to ten weeks, within a single term, and involved mostly homework with occasional tutorials. The course proved highly motivating for mature students, who particularly liked the recognition of their ability to study effectively and autonomously.

The starting point in the design process was to identify rhetorical functions which would provide recycling and rapid development of language through simple, specially written texts. Rhetorical functions are a useful basis for EAP for learners with an initially low level of English because they concentrate learning and teaching effort on development of language in context. The course was demanding in terms of materials development – one estimate for the time taken to write distance learning materials is that each student effort hour takes at least ten hours of tutor writing time[45] – but it solved the problem of restricted class time and was a one-off investment that proved useful for many years. Online delivery of this course would be an obvious next step.

In Scenario 2, initially, the engineering students were included in the existing wide-angled EAP writing course with a range of other postgraduates. The syllabus had been designed around rhetorical functions as the starting point, but was evolving and beginning to include useful genres, such as literature reviews. By encouraging students to bring in their specialist course materials, it was possible to identify generic features of specialist academic texts.[46] Feedback from the engineering students made it clear that they would prefer to study as a specialist group in order to benefit more from this type of input.

In the following year, feedback from the first cohort of students and the engineering tutors prompted the EAP team to develop a narrow-angled ESAP course. Course review documents and interviews with tutors and students provided information on perceived needs. The starting point in the design process was to identify two key genres for the EAP assessment that the students would need to produce later for their engineering coursework and in professional practice. A poster presentation based on a problem in their field and a literature review of a topic of their choice were selected, giving an assessment-aligned syllabus. Without time to write the course in advance, the team adopted the approach of sketching out a rough syllabus and writing the detail as the course proceeded. Teaching and learning focused on what was needed to produce the assessed EAP coursework. Using authentic materials from students and subject tutors helped to minimize materials writing. This approach provided authentic genres combined with the rhetorical functions needed particularly by engineers (for example, describing objects and processes, presenting problems and evaluating solutions). The syllabus unfolded through a research partnership between students and teachers. The teachers provided the linguistic and skills framework whilst the students researched the distinct genres and the rhetorical functions of their field, collaborating in fine-tuning the syllabus to match their needs.

The starting point in the course design process for Scenario 3 was to identify genres and tasks typical of undergraduate courses: timed examination writing, coursework writing and projects, lectures, presentations and seminar discussions. For the course designers, however, it was important that students additionally had background knowledge to reflect the international nature of the target degree courses. They used a sixth-form level textbook[47] for native speakers of English to provide themes for exam questions, coursework assignments and discussion tasks. The necessary language and skills practice was derived from this book and related texts on the same themes. The whole course was delivered in the same way as a first-year undergraduate course would be in the UK. For example, there was an expectation of developing student responsibility for study and the university's policies on submission deadlines and plagiarism were strictly adhered to. In addition to language and study skills, the exams also assessed retrieval of the textbook content which had been taught, thus providing an authentic undergraduate experience.

Scenario 4 led to an initiative intended to support those students identified as having weaker written and spoken English. What follows is a summary based on the published report.[48] Ten hours per week of EAP were provided. Details of the syllabus used are not presented in the source paper, but the starting point in the design process was to identify weaknesses in terms of academic skills, writing style and basic grammar. The initiative proved disappointing because very few students attended and those that did included a significant proportion of the 'worried well',[49] i.e., reasonably able students who were worried about their skills, rather than the intended target, i.e., students who were experiencing real difficulties. Overall gains in terms of assessments were barely significant.

The analysis of what went wrong is a good illustration of how institutional attitudes and practices can undermine the best intentions in syllabus design. Students, particularly those struggling to keep up, had no incentive to take time away from their core studies to attend long hours of an optional extra course. Recruiting for the support course depended on Management Studies lecturers communicating sensitively to students the importance and benefits of attending. However, the benefits were not made clear, and official communications instead focused negatively on the 'problems' of the students. The first writing exercise, intended to help students to self-select onto the course, involved writing about a culturally loaded case study of a UK football manager. The later EAP sessions clashed with Management Studies coursework deadlines.

Many of these issues were subsequently addressed. Some of the key skills were embedded into credit-bearing modules in the degree course; attempts were made to align the learning outcomes of EAP with other degree course modules to improve the relevance of the EAP input; the timings were improved and a more positive approach to identifying and recruiting students was agreed. An important outcome of trying to resolve difficulties such as these is a realization that subject discipline lecturers bear a responsibility for making their lectures, notes, instructions and advice more accessible to all students. In particular, the whole institution benefits by internationalizing the curriculum through using case studies and examples 'from a wide range of countries and cultures'.[50] EAP courses cannot make up for institutional failings but EAP teachers have a responsibility to bring such failings to the attention of the institution. When this is done sensitively and in a spirit of cooperation, everyone benefits, as in the case of scenario 4.

The role of the classroom teacher in syllabus design

Generally, designing whole courses is the remit of more senior or more experienced EAP teachers. However, all teachers need to take a principled approach when evaluating and modifying course materials.

Task 7

Evaluate the syllabus of an EAP course book or course that you are familiar with in terms of the three principles of progression, recycling and transferability. You may need to look further than the contents page.

- How far does the course integrate critical thinking, student autonomy and experience of academic study in the course units?

Most experienced teachers adapt or supplement courses. Although published materials generally go through extensive review, redrafting and piloting, teachers rarely follow them uncritically and usually make adjustments for their own particular students and situation, i.e., their constraints. In making modifications to course materials, teachers are in fact embarking on small-scale course evaluation and design. Modifying any course has implications. The students should experience the syllabus not simply as a series of related activities and objectives but as a fully integrated whole. Most EAP courses take an eclectic approach in which several strands of analysis are combined to provide a syllabus. However, it should be clear to students and teachers how needs and constraints inform the organizing principles.

Task 8

List any reasons you have had for adapting or supplementing the materials, e.g., a course book, you have used to teach a course.

Reasons for modifying materials can relate to the materials and activities themselves, to the needs of the students in the class, to teacher preferences or to the institution to which the course belongs. Materials might appear dull or culturally inappropriate. They can seem inauthentic in content, style or purpose and, especially in the case of listening recordings, in delivery. Texts may not reflect genres that the students need to use. They may seem too difficult for the level of the class or have subject-specific content that challenges the teacher's expertise. Tasks may not have sufficiently clear instructions or need more steps to ensure successful completion; or they may be insufficiently challenging. Activities can also fail to exploit the possibilities of the materials and miss opportunities to meet key teaching objectives about language, content, student autonomy, or critical thinking. Materials generally might not recycle enough or ensure that learning is transferable to new situations. Sometimes, teachers feel that aspects of a course or course book do not suit their style of delivery or the students' learning styles.

Teachers can experience frustration when institutions dictate course content which is based on outdated views of teaching and learning. Increased internationalization of the discipline of language teaching means that teachers worldwide can share ideas and access professional development courses and online publications to a degree never seen before. Such teachers may want to develop their teaching practice accordingly. However, sometimes the syllabus and assessments are imposed by a higher authority and it can be difficult to challenge and change established practices from within an institution.[51]

Whatever the reason for modification, it is particularly important to avoid a *Pick and Mix* approach in which favourite bits of different course books are combined in an incoherent way. Supplementation or modifications to materials should not be based on intuition but on the principles of good course design outlined in the earlier sections of this chapter. It is important for teachers to understand these principles so that they can evaluate, justify and share confidently any changes they make. The following constructed case study illustrates a common dilemma faced by teachers new to EAP: whether to fall back on a tried and tested lesson or attempt a new and unfamiliar approach prescribed by the course material.

Case study B:
The Jim Twins: same topic, different approach

Teacher X was teaching EAP for the first time on a busy pre-sessional course with an in-house syllabus and set of materials. The next unit entitled *Research* contained a suggested text, with tasks, about research on the Jim Twins – twins who were separated at birth but met again in later life. The main aim of the unit was for students to learn how academic writers report and evaluate research. Teacher X read the material and did not feel very confident about using it with her intermediate level students. She was very short of time and so she turned to a unit in an EFL course book that she had used before, which covered the same topic of the Jim Twins and which she knew would stimulate a lot of discussion.

Task 9

Read the following extracts from Text X, chosen by Teacher X, and the course material, Text Y.

- Which would you prefer to use with your EAP students?

- Why?

Teacher X used an article about the Jim Twins of approximately 600 words in the EFL course book, *Cutting Edge Intermediate*.[52] Here are the first and last paragraphs.

Text X

It is well-known that twins are closer to each other than most brothers and sisters – after all, they probably spend more time with each other. Parents of twins often notice that they develop special ways of communicating: they invent their own words and can often finish the other's sentences. In exceptional circumstances, this closeness becomes more extreme: they invent a whole language of their own, as in the case of Grace and Virginia Kennedy from Georgia in the USA, who communicated so successfully in their own special language that they did not speak any English at all until after they started school. In Britain there was the famous case of the 'silent twins', June and Jennifer Gibbons, who were perfectly capable of normal speech, but for years refused to talk to anyone but each other …

… But what can be the explanation for these remarkable similarities? Is it all pure coincidence, or is the explanation in some way genetic? Research into the lives of twins is forcing some experts to admit that our personalities may be at least partly due to 'nature'. On the other hand, analysts are also anxious to emphasise that incredible coincidences do happen all the time, not just in the life of twins.

The course materials used an extract about the Jim Twins from a second year undergraduate text on Marketing entitled *Consumption and Identity*.[53] It is approximately 275 words. Here are the first and last paragraphs.

Text Y

Social scientists are especially keen to study monozygotic (identical) twins which have been separated from birth. As such twins are genetically identical, one would expect that any differences in behaviour would be due to the environment. By studying separated twins, scientists can remove the influence of a common upbringing in a family in studying the effects of inheritance and the environment with respect to personality formation …

… … The study of the 'Jim Twins' seems to indicate that inherited characteristics play a key role in determining identity and consumption behaviour. However, one must be cautious in interpreting such findings. For example, just as the fact that both boys were called 'Jim' is not an effect of heredity, so it is not at all unusual for middle-aged men from the USA to drive Chevrolets and drink beer. Fascinating coincidences about their lives do not link in any conclusive way to any contemporary theories about inheritance. In other research, twins have adopted quite different behaviours, for example one twin in the same study grew up to be a proficient pianist in a non-musical family while her sister who was adopted by a piano teacher did not take to the instrument.

Teacher X chose her text because she thought the extract from the Marketing course was too difficult for intermediate level students as it contained technical vocabulary (e.g. *monozygotic*). Text X was longer and therefore provided more extensive reading practice as well as giving a more detailed account of the research and having many more interesting examples of twins for discussion, illustrated with photographs. This text left the conclusion open, giving more opportunity for a balanced discussion. The course book lesson notes with Text X included some useful verb tense revision, which many of the students needed. In comparison, Text Y seemed rather dry and boring and the lesson notes directed the teacher to spend a lot of time going over the text several times.

Text Y was chosen by the course designer because it was in an introductory textbook written by one of the lecturers in the university's Business School in which some of the students would subsequently study. It seemed to be a key piece of research in the Marketing course. In addition, although it was short, the writer seemed to use a more academic style, defining key terms such as *monozygotic* in the text and presenting a closely argued but succinct justification for his conclusion. There were also more words from the Academic Word List[54] in the shorter text and more academic noun phrases. It seemed to offer many opportunities for language exploitation.

Task 10

Compare the aims and activities of Teacher X's lesson with those recommended in the course materials.

- What were the most important differences in how the texts were used?

Teacher X's lesson notes using text X Aims	Teaching notes for using text Y Aims
Review the present perfect simple (with *for, since* and *ago*) and past simple verbs. Learn the language for describing life experiences. Discuss the life experience of twins.	Identify the writer's stance when discussing research in a textbook. Learn the language for showing stance and evaluating evidence. Review the organization and language for rhetorical functions.
Revision: target verb tenses **Pre-reading** Clarifying the meaning of key vocabulary (e.g., *leave home*) and matching these life events to a time scale. Discussion of personal experience, personal wishes and cultural differences relating to life events. Lead-in: Discussion about how being a twin affects a person's life and personality.	**Pre-reading** Lead-in: discussion about two types of twins and how they differ. Sorting task: separate human features which are genetically determined (e.g., eye colour) and those which are environmentally determined (e.g., first language).[55] Critical thinking: Why might a marketer be interested in these questions?
Reading 1 (search reading) Matching six sentences to specific twins mentioned in the text, e.g., *They had their own special language* = the Kennedy twins. **Reading 2** (careful reading) Comprehension questions about the research, e.g., How do scientists explain the similarities between the sets of twins separated at birth?	**Reading 1** (search reading) Task to identify the writer's stance, i.e., Does the writer believe that consumer behaviour is genetically determined? **Reading 2** (careful reading) What three reasons does the writer give to support this stance? Write these in your own words.

Language focus
What language does the writer use to show his stance?

Record the key words in vocabulary notebooks.

Revision
Text organization: Match parts of the text with their rhetorical functions, e.g., defining, comparing and contrasting.

Verb tenses: Identify the different tenses and say why they were used.

Follow up
Discussion: Which coincidences were most surprising? Is there a genetic influence – what is your opinion? Are the personalities in your family similar or different?

Prepare to talk about the life of a famous person.

Follow up
Critical thinking: What other research questions could twin studies help to answer? Write some suggestions, with reasons why identical twins would be needed.

Teacher X followed the activities set out in the course book. This is a well-established, task-based EFL course book, reflecting the priority given in the EFL classroom to discussion. The article on which the unit is based is interesting and easy to relate to students' experience. The text has clearly been chosen to present language connected to life events. It focuses on the tenses needed for narration and the vocabulary for biographical information. It is ideal for stimulating discussion of personal experiences and personal opinions. The activities exploit the text fully for these purposes.

However, although both classes have covered the same topic, there are two different underlying syllabuses. Lesson X is task based, with some grammar analysis. There is built in recycling but minimal progression or transferability in terms of academic needs. The class Y syllabus is functionally based and uses an authentic genre. Students in class Y have begun to explore how research is described and evaluated by academics. There is recycling of rhetorical functions and associated verb tenses, progression in terms of the introduction of persuasive rhetorical functions and academic transferability through the opportunity to write a supported argument and to think critically – to go beyond knowledge telling and into knowledge transforming. Although class X had an interesting and enjoyable lesson, the students in class Y would see a clearer rationale for what they were doing. The authentic source and purpose of text Y would give it credibility, and justify the time spent exploiting the text for language.

This case study illustrates the danger inherent in using non-EAP materials. In deviating from an EAP syllabus, however good the material may be, a teacher might not meet the particular needs of the students. This is especially true in the case of general English or EFL materials, which are not targeted at academic study in English. By making this type of modification, the teacher has applied a syllabus that is hidden, less transparent, less principled and less coherent than the original, and one that is not easily accessed by students or teaching colleagues. However, teaching is only effective when the teacher is fully committed to the course and its materials. Teacher X's choice was probably made through a combination of lack of confidence, time and support. This means that the designer of this course has failed to take into account an important constraint: the experience of at least one of the course teachers. It is important for course designers to anticipate teacher-training needs and build into the course a convincing justification for every demand that the syllabus makes of both students and teachers. It is particularly important in EAP not to let teachers feel de-skilled.

Task 11

Look back to your answers to Task 8.

- Were your modifications justified?
- Did you share your rationale for these changes with colleagues or did you feel this was just a matter for you and your class?
- What are the implications of your decision?

A principled eclectic EAP syllabus addresses the specific needs of the students, within the constraints of the course. Teachers need to maintain unbroken the important strands in its design and follow its inherent principles of integration, progression, recycling and transferability. Teachers and course designers are likely to negotiate a syllabus with students, at least to some extent, and will evaluate and adjust the course as it proceeds and student needs change. However, these changes have to be principled and incorporated into the shared description of the course to ensure that it develops appropriately.

Methodology

The previous section dealt with the *what* of EAP, i.e., the way in which students' language needs can be incorporated into a coherent syllabus. This section looks at the *how* of EAP, i.e., the methodology for achieving the aims and objectives of the syllabus. This aspect has tended to receive less attention from EAP writers and researchers.[56] The teacher's role is to support students in identifying and learning the language they need to achieve their rhetorical purposes and to provide scaffolding and feedback for their performance in communicative tasks. Basturkmen[57] summarizes methodologies in English for Specific Purposes (ESP) in terms of the relationship between input, i.e., the point at which students are exposed to samples of language use, and output, i.e., the point at which they use the language in productive tasks. Either students are first presented with models of language use which they are then required to produce themselves, or they follow a 'deep-end strategy'[58] in which they struggle to communicate and, in so doing, recognize the gaps in their language and strategic knowledge. An example of the former is a text-based approach,[59] whereas the latter follows a task-based approach.[60] Both these approaches emphasize the collaborative and experiential nature of teaching and learning. These approaches are illustrated in the following case study of a writing lesson.

Task 12

- Which parts of the lesson below seem to you to be text-based (i.e., input before output) or task-based (i.e., output before input) or collaborative?

- Where in the lesson does the teacher focus on grammatical form?

Case study C:
Students in an EAP writing class have been working on data commentary, a sub-genre usually contained within a report or research article. In a previous lesson they have been introduced to the concept of data in tables and graphs and how these are used to represent relationships between real world entities or variables. They have analysed several example texts and are now ready to write a commentary.

Lesson phase 1: The teacher explains that the aim of this lesson is to construct a data commentary which could be used in an information pack for new students who might be interested in reading about changes in higher education in the UK. She shows on a visual display a pie chart showing the proportions of students at university in the UK who have to pay tuition fees.[61]

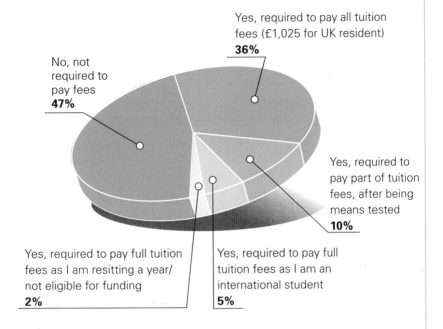

No, not required to pay fees **47%**

Yes, required to pay all tuition fees (£1,025 for UK resident) **36%**

Yes, required to pay part of tuition fees, after being means tested **10%**

Yes, required to pay full tuition fees as I am resitting a year/ not eligible for funding **2%**

Yes, required to pay full tuition fees as I am an international student **5%**

She asks the students if they are represented on the chart and they locate the segments which show the proportion of overseas students paying full fees or European students paying home fees.

Lesson phase 2: The teacher divides the students into groups of four and asks them to prepare, with their group members, a general statement that describes the main relationship in the pie chart. A scribe in each group prepares their statement for a visual. The teacher notices that students in some groups are discussing what to write but in two of the groups the scribe is writing and the other group members are not contributing. Each group then presents their statement and the class decides which one best represents the data in the chart. The class chooses the following statement:

The chart shows students who pay tuition fees and students who do not pay is the same.

Lesson phase 3: The teacher gives feedback by asking the questions below:

• Are the students really the same?

• Are the numbers exactly the same?

- How can we connect the chart to what it shows?

- How can we make a comparison between two categories in the chart?

Groups discuss the questions and the teacher guides whole class discussion to improve the general statement to the following:

> The chart _shows that_ the proportion of students who pay tuition fees is _about the same_ as the proportion who do not pay.

She underlines some of the words as shown and guides the class to identify the sentence patterns in which these collocations typically appear:

shows that + clause identifying the main relationship

first noun phrase + _be_ + _about the same as_ + second noun phrase

Lesson phase 4: From this general statement produced by the students, the teacher then completes the first part of the commentary herself, writing on the visual and eliciting suggestions from the class as she does so. As she writes, she talks aloud to let the students hear her thinking process. She decides that the commentary needs evidence from the chart to support the general statement. She also expresses surprise that so many students do not have to pay tuition fees (at the time these had just been introduced in England for home and European Union students) and suggests that the commentary needs to explain why many students still do not pay. As she writes and talks, she changes her mind about what language she wants to use and crosses out parts of her text. When she has finished she reads her text aloud and asks the students to comment on anything that does not seem clear. Finally, she guides the class to identify the genre moves in her text. These include:

- the general statement written by the students

- supporting data selected from the chart

- explanations for the main finding

Lesson phase 5: The teacher asks the students to complete the data commentary by writing about the remaining categories in the pie chart, using the same moves as the first part of the commentary. She suggests that they could also do this in their original groups but several students ask to write individually as they want to get feedback on their writing from the teacher rather than from other students.

In the sections which follow, text-based, task-based and collaborative approaches are explained in more detail and then related to the lesson in Case study C.

In a text-based approach, examples of genres which the students are likely to need in their studies are used as models for writing or speaking. These genre examples might be 'apprentice exemplars',[62] i.e., produced by students, if these are available. They constitute a more realistic target performance than professional genres such as textbooks or research articles. However, the teacher's writing, produced under time pressure without extensive polishing, is also a good example and it lets students see that even expert writers struggle to produce text. The cycle of learning and teaching activities[63] proceeds as follows: students are first oriented to the genre by discussing its purpose and audience in the context where it is used. Students analyse example texts in the genre to see how they are organized to achieve their purpose for the particular audience that they identified. Students map the organization by identifying the rhetorical moves. The teacher then models the genre and jointly constructs it with the students, using guided writing exercises. This is followed by independent writing on which students receive feedback from peers and the teacher. Finally, students examine other examples of the genre and reflect on the choices other writers made when writing in this genre. It is important to note that a text-based approach is not a template for a single lesson. The learning and teaching cycle might potentially last several weeks if students are working with genres such as documented essays or research reports, which contain sub-genres, e.g., introductions or data commentaries.

In this case study, the students are learning about a sub-genre, data commentary. They have been oriented to the genre in a previous lesson, where they discussed the purpose of data commentary and analysed the rhetorical moves in several example texts. In the lesson described in this case study, the teacher's aim is to model the genre. She introduces a purpose for writing about this data by asking the students to find whether they are represented in the chart. Their audience will be new students from similar cultural backgrounds to their own who might be interested in reading about changes to fees for higher education in the UK.

The teacher models the sub-genre first by guiding students to write the general statement in groups and then by jointly constructing the moves that follow with the class, thus giving students access to a wider range of possible language choices to realize this sub-genre. She then guides students to analyse the moves and to use the same move structure to write the remainder of the commentary. The teacher's initial feedback, in phase 3 of the lesson, focuses on accurate interpretation of the data, although she does decide to follow this with a quick focus on form for the general statement. The resulting sentence frames are used to scaffold the students' writing in phase 5 of this lesson. In a subsequent lesson, the teacher can focus on organization in her feedback by commenting on whether students have followed the genre moves and selected some data to support a general statement or merely described all the data they can see in the chart. Peer feedback allows students to decide whether the language they used is appropriate for a student audience.

This teaching and learning cycle can operate at the level of genre, e.g., report, and sub-genre, e.g., data commentary, but also at the level of rhetorical function. For example, students might work on the concept of comparing – which is required for data commentary – by first recognizing that data is often produced in order to compare the behaviour of one variable with another on which it depends. They can then identify comparisons in the general statements from a variety of data commentaries before constructing these statements jointly with the teacher, as in the case study above, and then independently.

Task-based learning and teaching: deep-end performance

In task-based learning, production usually comes before language input. Students are seen primarily as language users rather than language learners.[64] They work on authentic tasks, drawn from the target situation, which require them to use language to achieve the task goal through negotiation of meaning and problem solving. The EAP classroom is an ideal setting for a task-based approach, because it represents a practice situation designed as far as practicable to simulate the public performance situation in the target academic context.[65] Although the classroom settings in which research on task-based learning has been carried out are generally very different from EAP settings,[66] the approach offers a set of principles to inform classroom activities and reflect on their effectiveness.

A task-based approach generally involves pre-task activities to introduce the topic, activate existing knowledge of both language and content, and encourage planning for the task. The task cycle includes doing the task and planning and reporting the outcome to the class. The task can be quite short, as in this example. Students are free to do the task using the language resources available to them and the teacher does not intervene to correct errors. In the post-task phase, students reflect on their performance in the light of feedback from the teacher and their peers or observation of their own recorded performance. At this stage, they can be guided to notice the gap between the language they used and target language forms.[67] However, in keeping with the performance nature of EAP, the feedback should be driven by function rather than grammar, e.g., in the case study: 'How can we make a comparison between two categories in the chart?'

In the case study above, the students are given a task in which they write the general statement that introduces the data commentary. The teacher orients them to the task by asking them to find where they are represented in the data. The task requires collaboration and negotiation to reach a shared understanding of the data so that the focus is clearly based on meaning not language, although groups must use language to do the task. Groups report their task outcome, i.e., the statement, to the class and the feedback concentrates on task performance, i.e., choosing the statement which best reflects the data, and also on meaning, as the teacher guides students to decide if the statement they have chosen really does represent the data. It is only after focusing on meaning that the teacher focuses on the form of the statement, doing this by questioning whether it achieves its rhetorical purpose.

Focus on grammatical form

EAP students are learning how to do communicative tasks which require them to use language. The main focus is on the successful outcome of the task and not on the language itself, although grammar and vocabulary knowledge is needed to be able to perform the tasks. Therefore, the position of explicit grammar instruction in an EAP syllabus tends to be very different from its position in a traditional grammar syllabus.

General English instruction, even for students at an advanced language level, tends to follow an input before output method: presenting discrete grammar items, practising them in controlled circumstances when accuracy is important, and then allowing freer practice to encourage fluency, all within a single lesson. The grammar items tend to drive lesson planning, so the teacher starts by choosing a grammatical structure, e.g., *second conditional*, and searches for a context where it might be used, e.g., winning the lottery, in order to provide practice drills of the form. Grammar items are named and classified on the basis of form rather than meaning, e.g., *first, second* and *third conditionals*.

Text-based and task-based lessons are driven by meaning-based objectives, e.g., the need to understand and use genre conventions or successfully complete a task. Once this is achieved, a language focus guides students to examine choices that were available to a writer or speaker to achieve the purposes of the genre or the outcome of the task. This focus on form is best driven by functions which allow the performance to be connected to the rhetorical purposes in the text, as illustrated in the case study.

This kind of 'rhetorical consciousness raising',[68] encourages students to view texts as containers of content. When they have understood the content, they can examine the shape of the container, both at the level of social intention – whether the organization achieves the purpose for the specified audience, and at the level of language – whether the ideas are linked logically and coherently. When students come to construct their own texts, they can focus on their own aims and rhetorical purposes, rather than grammatical rules, and choose language to suit.

Collaborative learning and teaching

People learn naturally by cooperating in groups. In families, or special interest groups or in some workplaces, what a person understands and can do is constructed in relation to a community of novice and expert practitioners.[69] Learning arises from the interaction between an individual's current competence and their experience of the world and is mediated by conversations with practitioners in the community. This is effectively an apprenticeship model of learning in which novices have 'legitimate peripheral participation',[70] i.e., the right to share in and learn from the practices of the community. In this view, there is no direct cause and effect link between what is taught and what is learned. Instead, learning is seen as emergent, resulting from conversations between novices and experts or other novices, i.e., students can learn from peers, whose level of understanding is just above their own, or from experts, teachers or more advanced students, who can provide appropriate staging and scaffolding for tasks.[71]

The EAP classroom can become a community of practice for collaborative learning, but it is not enough just to put students in pairs or groups to do tasks as the case study above shows. Two of the groups did not work together effectively on the first writing task and several students decided to write individually at the end of the lesson because they did not think they could receive effective feedback from their peers. In order for a community of practice to develop, and for collaborative learning to be effective, students need to feel committed to achieving tasks they consider to be worthwhile and to take collective responsibility for the outcomes. Tasks should ideally be designed so that it is only possible to do them collaboratively with all group members making a contribution. Even so, students need training in effective group working strategies so they understand their responsibilities and the roles they can play. It takes time for individuals to trust each other, so groups should not be constantly changing. The teacher needs to build a classroom ethos that links shared goals and tasks with supportive feedback. The teacher in this case study is working towards this classroom ethos by encouraging peer feedback which focuses on meaning, e.g., when students choose the best general statement to describe the data, and by modelling collaboration in her joint construction of the data commentary.

An important feature of collaborative learning and teaching is the type and quality of interaction between students and teacher. Laurillard[72] describes the process of learning in an academic context as a collaborative conversation. The term *collaborative* here suggests working together towards a shared goal. Both teacher and student must be able to describe to each other their understanding of a concept and each must become aware of the difference between their descriptions. The teacher then has the responsibility of adapting her description to the level of understanding of the student, who then uses this feedback to attempt to change his own understanding. The teacher also provides an environment where the student can interact with a real-world task or problem and receive meaningful feedback on his performance so that he can reach a new understanding of the original concept. As the exchange proceeds, the student's developing understanding leads to a new focus for the continuing conversation. Students learning in a group can share the teacher's role of expert in this conversation because each person will have different areas of expertise which they can contribute to the collective understanding of the group.[73]

In the case study, the teacher has provided an environment in which students interact with an authentic task and receive feedback, i.e., interpreting the pie chart. The students describe their understanding of the chart in their general statement. The teacher then responds with questions which challenge their understanding, and the way they have represented it, e.g., with her question about what is actually shown in the chart. She provides an alternative description: *students* or *the proportion of students*. She then guides the class to produce a statement which more accurately describes the data.

Summary of learning and teaching approaches

Many EAP classes will have students going into a range of academic disciplines, and it will not be possible to focus on the disciplinary practices of one specific field. In this case, a general understanding of genres and functions can provide students with tools to analyse the specific texts in their disciplines, once they arrive there, in order to investigate how knowledge is constructed and communicated. Students need to work on tasks similar to those they will meet in the authentic academic context, e.g., writing an essay or participating in a seminar, with the initial focus on meaning and the task goal, followed by a focus on the language used to achieve the task. If possible, students should be given opportunities to research and write or speak about an aspect of their discipline, e.g., to make a concept or problem in their field of study comprehensible to their peers. The role of the teacher is to deconstruct texts through analysis, to model performance or facilitate tasks which require students to use genres or functions to communicate meaning, and to scaffold student learning through collaborative dialogue. Some of these roles can be supported with information and communications technology, as discussed in the next section.

Information and Communications Technology

E-learning is the term used to describe a variety of information and communications technology (ICT) which is used to support learning and teaching. It is an important part of EAP teaching, reflecting the fact that communicative language competence in the modern world now also includes the ability to communicate electronically.[74] The term covers a wide range of applications, which include generic word processing or data analysis software, interactive drill and practice routines on CD-ROM or DVD, and presentation technologies such as interactive whiteboards or Powerpoint™. It also includes the Internet, which can be used for information searching or for computer mediated conferencing (CMC), and can also support virtual learning environments (VLE) incorporating other media.[75] The terms *blended learning* and *distributed learning* refer to the combination of ICT with other media or face-to-face communication.

The advantages of e-learning for students include increased flexibility to study where, when and how often they want without needing to attend classes according to a fixed timetable. Individual needs can be catered for more easily. Activities and tasks which have specific answers can become interactive, giving students control over when to seek hints to guide problem-solving or reveal answers. The provision of large banks of such activities means students can work on as many or as few tasks as they need to master skills and knowledge. A variety of media – audiovisual, graphical, animation and text – can be integrated to provide a multi-sensory learning experience and increase motivation and involvement.[76] CMC via e-mail or discussion boards has the potential to encourage collaborative learning and to give shy students a voice in discussion. It can also give all students a greater sense of contact with a tutor because an e-mail can be sent to a group but can seem, to each individual, to be addressed to them personally.[77] Teaching can become more efficient as tutors can concentrate on facilitating interaction with software or with other students rather than providing content. They can monitor individual activity better and therefore guide students more effectively.

However, e-learning courses suffer from higher drop-out rates than traditional courses,[78] possibly due to a sense of isolation from tutors and peers. Students are obliged to rely on support from their peers in group discussions and assignments, but it is difficult to establish a sense of community, even in online discussion groups. Students are required to become more autonomous, directing their own learning, but e-learning does not automatically create more autonomous students, and it may be the case that 'learners require a degree of autonomy in advance in order to use new technologies effectively'.[79] Communication is usually written, via e-mail, which is more formal than face-to-face interaction, and the lack of non-verbal cues to support the message can lead to misunderstandings.

E-learning is rapidly becoming embedded in all aspects of university teaching but its potential is not always fully realized because of the gap in experience which can exist between students and lecturers. Students currently at university are likely to be 'digital natives'[80] who have grown up with videogames, mobile phones and the Internet. They feel comfortable with multi-tasking or random access reading, e.g., following hypertext links, and often prefer to learn using images or games. However, some university teachers may still be 'digital immigrants'[81] who value text-based resources, prefer reading sequentially on paper, and find it difficult to integrate ICT into their teaching. One consequence of this for e-learning is that VLEs and other electronic platforms can simply become dumping grounds for traditional lecture handouts and answers to tutorial questions, and are not fully exploited to improve the flexibility and quality of learning. Another more dangerous consequence is that university managers come to view e-learning as a way to teach more students at reduced costs using less well-qualified staff.

The Re-Engineering Assessment Practices (REAP) project, funded by the Scottish Funding Council, shows that e-learning can improve the efficient use of staff time in assessment.[82] In this project, online discussion forums have been used successfully with large classes of first-year native speaker undergraduates to enhance the quality of formative assessment and feedback, and help students to understand what is required for university study. However, e-learning does not save staff time or reduce the need for expert involvement. On the contrary, it requires considerable investment of time in learning new skills and approaches, including collaboration with ICT design specialists and moderation of online activities.

E-learning is not a methodology but a means of delivery that can support a variety of methods and approaches.[83] For example, Warschauer contrasted the practices of three writing teachers who were using ICT in their writing courses. One teacher emphasized the mastery of 'formal structures of what she considered the standard academic essay',[84] and gave explicit instructions for writing five paragraphs with five sentences each. A second was concerned 'to immerse students in a writing environment where they could learn as much as possible from their own writing experience'.[85] Her writing topics were personal or related to students' lives in their communities. Only the third, a non-native doctoral student who had experience conducting research, considered that teaching grammar and process writing would not benefit the students but instead they needed 'to realize what graduate life is about [and] how to become more academic in this system'.[86] She encouraged her students to explore and discuss the kinds of writing they were expected to produce at university. Although they had very different views of the best way to teach writing, all three teachers were able to use technology to support their teaching and considered their use of it to be effective.

There is not space to describe the wealth of e-learning technologies or to explain how they can be used. The pace of development in ICT is so rapid that the description would soon be out of date. However, a certain amount of caution is required when making claims about the potential of ICT to deliver better quality learning. It is necessary to be clear about the rationale for using ICT over other modes of delivery, even for distance learning, and to evaluate how it supports learning.

Task 13

Some examples of different types of ICT are listed below.

- Which ones are you familiar with and feel confident using?
- How much input is required from a teacher in setting up or supporting each type?
- How well do you consider that they support the EAP methodologies described above?

- language practice activities – on CD-ROM or on the Internet
- Internet search engines
- concordance software – used with purpose-built or web-based corpora[87]
- web pages – providing information on a subject or advice, e.g., about writing
- e-mail – both one-to-one and distribution lists
- online discussion forums – chat rooms, class forums and academic forums
- presentation software such as Word™ or Powerpoint™
- blogs, wikis and podcasts[88]
- virtual learning environments

Some forms of ICT need considerably more time for preparation and development than they require at the point of use. For example, language practice activities require detailed analysis of the types of mistakes that language learners typically make and the kinds of hints that will be helpful when they are interacting with tasks. Teachers also need time to produce these materials themselves or to collaborate with specialist designers. Although the teacher will have to guide students to use these resources independently, and monitor their use at first, this support can be gradually withdrawn. In contrast, online activities, such as discussion forums and web publishing tools, are fairly easy to set up but are often labour-intensive for the teacher in moderating the on-going activity or providing feedback.

ICT can support the EAP methodologies discussed above to some extent. The Internet provides access to an enormous variety of academic texts ranging from prestige genres, such as research papers in online databases, to student projects published in personal web pages. Example texts relating to specific disciplines can be analysed and used as models or prompts for writing tasks. Texts which contain particular rhetorical functions can be found by inserting functional search terms into an Internet search engine, e.g., *is a factor in* will find texts explaining cause and effect. The Internet also acts as a resource for task-based learning, encouraging exploration and research, for example, to find information for a project or advice on citation practices or typical uses and collocations for vocabulary items. The main problem with the Internet is the huge variation in the quality of material published online so teachers need to support students in careful choice and evaluation of resources.

E-mail and discussion forums enable teacher and students to come together online to discuss their understandings, and give and receive feedback in a collaborative conversation. This is the technology that is currently the most useful for EAP teachers and is increasingly used by students in their real lives. It creates a new dynamic between teacher and students because they are participating in a mental space and are not physically together. The teacher is no longer the focus of attention, as in the classroom, or the main source of motivation. Students have to imagine their audience, both teacher and peers, as they write. They can provide support for peers whose level of understanding is just below their own. The teacher becomes a moderator,[89] setting the scope and aims of the discussion and any tasks it is based on, establishing a collaborative environment, defining the code of conduct, providing access to experts, and ensuring that relevant contributions receive an adequate response. This moderating role usually means the teacher is more facilitating than directing and feels less pressure to fill silences, but can wait for students to contribute.

However, simply interacting online does not guarantee that students will be learning skills that are useful for university study, e.g., the language and conventions of a chat room will not be much use for an academic seminar. Students also have to see a clear purpose and evident benefits to make the time required for online communication worthwhile. This means that discussion forums have to be integrated into the syllabus and assessment tasks of the course. The decision to use ICT needs to be based on sound principles which address the needs of students within the constraints of a course.

Conclusion

Course design is a process in which all EAP practitioners are involved, whether designing a comprehensive syllabus or adapting and supplementing materials. The syllabus is generated from descriptions of student needs, and shaped by the constraints of the course context. Needs can be described using a range of levels and types of analysis, but choices of analysis must be principled and transparent. Three important principles in course design, which any EAP syllabus must demonstrate, are progression, recycling, and transferability to other contexts. No syllabus is ever perfect and the best course designs are always evolving, with the relationships between the elements – assessments, materials, methods and syllabus – under constant review by all the stakeholders in the course. The syllabus is implemented through appropriate methodology in classrooms and through individual study and computer-mediated learning. The role of the teacher is to support students in analysing texts, to model performance or facilitate tasks which require students to use genres or functions to communicate meaning, and to scaffold student learning through collaborative dialogue.

Further reading

Feez, S. (1998) *Text-based Syllabus Design*. Sydney: NCELTR, Macquarie University.

Hewings, M. and Dudley-Evans, T. (Eds.) (1996) *Evaluation and Course Design in EAP*. Hemel Hempstead: Prentice Hall.

Hyland, K. (2006) *English for Academic Purposes: An Advanced Resource Book*. Abingdon: Routledge.

Chapter 4: Reading

This chapter will examine:

- the nature and purposes of academic reading

- principles for selecting and using academic texts in the classroom

- a framework of tasks for using texts to develop academic readers

You will have the opportunity to:

- devise criteria for selecting academic texts to use in the EAP classroom

- devise tasks for texts that students bring in to class

Reading is a core requirement at all levels of academic study and may take up the largest part of a student's time.

Task 1

- What are the main difficulties EAP students face in becoming academic readers?

- How are these difficulties different from those encountered in non-academic reading?

Some aspects include:

- difficulty in understanding unknown vocabulary
- difficulty in decoding complex sentences
- reading too slowly because of word-by-word reading
- lack of awareness of different types of academic texts
- not understanding what the text is really about, i.e., the author's purpose
- difficulty in identifying the main points of the text
- lack of awareness of their own purpose for reading
- lack of flexibility in adjusting their reading strategy to their purpose
- inexperience in recording key information in a form which enables it to be used in future work

The first three difficulties relate particularly to reading in a second language. The third is a serious problem in an academic context, where inability to cope with the necessary amount of reading can lead to failure on a course. EAP students often identify slow reading as a problem but they may also report that they have been taught to read slowly because this is necessary for comprehension. The reading speed of an average native speaker is likely to be around 300 words per minute (wpm) when reading quickly, but university students studying in a second language can have reading speeds as low as 60 wpm[1] and research in China on classes preparing for the College English Test found reading speeds of only 80–120 wpm set as a target.[2] In fact, slow readers are likely to have poorer levels of comprehension as they lose the overall meaning of the text, and there is a correlation between faster speed and successful reading for foreign language learners.[3]

Reading speed is related to the skills involved in reading. Skills are sequences of actions that can be learnt and become routine. These automatic and less conscious aspects of reading include word recognition, decoding simple sentences, and the fluent eye movements needed to read quickly. When meeting an unknown word in a text, reading skills enable the reader to relate the form to meaning through accessing the reader's mental lexicon of previously known words and using clues such as affixes and grammatical inflexions. When an unconscious reading sequence is disrupted, strategies have to be used to compensate. These are conscious processes aimed to address a reader's purpose and solve problems presented by a particular text.[4] Such strategies might include judging whether a word is critical to the meaning of the text and searching for a definition in the surrounding text or consulting the index or a dictionary. EAP students can be helped to improve reading skills by training in strategies that help them to deal with unfamiliar vocabulary and sentences which are difficult to understand.

The remaining difficulties listed above are experienced when students are not employing wider strategic approaches that can help them to read efficiently. In everyday life, essential reading involves short, quite accessible texts, such as instructions or letters. Long, difficult texts such as novels are read for recreation and can be abandoned if they are too taxing. As academic readers, students will have to develop strategies to deal with long texts that may be beyond their language competence. Rather than seeing a text as simply providing information which can be retrieved by successfully processing its linguistic elements, students need to able to read strategically in a global way to understand the wider meaning of a text and match it to their purpose in reading. Global reading involves looking for the big picture and recognizing the main points made by the writer so that they can be recorded effectively in notes which reflect the reading purpose.

In the EAP classroom, texts have two distinct uses. The first is to train students in effective reading skills and strategies. When texts are used in this way, the teaching focus is on productive tasks requiring understanding of content. Texts also provide models of language use and can be studied for their organization and functional vocabulary. Often, a particular text can serve both these purposes, but both teacher and students need to be clear about the purpose for using a text at a particular time. This chapter focuses mainly on the text as a carrier of content, and the skills and strategies needed to read in an academic way. Chapter 5: *Vocabulary* and Chapter 6: *Writing* will consider texts as sources of language and as models for writing.

Reading at university

EAP students' previous reading experiences in English are likely to include textbooks which provide all the material needed for a course, newspapers or magazines, and web pages which contain quite short stretches of text and are multi-modal or interactive, i.e., with sound and video clips, images, and online conversations. Many students find the range of academic texts unfamiliar and are unsure how they should approach these. Reading on EAP courses needs to reflect text types which students will meet and also the purposes for which they will read them. Teachers, therefore, need to understand the status and roles of texts in university study and the way academic readers approach texts.

Academic literature and literacy

The type of texts students need to read at university varies across different disciplines and according to the level of study.

Task 2

Below is a list of a number of types of academic texts.

- Which of these might students need to read on undergraduate or postgraduate courses and for what purposes?

---

course books	textbooks
case studies	company or government reports
reference books	guidebooks or manuals
handouts of lecture notes	edited collections of papers
academic journals	conference papers or reports

At the beginning of undergraduate studies, textbooks aimed at introducing important areas of a subject to a student audience are the main reading material.

Lecturers' notes may provide a framework for a unit of the course. In many disciplines, e.g., in business, medical and engineering courses, students are also likely to encounter case studies, government or company reports, reference books, laboratory manuals and guidebooks. Academic reading at postgraduate level will vary according to the field and type of research. Although it will include the types of texts used at undergraduate level, it will be drawn predominantly from texts directed to the academic community of research professionals. Examples of these are articles in academic journals, conference reports, and edited collections of papers representing important research or discussion of a particular issue.

An important element of all these types of academic text is their intertextuality, that is, their interdependence. Academic writers and readers are part of the same discourse community, so authors address their writing either to novices in this community, that is students, or to their peers, who are practising academics and professionals. In both these cases, they constantly draw on the ideas and writing of other academics. Authors of undergraduate textbooks will have read the research and discussions of other writers in the discipline in order to present the prevailing consensus or a range of alternative viewpoints. Academic papers will be explicitly referenced to show that the writers are aware of the research of others. Lecture notes may be based on the writing of other academics. Even reference books and government reports not written specifically for the academic community have their origins in academic research. To read effectively, students need to be aware of this intertextual aspect of academic texts, as the outcome of their reading will usually involve some form of writing which acknowledges its relationship with this network of other sources. In linking their reading and writing in this way, students become literate in their own academic disciplines. In order to acquire academic literacy, students need to understand that academic texts are situated within the social practices and power hierarchy of the academic and professional community. This involves being aware of, and being able to participate in, the academic practices of the discipline, evaluating the purpose and status of texts, and responding to them in an appropriate way.

The developing academic reader

As well as developing the ability to read different types of text, students also need to be able to adopt different approaches to reading as they progress through the stages of academic study and read for a range of purposes. Here are some comments from subject lecturers about their students' reading needs and abilities.[5] The first five concern undergraduate students in mechanical engineering. Comments 6 to 8 refer to postgraduate students in management.

1 *They need to read fast in a critical way.*

2 *Even my final year students are still library shy – some of them don't even know where the library is!*

3 *They need to look for authoritative validated sources.*

4 *They lack creativity to take their own notes.*

5 *If I give them lemons, I expect them to give me back the juice not the lemons!*

6 *They have to be able to start at 100 miles per hour and keep going.*

7 *We give them maybe 30–40% of the reading they need. They have to find the rest for themselves.*

8 *They have to operate in a varied landscape – our discipline crosses with many others.*

At the beginning of an undergraduate course, students read mainly to follow up lectures and prepare for assessment, consolidating and expanding their understanding of the concepts and facts which constitute the core of the subject. At this stage, their reading is likely to be quite directed, and involve recommended textbooks, handouts supplied in lectures, case studies, and company or government reports related to professional aspects of the subject. However, as the lecturer points out in comment 1, they still have to read fast and in a critical way. The ability to read critically develops throughout the period of academic study. At first, the critical focus is likely to involve making connections with previous knowledge or thinking of examples or applications. However, as they progress through their courses, rather than using texts simply as sources of information, students will increasingly be expected to evaluate the basis of that knowledge and the conclusions of other authors. Using texts in more complex ways to support their own research and conclusions requires more sophisticated note-taking and recording strategies. In comment 4, the lecturer points out that the ability to take notes that reflect the reader's purpose needs to be developed from an early stage of academic study.

During their studies at university, what students read and what they need to do with the material become gradually more complex. The outcome of academic reading is usually a task which requires applying or transforming knowledge[6] to solve problems characteristic of the academic field or their future profession. The lecturer uses the analogy of the lemons to help her students see the importance of this process of knowledge transformation. For example, memorizing and re-presenting the content of a case study in paraphrased form would not be satisfactory in an examination answer. That would be 'giving back the lemons'. Students would be expected to extract 'the juice', that is, to select certain elements of the case study to illustrate their understanding of an aspect of the theory of the subject.

As students proceed through their courses, they will be expected to read more widely and independently. In comment 2, the engineering lecturer is concerned about her undergraduate students' inexperience and reluctance to use the university library when they need to read around a topic for their research projects. She expects them to be familiar with the location in the library of academic journals in their field and to be aware that, unlike many websites, these are key credible sources for their subject (comment 3). Interested students at all levels will keep up with developments in the field through general interest professional magazines, such as *New Scientist* or *The Economist*, but they need to be aware that these do not have the same status as peer reviewed (refereed) academic journals.

By the time they undertake postgraduate courses, students need to be able to read very fast and efficiently in a highly autonomous way, as comments 6 and 7 emphasize. Although there will be some required reading, most of their reading will be self-directed, as they formulate their own research question and then carry out the research. At both undergraduate and postgraduate level, students may have to read texts from a range of disciplines. Comment 8 points out that much research in applied subjects is multidisciplinary. For example, a textile engineer on a masters course needed to read a paper entitled *Structural and Mechanical Aspects of Embroidered Textile Scaffolds for Tissue Engineering*. To understand this research, the student had first to read about the structure of bone cells to understand how the mechanical properties of textiles could be matched with those of bone tissue to help heal bones. This student's research topic crossed three disciplines: mechanical engineering, textiles and medicine. Reading about the methodology needed for their research may also take students into different disciplines. For example, an undergraduate IT student, carrying out a final year research project which involved designing an online technical glossary, had to become familiar with learning theories. He had to find this information himself without guidance from his tutor.

Selecting and evaluating sources

As soon as students are required to undertake individual assignments and projects, they will find a huge amount of reading that may be useful to them and they need to be equipped to make judgements about the status and relevance of an array of competing texts. The advent of Internet searching has increased this problem because texts are instantly available without the mediation of gatekeepers such as libraries, publishers or booksellers. Previously, these agencies have exercised some discrimination with respect to the credibility and authority of writers and their works. This role is now fulfilled by academic databases, which act as a filter for credible sources, and students need to be taught how to use these. An example of the type of independent reading expected on academic courses is shown in these specifications for a final year undergraduate dissertation:[7]

> Students are required to undertake an appropriate literature review. This will require a focused review of the relevant literature. Students will be judged on their skills in selecting relevant aspects of the material read.

This assignment requires students to find their own sources and make critical judgements about the credibility and relevance of the sources.

Task 3

An undergraduate student has decided to do a dissertation on company mergers in the field of finance. Below are some titles of texts resulting from his search of a library catalogue and an Internet search.

What clues can you find in the titles and references that might help him to identify which texts are credible sources?

Which words in the titles might indicate the focus and scope of each source?

1. Fairburn, J. A. (1990) The Evolution of Merger Policy in Britain. In Fairburn J. A. and Kay J. A. (1990) *Mergers and Merger Policy* Oxford: Oxford University Press, pages 193–230.

2. Fama, E. F. (1980) Agency Problems and the Theory of the Firm. *Journal of Political Economy*, Vol 88: 21, pages 288–307.

3. Fama, E. F., Fisher L., Jensen M. C., and Roll R. (1969) The Adjustment of Stock Prices to New Information. *International Economic Review* Vol 10:1 (February) pages 1–21.

4. Jonquieres, G. D. (1992) Decline in Cross-Border Deals. *Financial Times*, January 10 Section II:17.

5. Rossi, S. and Volpin, P. (2004) Cross-Country Determinants of Mergers and Acquisitions. *Journal of Economics*, Vol 74:2 (November) pages 277–304.

6. Very, P. and Schweiger, D. M. (2001) The acquisition process as a learning process: Evidence from a study of critical problems and solutions in domestic and cross-border deals. *Journal of World Business*, Volume 36, Number 1, Spring 2001, pages 11–31.

7. Betancourt, M. C., Pablo, E. and Pileggi, V. (2006) Determinants of M&A Transactions in Latin America. Available online http://servicios.iesa.edu.ve/newsite/academia/pdf/EduardoPablo.pdf

8. *Economist* (1992a) Mad Mergers in Europe. February 1, page 18.

9. *Economist* (1992b) Perrier Bottled. March 21, page 107.

10. Reuters (1996) EC says no to 'gentleman's agreement' with UEFA over Bosman. *Internet Soccer Features.* Available online http://www.nando.net/newsroom/sports/oht/1996/oth/soc/feat/archive/020196/soc/ Latin America

Students could guess that some of these publications are academic sources, from words such as *journal* and *volume*. However, without prior knowledge, students from different cultures might assume that publications such as *The Economist* and *Financial Times* are academic publications. Not all academic journals have the word *Journal* in their titles. For example, *Nature* is a prestigious natural science journal despite its simple title. Students would have to look for further clues to see that 8 and 9 are clearly magazine articles. They could guess from the titles and also from the very specific topic, with its reference to the trade name Perrier. A similar judgement could be made about the Internet source 10.

To make guesses about the remaining sources, students would need some awareness of the way titles of different academic publications indicate their scope, i.e., exactly what they cover in terms of the specificity of the topic, and what is presented about it. Although the language of title 4 may sound academic, it does not seem to be aiming to do more than report a decline at a particular time, suggesting it is a newspaper report. The fact that 1, *Mergers and Merger Policy*, is published by Oxford suggests an introductory text on the topic. The scope of the chapter title (*evolution, in Britain*) suggests a focus on historical development typical at the beginning of an introductory book. The remaining sources are articles in academic journals and one website of a lecturer or professor, which can be guessed from *edu* in the url.

What is noticeable in the academic titles is the presence of words indicating rhetorical functions, such as causes, problems and development, or words representing academic activities and constructs. The articles are not simply about *mergers* but about the *determinants, evolution, adjustment, problems, solutions, evidence, process, study* and *theory* of mergers or related items. These words provide quite precise detail about the scope of the text. Unlike newspapers, academic texts do not present information for interest or entertainment; they aim to present information in a way that will advance the understanding of that topic, and provide explicit titles to show how they will do this. Students who focus on topic-related vocabulary might ignore *Agency Problems and the Theory of the Firm* as irrelevant because there is no mention of mergers. However, if they are alerted by *problems* and *theory*, they might check the abstract of the article and discover that *agency* refers to ownership and control, and that the text is relevant to mergers and acquisitions. To judge the relevance of a text, effective academic readers identify not only the main topic but also the communicative purpose in terms of intended audience and scope, signalled by words that indicate rhetorical functions, that is, the relationship between the ideas being discussed. Developing EAP students' awareness of these thematic levels of *aboutness* in academic texts is a step towards equipping them with the autonomy needed to function independently in their future academic context.

Understanding the status of academic texts

Academic readers also need to be aware of the status of the texts they read. Status includes aspects of credibility, such as whether an academic article is from a peer-reviewed journal, and whether a textbook is well-known and the author authoritative. Status is an aspect of academic texts which may be new to students who are not accustomed to selecting their own academic reading. Students who perceive all published texts as equally valid sources of information are likely to read and use indiscriminately any text which appears in a Google™ search for that topic, often the shortest article or one in a format that is easy to download. On this basis, they might choose *Mad Mergers* rather than *Mergers and Merger Policy* as a starting point to understand this topic. In the case of the textbook *Mergers and Merger Policy*, an Internet search reveals that it is cited in several journal articles, suggesting that it is considered to be an authoritative and useful source by other academic writers. It is also important to consider the publisher. As well as recognizing major publishers of academic books, such as Cambridge University Press and Oxford University Press, it is useful to know names of specialist or niche publishers in a particular field. The date of a text is not necessarily an indicator of its status. A text which is not very recent may be out of date, but it could be a seminal work which has influenced the way the understanding of the subject has developed, or a classic which is still regarded as significant in the field. A very recent text could represent state-of-the-art development or it may be an obscure item of research unlikely to affect mainstream thinking in that field.

Another element of status concerns the reader response required by the text and the context. Students need to know to what extent their discipline expects them to engage with or challenge texts. Swales discusses the relationship a textbook might have with a lecture course.[8] He notes that students might be expected to alternate between uncritical and critical responses to the text, depending on whether the lecturer intends the book to be accepted as representing received ideas or challenged as an outdated approach. First-year chemistry students are unlikely to be able to challenge a textbook on thermodynamics whereas first-year philosophy students may be expected to take a critical approach towards the ideas of Kant or Locke. Textbooks may be written in an authoritative style with few references when presenting the current accepted ideas in that field.

Classroom materials 4.1
What is academic literature?
introduces students to some text types and ways of evaluating their scope and status.

However, research papers are written in the expectation that their conclusions, methodology, and even their assumptions, may be challenged, hence the cautious use of language and the inclusion of references to support claims.

To read effectively, students need to be aware of the role academic texts play in enabling the writer, the reader and the wider academic community to communicate. To become academically literate and understand the requirements of the discipline when selecting, evaluating and using texts, students need to be able to:

- recognize the genre of texts commonly encountered in their disciplines
- check the source of any text to decide if it is appropriate and credible for the academic purpose
- look for specific clues which indicate the scope and focus of a text
- consider the status of the text and how this affects the way they will use it in their writing
- be aware of their role as readers and the type of response expected

Approaches of academic readers

Developing academic literacy appropriate to their field and level of study enables students to approach texts in a different way. Instead of a text-driven approach, in which the reader takes a submissive attitude to the text and focuses mainly on retrieving and understanding information, they can adopt a dominant, reader-driven approach, deciding on their own reading purpose. Submissive readers read simply according to the writer's intention. Dominant readers go beyond this to formulate their own questions, read the text to answer these, and evaluate the author's credibility and sources of knowledge.[9] Students need to accept that a purposeful, selective approach to reading is essential to cope with the time constraints of academic and professional research. In the following examples experienced academic readers describe their strategies.

Task 4

These readers all adopt a dominant reading approach.

- What strategies do they use to achieve their reading purposes?

Case study A:
Experiences of academic readers

1 I wanted to know how the interlayer pressure builds as the size of a roll of plastic film builds up. I found a book called 'The Mechanics of Winding'. I looked at the contents page and picked one chapter that seemed relevant to answer my question according to its title, 'Winding Models'. I read that chapter in depth. I skipped through the rest of the book and the index to see if there was anything interesting and I also read bits of other chapters whose input was directly related to the chapter I wanted.

(professional process engineer working in research and development)

2 Teachers can direct you to sources but you have to come to your own conclusions. I went through library journals typing search words into the library catalogue. There were a lot of sources so I had to use my own judgement. I read the abstracts. Some weren't related to my topic but in fact it helped me narrow down my topic. When I got an on-line article, I used 'find' to look for the key word and read the bit around that. I located text books through their titles. I spent a lot of time filtering, matching what I was trying to say and backing it up with a reference. It took about a month but I was always thinking about it.

(final year undergraduate preparing a dissertation project)

3 This is a project, which means I should do some research. Thus I should find a lot of materials, such as journals and books. In fact, if you want to read all things that you find, it is impossible. So during these weeks, I learnt how to read effectively and get my necessary information. For example, an article from a journal contains lots of content but sometime I just use the conclusion of the articles and read one paragraph or one sentence.

(EAP student preparing a course assignment)

4 When I began to research a new topic I found some introductory texts and a set of conference proceedings which gave me an overview and highlighted the key issues. I took a lot of notes to begin with to try to fix some of these ideas in my head. I found a book that looked like an introduction but found the ideas too difficult. I came back to that book later, after I had read some research papers, and it was a lot easier to understand. I found some review articles and used their bibliographies to find other books and articles in the field. Some of these turned out to be too detailed for my purposes but they helped me decide what level of detail was appropriate. I kept looking

> at the bibliographies to see which sources all the authors referred to so I could identify the key texts. When later articles referred to the same texts, I knew I had probably found most of the key sources.
>
> (academic writer researching a chapter for a book)

These are dominant readers who have learnt to shop for information and ideas. This does not mean that they ignore the writer's purpose, as can be seen from the first example. While reading mainly to answer his own question, the reader skims through to see if there is anything he needs to know that he was not aware of previously.

All the readers had clear purposes and specific questions to answer: 'I wanted to know how the interlayer pressure builds'. They first searched in a systematic way to find texts or parts of texts that were likely to answer their questions, using library catalogues, bibliographies, reviews and key word searches to find journal articles and specialist textbooks. They refer to books by genre names (*abstracts, text books, conference proceedings, review articles*) showing that they base their expectations on the purpose of these genres. They used their awareness of text status and intertextuality: 'When subsequent articles referred to the same key texts, I knew I had probably found most of the important sources'. They surveyed texts, using strategies such as analysing the title and scanning the contents page or index. They all read in a non-linear way, choosing the order that suited their purpose to save time – for example, reading only the abstract or the conclusion.

To make the sources serve their purposes, these readers were able to read flexibly, combining global strategies to find important points with careful reading for maximum comprehension. They used a technique called search reading to find the most relevant passages.[10] Search reading involves reading the text to answer a target question. This requires some prediction of how the target question might be answered in the text and the concepts that might be mentioned. The reader searches for a mention of particular items or concepts, looking for key phrases, clusters of related words and phrases (lexical chains), or titles of graphs and diagrams in the text. In example 1, the process engineer wanted to answer a question about a relationship between pressure and size. He predicted that this would be represented as a mathematical model, so *model* was one of the words in his mind as he searched the text. Having found the relevant passage, he read it in depth. These readers used other global fast-reading strategies, such as sampling, skimming and scanning to gain an overview of the text: 'I skipped through the text'. Skimming describes a more open process than search reading. The aim is getting an overview of the author's main points, for example, by reading the beginnings or ends of paragraphs, rather than searching for answers to specific questions. In search reading, the reader looks for a range of possible signals in the text that might indicate an answer to the target questions. Scanning is a narrower form of searching in which the reader scans the text for mention of one particular word or phrase. Scanning may be one strategy employed in search reading. In example 2, the student mechanized the scanning process by using the *find* tool in Word™. In all these cases, the strategy of careful local reading follows the search process: 'I read that chapter in depth'.

Dominant readers are able to use academic texts critically as a foundation to create their own texts, making the reading sources their servants not their masters: 'I spent a lot of time filtering, matching what I was trying to say and backing it up with a reference'. Inexperienced academic readers, or those from different academic cultures, tend to accept published texts as authoritative and feel that they must respect and reproduce the information they contain. Hyland points out that these readers may have 'different understandings of text uses and the social value of different text types'.[11] To operate as successful practitioners in an English-medium academic context, students need to learn to use sources as servants to support their own ideas or findings, and sometimes even as opponents to be critically evaluated in order to allow the student writer to present an alternative point of view.

These experienced readers were aware of the intertextual relationship between their academic reading and the texts they needed to produce. They employed critical thinking to judge the relevance of information and evaluate texts: 'you have to come to your own conclusions'; 'I had to use my own judgement'. Their aim was to use their reading to generate their own writing, so they were not afraid to reject what did not fit in with their purposes.

The strategies of dominant readers are summarized below:

- identifying a clear reading purpose before they begin
- searching systematically for relevant texts using appropriate resources, such as bibliographies, library catalogues and online databases
- using their awareness of the way academic texts are interrelated
- surveying texts using resources provided, e.g., contents pages and text layout features
- reading flexibly, that is, using global strategies for fast reading (prediction, search reading to answer specific questions, sampling information, skimming for the main ideas and scanning for key words) before reading the important passages carefully
- reading critically and taking appropriate notes that reflect the required outcomes and enable sources to be used to support their own points in subsequent writing

Reading in the EAP classroom

Reading in an EAP course needs to incorporate three levels:

- introducing students to the purposes of academic texts and of academic reading
- providing students with training and practice in the skills and strategies needed to develop as academic readers
- helping students to use texts as examples of genres, focusing on purpose, rhetorical functions, organization and academic vocabulary

Students tend to see the purpose of an EAP reading course as acquiring the ability to extract information from complex texts. They may feel that this will prepare them sufficiently for the demands of reading on their degree course. This perception may have been reinforced in their earlier experiences of general English classes where texts were presented in isolation, used mainly as a vehicle for studying language forms and testing comprehension, with little consideration of genre and source. However, as the previous section has shown, to become academically literate students need a different approach to reading and to texts. Developing academic literacy is best achieved using academic texts. Therefore, a first concern for the teacher is which texts to select for classroom use and where to find these.

Selecting academic texts for the classroom

Task 5

Look back to the text in Chapter 2 about Vibrios.

- What concerns would you have about using academic texts such as this one in the classroom?
- What are your criteria for selecting texts to use in the classroom?
- Where would you find suitable texts?
- Would you write your own texts?
- How would you select and use texts for a mixed subject class?

Using a technical text like this in the classroom can seem problematic. Some questions which concern EAP teachers include:

- How can my students cope with the length and difficulty of academic texts?
- Is it all right to adapt or write texts or should they always be authentic?

Chapter 2 showed how teachers can approach academic texts more confidently by becoming aware of text purposes, as well as the patterns and language features which show rhetorical functions and carry the flow of information. These aspects can form criteria for selecting texts. Teachers can choose texts which exemplify these purposes and provide students with opportunities to read in an academic way, as well as serving as models for the features and language of writing genres they will have to produce.

Authenticity

A first concern of EAP teachers when selecting texts is often authenticity. There are a number of different aspects of text authenticity, e.g., topic, genre, purpose, process and outcomes. However, teachers often choose texts on the basis of topic. They tend to look for texts on topics related to science, business or social sciences, and may be tempted to use journalistic sources, as these seem to be easier and are a convenient length for a single lesson. In fact, genre is a more helpful basis for teachers to use to identify academic texts that will contain the typical language and text organization which students need to be familiar with in order to read and write successfully in an academic context. Genres such as textbooks and research papers, which students are likely to meet in their studies, are good sources of authentic texts. Teachers may be concerned that the content and vocabulary of such texts will present too many difficulties and should be left until a later stage, but the reality is that, for EAP students, there is no later stage. As Lewis comments: 'Too many courses are constructed on the implicit assumption that they are intermediate stages on the way to full language competence'.[12] Only if they are introduced to the forms and features of academic texts as early as possible can EAP students discover the difficulties they have to face and the strategies that might help them overcome these.

It is possible to find academic texts that deal with accessible subject matter which lends itself to discussion and analysis in the classroom. In a mixed subject class, it will not be possible to cater for individual subject disciplines, but this is not necessarily inauthentic. The multidisciplinary nature of modern academic study means that students will need to read outside the boundaries of their own subjects. Most students will need some knowledge of topics relating to IT and management, as well as types of research methodology. Teachers should also think about their pedagogical purposes when selecting texts. Texts should be suitable for practising reading strategies and/or may be chosen as models for writing that students need to produce. Texts selected for a course also need to be related to each other to allow systematic progression in developing both reading skills and the appropriate writing outcomes which are linked to them.

Important sources of texts are those suggested by academic staff in target subject departments, and also texts brought in by students themselves. Departments supply reading lists for different courses and may have a bank of online support materials which can be adapted. Suitable texts include introductory sections from chapters of textbooks, which usually contain definitions and explanations that make them more accessible to the non-specialist reader, case studies, dissertations, and abstracts from research papers. Abstracts are easily accessible online and are useful as miniaturized texts, providing a rich source of characteristic patterns of text organization and language.[13] Past undergraduate and masters dissertations may be obtained from departments, or from the university library. Some EAP teachers have themselves written dissertations in English. Using extracts from these can produce examples in a range of topics. Where possible, students should be encouraged to bring in their own texts for study. These can be texts they need to read but find difficult or texts that they find interesting and want to understand better.

Writing texts for the classroom

There are special considerations in selecting texts for pre-undergraduate use, as these students are at an earlier stage of development in their academic literacy, and are less likely to be able to choose texts to bring to class. Textbook extracts are suitable, and used in some reading course books.[14] Teachers can also adapt or write their own texts, modelled on a suitable genre. For example, a report from a journalistic source can be re-written in a more academic style to provide an accessible text for classroom use. Such constructed texts are particularly useful when introducing new rhetorical functions. Authentic texts can be confusing because they are multifunctional, so it is useful for teachers to adapt a text which highlights the main rhetorical purpose without the burden of difficult vocabulary or content.

The following case study illustrates some of the principles for producing constructed texts for classroom study.

Task 6

Look back to the case study of *The Metropole and the Luxus Hotels* in Chapter 2. This is a constructed text.

- Where do you think the writer found ideas about what to include?

- What principles do you think the writer used to write the text?

This text was written for an undergraduate EAP course. Its pedagogical purpose was to introduce the function of comparison within a genre that students would meet in their studies, a case study. The students on this distance-learning course were studying in different contexts around the world, so the topic needed to be accessible and the introduction to the function clear. Here is the teacher's reflection on the process of writing.

Case study B:
Writing an EAP text – a teacher's reflection

In order to model the text on an authentic genre used in business courses, I studied the content and register of case studies and noticed that the style was simple and factual. It was similar to the style I would use in my own professional writing, e.g., in a course report. One issue which was mentioned in the case studies was how management styles affected businesses. I also noticed a news item about problems experienced by some hotels following the destruction of the World Trade Centre. That provided the theme and scope: a comparison of how different types of management affect company performance.

Having decided on the genre and content, I decided to write the text from information available on real hotel websites, so that the content was authentic, but changed the names. I did not focus on the fact that the text was for teaching purposes and made no conscious decisions about language or structure.

I wondered whether the topic would upset some students, but decided that the way it was mentioned was sufficiently neutral and avoided using the emotive expression 9/11. I thought about the life span of the text and decided that although it dealt with a topical theme, it could be adapted to incorporate some other major event at a later date. While designing the tasks to exploit the text, I allowed two minor changes, adding comparison expressions which my research had shown to be frequent in the target texts and which would be useful to introduce at this stage.

When constructing or adapting texts, teachers should focus on suitability of genre and function which can lead to authentic tasks as well as the opportunity to study transferable features of text organization and vocabulary. Teachers need to find and study real examples of target genres. Thought needs to be given to whether topics are appropriate to the culture and background knowledge of students or other colleagues who might use the text. The actual writing process should be as authentic as possible, avoiding contrived use of language or form to fit the teaching purpose. The lifespan and transferability of materials produced has to be considered to justify the time spent writing them and to make sure they can be re-used in subsequent courses.

In summary, teachers should select texts representing a range of genres and functions that reflect the reading and writing their students will need to do on academic courses. The tasks based on these texts should involve authentic academic goals, processes and outcomes.

Developing academic literacy

If students are to become academically literate, the ways they study and use texts in the EAP classroom should parallel as closely as possible those they will need in their degree studies. Writing assignments should be modelled on those at university, and involve drawing on information from several sources in order to present a problem or argument, or answer a question. Development of writing from reading sources can be staged. Initially, teachers supply reading materials for tasks. In later assignments, the framework and purpose are set by the teacher, e.g., to prepare a poster comparing two concepts or items in their field to inform high school students coming to a university open day, but students are responsible for choosing a topic and finding sources. In the final stage, students devise their own research or essay question, so that the purpose of the reading and selection of texts is entirely driven by the student. At each stage, reading and writing are presented as interdependent aspects of academic study, to prepare students for the literacy practices of their target academic communities.

The first consideration in developing academic literacy through reading in the classroom is providing students with an authentic reading purpose so that they have clear goals beyond simply understanding the content of the text. This involves formulating specific questions that they need to answer to achieve a particular outcome. For example, reading to find information for an assignment is an authentic academic purpose, whereas reading a text to answer a set of comprehension questions is not. The second consideration is that the tasks should require an authentic reading process, i.e., reading flexibly to suit the purpose, using the strategies employed by academic readers. Finally, selected texts should lend themselves to being integrated with authentic writing outcomes, such as note-taking and summarizing the author's main points. Outcomes which might be carried out over a series of lessons include combining or synthesizing ideas or information from different sources to present points in essays, and incorporating information to answer exam questions.

The most effective way to achieve reading purposes which will simulate the demands of academic literacy is through a task-based approach which simulates target performance, i.e., a project or report based on independent reading and research. However, this is not always possible and teachers need to find a balance between authenticity and particular teaching aims. If difficult skills are being attempted, e.g., when students first try summarizing and synthesizing ideas from different sources to use in their own texts, less authentic reading texts can be used to reduce the difficulty of the content. When more difficult authentic texts, such as research articles, are introduced, tasks can be used which give more support and do not require complete understanding of the content.

Task 7

For each of the lessons described in the case study below:

- How authentic do you think the texts and activities were?

- To what extent did the lesson develop students' academic literacy?

Case study C: Two lessons

Lesson A

This was part of a short course aimed at helping postgraduate students acquire a basic knowledge of key concepts and vocabulary for business related disciplines. Texts were specially written by subject lecturers and adapted by EAP teachers.

After a lead-in activity to activate prior knowledge, students formed two groups and each read a text on either financial accounting or management accounting. There were supporting tasks to help them focus on relevant information and take notes while reading. After reading, students checked their understanding in the group, before giving a short oral explanation of the topic to a partner who had read a different text. The partner was given a note-taking framework to record differences between the two types of accounting. Finally, students identified topical words and collocations from the text and recorded them on a vocabulary reference page.

Lesson B

This was a postgraduate reading class. The text, from an early unit in an EAP reading course book, was entitled *The influence of class size on educational achievement*.[15] The teacher asked the class to find the source of the text, which required noticing a footnote at the end of the text. Students were then asked to decide from the title what questions they would expect the author to answer. The elicitation took a long time as students mostly made suggestions related to the details of the topic, e.g., *Do students get less individual attention?* rather than the author's purpose. Finally, with a lot of prompting from the teacher, the students decided that the author would need to cite research to answer two questions: *Does class size influence achievement? If so, how does it do this?* The teacher asked students to search the text for answers to these questions. Students approached this task with varying degrees of success. Some found it difficult and confusing and wanted to read the introduction carefully or just focus on looking up words they did not know. About half the class were able to locate the answers. During discussion, the teacher asked what they thought the US-based writer actually meant by large class sizes. It emerged that the students had not thought about this. Ideas about what constituted a large class varied from 20 to 70 pupils, depending on their country of origin. Even students from the same country discovered that they had different ideas, depending on their age and social background. This discussion took so long that the class only achieved half the originally intended tasks. The teacher felt that the lesson had been rather inconclusive and messy.

Lesson A focused on practising skills and strategies and exploiting the text for language learning. The texts were reasonably authentic and the tasks represented simple versions of authentic outcomes, in that students had to take notes for a purpose and present the information orally to an audience, thus briefly taking ownership of the text and becoming the experts. Reading in a fixed time encouraged them to read quickly and avoid word-by-word reading. However, the well-controlled structure of the lesson prompted the students to be submissive readers, seeking only to understand the information content of the text. This type of lesson has a place in EAP courses, supporting students in an understanding of the concepts and vocabulary they will meet in their courses. However, to equip them to be independent readers, this type of structured approach to reading needs to be supplemented by more challenging encounters with texts, in which they also have to evaluate the purpose or context of the text.

In lesson B, the focus was on raising students' awareness of purposes they might have in reading. The aim was to help them become dominant readers, able to formulate questions and use flexible reading strategies to achieve their purposes. The text was less authentic, from a journalistic source, and the topic accessible to allow the introduction of two strategies: formulating questions to give a reading purpose, and searching for answers in the text. When approaching texts which describe research, the teacher should encourage students to formulate questions that focus on the purpose of the research and the likely questions which the writer will answer. In lesson B, answering questions about the research findings required a reading strategy which involved searching for information in different parts of the text without reading what was in between. Students found this non-linear approach to a text counter-intuitive and challenging. Some of them succeeded in locating the information they were searching for, but found they did not have the close reading skills necessary to actually decide what the answer was. In these tasks, students were encouraged to look outside the classroom to see the world of real academic reading in which readers have to make their own purposes, evaluate the foundation of knowledge underlying the text, and monitor their own understanding. The fact that some students did not like what they saw did not mean that they did not need to look. The discussion of what constituted a large class seemed rather time-consuming, but it was a step towards the critical approach to reading which is essential for postgraduate study. Realizing that the text did not in fact define what was meant by a large class size showed students how academic readers constantly have to question rather than accept texts they read. The objectives of this lesson aimed to develop academic literacy by raising awareness of the strategies required for purposeful academic reading. These are long-term objectives, not achievable as a measurable outcome of one lesson as the objectives of lesson A were. Training students to use more critical and purposeful approaches to reading requires persistence, and students need to learn through unsuccessful as well as successful experience. The teacher allowed the students to struggle so that they could experience the problem, diagnose some of their own difficulties, and gauge their real degree of understanding of the key information. When this approach is tried, it can result in EAP lessons which appear messy and inconclusive, but it is essential to emancipate students from being text and teacher dependent. This course is likely to be the last English course they attend, so they must become independent self-motivated readers without the help of a teacher to set reading purposes. Students also need to become less dependent on the text as the writer has structured it, and be prepared to ignore some sections, focusing only on what suits their purposes.

Reading outside the classroom

Developing the independence needed for academic reading can also be approached by finding opportunities for students to explore the reading needs they will encounter as members of the academic community. When working with EAP students in Thailand, Holme and Chalauiseng used the strategy of making their students actually 'walk through' the territory they would have to inhabit. The teacher took the students outside the classroom to interview senior students in their target pharmacy course, as well as practising professionals. The students learnt that their reading class was not just 'a forum for collective translation' but a place where they could prepare to participate in the academic and professional community they were aiming to join.[16] This type of interaction with the target situation is not always possible but teachers need to give students every opportunity to gain first-hand information about academic reading demands and practices through visits from academic lecturers or by putting students in touch with former EAP students who are now studying on academic courses. Looking outside the classroom to increase students' understanding of what they really need to do is always more effective than being told what is needed by the teacher.

EAP teachers need to encourage students to look beyond the extracts used for classroom tasks and think about the nature of the academic source texts. Students with little experience of academic texts need training in finding the range of academic sources available, through organized visits to the institution's library, with a talk from the librarian to make them aware of how resources can be accessed. Students can also be sent to the library independently to find texts in their subject and bring them to class. Postgraduate students can record their results in the form of an annotated bibliography of texts relevant to their research interest.

Skills and strategies for academic reading

To read fluently with an appropriate level of comprehension, most students also need help in developing their reading skills. This involves tackling the problem of slow reading speed and the difficulties of decoding complex sentences.

Skills

The existing skills EAP students bring to reading may vary considerably, depending on the degree of affinity of their first language with English, and their previous exposure to reading English texts. However, most students will need to work on vocabulary, grammar and reading speed. Research has found that vocabulary size is a key component in reading ability, even when the reader is familiar with the topic,[17] and Nation suggests that at least ninety-five per cent of running words[18] need to be known to comprehend a text.[19] Many EAP students are likely to have to manage with less than this target and so building transferable academic vocabulary and strategies for dealing with unknown vocabulary are important in EAP. These will be the subject of Chapter 5: *Vocabulary*. Students can also work on employing conscious strategies to help in dealing with features of academic texts such as long noun phrases, complex sentences with embedded clauses, and the cohesive role of general nouns. Exercises that focus on recognizing word class are helpful for decoding complex sentences. Finding the main verb in a sentence, identifying the boundaries of noun phrases, and deciding whether they are acting as the subject or object of the verb or the object of a preposition are effective ways to familiarize students with typical sentence patterns in academic texts. Students can also be encouraged to find embedded clauses and reduced relative clauses and identify what they refer to. As Chapter 2: *Text analysis* illustrates, these aspects of grammar study are much more useful in academic English than the verb grammar given prominence in general English course books.

Most students can improve their ability to read fluently at moderate speed with very explicit training.[20] Students begin by calculating their reading speed for a text which is at a slightly lower level of complexity than those they currently read in class. They record this speed and, after a period in which they practise reading texts of a similar level, they test their speed again. After each test of their reading speed, they complete a simple comprehension test, such as a gapped summary of the text or true/false questions and record their comprehension score. Nuttall suggests a target of about seventy per cent comprehension. The aim is to record their progress. This is accompanied by introducing techniques that can help them to read more quickly. A major cause of slow reading and poor comprehension is word-by-word reading. Good readers fix their eyes on meaningful chunks of the text as they read. For example,

As noted   by many teachers   a major cause of   slow reading

and   poor comprehension is word-by-word reading.

Students can be encouraged to develop this ability by presenting the phrases in a column on a visual, so that the students have to move their eyes down the column. The teacher can also reveal each phrase for a fraction of a second to show students that they can in fact process language in chunks. They can start by recognizing well-known phrases such as *a major cause of, the reason for*. Students are usually surprised at how successfully they can do this and are willing to try the strategy in their reading. The target of seventy per cent comprehension is important in helping students to let go of the belief that they must understand every word.

This ability to read in chunks can be reinforced by language exploitation that focuses on phrases, i.e., noun and verb phrases and collocations, rather than individual words. These natural groupings provide the meaningful chunks which the reader can process as units. Another strategy for improving students' ability to focus on meaningful chunks is to have prepared reading-aloud sessions as an occasional classroom activity. The teacher divides a text into short sections (paragraphs or half-paragraphs) corresponding to the number of students in the class, and assigns each one a section. Students have a few minutes to prepare their section by reading silently to understand the meaning and can consult the teacher or use a dictionary for the pronunciation of words they do not know. As part of their preparation, students can be encouraged to

Classroom materials 4.2 *How can I read faster?* shows how students can be introduced to reading in meaningful phrases.

mark the section of the text in meaningful chunks. This develops an inner voice for the rhythms and divisions of English sentences to help them when they read silently or write. Unprepared reading aloud has only negative effects, exposing weak readers to embarrassment and boring the class, but prepared reading aloud can be motivating. The time for preparation means that students read in a meaningful way and they briefly take ownership of a piece of text as they present it to the class.

The focus on reading quickly needs to be carried over into the reading of texts studied in class. This can be fostered by routinely providing a word count for texts and negotiating realistic time limits for global reading tasks. For example, an appropriate target for reading a 200 word extract to find the big picture or the author's main points might be one minute. Once students are aware of their own reading speeds and the need to increase them, they are willing to do this. Persuading students to avoid word-by-word reading is one of the most important contributions teachers can make to improve reading skills.

Flexible reading strategies

To read in a purposeful way, students need explicit teaching and practice of the flexible strategies required for academic reading, which include looking for the big picture, prediction, search reading, and close reading.

The first aim of strategic reading is to grasp the big picture, that is, to understand the purpose of the text and how that relates to the main points of the content. The big picture provides a point of reference in the reader's mind, which can be used to generate predictions or questions that provide a purpose for reading, and to monitor understanding while reading the text. It also provides a mental framework which can be filled in with as much detail as the reading purpose requires. Even readers with good first language reading strategies tend to panic and focus mainly on unknown vocabulary when faced with difficult texts in another language. Identifying and focusing on the big picture is an important initial strategy for students to develop in order to become dominant readers in control of their own reading purposes.

Once the big picture is grasped, the reader can use other strategies for reading, including prediction, search reading, and close reading. Search reading, based on prediction followed by close reading of relevant passages, is probably the most authentic academic reading strategy. Readers use their knowledge of the expected content and form of the genre to predict which questions might be answered in the text and where. Their search of the text is assisted by their awareness of sentence structure and information flow in academic texts. Chapter 2 describes how the general to specific organization of information can be used to distinguish the writer's general claims from the supporting detail. Searching for clusters of functional vocabulary can also provide clues to the location of required information. For example, in the text *The influence of class size on achievement*, from Case study C, expressions for evaluating, e.g., *however, in fact, unfortunately*, identify paragraphs that contain the author's evaluation of the studies of class size.

Classroom materials 4.3 *How do you read?* introduces students to these flexible reading strategies and their purposes.

Close reading involves engaging reading skills with knowledge of the content, to come to an understanding of what exactly is being said. Readers may need to read only a short relevant section of the text or they may need to read the whole text carefully. It should be made clear to students that close reading of a whole text is never an initial strategy. The investment of time and effort is only worthwhile once they are satisfied that this is essential to their purpose. The academic reader in Case study A decided to return to a difficult key book and read it in depth only after she had read other articles on that topic. The strategies described above for sentence level reading can help with close reading. However, students also need to monitor how the meaning they obtain from close reading is consistent with the big picture in the text.

In general English classrooms, skimming and scanning are widely advocated, but may lack authentic purpose when a text is presented in isolation, with little indication of source or context. Students are often asked to skim to identify the topic. In a university context, where students are likely to know already what the topic is, a more authentic use of skimming is to interrogate a text, asking, 'Do I need to read this?' When providing a range of suggested source texts for an assignment, teachers can include a few irrelevant items to give students practice in selecting what to read. Skimming can involve some of the strategies involved in search reading, particularly identifying the author's main claims and ignoring detail. Scanning, looking for instances of a particular word, phrase or figure, is used for finding information from indexes in books and online databases, and should be practised in those contexts, where it is more authentic.

Taking notes and summarizing relevant parts of a text in a way that reflects the reading purpose are also important conscious strategies to be used while reading.

Task 8

- Why might students take notes while reading?

- How might the purpose of note-taking affect the form in which notes are recorded?

Notes may serve as a learning aid in order to help understanding, record key points for revision purposes, or be used as the basis of written assignments or research. In all cases, the expected outcome of reading will involve knowledge-transforming rather than knowledge-telling. If the notes are taken to assist personal understanding, they need to be recorded in a way that is meaningful for the individual student. Notes for revision need to be very clearly organized into a format which will be easy to memorize, and should contain an appropriate amount of detail for what is likely to be required in an exam answer. Notes for a written assignment will be more detailed, as they do not need to be memorized and will reflect the focus of the particular assignment.

Students need to develop a flexible range of frameworks for note-taking, to reflect their reading purposes and the rhetorical purpose of the text. For example, if their purpose is to investigate why a problem occurs, the notes might be recorded as a cause and effect chain. However, if they are more interested in evaluating possible solutions, a table enabling them to be compared is more useful. Tree diagrams are suitable for classification, or flow charts are useful for processes. As these techniques become routine, they are incorporated into the students' repertoire of reading skills. Notes for research or assignments should include an exact record of sources for referencing purposes. Good notes which reflect the reader's purpose, and the author's key points, can form the basis of effective summarizing and synthesizing of information, and help to avoid plagiarism.

A framework for exploiting texts in the classroom

Text selection in general English is often based on topic, and the classroom exploitation is often about clarifying meaning and discussion of the topic. Sometimes, the main purpose of reading a text is to introduce vocabulary or particular language points. Any written outcomes may be focused on the students' personal reactions to the points in the text. In EAP, text selection is based on the genre and rhetorical functions of the text. Written outcomes are likely to involve using the content as a source to be summarized and incorporated into other texts, or using a text as a model for a piece of parallel writing in which students write in a similar genre about topics related to their field of study. Exploiting an academic text in the classroom will involve reading it several times on different occasions for different purposes. In general English classes, reading texts are expected to be entertaining and provide stimulus for discussion, so the notion of returning to a text might be considered boring and de-motivating. However, EAP students have to make a considerable investment of effort to understand an academic text, and re-using it can help them to tackle more difficult aspects once they have grasped the general ideas. They will have to get used to returning to texts and re-reading them many times in their academic study. Being able to tackle a text in different ways, and for different purposes, is an essential part of becoming an independent dominant reader.

Classroom materials 4.4 *The Metropole and the Luxus* illustrates how elements of this framework are used in exploiting a text for the classroom.

Using a text to help students develop as academic readers requires a framework of tasks which encourage top-down global reading, and enable the text to be used for authentic purposes before it is exploited for its organization and language. Global understanding begins with awareness of the genre and academic context of a text. Before reading, students can be encouraged to make predictions about what might be covered using the source, genre, title, and any other clues. The topic may be discussed to activate prior knowledge and vocabulary. At this stage pre-teaching of vocabulary can take place, if the teacher thinks this is necessary.

Tasks for the first reading should focus on an aspect of the big picture. Depending on the difficulty of the text, students can be given a specific question to answer or asked to formulate their own questions based on predictions of the content. For more difficult texts, tasks can be devised to give extra support in achieving this understanding. For example, students can be given a list of possibilities from which to identify the genre, scope or main functional purpose of the text. Another way to focus on the big picture is to ask students to search for key information such as the writer's preferred solution to the problem. It should not be assumed that the main points can always be identified by a quick survey, so the teacher needs to select a task suitable for the particular text. However, it is important that students should always undertake some type of overview task before reading intensively. Negotiating a realistic time based on the word count of the text helps to focus students on the need for a fast-reading approach at this stage.

The next stage of reading should give students an authentic purpose, which involves understanding the main points in the text in order to produce a specific outcome, rather than simply testing comprehension. Students can be given as much support as they need to understand the important content of the text, and enable them to read beyond their language competence. Tasks can be designed to provide students with mental maps or outlines of difficult texts before they read them at a more detailed level. For example, students can be given the important points of the text as a jumbled series of sentences, which they put in order to form a summary of the text. Alternatively, a summary can be presented with gaps which focus on content rather than language. Gapped diagrams, e.g., cause and effect chains, timelines, flow charts, or comparison tables can also be filled in. Note-taking tasks should reflect an authentic reading purpose involving elements of knowledge-transforming. This could be to write a summary of the main ideas to include in a further piece of writing, or to take notes that can form the basis of an answer to an exam question. Initially, suitable formats for note-taking can be presented to support students in developing this skill. Later, they can be encouraged to devise formats to match their reading purposes. Students can collaborate in reading a section of the text in detail, comparing the notes they have taken, and monitoring their comprehension through discussion, before presenting the main points to a new partner. This models the authentic academic context of a team assignment, where different group members take responsibility for finding and presenting specific information. This is in contrast to jigsaw tasks used in general English, which tend to be based on a more transactional model, where participants exchange specific items of information. Students can also write parallel texts from a similar input. For example, after studying a text commenting on a table or graph, they can be given a similar table or graph and asked to write a text explaining this data, using the text they have studied as a model.[21] This is an authentic way to link reading and writing, as writers needing to write in a new genre for professional or academic purposes usually look at existing examples of the genre as models – for example, new teachers will check how end-of-term reports are written and what sort of information is usually included before writing reports on their own students' progress.

Once the students have understood the main content of the text, they can be asked to identify the language and organizational features which helped them understand the text. This will focus on the features associated with the genre, and with the main functions in the text. In practice, language study is likely to be carried out before the final writing outcomes, to provide support for the writing. Such tasks can include identifying features of academic texts described in Chapter 2, e.g., the *general to specific* moves, or the flow of ideas from what is *given* to what is *new*. Students can also study the way cohesion is achieved using noun phrases and general nouns. This is particularly helpful for improving decoding skills for dealing with dense and difficult texts. Students can identify sentences they find particularly difficult and try to deconstruct them in this way. Finally, students can identify and record useful academic vocabulary, which they can use in their writing, mainly based on the key rhetorical functions of the text. Chapter 5: *Vocabulary* deals with the principles of selecting such vocabulary and the tasks which can be used for identifying and learning expressions.

In summary, a framework for exploiting texts in the EAP classroom will include some or all of these elements:

- a task or elicitation to promote prediction and awareness of reading purposes based on the genre, source or title of the text
- tasks requiring global reading to understand the big picture
- activities which promote comprehension of significant points and give students an authentic academic purpose for reading, with as much support as necessary
- close study of sentences and phrases to practise and develop reading skills
- exploitation of the text for vocabulary and features associated with the genre and rhetorical functions
- writing tasks which enable students to use the text content in authentic ways, and see how the language they have been working on can be transferred to other tasks relevant to their future studies

The following case study illustrates how elements of this framework were used to exploit an academic text. An electronics student, studying in a mixed class of postgraduate students, brought the text below to class in response to an invitation to find and bring to class texts from their own subjects.

Task 9

- What is the main rhetorical function in the text?
- What aspects of the text would you focus on?
- What tasks would you devise?

Case study D:
Adaptive real-time particle filters for robot localization[22]

Abstract

1 Particle filters have recently been applied with great success to mobile robot localization. **2** This success is mostly due to their simplicity and their ability to represent arbitrary, multi-modal densities over a robot's state space. **3** The increased representational power, however, comes at the cost of higher computational complexity. **4** In this paper we introduce adaptive real-time particle filters that greatly increase the performance of particle filters under limited computational resources. **5** Our approach improves the efficiency of state estimation by adapting the size of sample sets on-the-fly. **6** Furthermore, even when large sample sets are needed to represent a robot's uncertainty, the approach takes every sensor measurement into account, thereby avoiding the risk of losing valuable sensor information during the update of the filter. **7** We demonstrate empirically that this new algorithm drastically improves the performance of particle filters for robot localization.

(173 words. Sentences are numbered for ease of reference.)

The teacher photocopied the texts brought in and, in the next lesson, students brainstormed a list of the features of academic English, then checked their texts in groups to see how academic they were. One of the features was long noun phrases, and the teacher set up a contest to find the longest. This text contained the longest noun phrase. Later in the course, a colleague needed a text to introduce a particular rhetorical function, problem and solution, to a specialist EAP group of electronics students, and the two teachers worked out a series of tasks to exploit this text.

This text can be regarded as an example of its genre, an abstract, and also as an example of a function, problem and solution. The pre-reading elicitation focused on the purpose of abstracts. Some students said it was to summarize the report, but others noticed that abstracts act rather like advertisements or trailers for a film, so that potential readers can decide if they want to read the full report. Once students had established some expectations about the content, they could test their expectations. As a big picture task, students were given one minute's search reading time to find the sentence containing the problem that the research set out to solve. Students recognized *computational complexity* (sentence 3) as something usually considered to be a problem in their field.

The students could now consider this as a problem-solution text and look for other features of this function, based on the framework: situation→ problem→ solution→ evaluation. They were given the following task to match individual sentences to their role in this framework. (The answers are given in brackets.)

Identify the sentence that:

- states the problem (3)

- gives a possible solution to the problem (4)

- explains the background situation and recent developments (1)

- states the outcome of the research (7)

- describes the method used in the research (5)

- explains the background reason for the problem (2)

- evaluates and justifies the method (6)

The students now had an overview of the main points of the text and could study it as model of a research genre they needed to produce: the abstract. They noticed how the authors justify and evaluate their method and, in the final sentence, emphasize their success. Finally, they identified persuasive vocabulary, *even when, every, demonstrate empirically,* and related it to the purpose of the abstract as an 'advertisement' for the research.

Abstracts are miniature texts containing a concentration of the features of academic writing and are written in a concise style which uses general nouns as cohesive devices. This text gave an opportunity to draw students attention to the way academic texts use a *given* to *new* pattern to control the topic and maintain the flow of information. Students were asked to find summarizing general nouns or noun phrases which refer back (shown in bold in the text), and underline the phrases they referred to. As a hint, they were told to look for cohesive devices *this, the*, and phrases containing the same word or a different class of that word. They found these examples of cohesion:

> Particle filters have recently been applied with great success to mobile robot localization. **This success** is mostly due to their simplicity and their ability to **represent** arbitrary, multimodal densities over a robot's state space. **The increased representational power**, however, comes at the cost of higher computational complexity. In this paper we introduce adaptive real-time particle filters that greatly increase the performance of particle filters under limited computational resources. Our approach improves **the efficiency** of state estimation by adapting the size of sample sets on-the-fly…

Exercises like this help students to recognize how authors repackage information by using different word classes, in particular the way verbs are replaced by adjectives or nouns as the information is repackaged into noun phrases, e.g., *represent/representational*. Synonyms (*ability power*) also provide lexical cohesion.[23]

Students were asked to find other examples of abstracts in their field, bring them to class for comparison, and try similar strategies to analyse them. This involved independent reading and allowed students to identify some typical patterns of abstracts in their field. This was an authentic use of the abstracts as a model for a genre they would have to write. As a further authentic activity, students wrote a summary, as if they were citing the text in an assignment they were writing. They were given a framework to support them in doing this:

Kwok *et al.* (2003) applied _____
to solve the problem of _____
and found that _____

Students might produce something like this:

*Kwok et al. (2003) applied adaptive particle filters which adapt the size
of sample sets on-the-fly to solve the problem of limited computational
resources when using particle filters for mobile robot localisation and
found that these improved the performance of particle filters for this
purpose.*

Students then wrote similar citations based on abstracts that they
brought to class, and finally wrote short abstracts of a piece of research
or project they had done previously.

This is an example of how a teacher can usefully exploit a difficult text
with little knowledge of the subject matter. Although the students did
not understand the text fully, they were given tools to understand it
better when they have more knowledge of the subject.

Conclusion

Academic reading is part of the social communicative practice of academic
disciplines. EAP teachers should train students for the wider academic context
where they will have to read independently and become dominant readers,
critically aware of the status, purpose and significance of what they are reading.
Texts and tasks used in EAP reading should help students to acquire this wider
perspective and to experience reading as a crucial part of the research process.
Texts are a major resource through which authentic academic genres and
activities can be brought into the classroom, and therefore need to be carefully
selected and exploited very fully for their characteristic features of organization
and language. There should be a balance of authenticity between the tasks and
texts, so that activities can be devised which support students in dealing with
texts that are beyond their initial language competence. This will help them to
read academic texts in their own disciplines with better understanding, and also
provide a foundation for the types of writing they will need to produce.

Further reading

Nuttall, C. (1996) *Teaching Reading Skills*. Oxford: Macmillan Education.

Swales, J. M. (2005) *Genre Analysis* 2nd edition. Cambridge: Cambridge University Press.

Urquhart, A. H. and Weir, C. J. (1998) *Reading in a Second Language*. London: Longman.

Course books which have the development of academic reading as a stated aim

Glendinning, E. H. and Holmstrom, B. (2004) *Study Reading*. Cambridge: Cambridge University Press.

Slaght, J. (2004) *English for Academic Study: Reading Source Book*. Reading: Garnet Publishing.

Chapter 5: Vocabulary

This chapter will examine:

- types of vocabulary frequently found in academic texts

- what students need to know to use this vocabulary effectively

- ways to select, organize and teach academic vocabulary

You will have the opportunity to:

- reflect on your criteria for selecting vocabulary

- analyse a text and devise recording formats and tasks which promote learning

Acquiring an academic vocabulary is a key aim for many students preparing for academic courses. Research has found that vocabulary is a significant area of concern for students and that subject lecturers find students' use of vocabulary causes problems in understanding their written work.[1] Here are some difficulties reported by students:

- *I can't read quickly enough because I am always stopping to look up new words.*

- *I know what each word in the phrase means, but I don't understand them when they are together.*

- *I know what I want to say in my writing but I can't find the right words.*

- *I know the symbols for the chemical elements but I don't understand the English names like sodium and sulphur.*

The main resource for vocabulary learning in the classroom is the reading text in which the language occurs in context. However, the high frequency of technical terms, together with the complex interactions of words, can make academic texts rather daunting for both students and for EAP teachers, who may feel unsure of which types of vocabulary are most helpful to their students. On EAP courses, time is limited, so an approach needs to be based on clear principles for identifying the most useful language and organizing it in a way which will facilitate understanding and learning. Teachers need strategies to exploit fully the vocabulary potential of texts, and confidence in directing students to vocabulary they really need. Teachers also need to know what their students' vocabulary learning strategies and experience have been in the past.

Task 1

The text below, which you met in Chapter 4, is an abstract from a research article, brought to class by an engineering student.

- Which vocabulary items would you select for EAP students to record and learn?

- Which criteria did you use to select these words?

Keep your list beside you and review it as you read through this chapter.

Adaptive real-time particle filters for robot localization[2]

Particle filters have recently been applied with great success to mobile robot localization. This success is mostly due to their simplicity and their ability to represent arbitrary, multi-modal densities over a robot's state space. The increased representational power, however, comes at the cost of higher computational complexity. In this paper we introduce adaptive real-time particle filters that greatly increase the performance of particle filters under limited computational resources. Our approach improves the efficiency of state estimation by adapting the size of sample sets on-the-fly. Furthermore, even when large sample sets are needed to represent a robot's uncertainty, the approach takes every sensor measurement into account, thereby avoiding the risk of losing valuable sensor information during the update of the filter. We demonstrate empirically that this new algorithm drastically improves the performance of particle filters for robot localization.

Types of vocabulary in academic texts

It is necessary to classify academic vocabulary in order to determine the roles of different types of vocabulary, and how these will influence decisions about what to select for teaching. Different approaches have been used to identify and classify the vocabulary which characterizes academic texts. The table below shows the categories used in this chapter.[3] Some examples from the text *Particle filters* are given to illustrate the categories.

Type of vocabulary	Explanation	Examples from the text
Technical	terms specific to a discipline or a particular area of a discipline, which would not usually be understood by a non-specialist outside that discipline	particle filters, algorithm, state space, on-the-fly, multi modal densities
Semi-technical	words or phrases in general use which also have a restricted or special meaning in a particular discipline, or different meanings in different disciplines	particle, filter, set, sensor, sample, state
General academic vocabulary	vocabulary that represents academic activities or academic register, or which signals rhetorical functions or text organization	approach, complexity, estimation, furthermore, due to, even, measurement, in this paper, clearly, result

Technical vocabulary

Some expressions, such as *algorithm*, are clearly technical. Others, such as *particle filters*, are composed of words familiar to the non-specialist reader but are not understandable without specialist knowledge. Nation[4] estimates that technical vocabulary accounts for about five per cent of the words used in an academic text. However, this may be an underestimation if technical terms that are noun phrases built from semi-technical words, such as the two examples in the table, are taken into consideration.[5] During a specialist course, lecturers will normally define new concepts and terms as they are introduced in lectures, but problems can arise with vocabulary that is assumed to be known from previous study or general language knowledge.

It is a useful principle that students have some responsibility for finding out the English equivalents of basic concepts in their subjects before they begin a specialist course. The student who does not know the names of the chemical elements simply needs to acquire a copy of the Periodic Table and learn the English names. However, this may be a problem where students' intended study is in an area different from their previous study, and also in subject areas such as the arts or social sciences, where terms may be difficult to translate across cultural boundaries.

Task 2

The student in the case study below did not understand the term *National Insurance contributions* when she met it in her reading.

- What could be the reason for this?

Case study A:
Understanding a technical term

A student from China produced the following research question, 'What are the major companies providing unemployment insurance in the UK?' She was having difficulty finding names of companies specializing in this field. She approached her EAP teacher and a comparison of the Chinese and British systems uncovered the fact that the term *National Insurance* did not convey anything to her because the concept of a government insuring its citizens was something she had not come across before. Once she was aware of the existence of National Insurance contributions as the basis for social security provision in the UK she was able to find a large amount of data available on this subject.

This is an example of how noun phrases can cause confusion, especially when they carry cultural assumptions. The student had met the phrase *National Insurance contributions* in her research, but had interpreted it as a vague description suggesting that

> *insurance contributes to (i.e., benefits) the nation.*

She had not thought of an alternative way to unpack this phrase:

> *contributions people pay towards a national system of insurance.*

Classroom materials 5.1 *Unpacking noun phrases* shows an example of how this type of technical noun phrase can be explored in class.

Technical terms which occur as reduced noun phrases like this are frequent, so EAP teachers need to be aware of this feature of technical English and help students develop strategies to unpack such phrases and check their exact meanings.

Semi-technical vocabulary

Words in this category are likely to be already in the vocabulary of native speakers, who may be aware that there is also a specialist meaning, even if they could not give a precise definition. A problem arises for non-native speakers where subject lecturers use specialized meanings of common words, e.g., *state* as it is used in physical science, rather than in its everyday meaning of a country or nation.

Task 3

The students in the case study below ignored a key term used by their economics lecturer.

- What could be the reason for this?

> ### Case study B:
> ### Understanding a semi-technical term
>
> I attended an economics lecture with a group of EAP students to observe their note-taking techniques. The topic of the lecture was fiscal policy and one of the main points the lecturer mentioned concerned 'the different statutory instruments available to governments'. Afterwards I noticed that none of them had recorded this key phrase in their notes.
>
> After the lecture, I asked the students what they understood by *instruments*. 'Something to do with music,' they answered. They had ignored a key term because they had no idea how it related to the topic of the lecture. This area of vocabulary often presents difficulties. For example, students intending to follow a business studies course might not know the word *firm* for a UK company, or *plant* for a factory.

It must be noted that these two categories of technical academic vocabulary are considered separately in order to assist language awareness. In practice, it is difficult to draw a clear line between technical and semi-technical vocabulary as their classification may depend on the readership of the text. What would be regarded as technical vocabulary at high school or first-year undergraduate level may differ from what would be considered as technical in a research paper in the same subject area. Furthermore, the language itself is constantly evolving, as technical expressions such as *GM crops* or *megabytes* become part of our everyday speech, and common expressions such as *real time* or *network* acquire restricted technical meanings.

General academic vocabulary

This type of language represents a neutral, formal register which expert users may intuitively feel sounds academic. It is the language that allows the writer or speaker to make clear what is being said about the technical topics in their texts, to discuss abstract concepts and to describe academic activities. It is also used to organize texts into an appropriate form to support the writer's main points and to make this organization explicit to the reader.

Task 4

Look back at the text *Particle filters* on page 153.

- Which parts of the text might be transferred to an abstract about a different topic?

KEY

... have recently been applied with great success...

This success is mostly due to...

... however, comes at the cost of...

In this paper we introduce...

Our approach improves...

Furthermore,...

We demonstrate empirically that ...

General academic vocabulary provides a resource for students to use when reading or writing many types of academic text.

Selecting vocabulary for classroom study

The examples in tasks 2, 3 and 4 show that there are vocabulary items which are characteristic of academic texts, and which are worth studying on an EAP course and beyond. It is important to have a systematic way of selecting this vocabulary for teaching, so that it forms a developing part of a principled syllabus rather than a haphazard collection of words which happen to be encountered in the texts studied in class.

Frequency

The first principle for selecting vocabulary is frequency. There is little point in students investing time in the thorough exploration necessary to learn vocabulary items unless they are likely to encounter them frequently in their academic reading. Task 4 suggests that there are types of words which occur frequently across many academic texts and seem to be typical of the academic register. Teachers need a way to corroborate their intuitions about vocabulary.

Task 5

- Which do you think are the six most common adjectives in academic texts?

  Note your suggestions and then read on to find an answer.

An important development in identifying words which are characteristic of academic texts has been the corpus-based Academic Word List. This list followed the earlier development of a General Service Word List (GSL) which identified the most frequent words in English texts.[6] The first 2,000 words on the GSL give about eighty per cent coverage of most English texts. More recently, Coxhead compiled a large electronic corpus of academic texts from the disciplines of arts, commerce, law, and science, and identified 570 word families which are more frequent across all the disciplines and text types in this corpus than in other non-specialized corpora of written English texts.[7] The list of these words is known as the Academic Word List (AWL). A word family in this sense is a group of closely related words consisting of 'a stem plus all closely related affixed forms'.[8] The list does not include words which occur in the first 2,000 words of the GSL nor specialist words whose range is limited to certain disciplines only. The AWL is divided into ten sub-lists in descending order of frequency, so that very high frequency words can be prioritized for learning. For example, in sub-list 1, representing the 60 most frequent word families from the corpus, just six adjectives with a general meaning are found: *available, consistent, major, significant, similar* and *specific*.[9] There are also groups of verbs in the AWL which represent the more formal, neutral register of academic English, such as *occur, obtain, achieve, assist, create* and *generate*. Being able to use these as substitutes for verbs such as *happen, get, help* and *make* enables students to achieve a more academic style. Haywood has devised an online tool, the AWL Highlighter, which will highlight all the words from the AWL in any text.[10] This can be used to determine if a text is academic in its language, and help to decide whether a non-academic text such as a newspaper article on a particular topic is likely to produce useful vocabulary for EAP students to study.

Word lists identify key words for study but, on their own, they are not enough. They do not supply information about why these words are frequent in academic texts or how they relate to other language items, because there is no contextual evidence to make clear what it is about their meaning or function that makes them important in expressing academic ideas. High frequency words which are found from corpus studies should be regarded as 'facts that require explanation'.[11] Because only individual words are recorded, phrasal groupings and the meanings they represent are lost. In the case of *account*, which appears in the text *Particle filters*, the AWL does not indicate that it usually appears as part of two phrasal verbs, *take into account* (as in that text) or *account for*, or that it also commonly appears in the fixed noun phrase *on account of*. Word lists give no indication of the strong word partnerships, known as collocations, which exist between words and form a key element of the expert speaker's mental lexicon, e.g. *significant development* or *no significant difference*. Although learning words from the same family is a productive way of increasing vocabulary, it should be approached cautiously. The stem form, given as the headword for each family in the AWL, may not actually be the form most frequently found in academic texts in the corpus, and may even have a meaning quite remote from that form. For example, the headword *convene* has a meaning quite different from the most frequent form, *convention*, meaning a standard way of doing things.[12]

The source corpora themselves also have inevitable limitations because they may not represent the type of texts most relevant to particular target groups. For example, the original corpus for the AWL included law as a whole discipline area, but did not contain applied science or engineering texts although it does in fact give good coverage of such texts.[13] Teachers need to research texts relevant to their students in order to select appropriate vocabulary for teaching.

Function

Classroom materials 5.2 *Exploring the academic word list* shows how students can study the academic word list through a functional approach.

In order to write, students will need to understand how frequently occurring words are used in combination to express particular ideas. Chapter 2 shows how the rhetorical functions form the building blocks of all texts. An approach to vocabulary based on rhetorical functions focuses on how the selected words relate to other lexical items in the text. This provides a more discriminating basis for selecting vocabulary to teach in EAP classes and draws on the principles of the Lexical Approach, which views encountering and learning vocabulary in context as key elements in developing language competence.[14] The meaning of *context* here is 'the totality of the event which surrounds the use of a particular piece of language'.[15] This includes both the situation, that is, the purpose and readership of the text, and the co-text (all the words surrounding the language being studied).

A context-based approach to vocabulary learning involves choosing texts for their functional purpose, as recommended in Chapter 4, and then examining the vocabulary that carries out that purpose, so that learning is genuinely context driven. Focusing on function takes us into the purpose of the text and to the language students need to understand and use. Rather than being encouraged to see vocabulary as a set of words that have to be individually learned and dropped into a grammatical framework to create different meanings, students can observe the way vocabulary items interact to create meaning as the text develops.

Adopting a functional approach to selecting vocabulary also reveals a group of words from the first 2,000 of the GSL which are particularly frequent in academic texts.[16] These include words such as *cause, result, solution* and *if,*[17] and formal register verbs such as *exist, experience* and *include*. Students can find these words difficult to use effectively and accurately. Subject lecturers refer to 'style' and 'grammar' as problems with students' written work but in fact, on examination of student scripts, the problem can often be more accurately identified as inability to use functional vocabulary appropriately (see Case study C in Chapter 1). This is the vocabulary which helps to create the structure and overall meaning of the text. Enabling students to use this type of vocabulary effectively is one of the most empowering results of a functional approach to selecting and studying vocabulary.[18] Students develop confidence in using a core of vocabulary whose meaning and purpose they clearly understand. They can also build their language knowledge around this core through noticing and learning collocations and typical grammar structures with which the key words are frequently associated.

Subject-related vocabulary

Classroom materials 5.3 *Product costing: studying subject-related vocabulary* shows an example of how key words can be explored in the classroom.

In addition to focusing on frequency and function in selecting language for classroom study, there is also the issue of whether to include technical or semi-technical vocabulary which occurs in a text. Technical expressions that are necessary only to understand that particular text can be glossed if they are not relevant to students' subjects. However, students may ask for help with technical or semi-technical expressions they need to learn. The two case studies above illustrated the importance of the teacher being aware of the problems that can arise when students encounter such terms. Although it can be argued that teaching this type of vocabulary is not the responsibility of EAP teachers, there are elements of technical vocabulary which can be usefully tackled in the EAP classroom.[19] Teachers need to develop teaching strategies for dealing with this type of language, provided that they remain within their competence as language specialists rather than subject specialists. Words from the semi-technical category need to be included, because they can cause difficulties and are likely to be of high frequency in students' specialist texts. They are often key words in a particular text, that is, words which are important to that topic and are therefore repeated throughout the text or certain sections of the text. These words can be selected for study in themed English courses for areas such as business studies, science or IT.

Task 6

The list below summarizes the main criteria that have been proposed for selecting vocabulary to study in the EAP classroom.

- Compare the words you chose from the *Particle filters* text in Task 1 and decide which criteria each one meets.

- Would you change any of the words you have chosen in the light of this discussion?

A word or phrase could be chosen for recording and learning for one or more of these reasons:

- It occurs with higher frequency in academic texts than in other types of texts.
- It is transferable across different academic topics and contexts.
- It is useful as productive as well as receptive vocabulary.
- It helps to create the structure and cohesion of the text.
- It is useful for the students' specific academic field or purposes.
- In the teacher's experience, it is frequently misunderstood by students, or can cause ambiguity or other problems if it is misunderstood or misused.
- Students have asked for help with this word or phrase.

Selecting vocabulary on the basis of rhetorical functions fulfils most of these criteria. This vocabulary is critical to an understanding of the relationship of ideas in the text, and is transferable across subject areas and different reading and writing genres. Knowledge of this type of vocabulary and proficiency in using it can build a secure bridge between reading and writing in academic contexts.[20]

Knowledge about words

It is usual to distinguish two levels of vocabulary knowledge: receptive and productive. The general reader of English needs a very wide range of receptive vocabulary, for instance, to read a newspaper, where the topics range widely, or a novel, where the writer may consciously employ metaphors or lead the characters into unusual situations. The academic reader is likely to need a much narrower range of vocabulary, but a much higher level of productive knowledge of that vocabulary. Most academic writing builds on and incorporates information from other published texts, so students need to be able to master and re-use much of the vocabulary they meet in their reading within a relatively short space of time. They also need to be able to use this vocabulary to create texts: they need to understand the way words can work together to create cohesion and coherence in a text.

Meaning, register and connotation

Students' mistakes indicate which aspects of word knowledge they need to work on.

Task 7

Below are some examples of sentences from the writing of students on pre-sessional courses.

- What types of error can you see?
- What information about the language would enable the student to avoid this type of error?

---

1 *The company will probably locate in a living area near bourgeois place.*

2 *The second reform issue is opening trade to let foreign merchantmen enter the Chinese market.*

3 *Most of the students have a relative background: only one student hasn't studied in the related area before.*

Students need to know the register and connotations of a word, and also the degree to which it is interchangeable with other expressions. Students often equate knowing the meaning of a word with being able to make a one-to-one correspondence with a word in their own language as they read and write. However, relatively few words in English are highly lexical (i.e., having a meaning which defines just one exact thing, such as *cyclohexane*) and can therefore be easily translated. Such vocabulary is quite easy to learn because little information is required to use the word.[21] The sentences above show what can happen when students try to make simple correspondences with L1 words. This may result from their dependence on bilingual dictionaries, which often lack examples to illustrate and explore meaning. Such dictionaries may not identify the most frequent meaning or may lack information about register and out-of-date or pejorative uses such as that for *bourgeois* in sentence 1. They may give incorrect meanings for different members of a word family, which proved to be the case in sentence 2, where the student's dictionary did not specify that *merchantmen* referred to ships not people. There even appear to be some electronic dictionaries which generate a set of possible members of word families regardless of whether these words exist in English.

Students need to know which transformations are possible within a word family, and whether they affect meaning. The student who wrote sentence 3 clearly thought that, as adjectives from the same family, *relative* and *related* could be used interchangeably to avoid repetition. In this case, the student needed to be aware of the effect of word order on meaning, as *relative* is used to indicate comparison before a noun, *relative merits*, but indicates connection when used after a noun, *facts relative to this issue*.[22] This feature would be revealed by studying examples in a good dictionary.

Collocation, metaphor and grammar patterns

Task 8

Here are further examples of sentences from the writing of students on pre-sessional courses.

• What types of error can you see?

4 *They are likely to make more mistakes or they could produce some accident.*

5 *The fax machine will not be a very good demand in the future.*

6 *There are many problems appear to these students.*

7 *This research occurs to contrast groups of different ages in order to get several conclusions.*

8 *This also would help the whole development control operation working more effective.*

Sentences 4 and 5 contain errors of collocation. Although they do not break any grammar rules, they sound wrong. In academic English particularly, where writing is expected to conform to predictable patterns, mis-collocation can be one of the most distracting advertisements that the writer is not a competent writer in English, and can lead to a different meaning from that intended. Learners need to learn collocations, *cause an accident*, and fixed phrases, *in demand*. Because *demand* is an important concept in business and economics, students in those fields need to know its other collocations, for example, *high demand*, and *demand for*. Knowing the collocations of terms in a field is part of knowing the technical terms themselves, which often consist of noun phrase collocations.

Appropriate collocations also create fluency by keeping a metaphorical flow through a topic – for example, *face / run into / encounter a problem* all keep the reader focused on the idea that a problem is like an obstacle in the road, whereas *reach / come to / point to a conclusion* use the metaphor that a conclusion is a destination or end point. In academic texts, students will not often meet metaphors used as stylistic devices, as in literature or journalism, but they need to be aware of the basic metaphors that underpin the concepts they are writing about.[23] A characteristic of academic discourse is that the concrete processes in verb phrases are transformed into abstract concepts represented by nouns or noun phrases as a text develops:

'The data was *analysed.*'   is followed by   'The *analysis* revealed...'

This nominalization creates an abstract entity, *the analysis*, that needs to perform or be the object of actions. This raises a whole area of difficulty for EAP students, who must therefore learn the underlying metaphors for what *analysis* can do or have done to it so that they can choose the right collocations. They need to know which concepts are agents and behave rather like people, *this research aims to*, *the analysis revealed*, and which are phenomena that just happen, e.g., *problems arise*. Knowing appropriate collocating verbs to match the nouns they need to use is just as essential for writing successful academic English as knowing the tensed forms of verbs. Students also need to know how an abstract entity is measured. There may be scales (or clines) of height, extent or degree of importance. For example, students can see that a building can be high or tall, but it is not obvious why success can be *great* or *significant* but not *high.*

The language of business is permeated with metaphors from shipping, from the time when a company is *launched* to the time when it finally *goes under.* However, connecting *launch a company* with *launch a boat* may not be particularly useful to a business student whose language does not include much nautical metaphor. It might be easier to just remember the collocation *launch a company.* In technical subjects, metaphor can permeate a particular topic. In the field of machine learning, *branch, node, rooted* and other tree-related metaphors are used to describe the operation of decision tree learning. The discipline of logistics uses the key metaphor of *hub* and *spokes* to describe transport networks. Such patterns of metaphor are unlikely to be found in a dictionary, so the teacher can help students to notice them.

Sentence 5 appears to contain grammar errors. However, the grammar problem arises from the presence of a particular word in the sentence, *help*, which requires the form:

help + someone/something + to do + something.

This pattern is also associated with words with a similar meaning, such as *assist, enable* and *allow.* If students record such groups of words which show grammatical patterns together, they can learn and produce these more easily. Integrating grammar knowledge into the learning of a particular word can be more productive than focusing mainly on verb grammar, as is commonly done in ELT classrooms. Proponents of the lexical approach suggest that words such as *would* and *if* are better taught as lexical items rather than focusing on the forms of the conditional presented in traditional grammar books.[24] Teachers need to analyse student errors carefully to avoid misdiagnosing vocabulary difficulties as grammar errors and wasting time on unnecessary study of grammar points. Knowledge of vocabulary patterns can be a more efficient way of improving students' success in expressing their ideas.[25]

Researching language

The examples in the above tasks emphasize the importance of students knowing the associated collocations and grammar patterns needed to use vocabulary in context. A certain amount of information may be found in a good corpus-based dictionary, but only a few examples are usually given. To study collocations, grammar patterns, connotations and the boundaries of meaning, teachers need access to more information. Their expert user's knowledge of language applied to examples encountered in texts is a starting point, but they need to be able to check their own intuitions about language and find out whether the use in a particular text is typical.

An important method to explore the frequency, use and patterns of vocabulary items is electronic concordancing.[26] This software can analyse a large corpus of electronic texts to retrieve all the examples of a selected word (the keyword) together with the surrounding words. Using concordance tools, it is possible to access many individual examples of a vocabulary item to check existing intuitions about the patterns and meanings of a particular word and how it interacts with the text around it.

> ### Case study C:
> ### Investigating an important word
>
> A group of students were using the word *hypothesis* in written coursework about their subject. I wanted to test my intuitions about what we can do to a hypothesis and what a hypothesis can do. I was not sure if they were always using the correct collocations. My intuitions suggested *frame / prove a hypothesis*. I also wanted to see if there were any characteristic collocations or sentence forms associated with this word.

Task 9

Figure 1 shows the results of a search for *hypothesis* in a corpus of academic texts used in Heriot-Watt University courses, using the WordSmith software.[27]

- What information about this word can you see that would be useful for students to know?

Check your ideas with the Key which follows.

this assumption is called the induction	hypothesis	-I.H.). Then we show
calculated using the induction	hypothesis	and the chain rule,
pothesis, followed by the testing of the	hypothesis	against empirical data
(we call this assumption the induction	hypothesis)	and show that it
deductive reasoning to generate a	hypothesis,	followed by the testing
enditure, from which some (then) new	hypotheses	emerged. We will consider
statement, it is possible to test the	hypothesis	that one form of income
is more efficient than another. The	hypothesis	that lump sum payments t
employment of the economic laws and	hypotheses	to predict the outcome of
patterns of consumption. The Linder	hypothesis	also implies something
Second, frame a logically derived	hypothesis	on the connection between
verlapping and sometimes competing	hypotheses.	The best we can hope for
lead from it. The first is that the	hypothesis	is presented as an econo
an NTB. This section opens with the	hypothesis	that the size of the
referred to as the efficient markets	hypothesis,	which is a statement that
to develop economic laws and	hypotheses	in order to explain econo
generally referred to as the life cycle	hypothesis.	The analysis has its
referred to as the permanent income	hypothesis.	The analysis is essent
We simplify the life cycle	hypothesis	merely to seek an overvie
words, we expect, from Linder's	hypothesis,	trade to be intra

Figure 1: *Concordance for hypothesis*

KEY

verb collocations

what can be done to a hypothesis

use / generate / frame / present / develop / simplify a hypothesis

test a hypothesis against empirical data

what a hypothesis can do

emerge, predict or imply (something)

adjective collocations

logically derived hypothesis and a competing hypothesis

grammar patterns

the hypothesis that + clause

Other features noticed

The association with a definition, which occurs three times.

we call / is called / referred to as

This drew my attention to the most frequent and unexpected feature – the instances of the name of a particular hypothesis: *the induction hypothesis, the life cycle hypothesis, the permanent income hypothesis, the efficient markets hypothesis, The Linder hypothesis.*

This use of the word as part of a technical term in a noun phrase was something which could be explored with students. They often seem uncertain whether to use capital letters or small case for such terms. These examples would help them to be clear about this. I could also access the source texts for such terms and possibly find examples of definitions to study that function.

Using the software, the lines can be sorted in different ways. For example, a left sort will reveal collocations with adjectives or determiners, as the words immediately to the left of the key word will be in alphabetical order, so that frequent collocations appear in groups. A right sort will reveal prepositions or verbs that follow a noun. It is also possible to access the full text from which a particular example is taken so that teachers can discover more about the context. In addition to producing a list like the example above with the key word in context (KWIC), concordance tools can perform other more sophisticated analyses of frequency and language patterns. Programs can be accessed online which can be used to search various existing corpora.[28] There are very large corpora such as the British National Corpus,[29] as well as smaller corpora, such as the Brown corpus, which is based on academic texts. Alternatively, teachers can assemble a corpus of academic texts from within their institution, and then use software packages such as *WordSmith Tools* or *Sketch Engine*[30] to investigate the language most relevant to their students. It is worth exploring and becoming familiar with this resource, and discovering appropriate programs and corpora for the needs of teachers and students.[31]

Vocabulary in the EAP classroom

This section will suggest effective ways for learners to notice, record and explore vocabulary for learning. The main focus will be on functional language. However, it will also examine how to use the Academic Word List as a tool for language development, as well as several approaches to technical vocabulary.

Research into vocabulary learning has found that in order for a vocabulary item to be acquired, it must first be noticed, and then needs to be retrieved at spaced intervals.[32] Opportunities to retrieve an item (that is, to identify or recall the word when the meaning is given, or remember the meaning when the word is present) need to occur about five to seven times over a reasonably short period of time during vocabulary learning. An approach which encourages the student to take an active role in observing language and hypothesizing about the way it works, and then experimenting with it to find the boundaries of meaning and usage, will help this process.[33] This observe–hypothesize–experiment approach contrasts with the traditional teacher-centred present–practice–produce general English methodology which does not allow sufficient time for development of the learner's mental lexicon through experimenting and making mistakes.[34] Teachers need to devise tasks that provide opportunities for these different elements of the learning process to occur. They also need to devise formats for recording the vocabulary in ways that provide helpful information about the word or phrase.

Noticing and recording vocabulary

Task 10

In Chapter 4, the text *Adaptive real time particle filters for robot localization* was presented as an example of a problem-solution text. Refer back to the text at the beginning of this chapter.

- Which problem–solution vocabulary would you select as the focus for study?

- How would you get the students to notice the language items?

- How would they record these? What would the recording format look like?

In their reading tasks, students have identified the main problem in the text (the computational complexity), and the solution (the use of adaptive particle filters). They can now be given the task of highlighting words and phrases indicating a problem in one colour, and those indicating or evaluating a solution in another.

This method of noticing vocabulary involves students using their awareness of the main functional purpose of the text or section to search for and identify language connected with that function. At this stage, the meanings of new words may be only approximately known, but the fact that these words will be noticed, along with familiar words expressing the same function, provides the basis for building a hypothesis about the meaning and usage of each item. This process of exploring language items allows students to observe and hypothesize.

When this text was originally used with a class, students were given the table shown below as a recording format, with the left-hand column ready-labelled with word class and functional indications. They then filled in the right-hand column to create a language reference page as a basis for future study. The teacher's target examples of problem and solution language are shown in bold on the right-hand side.[35] The other items were suggested by the students. The fact that the students identified eight extra items emphasizes the fact that students may have a deeper knowledge than the teacher of what constitutes vocabulary for problems and solutions in their field.

Vocabulary reference page	Problem and solution expressions
Expressions for a problem nouns	**cost, complexity, risk**
adjectives	**limited,** uncertainty, losing, arbitrary
Expressions for a solution nouns	**ability, approach,** algorithm
verbs	**adapting, avoiding, improves**
adjective	adaptive
maximizers used in evaluating a solution	**even, furthermore, every**
Collocations collocation indicating a problem	comes at the cost of
collocations evaluating solutions	**increase performance** **improves efficiency** **drastically improves** ** performance** **improves performance** **avoiding the risk of** increased representational power demonstrates empirically

Recording vocabulary in a format that includes functional purpose, word class, collocations, and grammar patterns preserves the contextual aspects of the items. Trying to record vocabulary in a simplified, 'cleaned-up' form may discard valuable clues about the way the item operates in texts. Students can be encouraged to explore further to find out if the examples they have collected are really typical and to use the open-ended format to record vocabulary met outside the classroom. Rather than simply noticing language in a visual way, e.g., when pre-selected target words are marked in bold in a text, students are intellectually engaged. They know there must be problem and solution terms in this text; the challenge is to find them. An advanced group, asked if they found this type of language awareness activity boring, said 'No, it's like Sudoko. It's a puzzle!'

Classroom materials 5.2 *Exploring the Academic Word List*, 5.3 *Product costing: studying subject-related vocabulary* and 5.4 *Gender differences: studying functional vocabulary in context* give examples of different recording formats.

Language reference pages such as the one above can be added to as the course proceeds, to form a resource for students to keep and refer to. Students often overload their files with ephemeral classroom materials which were only intended for one-off use. Presenting a set of functional reference pages at the beginning of a course, to be filled in as the course progresses, gives a sense of purpose to vocabulary learning, showing students that there is a body of useful language for academic study which they are going to learn. Studying a series of texts with the same functional focus in a short space of time exposes students to a range of examples, deepens their knowledge of previously known items and also provides an opportunity for the spaced retrieval needed to help acquisition. The outcome of a vocabulary study session might be that students now understand how to use words that they thought they already knew, rather than that they learnt ten new words.

Formats for recording vocabulary can vary depending on students' needs and level of English or the length of the text. For example, clues such as first letters of words can be given, or one half of a collocation word can be supplied. Some definitions could be added in the left-hand column if the teacher felt the class needed more support in the noticing and recording stages. However, it is important that meaning emerges through discussion and exploration. Degrees of collaboration in class can range from individual study to competitive group activities to see which group finds the most target language.

Devising different formats for recording vocabulary is an opportunity for teachers to exercise their creativity and enlist the students' ideas as well. Some functions lend themselves to formats which discriminate differences or opposites such as cause and effect, similarity and difference or problem and solution. Others lend themselves to placing words on a cline according to strength of meaning, or positive or negative connotations. Clines are particularly suitable for language used to indicate caution and hedging, e.g., possible→ likely→ probable→ certain. Word spiders can also be used, and diagrams can indicate metaphorical aspects of meaning. Words can also be sorted according to the 'what can something do/what can be done to it' principle. For example, when using the word *research,* students need to distinguish:

scientists *carried out / undertook* research, or experiments or studies

research *investigated, found that…*

2.3 Identifying general nouns *and* **2.4 The role of general nouns** gives practice in identifying and using general nouns.

Language record sheets provide a bridge between reading and writing. Students can use these to help them during the writing process and can also record new words that they needed to use. Well-designed vocabulary reference pages should be open ended and provide a model for students' personal vocabulary records. Another step in bridging reading and writing and raising student awareness of cohesive aspects of vocabulary is studying the way general nouns are used in texts. General nouns or noun phrases which have a signalling function can be highlighted and the information they refer to in the text underlined. The text can also be re-presented with the general nouns omitted for the students to complete.

Activities for using vocabulary

Task 11

- What classroom strategies do you use to help students learn and use vocabulary they have recorded?

- How do you ensure that they meet these items again in the near future?

Retrieval and production are the next important steps in the acquisition of vocabulary items. The recording process has involved some instances of retrieval. Further activities can involve matching words with their collocations, sorting vocabulary expressions on a cline according to some aspect of meaning such as intensity or frequency, and completing gapped texts. A meaningful piece of text rather than a set of de-contextualized sentences should be selected. A gapped version of part of the original text can be used, or the teacher can write a brief summary of the original text. Gapped summaries check understanding of global meaning at the same time as prompting retrieval of the target items. They can also activate other language. Students may suggest alternative answers for the gaps, which will prompt discussion about the meanings of similar words.

Task 12

Read the text *Product costing* in the Classroom materials 5.3. The final activity in this set of materials is a gap-fill activity designed to test the students' vocabulary learning. Here is a summary of the text the teacher wrote to use as a gapped text.

- Which words would you choose to gap for student vocabulary practice?
- How did you select the words?

Product costing – summary

Accountants have two main ways of classifying costs. They can consider the cost of producing a particular product, for example, by calculating the cost of the materials and the direct labour costs (the wages and salaries that have to be paid to the employees who make the products). They also have to consider the costs of other items used in production that are difficult to work out. These are called indirect costs.

Another method used to classify costs is to distinguish costs that vary with the amount of goods that are produced, i.e., variable costs, from fixed costs incurred whether a large or small number of products are manufactured.

When preparing materials, a teacher needs to make a series of principled choices which reflect the learning purpose of the activity. Here is a record of my thinking when creating a gap-fill self-test exercise for students after they had studied the text and vocabulary.

Case study D:
A teacher's thinking process

I want students to be able to test their knowledge of some strong collocations of *cost*. What can accountants do? *Calculate / work out costs.* What can *costs* do? *Vary* is a useful word which may not be familiar to students, and it occurs with another word from the same family, *variable. The cost of producing + something* is a useful grammar pattern which can be transferred to other verbs. *The cost of produce + something* is a common student error.

This text and the tasks are aimed at helping students with the technical vocabulary for their course, so noun phrases which form technical terms such as *variable/fixed, direct/indirect, labour costs* are important. *Labour* is a good word to gap as examples are given which will be clues for the students. *Costs incurred* is a new and difficult expression but very frequent in this subject area. They are unlikely to fill that gap correctly, but that will make them re-check it and prioritize it for learning.

I asked a colleague to try out the gap-fill (see the final task in Classroom materials 5.3). She couldn't supply *incurred* and also suggested I should gap some classification vocabulary, as this is a classification text. I decided to gap *distinguish* as it forms part of the useful sentence structure *distinguish X from Y.* However, this extra word near the beginning of a long sentence might impose a heavy conceptual load on the students. I decided to compromise by adding some clues in the form of initial letters for *distinguished, vary, variable* and *incurred.*

The next stage is to set up writing activities that generate production of the target language. Depending on students' level of competence, this could involve writing summaries from memory using the gap-fill as a model, or writing their own summaries before comparing them with the teacher's version. Writing summaries is an authentic outcome of studying a text as it can be the basis of note-taking or citing the text in an assignment. It is often tempting to devise exercises that use words in different grammar patterns or forms. Such substitution exercises can be rather seductive to teachers but may have little learning benefit. In fact, having met the language in context, it is better to reproduce it in a closely similar context to reinforce it and aid memory, rather than try to generate what might prove to be unnatural usages.

Students now need to attempt free writing which generates the target vocabulary. Sometimes they are instructed to 'write a paragraph using these words'. This is artificial and unlikely to result in students producing vocabulary in ways they will actually need. A more productive approach is to write a parallel text about some aspect of their intended field or a topic relevant to their interest.

Classroom materials 5.2 *Exploring the academic word list* **and 5.3** *Product costing: studying topic-related vocabulary* both have examples of writing parallel texts.

The first writing task based on the *Particle filters* text was to write a short abstract of a project or piece of research the students had done previously. This involved writing in a problem–solution–evaluation format, using the text as a model. As an extended coursework assignment, they then had to read and write about a problem in their field and an evaluation of the possible solutions. Such tasks generated a large amount of the vocabulary studied and enabled students to add specialist vocabulary relevant to their own particular fields. These were electronics students and they found a variety of terms for problems, *loopholes, security threats, time constraints*, and for solutions, *guarantee the stability of the system, firewall, robust system*. The effectiveness of the functional approach to vocabulary is that students are encouraged to use language in an appropriate context, writing and talking about topics relevant to their specialist subjects. A common assumption is that studying topical vocabulary enables students to write about topics. In fact, what is needed is language for saying something about those topics, i.e., functional language. The students produced the examples above because they were given a framework to express what they wanted to say about a topic. After writing, students can increase their exposure to the vocabulary they have studied by going though their own texts and underlining the target vocabulary they have used, as well as collecting further examples of functional vocabulary they needed.

Exploring vocabulary

The process of vocabulary learning should not end in the classroom. Most ELT teachers are already used to encouraging students to notice, study and record vocabulary outside the classroom. This is particularly important for EAP students, partly because their use of vocabulary has such potential to help them succeed in their chosen course of study, but also because once they have started their academic subject they will need to continue developing their vocabulary to keep pace with the demands of the course. The EAP teacher can prepare them with some useful vocabulary, but it is equally important to supply them with strategies for effective vocabulary learning. Good general English strategies include keeping word cards to record information on aspects of meaning and use, and gradually moving the cards to the back of the filing box as students become confident about their knowledge of that word. Vocabulary notebooks are also useful, provided that information is recorded in a format which facilitates retrieval and revision. Many EAP course books have introductory chapters to help train students in these strategies and in dictionary use. Students also need to be able to choose suitable English–English dictionaries and use them effectively rather than relying on bilingual dictionaries. Comparing and evaluating information from different dictionaries helps students to regard them as a source of data about words rather than simply lists of meanings.

Classroom materials 8.8 *Critical analysis: evaluating dictionaries* is designed to help students to evaluate different dictionaries.

There is a range of good corpus-based English advanced learners' dictionaries. Most of these give information about collocations, and grammatical patterns and usage, and the Macmillan dictionary[36] gives information about underlying metaphors. The EAP teacher can direct students to other sources of self-help such as specialist dictionaries and online glossaries.

An important principle for developing autonomy is encouraging students to use the same sources of data as teachers, and to go beyond the teacher's expertise. As their academic studies will require them to become researchers, who base their knowledge and understanding on research, using this approach to learn about language will help to train them in these techniques. The AWL can be an aid to self-study and can usefully harness the addiction of some students to lists. Many functional or cohesive words selected for study in class will also be found in the AWL. Students can tick off these words on their own copy of the list as they meet them. The growing list of ticks will reassure them that these words really are frequent and useful to learn. Most texts will probably contain additional words from the AWL which do not relate to the particular focus chosen for the lesson. Students can try to predict which extra words might be considered academic vocabulary, check them on the list and add them to their notebooks, together with any collocations they can find. They can also be trained to use the AWL Highlighter mentioned above. This website also includes a programme called the Gapmaker which will gap words from the AWL in a text which is submitted, so that students can create their own self-test exercise.

Students can be introduced to concordancing as a way of exploring language. This encourages them to use the observe–hypothesize–experiment model in an autonomous way. This technique requires initial training.[37] At first, teachers may wish to edit concordance lines to help students see the types of information available before progressing to unedited sources. This can be a motivating way of exploring vocabulary, especially if students become skilled in manipulating the concordance lines to generate the information they want. Students can report on their findings, and even take responsibility for some of the vocabulary research needed by a class.

Task 13

Review task

Read this text from an undergraduate marketing course. Using the ideas from this chapter:

- select vocabulary to study

- devise a format for a vocabulary reference sheet to record your selection

- develop some tasks which will allow students to use the vocabulary to write a parallel or related text

Text: Gender and the Web

The Graphic Visualization and Usability Center (GVU) of the Georgia Tech Research Corporation carried out a number of surveys of the Web. Their 1995 survey found that only 29% of users were female. By comparison the 1998 survey findings indicated that females now accounted for 39% of all users. This is evidence to support the view that the male domination of the Web is beginning to wane.

One assumption that is frequently used in marketing is that there is a difference in Web use between men and women. This issue was explored in a study carried out by Hawfield and Lyons (1998). They looked at four common assumptions.

The first claim was that women seek relationships or "community" on the Web, but the Hawfield and Lyons research suggests that there is no real difference between men and women in this respect.

With respect to the second conventional belief that women are uncomfortable with technology, Hawfield and Lyons found that research findings suggest that it is rather general experience with technology that matters and that gender does not play a role.

As regards the third belief, that women love to shop, Hawfield and Lyons found that most women do not fit this stereotype. This is backed by the GVU study which found that marginally more male than female respondents reported using the Web for shopping purposes.

Finally, the researchers examined the idea that women are drawn to the Web to purchase retail items such as cosmetics and clothing. The authors found little evidence of this.

Classroom materials 5.4 Gender differences: studying functional vocabulary gives examples of tasks which have been developed to exploit this text.

Conclusion

This chapter has advocated an approach that starts with language in its context, and encourages students to take an active approach to language learning and development. It is suggested that studying a core of systematically selected functional vocabulary in depth is an effective basis for providing EAP students with the academic vocabulary they need. EAP courses can also provide some support for students in dealing with vocabulary for their specialist subjects. Students need to be aware of the different dimensions of knowing a word and be given frequent opportunities to retrieve and re-use this vocabulary in contexts similar to their target contexts, in order to learn boundaries of meaning and usage of vocabulary items. An approach to vocabulary study which begins with carefully chosen reading texts and takes students through planned stages of development to writing parallel texts is an effective bridge between reading and writing skills. By observing and experimenting with language, students can explore vocabulary both in the classroom and beyond.

Further reading

Coxhead, A. (2006) *Essentials of Teaching Academic Vocabulary.* Massachusetts: Houghton Mifflin.

Jordan, R. R. (2002) *English for Academic Purposes.* Cambridge: Cambridge University Press.

Lewis, M., Ed. (2000) *Teaching Collocation: Further Developments in the Lexical Approach.* Hove: Language Teaching Publications.

McCarthy, M. and O'Dell, F. (2008) *Academic Vocabulary in Use.* Cambridge University Press

Nation, I. S. P. (2001) *Learning Vocabulary in Another Language.* Cambridge: Cambridge University Press.

Thurstun, J. and Candlin, C. N. (1998) *Exploring Academic English: A Workbook for Student Essay Writing.* Sydney: Macquarie University.

Chapter 6: Writing

This chapter will examine:

- the nature and purposes of academic writing
- ways to develop academic writers
- principles and techniques for giving feedback on academic writing

You will have the opportunity to:

- devise tasks to support academic writing
- develop strategies for giving effective feedback to support writing

Writing is the most crucial of the skills needed in an academic context, where written texts are the main means of communication. Academic English is currently the lingua franca, and academic writing is the currency required for entry to academic study and for progression through all stages. In the form of publication, writing provides academic capital, conferring status on published authors, especially if their work is widely cited. The skill of academic writing is generally regarded as difficult to acquire by native and expert users in any language, and requires a considerable period of development through all stages of academic study.

Task 1

- What are the main concerns of EAP students when approaching academic writing?

- What are your main concerns when preparing to teach students to write academic texts?

Here are some examples of students' comments and concerns:

1 *Lack of experience of writing: a dissertation for me is a completely new thing.*

2 *In the literature review I should summarize previous research. The problem was, I was required to use own words to express other person's ideas.*

3 *It's very hard for me to write something: actually I sometimes spend ten minutes on one sentence.*

4 *I don't know how to start sentences and paragraphs.*

5 *I don't know the correct academic style.*

6 *I try to avoid repetition but then I can't find other words or my grammar becomes confused.*

7 *I try to use unusual words to get the reader's attention.*

Comments 1 and 2 illustrate the problems EAP students have in attempting to write genres such as literature reviews and dissertations, which they may never have written in their first language, or which may take a different form in that language. They are not sure what is expected in terms of content or formal requirements. Additionally, incorporating material from other texts in a way that demonstrates understanding of both the content and significance, and avoids copying, represents a major challenge to their language resources. Comments 3 and 4 refer to the fact that students may be limited by lack of skill in controlling aspects such as information flow and sentence construction,[1] and so for them the process of writing takes a long time. However, many expert writers of English write slowly, revising, rewriting sentences, and carefully selecting vocabulary to try to express their ideas more clearly. EAP students may also be hampered by inaccurate information about academic style as revealed in the final three comments. For example, they may have been told that they should model their writing on literary styles or serious newspapers, as these are regarded as good writing. Students who worry about not repeating words or about catching the reader's attention by using original language have been misinformed about the expectations of academic readers in English. Academic writing should be transparent, like a pane of glass, so that the ideas can be clearly seen without the language intruding. In fact, if the language is noticeable, it is often a sign that the ideas are not clearly expressed. It is possible for students to write clearly and simply within their level of competence. Although repetition of the same information is regarded as undesirable digression, repetition of key words or phrases, particularly technical terms, is often essential to avoid confusion. Using a thesaurus or dictionary to avoid repeating words can lead to unintentionally comic effects. For example, concerned about repeating the phrase *wind farms* in a report on this topic, a student consulted a bilingual dictionary and arrived at the phrase *Aeolian plants*.

Classroom materials 6.1 *Quiz: do I have a good academic writing style* helps students to clarify misconceptions about academic writing style.

Concerns expressed by EAP teachers include:

1 *How can I find out what students will need to write on degree courses?*
2 *How do I know what standards their lecturers will expect?*
3 *How can I give them something to write about in class?*
4 *How can I stop them plagiarizing?*
5 *How should I teach paraphrasing?*
6 *I worry that I am writing their essays for them.*
7 *How can I give effective feedback?*
8 *How can I assess writing where students use a lot of technical terms?*
9 *What's the point of teaching academic writing when they can't write at sentence level?*

The key issues for EAP teachers are knowing what the expectations of academic departments are, and what types of texts students actually need to write, so they can provide students with appropriate writing activities. Teachers also worry about issues of plagiarism. However, numbers 4 and 5 above are the wrong questions, as they suggest that plagiarism is intentional and paraphrasing is a cure for it. In fact, plagiarism often results from students not knowing why they are including information or what they really want to say. The intertextual nature of academic texts means that incorporating information and opinions from other authors is an obligatory element of academic writing.[2] It is important for teachers to understand the role of citation, and help students to investigate the citation practices that are appropriate in their disciplines. Another key component in developing writing is feedback. Teachers need principles to identify which aspects to focus on when giving feedback, and techniques which assist students' development as academic writers but do not appropriate their texts. Comment 8 is sometimes used as an argument for avoiding subject-specific texts and tasks. However, as Chapters 2, 3 and 4 show, the way into subject-specific texts is through genre or rhetorical functions. These aspects are also more useful for EAP students than sentence-level language features. Students often have a long history of being taught English through grammar and translation methods.[3] Focusing on the content and purpose of academic writing, and on managing information flow in texts, will help them more effectively than trying to achieve complete mastery of grammar items.

In order to address the concerns of both students and teachers, this chapter will first look at the requirements and expectations of academic departments and the nature of academic writing, before looking at classroom approaches and tasks which can help students to develop as academic writers. The chapters on *Text analysis, Reading* and *Vocabulary* have introduced a way of analysing texts in terms of the features and language associated with their genre and rhetorical functions. This chapter applies this analysis to preparing students for the writing required at university.

Writing at university

To understand what is involved in writing at undergraduate and postgraduate level, students and teachers need to know what texts are produced and what lecturers actually expect the content and language of these texts to be like. They especially want to know what is regarded as good writing within particular academic disciplines.

Task 2

- What do students need to write at university?

- What are the differences between writing required on undergraduate and postgraduate courses?

University courses are now very diverse, with a range of applied subjects covering topics which would not have formed part of academic study in the past. First degree and masters courses in subjects such as hospitality studies, logistics, energy studies, and fashion marketing are offered alongside traditional subjects such as chemistry or history. Developments in computer technology are opening up new areas of knowledge and practice. These newer subject areas are often multidisciplinary and strongly focused on the future professional needs of the students. This trend is reflected in the diversity of written genres that students are required to produce.

Here are examples of writing which might be required in coursework assignments and exams in a range of subject areas, including IT, mechanical and electronic engineering, modern languages, translation studies, logistics, fashion marketing, nursing, and strategic project management.[4]

critical essay	dissertation	business report
examination essay	project	poster presentation
case study essay	lab report	team assignments
literature review	research proposal	management brief
reflective assessment	case notes	website

This list shows the wide diversity of genres that students need to produce. Some may be more typical of certain levels, e.g., some masters courses are assessed only by a research dissertation, while examination essays are more frequently set at undergraduate level. However, final-year undergraduate dissertations based on direct research or exploration of the literature are also common. In practice, it is difficult to draw a distinction between postgraduate and undergraduate writing requirements, and portfolios which include emerging genres such as reflective assignments and poster presentations are becoming more widely required at all levels of study as universities adopt more eclectic approaches to teaching and assessment. The names given to different types of assessment are often ambiguous. Studies across disciplines have found widely differing meanings of these labels even within the same institution. For example, a study in one university[5] found that an essay in animal science and a project report in chemistry were both based on secondary data obtained from a literature search, and required similar formats. The terms *critical essay* or *project*, in the list above, are also used to refer to this format.

The word *essay* is problematic when used in academic writing. The type of traditional essay often used in school or in general English contexts, in which students simply display the ability to write and construct an argument based on their own opinions, is rare in academic coursework or exams. This is particularly true in the UK, where students specialize early in their studies and assignments are subject-orientated or may be in a genre related to future professional requirements. Jackson *et al.* suggest that the defining feature of an academic essay is that it involves 'a written response to a focused question',[6] drawing information from a number of sources. Another term suggested for this type of assignment, in which students are required to use a range of sources to answer a question, is *documented essay*.[7] An essay is simply a tool for learning. Preparing one is intended to deepen students' understanding of the field, and the finished text provides evidence of their ability to apply the concepts, models or theories they have been studying to real-life cases. Teachers can then assess students' progress and give feedback. However, unlike other genres, such as reports, essays rarely mirror real-life writing contexts. This makes it difficult to teach students what is required in terms of content and focus. Students are writing for a subject teacher who already knows more than the writer, but they must imagine an audience with a similar level of knowledge to their own.

Further confusion can occur when professional genres are adapted for pedagogical uses. Thaiss and Zawacki[8] observed an environmental science lecturer who asked first-year students who were not majoring in science to prepare a poster presentation on a scientific topic. The assignment required students to compare the way the topic was covered in newspapers and in validated sources, and to present the differences between these. The aim was to help students understand what scientific thinking means, and make them more critical of the way science is communicated in popular media. However, the form of this poster was very different from the usual poster presentation seen at conferences, which is a tightly summarized display of research outcomes. Introducing students to these alternative genres is useful provided that they are aware of how the classroom version might differ from what they will produce in their later study or research. Another study found confusion when professional genres were embedded in coursework assignments.[9] A law student had to write an essay advising particular clients of their rights. She found it difficult to write the essay in a way which would show her knowledge of the relevant cases or laws by referring to them in a fully referenced way, with dates. This would be unrealistic if she were advising real clients, who would not require or understand this information. Such embedded genres require strategies for combining elements of the professional genre in an academic framework which includes reference to theories or models and cites academic sources. These types of assignment are often used in professionally oriented courses such as finance and accountancy.[10]

Examination answers are also difficult to characterize as the language of examination questions can be particularly unclear and the required answers may vary widely. For example, Chapter 1 showed that the instruction *discuss* could require a range of different responses from a simple description or list to an evaluation of different views. Examination questions can be analysed to identify the topic and focus and the expected response.[11] This is usually indicated by the function of any instruction words. For example, *contrast* or *differences* indicate that comparison is required, whereas *reasons* or *factors* require an explanation of the causes of a situation or phenomenon.

Task 3

Below are examples of undergraduate examination questions.

- Identify the topic and its specific focus, and any instruction words.
- What might students be expected to include in their answers?
- What difference would the number of marks allocated make to the expected response?

1 Outline and discuss the composition and functions of the main EU institutions.
2 Explain the differences between 'void' and 'voidable' contracts.
3 Adam Smith wrote: 'It is not from the benevolence of the butcher, the brewer, or the baker that we expect our dinner, but from their regard to their own interest'. Discuss.

In question 1, the topic is EU institutions, and the focus is *composition and functions*. The instruction *outline* suggests that a description is required. The word *discuss* is ambiguous, but students might guess that this invites some sort of evaluation, e.g., identifying the limits of the functions, otherwise the essay would be simply a memory-based exercise in knowledge-telling. In question 2, the topic is particular types of contracts. The instruction to *explain the differences* seems to ask for a comparison, but in fact it requires a definition of each term, and an explanation of how they differ in order to make them clear. The number of marks allocated also indicates the depth required. For instance, for 5 marks, question 2 might simply require a comparison of the two definitions whereas, for 20 marks, a more extended and analytical explanation might be required, with a sequence of paragraphs expected in an essay. Question

3 illustrates the importance of understanding the whole communicative context of a genre. The prompt for this sub-genre (the essay which responds to a quotation) is usually a quotation from a famous text or author. However, this question does not require a critique of the views of the 18th century economist Adam Smith, but is a coded way of referring to the arguments among 20th century economists about the virtues of a free market economy versus a state-controlled economy. The answer expected would be an essay presenting and evaluating these arguments, and mentioning influential modern economists. Students have to recognize the quotation and show understanding of the role of such seminal texts in their discipline.[12]

When designing tasks and assignments for EAP writing courses, teachers need to keep in mind the wide range of genres required at university. They should also make clear to students that the labels given to academic assignments do not always correspond to clearly identifiable genres, but vary across and within disciplines. A genre comprises not only the text itself but also its role in a sequence of connected activities within a discourse community[13] (known as a genre chain or genre system). These activities shape the conventions of the genre, giving rise to differences in audience, purpose and organization. In order to understand a new genre, students need to be aware of important elements of this genre chain or system, i.e., how the text fits into its context. One way to explore this is to talk to lecturers about their assignments.

Expectations of lecturers

Students and EAP teachers are often concerned about exactly what subject lecturers require in terms of the content, style and quality of written work.

Task 4

- What questions would you like to ask a group of subject lecturers about their expectations of student writing?

- Read the comments below from lecturers from different subject areas,[14] and try to find answers to your questions.

1 Students need to be able to clearly express complex ideas to a non expert.

2 Masters level literature reviews should be appropriately critical, recognizing limitations as well as advantages of the approaches, and thus going beyond a simple presentation of past work.

3 Don't just produce your own opinion – substantiate what you say by academic data or a source.

4 *If I see Wikipedia, I put a line through it!*

5 *The ability to summarize a lot of information in a short coherent document, e.g., a literature review, is a real problem for students in general.*

6 *It's not about describing; it's about analysing, evaluation, synthesis.*

7 *Populate a theoretical framework with what you are doing: apply theoretical models to a piece of data you are using.*

8 *Clear and logical argument, i.e., show how that is related to what you just said.*

9 *They need to be able to structure a document and ideas in a coherent manner.*

10 *I like it succinct and snappy – if there are three issues, have three paragraphs!*

11 *Competency in English is critical for success, but it is not a critical part of the assessment process.*

12 *I look for a good academic style – you know what it is when you see it.*

These lecturers' comments show their concern for all levels of writing: *what* to write as well as *how* to write. They expect students to be aware of the needs of their audience, as the first comment notes, and to understand the type of content expected in a particular genre and context. In comment 2 the lecturer expects her students to know the appropriate scope and depth required in a literature review at this academic level.

Expectations for sourcing and using information are very clear in comments 3, 4 and 5. As explained in Chapter 4: *Reading*, writers are expected to draw on and use authoritative academic sources to support their own ideas, and to be able to summarize and comment on relevant points from their reading. Comments 6 and 7 show the importance attached to knowledge transformation in academic writing. Chapter 4 showed how academic texts are intertextual, referring to each other to build the body of knowledge in a discipline. Even at undergraduate level, student writers are expected to behave as if they are part of that discourse community, acknowledging and transforming previous knowledge and theory built up by the community, and showing how it interacts with their own activities and ideas. This is what is meant by 'Populate a theoretical framework with what you are doing'.

Comments 8 to 12 deal with the *how* of writing. Structure and organization take priority over mechanical accuracy, and lecturers can be forgiving of some weakness in language, provided it does not impede the reader's understanding. This may be specified in the marking criteria. The lecturer who made comment 11 explained, 'I give 95% for comprehensiveness, analysis, quality of argument, structure, and literature references. Only 5% is for style, i.e., getting the words and the vocabulary right. But, of course, that enables everything else.' This emphasizes the importance of encouraging students to write in a simple, clear way, within their level of competence, with the main focus on the quality of their ideas.

Expressions such as *clear, logical* and *academic style* can be ambiguous, and their exact meaning has to be investigated. The lecturer who offered comment 12 reflected afterwards, 'So if I only know what I mean by good academic style when I see it, how do the students know what I want? Does that mean we don't really teach them what academic style is?'[15] Lecturers from disciplines other than languages rely on intuitions about academic style which may not accurately reflect their own or general usage. In practice, only students of maths or philosophy are likely to write logically, in the strictest sense of the word. Thaiss and Zawacki[16] surveyed a group of lecturers from different disciplines, and found these terms and others such as *organized* and *evidence* were widely used to describe how students should write. However, when lecturers were brought together in focus groups, they discovered that each faculty, and even individuals within the same faculty, had different ideas about the meaning of these terms. The differences were often related to the differing goals which lecturers had for the students. For example, some wanted their students to learn and express scientific ways of observation and analysis, while others wanted their students to be aware of the different audiences they would encounter in their professional life and the way the discipline interacted with the wider public.

These findings reflect the experience of many EAP teachers who have struggled to find out what colleagues in other disciplines, and even in their own speciality, regard as good writing.[17] However, as Chapter 2: *Text analysis* explained, there are general tendencies in most academic texts which can encompass concepts such as *clear* and *logical*. Texts which are instances of a particular genre will tend to follow the organization expected for that genre, e.g., the introduction, methods, results and discussion of a research report. Paragraphs will develop from general to specific ideas, and information that is familiar to readers will form the starting point for new information. Rhetorical functions will provide patterns of language which show the relationships between ideas. The words *related, structure* and *coherent* in comments 8 and 9 refer to these general tendencies. Although disciplines may have different priorities in what needs to be explained or made clear, Thaiss and Zawacki[18] were able to identify three overarching principles which they felt characterized academic writing and distilled the concerns and requirements of the academic lecturers in their study:

1. evidence in writing of a disciplined open-minded approach to study, which seeks to achieve in-depth understanding rather than taking a casual or shallow approach
2. the dominance of reason over emotion, showing that a writer can step back to analyse and evaluate ideas in a rational way
3. an imagined reader who questions the text in a rational way, reading for information, and looking for flaws in logic or gaps in observation

Evidence for a disciplined open-minded approach to study would be seen in the use of sources which present an alternative viewpoint or interpretation, as well as those which support the writer's points. Students would have searched for sources, rather than just using those which were provided or easily found. Principles 2 and 3 require that the content is based on theories, facts and data which are organized in a framework that allows the relationship of ideas to be understood by a questioning reader. Effective academic writers will have this reader in mind, making sure that their intentions are clearly signalled, and appropriate content is included to meet possible questions or objections that the critical reader may raise.

Academic writers

The term *academic writers* covers a wide variety of individual situations, from undergraduates hastily writing assignments in the middle of the night for a morning deadline, to professors on sabbatical leave, for whom writing is a full-time activity.

Task 5

Think about your own writing experience.

- What kind of writing do you routinely do?

- How confident do you feel about this writing?

- Would you describe any of your writing as academic?

- Can you recognize any stages in the development of your writing skills?

Becoming an academic writer requires a long period of development through stages of gradually increasing commitment. Many students and academics have made this journey using English as a second language. In a reflective study by a multinational group of such language practitioners,[19] patterns and stages in this journey emerge. These writers speak about their initial experience of using English, where it was regarded 'not as a means of communication, but rather as a subject to be tested in the entrance exam'.[20] At this stage, they focused on grammatical forms, and their only purpose in producing a text was to satisfy the marker's demand for grammatical accuracy. They report basing their writing heavily on direct translation from their first language, and making one-to-one correspondence of words, using a bilingual dictionary. There was little focus on the organization of writing. Another study found that students used frameworks from their first language, with no awareness that these would be unfamiliar to an English-speaking reader, e.g., using a series of direct questions or leaving the statement of their main point until quite far into the text.[21]

As they entered English-medium academic study, these students became aware of the limitations of their approaches. They started to use English–English dictionaries, and paid more attention to organization as an important aspect of writing. At this point in time, students were often heavily reliant on feedback from their English teachers or subject lecturers to show them what was expected, and to build their confidence. Thaiss and Zawacki,[22] in another study which included both first and second language undergraduates, found that students formed generalized rules based on the experience of their early courses. However, as they experienced the variety of expectations in different disciplines, they became confused, and even resentful, at the apparent lack of consistency in these expectations. A major revelation for the students in both surveys was the understanding that there is an audience that they have to consider when deciding what to put into their text, how to organize it, and how to provide signals to indicate their organization. A Japanese student explained, 'For me, writing is a process of making my ideas accessible to readers... Having linking paragraphs and explaining what I would write about next, and what I had just written about, are a few examples of this idea.'[23]

Once students begin to understand that texts are constructed on the foundations of knowledge established by others, they can appreciate the overwhelming importance of reading as the foundation for their writing. At this juncture, students move from a rather mechanistic approach, simply reproducing ideas they have collected, and including as much information as possible, to a stage where they try to weave the results of their reading into a narrative which reveals their own voice and purposes. They realize the importance of making clear claims, and transforming what they read to support these claims. A Spanish speaker who progressed through the system to become a lecturer, teaching and writing in English in the USA, reflects on the development of her writing:

> • *I gained insights about the writing process in general and mine in particular. So I started doing more in the way of summarizing and synthesizing my sources after reading. I found that this practice sped up my writing a great deal... I got my processed reading down on paper, and I was able to use it later in my writing... I can probably improve my approach to writing in ways I am not aware of yet.*[24]

As they struggle to find ways of expressing their own voice amid the density of citations and data that are their sources, effective student writers look for models, and observe how their lecturers and other authors in their discipline manage different aspects of academic writing. They come to understand that academic writing is an apprenticeship in a particular disciplinary discourse community in which they too can have a voice, while keeping within the framework of its conventions. As a final-year student explained:

- *All the rules you worry about following when you're just beginning to write sort of fade into the background and become the foundation from which you work. I guess that's how you feel like you have more freedom to say what you want to say.[25]*

The help and example of peers and mentors can support students' development in academic writing, particularly at postgraduate level. Mature academic writers routinely collaborate, exchange ideas, share reading texts, and ask colleagues to review and check their work. This network of support may not initially be visible to students and discovering it is one more stage in their entry into the discourse community.

These perspectives on the nature of academic writing, and the processes through which student writers develop, contain recurring elements which are the core of what academic writers need to be able to do:

- write for a purpose and an audience
- write from sources
- find their own voice as participants in their academic discourse community

Developing academic writers

In order to develop as academic writers, students must learn how to select and organize information to meet the purpose and the audience expectations of a range of genres. They also need to develop fluency in writing. Fluency involves having sufficient language resources to be able to control the flow of information in a text, and communicate ideas effectively to readers. Students also need to see writing as a cyclical process in which they take responsibility for critically reviewing and redrafting their own work. They need to view both their peers and their teacher as part of a support network that can give feedback on their writing. The role of the EAP teacher is to support students in their journey to become academic writers by making explicit what is happening in the stages described above, and helping students to acquire the language resources they need at each stage.

Task 6

Read the case study below.

- Which aspects of writing does the student need help with?

- What did the teacher fail to do?

Case study A:

In the second week of an EAP writing course, a teacher introduced the rhetorical function of classifying. The class studied a simple text which involved classification, and identified expressions for classifying, e.g., *based on, category*. In a rush at the end of a lesson, the teacher decided to set a writing task for homework. She asked students to write a short text explaining how some items in their subject field are classified. For those students entering courses unrelated to their previous degrees who did not have enough knowledge to do this, the teacher suggested that they could write a classification of sport. Here is the opening of one student's writing.

Common sport can classify in following categories based on how sport is played: athletics, combat sport, target sport, power sport, racquet sport, water sport, snow sport and team sport. However, this classification have disadvantage is no matter how to classify, there are always some sport cannot fit in any category or can fit more than one categories.

Athletics, also know as track and field, has long history that can retrospect to ancient Greek period. Normally, it is deemed to consist by jumping, running, throwing and walking. Combat sport is one-on-one competition of fight or combat, most of martial arts like judo, karate, and kung-fu can range in this sport, however, there are some other sports such as boxing, wrestling, even fencing and kendo can put on this category.

This student is at the first stage of academic writing, focused mainly on demonstrating his ability to incorporate the language learnt into a text to satisfy the teacher. He has attempted to use the target language involved in classification, and has remembered collocations such as *following categories* and *fit/put into categories*. However, there are some grammatical errors, and words such as *deemed* and *retrospect* suggest that he is relying on a bilingual dictionary to try to achieve one-to-one correspondence with his first language. The student is starting to use linking and cohesive expressions to achieve a flow of information, e.g., *However, this classification.* Despite this, the text is difficult to read and the structure difficult to follow. For example, the second sentence leads the reader to expect that the topic of the disadvantages of this classification will be developed in the next paragraph, but in fact the second paragraph begins with a statement about the history of athletics. The student is effectively writing the text for himself – thinking aloud to answer the question, 'So how can I classify sport?' There is no thought at all of a reader for this text. The writer includes everything he can think of about the topic without asking, for example, if the reader really needs a definition of athletics.

The teacher inadvertently set up this situation by omitting to give the student any purpose for writing other than to recycle the language learnt. She supplied the framework of a rhetorical function, classification, and some associated vocabulary but did not suggest an audience for the text. The student's voice is not evident in this writing because there is nothing he really wants to say about this topic. He wrote the text only for the teacher to mark, not for the teacher to read. Interestingly, the students who were able to write about their own field handled this task more successfully, probably because they had a more realistic writing purpose, i.e., to communicate something they knew to a non-expert. This case study is a reminder that students cannot be assisted in their progress towards writing for an audience and a purpose unless they are given regular tasks which clearly specify these. Responsibility can be shared with students and motivation for writing can be increased by negotiating a real-world audience and purpose, e.g., for this assignment: classifying sports as part of a report for a committee who will decide the types of venues required for the Olympic Games.

Writing for a purpose and an audience requires awareness of the genre specified in the task, and how it is realized in its disciplinary context. Chapter 3: *Course design* showed how a genre can be modelled in the EAP classroom to support writing. However, students should not be given the impression that writing in an academic genre involves simply applying a standard framework which can be filled in with content, as can be done when writing formulaic genres such as a recipe or a letter of enquiry. Students need to understand that their ability to write a particular genre develops gradually, and may never be complete, as genres themselves are constantly evolving. Students at postgraduate level often say, 'I want to know how to write a research report.' They are disappointed at the answer, 'I can't show you how to write a research report, but I hope I can equip you with the tools to discover how research reports are written in your discipline.' Students need to go through a gradual process of engagement with their discourse community in order to understand the purposes and audiences for genres in their discipline. How far they get with this process of acculturation may depend largely on their closeness to their target situation. EAP classes cannot produce fully developed academic writers. They can only produce students who are aware of what academic writing involves and understand how they can become academic writers.

Prospective postgraduates will already have some awareness of communication practices in their academic discipline. They may also have access to their subject department or some contact with their supervisors. At the least, they can access online materials, such as academic journals, to develop an understanding of how their discipline builds and communicates knowledge. Intending undergraduates, on the other hand, may be far from their future subject area, with insufficient knowledge to access the type of materials which would be helpful. They may not even know in which university or course they will finally study. Acculturation exercises, such as those described in Chapter 4: *Reading*, where teachers actively set up contacts with academic departments, are desirable, but not always possible. In this case, writing for the readers at hand, i.e., the teacher and classmates, or other easily imagined readers, is the first step towards writing for an audience.

Writing from sources

The writers in the surveys by Thaiss and Zawacki[26] and Silva *et al.*[27] described how they progressed from using sources in a merely mechanical way to being able to process and use their reading as part of their own narrative, making the ideas and findings of other authors serve their own purposes. These skills are at the heart of academic study, linking the learning and membership of the academic community obtained through lectures and reading to written output which is the evidence of that learning and membership. Teachers may identify student needs in this respect as awareness of referencing conventions, and avoiding plagiarism in the form of sections of unacknowledged quotation in their texts. In fact, to write successfully from sources, students need to engage intellectually with what they are reading. This means they must focus on understanding the ideas thoroughly rather than quoting them in a superficial way. They also need to evaluate the basis of the knowledge in a way that is appropriate to the discipline. For example, in a physical science subject, students might consider critically the methodology or the conditions under which an experiment was performed, whereas, in a social science context, students might try to identify the school of thinking on which the writer's interpretations are based. Students have to show awareness of the status of their sources and indicate their own stance, as well as the relationship between the citations and their own text purposes. Just as they need to become *dominant readers*, they also need to become *dominant writers*, creating and controlling their own narrative.

In a study of the citation practices of a small international group of postgraduate students in IT, Perry[28] observed that, as well as failing to acknowledge sources and follow referencing conventions, students experienced problems in the following areas:

- making clear the extent of attributions, i.e., distinguishing the words or views of the writer from those of the author of the cited text
- making clear the function of the cited text or ideas in the writer's argument
- including a reference to substantiate statements made

Task 7

Extracts A and B are from the first draft and the final draft of a literature review written by a postgraduate EAP student as part of a small research project in the final term of a one-year course.

- What is better about the final draft when compared with the first?
- Where does the student locate each reference in the sentence?
- How far is she able to show her own voice?

A First draft

The literature review is divided into 2 sections. Firstly the report into organisations of UK and Chinese health care systems will be mentioned and then a more detailed review of characters of these two health care system finances will be discussed.

According to NHS in England website (2006), National Health Service was set up in 1948 to provide health care for all citizens. NHS includes three kinds of services: hospital, family (e.g. General Practitioner, dentists, opticians and pharmacies) and local authority health services (e.g. community nursing and health visiting). Ranade (1995 p.5) identifies the structure of NHS which has two kinds of relationships: managerial and coordinating relationship.

B Final draft

In order to solving financing problems, it is beneficial for China to look at other health systems in developed countries. The UK health care system has developed for a long time and is mature. The National Health Service in the UK was set up in 1948 (NHS website 2006). Most of the money for the NHS derives from taxes and a large number of residents in the UK are covered by the NHS (Ham 1991). The NHS is considered to be an effective system to provide health services. According to the NHS reform and investment plan (2000), Americans, Canadians and Australians are 50% more worried than British people about affording medical charge. Because the NHS has developed for a long time and has better approach of financing, comparison of the UK and the Chinese health care systems can be useful.

Ranade (1995 p 55) argues NHS has strengths which provide "a reasonably equitable and comprehensive service to the whole population at remarkably small cost". Because of central management, Ranade (1995 p 55) emphasizes that hospital charge is easy to control and compares British and American hospital charge (Weiner 1987 in Ranade 1995). ... However, as Maynard (1993) argues NHS is not without pitfalls such as low effectiveness which is defined in the UK by the length of time to achieve the intended benefits in health care.

In the first draft, the student is merely presenting information from the sources she has consulted. Even though the information quoted is routine knowledge over which the two sources have no particular monopoly, the name of each source is given prominence at the beginning of the sentence, *According to NHS, Ranade ... identifies*. This 'author prominent' form of citing,[29] where the author is the subject of the verb, leaves little trace of the student's own voice. Her modest opening tells the reader about the organization of the paper, but makes no statement or claim indicating her own thesis. This writer is at a very tentative stage in her use of sources.

In the final draft, the student has grown in confidence and her voice is clear in the bold claim made in the opening sentence. She uses her sources to justify her choice of the UK system as a model for comparison. The citations are now controlled by her own narrative, and in her form of referencing. She has begun to discriminate between sources of factual information, referenced as non-integral[30] citations outside sentences, and statements of evaluation, in which the original authors are given prominence. She even dares to hint that she concurs with one author's view, *as Maynard argues*. A characteristic of academic writers identified by Thaiss and Zawacki in their study was 'passion'.[31] This student's commitment and conviction of the importance of her chosen topic is beginning to be visible in her writing.

Classroom materials 6.2 *What is research?* introduces students to the concept of synthesizing their own ideas from several sources.

The student needs to develop further skills in incorporating citations effectively. She still stays close to the original sources, using an unnecessary direct quote because she felt she could not paraphrase effectively. She is not able to summarize Ranade's points in a way that avoids multiple references, and she does not yet attempt to synthesize ideas from different authors, but keeps them separate. It is not clear if Maynard's view is in opposition to Ranade's or if she has simply juxtaposed them. She also needs to widen her repertoire and understanding of specific verbs for citing such as *argues*.[32]

Students need a range of skills to use sources effectively. The first and most important is to establish a narrative, led by the writer's voice, in the form of a series of clear statements or claims. The sources then become servants not masters[33] as they are incorporated and evaluated in appropriate ways to support or illustrate the claims. To establish a narrative, students need to know how to present citations, briefly acknowledging information which is factual or in the public domain, paraphrasing where they wish to stay close to the author's idea, summarizing wider points in a way that demonstrates real understanding, and synthesizing a group of relevant ideas from the sources to create their own points. They need to draw on their understanding of the status of different texts, e.g., in choosing when to employ direct quotation. They should be aware that quotations are like birthday cakes, to be brought in on special occasions only, e.g., when the author's words are particularly apposite in expressing an idea, or when this author is used as authoritative support for the writer's view.

There are also requirements in terms of language resources when students incorporate the author's ideas into their own sentences, e.g., the ability to manipulate grammar forms and sentence structure. This is sometimes taught as paraphrasing, and students are given the false impression that using sources simply requires them to rewrite as much of the original text as possible in their own words to avoid being accused of plagiarism. Approaching citation in this way prevents students from developing their own narrative and, as shown in Chapter 2: *Text analysis*, it can destroy the logical development of ideas in the original text. Summarizing a whole text is equally unhelpful as it does not train students to select the information they need for their own purposes. Summarizing and paraphrasing, like all other forms of writing, need a clear purpose.

Citation also requires knowledge of formal conventions for in-text referencing and references lists. Students need to be aware that different referencing systems, e.g., the American Psychological Association (APA), Institute of Electrical and Electronic Engineers (IEEE), Numerical, or Havard systems are used in different disciplines. Students can find the relevant system online or check what their department uses. Classroom time should not be wasted on mechanical exercises to master a particular system that may not be relevant to their future needs.[34]

Writing from data

When writing a data commentary,[35] as with writing from other sources, students have to establish their own purpose and voice, and not let their writing be driven by the data. In EAP classes, students are often given tasks to write an assignment based on a group of graphs or tables. In the following example, students were given data from the UK Office of National Statistics about types of leisure activity in the UK, such as sports, watching TV and cinema attendance, and were asked to write a report aimed at educated readers, on patterns of change in these leisure activities.

Task 8

The extract below is one paragraph of a student's answer, based on a graph comparing cinema attendance for different age groups over a period of years.

- What makes the paragraph difficult to read?

- What would help the student to write more clearly about data in terms of

  a making clear the purpose of the graph

  b organization of information

  c accuracy in referring to data?

Over the period of 19 years that is to say 1984 to 2003, cinema visits rose rapidly from just over 15% to 45% in 1992 concerning the age 15–24 because new movies can be seen only at cinema and also the sensation of the public and then fluctuated throughout most of the year within two small periods of stabilisation by reaching a peak at 50% in 1994 and approximately at 58% in 1999 due to the arrival of home cinema, DVD and video CD. Regarding the trends, the young people 7–14 and adolescent people 25–34 had almost the same variation dominated by fluctuations. Going to the cinema rose moderately from 5% in 1984 to just under 20% in 2003 for the age 35 and over may be because of their responsibility (home, job).

The lack of organization makes this text difficult to read. There is no initial reference to where the graph is located in the text, what it represents, or its purpose (comparison of cinema attendance in different age groups). There is no attempt to reflect this purpose in the text organization. There is no general to specific development in the text. It lacks a general (highlighting) statement[36] to indicate the main points in the data to which the writer intends to draw attention. It is difficult to distinguish between factual details and the writer's interpretation of the data. The first sentence moves confusingly between facts and interpretations, without any signalling. The lack of precise noun phrases to indicate exactly what is represented generates further confusion, and results in inappropriate subjects for the verbs or phrases that follow. The student claims that *cinema visits rose, young people ... had almost the same variation, going to the cinema rose moderately*, rather than using accurate noun phrases, e.g., *the number of people between the ages of 15 and 24 visiting the cinema rose.*

The student needs to understand why both data and commentary are included in academic texts. Graphs or other forms of data presentation are not ways of filling page space. Nor should they be accompanied by a summary of the content

Classroom materials
8.1 *Mystery graphs* and 8.4 *Speculating why* give practice in thinking critically about the purpose of graphs, identifying significant data, and suggesting possible interpretations.

of the graph. It is the writer's responsibility to impose a clear narrative, drawing the reader's attention to what is significant for the purposes of the particular text. Graphs or tables give the reader visual support, demonstrate that research has been done and, most importantly, allow the reader to interact with the text in a critical way, evaluating the writer's claims about the significance of the data, and considering alternative interpretations. The student needs to know how to signal and separate interpretation from facts. This involves being aware of the purpose of cautious language, known as hedging, to signal the writer's own suggestions, and developing a repertoire of such expressions, e.g., *possibly this could be / may be.*

Classroom materials 6.3 *Noun phrases for referring to data* gives practice in writing noun phrases which accurately describe data.

This student needs practice in forming noun phrases that can carry a large amount of information. He also needs to clarify the difference between what can be said about real world events and what can be said about numerical quantities and proportions. People and their activities cannot rise, fall or show variation, only numbers, measures or proportions can do these things, e.g., *the number of unemployed adults decreased; the price of oil / the proportion of world trade carried out by the developed countries rose.* These noun phrases transform real-world situations into abstract concepts which can be described in exact numerical terms and within exact limits of time or space, e.g., *the number of cinema visits by people aged 15–24 rose by 50% between 1984 and 2003.* There are also restrictions for some expressions. For example, *account for* can only be used in one direction, i.e., to link the real world to the numerical expression, but not vice versa, e.g., *Chinese students account for 18% of the overseas students in the EAP course.* Students often try to reverse this form resulting in an incorrect statement, e.g., *18% accounts for the Chinese students on the EAP course.*

Classroom materials 6.4 *A class profile* introduces students to writing from data and using highlighting statements as a narrative frame.

Students are often trained to write about data in a very descriptive way, mirroring the type of data and style of reporting used in financial news reports, perhaps because this is a readily available source for teachers, or because materials are borrowed from business English textbooks. The focus is on lists of exciting verbs (*soared, plummeted, fluctuated*) describing the variations of a single item (*shares* or *the dollar).* This specialized genre has been adopted too often as a model for data commentary, and does not equip students for the different types of data found at university and the ways in which these are described. The writing of the student in this example shows the result of this approach. Case study C in Chapter 3 shows one way to raise students' awareness of these aspects, helping them to form accurate noun phrases, and create their own narrative of significant points in the form of highlighting statements, which are then supported by appropriate detail and interpretation.

Data and numerical expressions occur in many forms in academic writing. EAP teaching materials tend to focus on a limited range of forms: pie charts, representing proportion or percentage; tables, usually involving comparison;

and graphs, which represent the behaviour of an item or group of items over a period of time, e.g., fluctuations in the rate of unemployment. However, these forms are by no means typical of many disciplines. In a one-million-word corpus of undergraduate management materials, including economics, finance, accounting and marketing modules, only one graph which represented change over time was found. Most data were presented in table form. However, in the economics texts in this corpus, another type of graph was frequent. This is the *relationship graph*, which represents a causal relationship between two or more variables. The graph shows how the value of one variable changes when the value of the other changes or is manipulated under certain conditions. This type of graph can also be represented by a mathematical equation. Examples of this type of graph are the supply and demand curve in economics, and graphs which represent the relationship between the volume and pressure of gases at particular temperatures in physics and chemistry. Graphs may also represent frequency distribution, e.g., the bell curve, or exponential relationships. These concepts may be more familiar to students than to their EAP teachers, but it is important that students know how to write about the graphs and relationships which occur in their disciplines. For instance, they need to be aware that, in English, the present tense is used to comment on graphs representing general causal relationships, whereas the simple past is used to explain the information in graphs representing events at a specific time.

Classroom materials 6.5 *The demand for chocolate cakes: graphical presentation* introduces an example of this type of graph, and the language used to explain it.

English terms for common mathematical expressions, operations and symbols are unlikely to have been encountered by EAP students, particularly undergraduates who have not previously undertaken English-medium study. It is worth spending time checking students' knowledge of terms such as *multiply* and *formula*, as dictionaries may not always reflect the precise usage.

Classroom materials 6.6 *Quiz: mathematical expressions* helps students to check their knowledge of some common mathematical terms.

EAP students need to be taught to write about the type of data and mathematically expressed information they are likely to meet in their target courses. The creation of a narrative through highlighting statements, and the clear separation of real-world objects and phenomena from mathematical or abstract concepts, are useful general principles, both at the organizational level and at the level of language choices. Students and EAP teachers need to collaborate in exploring the types of data and commentaries used in different disciplines.

Writing in the EAP classroom

The overall aim of an EAP course is to help students towards membership of their chosen academic community. The main way that students can demonstrate their academic credentials is through writing which shows evidence of in-depth exploration of a specific question or topic, the effective use of sources and data to support their claims, and the ability to imagine a questioning reader. This means that the main objectives of the EAP classroom will involve reading, research, analysis and, above all, writing for a purpose and audience. The academic texts students read provide the source of ideas for their writing, but are also used as models of the genres and rhetorical features of academic English.

It is because writing is such a crucial skill for students to acquire that many of the earlier chapters in this book also refer to it. Case study C in Chapter 1 identifies student needs through analysis of a poorly written essay. Chapter 2 shows how students can analyse texts to study academic register, genres, rhetorical functions and discourse patterns, together with the grammar that supports them, e.g., noun phrase construction, in order to use all these in their writing. Chapter 3 suggests that analysis of student needs, based on genres or rhetorical functions, forms the best starting point for EAP syllabus design, particularly for writing. Case study C in Chapter 3 shows a teaching and learning cycle in a writing class to illustrate the use of text-based, task-based and collaborative teaching approaches. Chapter 4 shows that writing is inextricably bound up with reading, which provides a source of ideas, as well as models for language analysis. Case study D in Chapter 4, together with Task 10 in Chapter 5, illustrates how an authentic genre, an abstract, can be analysed to discover the conventions of the genre, and then be used as a source of functional vocabulary and a prompt for a writing task.

Task 9

Think about your current teaching situation.

- How much time do you spend teaching writing?

- How would you describe your approach to teaching writing, e.g., do you use a process approach?

In English language teaching, learning to write has been approached from two different directions. One approach has been to start with what students need to write, the genre (product), modelling the elements of the genre using example texts, and supporting students in acquiring the necessary knowledge and skills to produce similar texts. The other approach focuses on the individual process of composition, i.e., first generating and organizing ideas, and then reviewing and redrafting the text. Teachers sometimes have the impression that these approaches are mutually exclusive, whereas in EAP they are both essential elements of learning to write effectively.[37]

Examples of the genres which students need to write can provide the learning content of an EAP course. Students can study the patterns of organization and language which will enable them to express their ideas, and achieve the purpose of the genre, for example, passing an exam. As Hyland points out:

> The whole edifice of education is premised on the idea that the knowledge and skills required for particular tasks can be identified, analyzed, and taught before engaging in those tasks.[38]

Learning about genres, and their associated rhetorical functions and discourse structure, and being aware of what to look for when analysing a text, enables students to become autonomous writers who can continue the language learning process when they leave the EAP classroom. As explained in Chapter 3, a course that neglects this analysis will fail to make students aware of the complexities of academic language in discipline-specific contexts.

The writing process is equally important. By developing good strategies for planning and reviewing their own work, students will ensure that they approach writing in an organized way. Reviewing and redrafting are also crucial steps in the process, and enable students to develop their capacity for self-evaluation and reflection, and the ability to learn from the comments of peers and teachers. However, if students have been taught to focus on the process of writing without considering carefully what is required for a particular genre in a specific context, the consequences can be disastrous, as the following case study shows.

Task 10

How did a focus on the writing process disadvantage the students described in the case study below?

Case study B:

An examiner regularly marked papers from an overseas centre delivering an English foundation course. The exam format included a reading text and two essays, the first one requiring students to apply concepts explained in the reading text to a real situation. Students were told to use their own examples, so that specialist topic knowledge was not required. The second essay was a report based on data supplied in a table or graph. Each year, the marker experienced the frustration of being obliged to fail two groups of students. The first group wrote satisfactory, sometimes very good, answers to the first essay question. They then crossed these out and redrafted the entire essay. Of course, this meant that they had no time to attempt the second essay, and were unable to gain enough marks to pass the exam. Comparing the two drafts, the examiner found that the students had never gained more than a maximum of one or two marks in this process, whereas even a hurried attempt at the second question would usually gain good students seven or eight marks. The second group wrote the first essay entirely from their own ideas, often very imaginatively, but failed to refer at all to the ideas in the source reading text, despite the clear instructions in the question to do so.

Classroom materials 4.4 *The Metropole and the Luxus* gives an example of how students can be helped to predict the expectations of an exam answer and write a text to meet these expectations.

At some earlier stage in their learning, both groups had been given the impression that there is a single approach to the process of writing, suitable for all contexts. They had been taught that brainstorming exciting ideas, and checking their work for minor language errors, would produce good writing. Of course, these are an essential part of the process of good writing, but this has to be contextualized for each genre. Swales[39] suggests that students need to learn to write in a way that reflects the *hard* process of accommodating to the requirements and reader expectations of genres rather than the *soft* process of focusing on their internal composing processes. These unlucky students may have thought that the examiner would be able to award extra marks for the accuracy of their expression or the originality of their ideas, but the proportion of marks and the requirements of the question were fixed so the examiner could not do this. Generally, a lower of level of accuracy and originality will be accepted in an examination script than in coursework, precisely because the writer is expected to have had little time for marshalling ideas or checking. If the students in this case study had been aware of the need to adapt their writing processes to accommodate the conventions of a variety of genres, and to relate their own ideas to concepts in a text, they might have been better able to understand what was required in the examination genre.

Using genre in the EAP writing classroom

Chapter 3: *Course design* describes the learning and teaching cycle for a genre approach, and illustrates this in Case study C. Students are oriented to the context of the genre through discussion, and analyse the organization of example texts by identifying the rhetorical moves. The teacher has to find example texts or encourage the students to bring these to class. She also has to analyse these texts prior to the class and prepare to model and jointly construct the genre with students by means of guided writing tasks. These might involve collaborative writing in groups, or pre-writing exercises, e.g., to construct accurate noun phrases to refer to data in a graph. The teacher must also provide – or negotiate with students – a writing assignment which specifies a purpose and audience appropriate for the genre. Students then write independently, and receive feedback from peers and the teacher. Students can be encouraged to become genre detectives, looking for other examples of the genre, and examining these to discover the range of possible options for writing in this genre. Genres, such as an essay or research report, can be studied over several weeks as part of a chain of activities:[40] reading about a topic – devising a research question – writing a proposal – collecting data – writing a report – making an oral presentation. The sections of a research report can be dealt with as sub-genres, each supported through the learning and teaching cycle described above.[41]

However, using a genre approach can be difficult when students are very far from their target context. For example, prospective undergraduates with a fairly low level of English may struggle with writing an essay based on sources. In this case, awareness of the activities required in the genre chain that leads to an essay has to be built up very slowly through supported reading of pre-selected source texts, and strongly scaffolded writing activities such as note-taking, summarizing and collaborative planning.[42] A more appropriate initial approach for these students might be a writing syllabus based on rhetorical functions, which provides regular practice in writing short focused paragraphs, using prompts such as note frameworks or selected short quotations. Later in the course, these paragraphs can be combined to produce a more complex genre such as an essay or report.

Even for postgraduate students who have a better understanding of the requirements of their future academic discipline, using authentic genres in the EAP classroom requires careful research and planning. There are many constraints to consider: the difficulty of understanding how a discourse community actually views a genre, e.g., a literature review; or finding examples of certain genres, e.g., project proposals; or the need to balance authenticity against pedagogical usefulness, e.g., dealing with texts of the length and complexity of dissertations and PhD theses.

Task 11

The following case study describes problems encountered in using a target genre as a writing outcome on a pre-sessional course.

• How could an EAP teacher handle these issues?

Case study C:
Students on a pre-sessional course were required to undertake a short research project related to their academic field, and modelled on the masters dissertation required in their target degree. There was a

considerable limitation in authenticity for the science and technology students as they could only produce literature-based research, whereas some business and finance students were able to undertake small surveys or case studies, or find secondary data such as company figures to analyse.

Student A, a microbiologist, discussed his project with the teacher, and agreed on a title which involved answering a question based on one aspect of his intended PhD topic. When he presented his first draft, the material appeared to be the whole draft of his PhD literature review. The teacher tried to persuade him that this would not fulfil the task for the EAP assignment as it covered aspects of the topic not specified in the project title, and would be impossibly long. The student argued that reducing his scope in this way was inauthentic, and there would be no point in such a 'dumbed down' version of his work.

Student B had already begun his postgraduate study in an applied science. He agreed on a specific title dealing with one aspect of his work. When he submitted his first draft, it appeared to be simply a lab report and contained details of research he had done with his supervisor rather than reference to the literature. It was also remarkably well written compared with his in-class writing. The teacher tried to deal with these issues, but the student became angry and said that the problem was due to her lack of understanding of his field.

Student C was a mathematician. He explained politely that there was no way that the teacher would be able to understand his text, as it would only be accessible to mathematicians because of the high number of mathematical expressions it would contain.

Initially, Student A simply saw the assignment as a way to obtain a proofreading for his PhD literature review. After conversations with the teacher, and after participating in collaborative class activities, he became aware of the way other students were using this opportunity to learn a general approach to writing literature reviews and reports rather than focusing only on this assignment. The student agreed to curtail his report to the agreed topic focus, and made it short and accessible enough for the teacher and other students to give useful feedback and identify ways in which he could improve his language and organization. At the end of the course, the student said he felt he had learnt some general principles and useful language for constructing a literature review.

Student B continued to present versions of the same lab report to the teacher, and avoided collaborative feedback activities, preferring to work alone. The teacher felt unable to give effective feedback because, whenever she made suggestions, the student fell back on the accusation that she did not understand the technical concepts. The student felt the course was not useful and left.

Student C gradually brought his mathematical text down to a level that was broadly accessible to the teacher, while keeping in the necessary equations. His report earned an A grade and he reported that he had gradually realized that he would not be communicating only with mathematicians when he went to work in a professional situation, so it would be useful to take this opportunity to learn to write for a less knowledgeable audience.

This case study illustrates some of the difficulties encountered when attempting to use authentic genres. Where students are very close to their target situation, it is difficult for the teacher not to collude in helping to write sections of the students' dissertations or theses. Apart from the ethical issues, this wastes an opportunity to develop wider academic writing skills, as Student A eventually realized. Teachers cannot always give students exactly what they want. It may not be within the remit of the EAP course, and the course director needs to deal with students such as Student B, who are not satisfied with the available provision. Sometimes the nature of the target genre makes real authenticity an impossible task. Student C was probably right in thinking that the teacher would be unable to give useful feedback on an authentic mathematics dissertation. However, a compromise enabled the student to develop his competence, particularly his ability to write for a non-specialist audience. As mentioned in the section on lecturer's expectations earlier in this chapter, this is also an important aspect of academic writing.

Adapting the process approach for the EAP classroom

The focus on reading, text analysis and writing in an EAP classroom can result in a very different emphasis from that in the general English classroom, where lively discussion and debate on topics of current interest are valued. Sometimes teachers from a general English background find it difficult to adapt to the different focus of the EAP classroom. However, it is important to encourage lively discussion and debate around reading, analysis, writing, and feedback tasks. EAP students will find this discussion stimulating and motivating if they can clearly see how it relates to their future studies.

Task 12

Think about the activities you use to develop students' writing ability.

- Which of these activities involve discussion?
- Which activities happen in class and which happen outside, e.g., for homework?
- What kind of feedback are students given on their writing?

The activities normally associated with a process approach to writing include brainstorming ideas, planning an outline of the content, writing a draft, redrafting on the basis of feedback from peers and the teacher, and revising the final draft for surface features such as spelling, punctuation and grammatical mistakes. It is often the case that the brainstorming phase takes up a good deal of class time precisely because it involves lively discussion and sharing of personal ideas. In contrast, individual writing is often done for homework, and students receive no support from peers or their teacher when they are actually writing. Feedback from peers is usually a classroom activity, but feedback from the teacher is not, although students may sometimes have writing tutorials with the teacher to discuss their work. The kind of teacher feedback students receive might focus more on their choice of vocabulary and grammatical structures rather than the organization of their text and whether it achieves its purpose for an audience. In the EAP classroom, all these activities can be adapted to provide more effective support for students in becoming writers of academic genres.

Discussion and brainstorming

Classroom materials 1.3 *Chocolate in the classroom* introduces the idea of citation and plagiarism in a fun way through a class discussion task.

Oral discussion is very important in the EAP classroom, not primarily to promote oral fluency, but because it helps students to put the ideas of other people into their own words, i.e., literally to develop their voice in writing. For example, students can be asked to discuss their views on a topic. Ideas from the discussion are then incorporated into a text, and students can decide how their own names should be cited in the text and in the list of references. This gives them an academic identity, and they start to see themselves as future academic writers.

Classroom materials 6.7 *In my own words* shows how oral summaries can help students to use citation in their writing.

When reading in class, students can be asked to provide an oral summary of what they have read. This encourages them to find their own words, rather than depending on the text. They can capture their own words by immediately writing down what they have said, or working with a partner who transcribes their summary. Searching through a text for the answer to a critical thinking question, and then discussing their ideas with a partner, as in Case study C in Chapter 4: *Reading*, helps students to develop the open-minded approach, which seeks in-depth understanding, that is valued at university.

When students begin to work with a new rhetorical function or genre, discussion is the first step in understanding why, and in what form, the function or genre might occur in their discipline. Subsequent tasks, such as analysing examples of the genre or finding useful functional language, can be performed collaboratively through discussion. In all of these examples, the students should have a specific purpose for the discussion which leads to the next stage in the learning and teaching cycle.

Supporting writing as students write is possibly the most neglected stage in the process. Writing is such a difficult task, even for expert native speakers, that the first attempt should always be supported in some way. Key elements of this support are:

- models of the genre
- resources to help at language level
- model answers for the particular task
- interaction with other students and with the teacher

Chapter 4: *Reading* outlined a series of steps for exploiting reading texts in the classroom as models of genre and language, finishing with writing tasks which enable students to use the content of a text in authentic ways, but also to see how the organization and language of the text can be transferred to other tasks relevant to their future studies. This transfer can be done at the level of sentences, e.g., identifying functional sentence frames in the text into which students can insert their own content: *The differences between … and … can be considered in terms of …* It can also be done at the level of paragraphs, e.g., making note frameworks appropriate to the content and function of the text, such as process flow charts, comparison and contrast tables, classification diagrams, cause and effect chains, and then using these as outlines for a parallel text with different content, but a similar rhetorical purpose. Case study C in Chapter 3: *Course design* showed an example where the teacher modelled the first part of a data commentary, and then asked students to use the same series of moves to write the rest of the commentary. These functional paragraph outlines are good preparation for quickly planning answers to examinations questions, which tend to specify a single function for the response. Students can also use whole texts, e.g., essays or research reports written by students in previous years, from which they can derive an outline plan to modify for their own essay or report.

It is not authentic to see writing as a test, so students should have a range of resources available to consult if they need them. For example, if they are writing a paragraph with a specific functional purpose, they should have the reference page for that function next to them as they write. The teacher might elicit some vocabulary and sentence frames from the whole class which could be used in the task. She can also act as a resource while the students are writing, helping to formulate ideas into sentences, or providing suggestions for vocabulary as requested. For lower level classes, model answers for a writing task, written by the teacher or based on a good student text, can be used to scaffold student writing. The model answer can be cut up into individual sentences which students have to reorder. When they reconstruct the model, students have to go through the same process as the writer, in deciding what to put next in order to maintain the topic and create a narrative of the main points and supporting detail or explanation. A gapped version can then be presented with functional language removed which students have to supply. These models and tasks are then removed, and students can try to write their own answers to the original assignment.

Classroom materials 2.9 ***General to specific*** shows an example of whole class writing which results in students producing individual paragraphs.

Many of the communicative groupwork activities common in general English classrooms can be adapted to support writing. The whole class can write a text together, with the teacher as scribe and shaper of the ideas. Students in a group can each be given responsibility for selecting significant ideas from one of several texts. The group then synthesizes these ideas into one or more paragraphs. This can be scaffolded for lower levels by instructing individual students to look for ideas related to specific functions, e.g., the problem, the solutions, the evaluation of each solution.

These group and whole class activities which support planning and drafting can be engaging and motivating for students because they are enabled to write beyond the level of their current competence, and can start to feel what it is like to be a competent academic writer. Regular support and advice from the teacher and peers creates a collaborative classroom atmosphere in which feedback on writing can be viewed positively. Teachers may be concerned that this level of support is inauthentic but, in fact, as pointed out above, academic writers routinely support their writing by strategies such as finding models of target genres, using dictionaries and glossaries, and consulting colleagues and supervisors.

Feedback on writing

Feedback is used here in the sense of reflection on or evaluation and discussion of a student's writing, which is not aimed at awarding a grade or satisfying institutional needs, but at shaping and changing the students' understanding and competence. This feedback should be an ongoing process built into the structure of the syllabus and teaching methodology as explicitly as any other course element. It involves self-assessment and peer assessment, as well as teacher assessment. In each of these cases, the focus and purpose of the feedback should be clear. The ability to assess their own writing in terms of the criteria against which it will be judged is essential in developing the autonomy students will need in their future academic study.[45] Self-assessment should be carried out before any other type of assessment is given.

Doing self- and peer-assessment in the classroom requires a climate of trust, and a sensitivity to group dynamics and individual feelings. Students may feel

Classroom materials 10.1 *Assessment criteria* shows how EAP students can be encouraged to negotiate assessment criteria. **Classroom materials 6.8 *EAP warmers 3: sentence auctions*** suggests a fun way to provide immediate feedback while the whole class constructs a text.

uncomfortable being asked how good they think their work is.[46] In order to overcome this, students should be given clear criteria for assessing their own and their peers' performance. It is helpful to begin by first assessing texts produced by a group, so that the work of one individual is not exposed to criticism. The teacher can ask the class to decide how far the group achieved each element of the task. This could relate to audience (*Is the information appropriate for target readers?*), organization (*Is there a general to specific flow?*), or target language (*Have they used cause and effect expressions appropriately?*). This task can be presented as a game, with points being scored for identifying or correcting problems. More formal self- and peer-assessment can be supported by negotiating specific criteria for giving feedback.

It is important to begin any type of feedback by focusing on the positive aspects. This is not a patronising way of softening criticism, but a means of reinforcing the good habits students already have or are acquiring. When people are learning a new skill, such as riding a bicycle or playing a musical instrument, there is a point at which they realize what it feels like to get it right. Teachers can create similar feelings about writing by displaying a text written by a group, and asking students to guess what the teacher liked about it. Students thus focus on the successful features of the text rather than criticizing its failings. They might identify the use of elements which have been recently taught such as summarizing noun phrases or general to specific structure.

Classroom materials 6.3 *A class profile* shows how students can use this technique to compare a model answer with their own or a partner's text.

Chapter 4: *Reading* encourages a global approach to reading which focuses on the purpose and main points in a text before close reading for details. This applies equally to self- or peer-assessment of students' writing. Students can be asked to highlight the main points or claims in their text in one colour, and then highlight in a different colour sections where these claims are expanded or justified. The main claims will often be functional generalizations or include language showing importance or significance, e.g., *The main reason for... is...; There are three factors which influence...; There are several differences between...* The patterns of the two alternating colours make the students' own narrative voice visible, and reveal how far the writing achieves its purpose. If there are large un-highlighted stretches in the text, students can reflect on whether this content is relevant. If the pattern of the two colours seems to be random, students can evaluate the development from general to specific ideas. Once they have assessed the text in this way, students can be given the teacher's feedback in the form of copies of their work marked by the teacher, or pro forma feedback sheets which list the assessment criteria, together with teacher comments on how far the writing meets these.

Students can also be encouraged to evaluate their writing process through reflective statements or blogs. This online form of reflection, with its absence of formality, is one with which they may feel more comfortable. Teachers can encourage this reflection by writing blogs themselves for tasks they set, which describe their own process of producing model answers. Teacher blogs can include an honest description of the difficulties of the task, and show how the teacher decided what content to include and how to organize it. This helps students to understand the choices writers make, and see that even expert writers experience difficulties and frustration when writing.

Model answers for an assignment are essential for giving feedback. Students can use the model to identify how the criteria for the task were achieved, and compare this with their own task achievement. Models written by the teacher should be written quickly, and not polished. This avoids setting standards that are impossible for students to achieve, and allows students to identify where improvements could be made. Student texts make excellent models because they showcase good student writing, and demonstrate that it is possible for students to achieve a task while writing within their competence, without expert command of language.

Despite the value of structured self- and peer-assessment, studies show that students value teacher-assessment.[47] The teacher's reading of EAP students' texts is probably their only opportunity to have their writing read by an expert questioning reader, responding to ideas that are interesting, and commenting on what is puzzling or unclear.[48] It is important for the teacher to respond first as a reader, interested in the ideas, and only second as an editor, looking for surface mistakes. The response needs to be captured as it occurs, as an audio recording while reading, or as an online comment, e.g., using the *insert comment* function in Word™, or in a writing conference, where the students can react to the comments in order to explain what they were trying to say. Teacher time is a scarce commodity and, therefore, should be used as efficiently as possible. This means that the teacher's response should be based on aspects of writing that the student can realistically improve in the time available.

Students are more likely to be able to correct global aspects of their writing in a short time than to improve grammatical accuracy. It is, therefore, more useful to focus on aspects such as text organization, topic maintenance, and the use of functional language to signal relationships between ideas. This means that teachers need a good understanding of text analysis, as outlined in Chapter 2, in order to identify exactly what is happening in student writing. Vague comments, such as 'Well, it just doesn't sound right' or 'The language doesn't help my understanding of what you are saying', are not helpful feedback for student writers.

Classroom
materials 9.2
*Correction code
and error log*
gives a sample
correction code
and suggestions
for training
students to
take responsibility
for correcting
their work.

The focus on surface language errors should form the final stage of feedback and is best dealt with by handing over the responsibility for these errors to students. A selection of common errors can be discussed and corrected, with the whole class using a correction code. Individuals can then log their recurring errors, and check their work for examples of these errors before it is submitted. Teachers can also negotiate with students what level of correction is required, e.g., by asking them to specify what they want the teacher to focus on in the feedback. There is no point in the teacher correcting every omission of the third person singular –s on present tense verbs or correcting every misuse of articles. It is more likely that correct usage of these items will be acquired gradually through daily exposure and use of the language, or may not be acquired at all.[49]

The most valued type of feedback is a personal writing conference. As time is so limited, this should be well prepared for, with an agenda, like any other important meeting.

Task 13

- How would you prepare for a feedback conference on a student's writing in order to make best use of the time available?

- Who would decide the focus of the feedback?

Preparing for an effective conference involves fixing a suitable time and a place which is private and free from interruption, and where the student feels comfortable. A fixed duration needs to be agreed so that some students do not get an unreasonable allocation of time. Students should be encouraged to make the most of conferences by taking responsibility for the focus of the discussion, e.g., making sure they understand and can respond to the teacher's feedback. The teacher must be given sufficient time to mark and return the text before the conference, so that the student can select aspects of the feedback they would like to discuss. A useful way to do this is by e-mail: the teacher sends the marked text to students, who then prepare their own questions or responses, and e-mail them back to the teacher or note them on their texts. This sets up a professional atmosphere and clear expectations on both sides about what will be discussed. A conference is a dialogue about writing, and any disciplinary issues or student complaints should be saved for other occasions.

It is important for the teacher to avoid dominating the conference and forcing the student to adopt a passive role. The conference should be a dialogue, with the student's text and its meaning as the focus, rather than features of the language which interest the teacher.

Task 14

Read the extract from a student's writing in the case study below.

- What general positive and negative points would you make about the student's essay in an e-mail in preparation for a conference?

- What problems would be useful to discuss in the conference?

- What questions could you ask to help the student?

Case study D:
Human resource management[50]

Human resource management (HRM) is generally broken down into three or more functions. The first one of these is recruitment such as selecting application and interviewing candidate. Training is essential function to HRM including on-job-training (OJT) and off-job-training form. The third one, performance assessment (PA), is one of the most important elements for company's management. HRM is multi-function approach supporting system for members and organization's development and benefit.

Recruitment is a process of hiring right people for suitable position. The first step is that job vacancy should be analyzed and discovers core properties belonged to the position...

The second category of HRM functions is training. ...

Probably the most important element of HRM function is PA. PA includes object formulating and assessment. The object formulating shall base on company's plan and be distributed responsibility to employees who is in charge. Recent performance of employees were compared with the object formulating and assessed. Consequently, the outcome of assessment connects with promotion and bonus given. Through PA, management becomes object approach. Not only dose a company manages employee easily, but also the employee is treated fair.

The teacher's initial observations e-mailed to the student were:

The organization at paragraph level is good and the content is interesting and informative. Sometimes it is difficult to understand your noun phrases and the exact meaning of your sentences or the relationships between them.

The student agreed to talk about these aspects in the conference. Here are some of the exchanges between the teacher and student.

- T *(reading aloud) HRM is multi-function approach supporting system for members and organization's development and benefit... I'm not sure,... is HRM an approach or a system?*

- S *Well, it's an approach to make a system.*

- T *You mean… it's an approach that provides a support system?*

- S *Yeah, it's an approach that provides a support system.*

- T *I see – an approach which provides a support system. Do you want to note that? (student writes)*

- T *(reading aloud) … The object formulating shall base on company's plan. That doesn't seem clear. What is object formulating? What sort of object?*

- S *Like the … aim for the company.*

- T *An objective? Is that the word they use in your management texts?*

- S *Yeah, I think it is – I thought object is the same meaning.*

- T *This seems to be a really important phrase in your subject. Can you check this phrase in the management books you read?*

- S *Mm… I'll maybe check that.*

- T *So the formulation of objectives is based on the company plan and then… be distributed responsibility to employees who is in charge. So what is distributed?*

- S *Responsibility… responsibility is distributed…*

- T *Who to?*

- S *The employees who in charge – like the managers…*

- T *So you mean the responsibility is distributed to the managers – is that the senior managers… or the HRM managers, or…?*

- S *No. The managers for the departments… who are recruiting.*

- T *Oh, I see. Do you want to write that down while you remember? (student writes)*

- T *Consequently… Why consequently?*

- S *Well… I don't know… I just thought I needed a word to join…*

- T *It seems clear without it… you say assessed… and then… the outcome of assessment… that seems to link back clearly… given to new information, remember?*

- S *Yeah. OK, maybe I don't need it.*

The teacher, as a questioning reader, found it difficult to understand the phrases that refer to the people and procedures in the student's field. Her protocol was to ask questions to elicit the student's intended meaning. She also reformulated the student's phrases, checking with him if this fitted his intended meaning. Once the student had expressed orally what he wanted to say, she encouraged him to capture it by writing it down. When discussing a technical phrase related to the student's field, *object formulating*, the teacher's intuition was that *objective formulation* was the correct phrase. However, she encouraged the student to go and check academic texts in his field. The EAP teacher is not the expert, and does not have the responsibility to teach technical language. The aim is to make the student more autonomous, and encourage interaction with his subject discipline. In the discussion about *responsibility*, she tried to make him think about the agents in his sentence – who does what to whom. The teacher also helped him reflect on the framework for his writing. The *given to new* information structure[51] he employed, in which the noun *assessment* connects the information given in the previous sentence (*performance is assessed*) to the new information about its connection with promotion and rewards, makes *consequently* unnecessary. He used this word because he had been told previously to use link words to create a structure. In fact, he used the function of classification to create an effective structure for the text, and used noun phrases effectively to maintain the topic flow. The teacher was aware that the student's command of grammar was weak. At the end of the conference, she gave him a copy of the text with the errors indicated, using a correction code, and suggested that as the content and organization were so good, it would be worth producing a more polished version.

While individual conferencing is desirable, it is not always possible. Even marking every student's assignment may be unrealistic for large classes. Solutions include marking only a sample of each assignment. Highlighting students' main points and supporting details in different colours, as described above for peer- and self-feedback, is also a quick marking method for a teacher with little time. A useful way of directing students to the problems of their text is reformulation, in which the teacher rewrites a section of the text as a native speaker would have written it.[52] The student can compare this with their original and note the similarities and differences, and try to decide why the changes were made.

Feedback should provide an opportunity for the student to experience the response of a questioning reader and promote student autonomy, especially through self-assessment and peer-assessment. Feedback should focus first on the purpose of the text and task achievement, and then on how language and organization contribute to these. Positive feedback should be given first so that students can see in which areas they are progressing. The main focus should be on drawing students' attention to aspects of their work they can realistically improve. Surface language corrections should be treated as a separate issue, if needed. After feedback, students should always have the opportunity to redraft their work and have it re-marked (this might take the form of a brief comment on the level of improvement observed), so that they can see the outcome of the feedback process.

Conclusion

The key requirements of academic writing are: the ability to demonstrate in-depth exploration of a specific question or topic; the ability to construct a personal narrative, drawing on sources and data to support claims; and the ability to imagine a questioning reader. Writing depends on reading as a stimulus for ideas, and as a source of information about the expectations of a range of academic genres. Students learn to write by analysing texts to discover their organization, the way ideas flow from one sentence to another, and the functional patterns that show the relationships between ideas. They can then consciously try to incorporate these structures and patterns into their own writing. Students also need to understand that writing is a process of reading and deciding what to say, followed by redrafting work in response to feedback. Oral discussion is an important aspect at all stages of this process. Teachers need to support students in writing with activities which scaffold performance, and provide opportunities for self, peer and teacher feedback. Feedback is most effective if the teacher has a sound understanding of text analysis, and can comment on global meaning and organization rather than surface features of the text.

Further reading

Hyland, K. (1999) Academic attribution: citation and the construction of disciplinary knowledge. *Journal of Applied Linguistics*, 20/3, pages 341–367.

Hyland, K. (2004) *Genre and Second Language Writing*. Michigan: University of Michigan Press.

Hyland, K. and Hyland, F. (2006) *Feedback in Second Language Writing*. Cambridge: Cambridge University Press.

Paltridge, B. (2001) *Genre and the Language Learning Classroom*. Michigan: University of Michigan Press.

Swales, J. M. (2005) *Genre Analysis*. 2nd edn. Cambridge: Cambridge University Press.

Thaiss, C. and Zawacki, T. M. (2006) *Engaged Writers and Dynamic Disciplines*. Portsmouth, New Hampshire: Boynton/Cook Heinemann.

Course books with a functional or genre approach to academic writing

Jordan, R. R. (2004) *Academic Writing Course*. Harlow: Longman.

McCormack, J. and Slaght, J. (2005) *English for Academic Study: Extended Writing and Research Skills*. Reading: Garnet Education.

Pallant, A. (2006) *English for Academic Study: Writing Course Book*. Reading: Garnet Education.

Swales, J. M. and Feak, C. (2004) *Academic Writing for Graduate Students*. 2nd edn. Ann Arbor: University of Michigan Press.

Weissberg, R., and Buker, S. (1990) *Writing Up Research: Experimental Research Report Writing for Students of English*. Eaglewood Cliffs, NJ: Prentice Hall.

Chapter 7: Listening and speaking

> **This chapter will examine:**
>
> - the nature and purposes of listening and speaking in academic contexts
>
> - the difficulties for students who have to cope with listening and speaking beyond their level of proficiency
>
> **You will have the opportunity to:**
>
> - reflect on strategies for teaching academic listening and speaking
>
> - understand how to develop listening and speaking materials for your students

Listening and speaking are usually the first skills international students need when they come to study overseas. However, these may have received less attention than reading and writing in the English classes they attended at home. Students may also be surprised to find that communicative group work is part of their degree studies, and not something peculiar to English classes. They often feel challenged in their first weeks, as the comments below illustrate:

- *I cannot forget the first week after my arrival here because I was in a very difficult situation in terms of speaking and listening in English language.*

- *When I just arrived to here I can't understand anything because of the strong accent. I dare not talk to others.*

- *I did not know we have to discuss with classmates in lectures. I think is very difficult to me.*

Although there is a range of good published EAP material to help students improve their academic listening and speaking skills, it is likely that you will also want to create materials targeted specifically at your students' degree subjects. This chapter looks at the principles underpinning materials design for listening and speaking. It provides suggestions for helping students to develop their listening and speaking proficiency, and to find strategies for coping when they do not understand.

Listening to lectures

Lectures remain an important teaching method at university, mainly because they are seen as an efficient way of delivering information to large groups of people. Although it is becoming increasingly possible to provide course information in electronic formats, 'students learn better by listening, selecting, organising, writing down and reviewing'.[1] Lecturers also try to develop a rapport with students, particularly over a series of lectures.[2] This enables them to check the understanding of the audience, and adjust their content and delivery to suit. For native speaker (NS) students, a lecture is arguably an easier medium through which to receive information, as its structure and language is likely to be less complex than written material.[3] For non-native speakers (NNS), however, a lecture can present a formidable challenge.

Case study A:
Observing non-native speakers in a lecture

I recently attended a two-hour postgraduate lecture which aimed to provide an overview of research techniques and methods required to produce a masters level dissertation. The lecturer had a regional accent and a delivery which included a number of asides and jokes. Over half of the audience comprised NNS, and during the lecture I observed the activities of several seated near me. They listened quietly for about ten minutes and then appeared to take no further notice of the lecturer. A couple talked softly together; one took out a mobile phone and showed it to a friend, and another opened a newspaper in his own language which he read for the rest of the session.

In addition to providing the audience with an overview of research methods, an underlying aim was to improve the efficiency of the supervision process for the dissertation, so that staff did not have to teach research methods to each individual student they supervised. At the end of the lecture, I asked the students beside me what they had understood. They looked a little embarrassed, but agreed that they had understood almost nothing. I asked them what they would do to get the information they needed for the course. They replied, 'Ask my supervisor.'

Task 1

- How far were the aims of the lecture fulfilled?

- What skills did I bring to the listening task which these students did not have?

The lecturer may have achieved his stated aims of providing an overview of research methods, but the underlying aim of the lecture was clearly not achieved for these students since they had understood very little, and intended to ask their supervisors for information about research methods. Of course, the exercise was not wasted as it is likely that the NS and some of the other NNS students had understood the lecture, and would not need so much individual tuition. Although I did not have the students' knowledge of the subject, I had an NS ability to understand most of what the lecturer was saying. I could follow the organization of the lecture, appreciate the jokes, decide what was important and record this in my notes. The following sections will consider this listening process in more detail.

The purpose of lectures

Lectures exhibit a wide range of structures and styles, which vary within and across disciplines.[4] The content may be divided into sections and subsections, or structured as a narrative leading to a conclusion. Alternatively, it may centre on a problem with proposed solutions and their evaluation; it might outline theoretical concepts and show how these can be applied; or it might present a thesis and its justification.[5] In the UK, lectures normally last 45 or 50 minutes, but some may be as long as three hours. The audience may number between 30 and 300 (anything less than 30 is more likely to be a seminar or tutorial, and anything greater than 300 depends on having lecture theatres to accommodate such numbers). Lecturers may read from a script or improvise around a set of notes. They may give dramatic performances, in which questions are purely rhetorical, or their delivery may be interactive, requiring participation from the student audience. Some lecturers include tasks and exercises with feedback. Lectures may involve some or all of these methods of delivery. There may be visual components such as a handout or slides or video, as well as more recent technologies, such as Powerpoint™ or interactive whiteboards.

Task 2

List the possible purposes of a lecture.

- Which of these purposes could be described as knowledge telling and which as knowledge transforming? (Refer back to Chapter 2 page 49 for an explanation of these terms.)

- Which of these purposes might your students be aware of?

Lectures at university may have some of the following purposes: [6]

- to present the subject matter of a course
- to engage students' enthusiasm for the subject
- to highlight, in the view of the lecturer, what is important in the subject
- to give a framework for study, and show how material from sources such as textbooks fits into this
- to explain difficult aspects of the subject, and give relevant examples
- to demonstrate how theoretical principles can be used to explain phenomena or solve practical problems, especially in science and engineering
- to present points of disagreement in the subject, and give the lecturer's stance
- to demonstrate how the discipline evaluates and uses knowledge
- to develop students' ability to think critically within the discipline, by challenging them or by demonstrating a critical approach

Only the first purpose above could be described as knowledge telling, i.e., direct transmission of the subject matter; the remainder are intended to promote deeper, transformational learning. However, students may not be aware of some of these purposes,[7] particularly the last two. They may have little experience of independent or critical enquiry. They may have come from educational contexts where they were required to learn a specified body of material, and where lectures were seen as no more than a means to provide this material.[8] This view may lead them to consider lectures to be unimportant if the material is available in textbooks. They may also have different priorities and levels of engagement with the subject, wanting only to note what will be in the exam or when their coursework submissions are due. This mismatch between students' and lecturers' purposes, together with the challenging task of listening, can make understanding lectures very difficult for students.

Skills for listening to lectures

Listening to lectures requires a number of activities, at different levels of processing, to be performed simultaneously.[9] In order to understand the content, students must use bottom-up processing skills to decode the stream of speech, and distinguish words and phrases which refer to the topic from those which, for example, signal the structure of the lecture or are intended to promote empathy with the audience. They must be able to ignore unknown vocabulary or to guess it – in real time – from the context. If the lecturer is improvising from a set of notes, they will have to cope with features of spoken language such as false starts, hesitation fillers and repetition. Parts of the lecture, for example, throwaway remarks, may be delivered more softly and quickly than the main points. The lecturer's accent and speed of delivery, or the informality of the language used, may affect students' ability to do these tasks.

In addition, students need to use top–down processing skills to understand the organization of the lecture and follow the development of the topic, recognizing the main points and their relationship to supporting ideas and examples. There may be a narrative thread or metaphor being used to structure the lecture which students need to recognize each time it is repeated. They need to understand the role of asides in explaining apparent contradictions between ideas, highlighting contrasts, or establishing relevance to the course.[10] They need to be able to infer relationships between ideas, e.g., cause and effect, and relate new ideas to their prior learning or experience. They also need to understand the attitude of the lecturer towards the ideas being presented and decide how this agrees with, or contradicts, other views of the topic, e.g., those they have read in textbooks.

Students must also recognize when the lecturer is injecting an interpersonal note, using jokes which are intended to lighten up a long monologue and reduce tension.[11] In a UK context, jokes and other cultural references might be used by lecturers to promote solidarity with the students, and reduce the power distance. Students from countries where teachers and learners are in a 'culturally established hierarchical relationship'[12] may not welcome this attempt, preferring the lecturer to remain aloof. Furthermore, when students cannot understand the jokes or references, the effect is the opposite of that intended, making them feel excluded from the group.

As they listen, students are expected to take notes, which will allow them to retrieve information later. Lecturers may try to help this process by indicating the overall structure and purpose of the lecture in visuals and handouts. They may vary their intonation to indicate the end of one section and the start of a new one. They may use textual signalling language: macro-markers, which state how the sections of the lecture fit together or link to other parts of a course, and micro-markers such as *but, well, now, so*. As well as signalling relations in meaning, these are also used to indicate where the lecturer moves to a new idea. However, students with a low proficiency level for listening may be unable to recognize the function of intonation, or distinguish signalling language from content language. They may find it difficult to listen, read and take notes at the same time. They may fail to recognize that they should supplement information contained in visuals and handouts with interpretive and evaluative comments made by the lecturer.[13]

Studies which attempt to assess student understanding of lectures[14] have found that the quality or quantity of students' notes does not necessarily reflect their level of understanding. Notes are sometimes simply a record of key words that students recognize and they do not capture the main points of a lecture. Rost[15] suggests that accurate understanding of the content may not be students' main goal while listening. Instead, they may be trying to identify areas of understanding into which they can integrate new ideas. King[16] found that students who formulated their own questions or summaries during the lecture were better able to remember the content than those who took notes. This may be because these generative strategies enhanced their ability to process the content.

Clearly, listening to lectures and taking notes is a challenging task, even for those who already have a native command of the language and can concentrate on the lecture content, new ideas and terminology. For non-native speakers, it represents a huge challenge, and many respond in the same way as the students in Case study A. Nevertheless, students do cope surprisingly well with lectures. How do they do this?

Task 3

Imagine that you have missed a lecture, either for study or work, that you really wanted to attend.

- What would you do to get the information presented in the lecture?

- How would you get a sense of the purpose of the lecture (see the list on page 219)?

You could ask your friends who attended for their notes, and discuss with them their understanding of the purpose of the lecture. Of course, it is always possible that they may not have recognized all the lecturer's intentions. In that case, you might look for other sources of information, such as books or papers that the lecturer has written. These are the strategies many students use when they have failed to understand a lecture, and they often set up informal study groups with friends for this purpose. Sometimes lecturers recognize and encourage this kind of study support.

Reducing students' anxiety about listening

When preparing students for university study, e.g., in pre-sessional courses, it is important to acknowledge the challenges of listening and the difficulty, even for fluent speakers, of taking accurate notes. Students need to be advised not to set themselves impossible goals when listening to lectures. Note-taking, although clearly important, can be given undue emphasis in EAP listening classes, perhaps because it has a set of exponents which can be easily presented and practised. Other activities, such as discussing listening strategies and then exploring their effectiveness, should be included to help to reduce students' anxiety about listening. Students also need to decide for themselves what counts as progress. Jordan[17] reported a survey in a UK university, in which students said listening was the main difficulty when they first arrived, but was much less a concern after six months of immersion in an English-speaking environment.

Differences between lectures and listening skills lessons

In this section, you will reflect on some of the differences between academic lectures as described above and listening skills lessons you have taught, either with EAP or general English (ELT) students. This will help you to evaluate the listening activities you use, and decide how far they would be useful for students preparing for university study.

Task 4

- What materials and tasks do you use to develop your students' listening skills?

- How similar are these materials and tasks to the purpose and content of authentic academic lectures as outlined above?

  Make notes in the left-hand side of the following table.

	EAP/ELT listening skills lesson	Academic lecture
Listening material		at least 50 minutes long
		topics covered in depth
		one of a series in which the subject matter is developed over several weeks
		considerable recycling of concepts and vocabulary

Delivery		often conversational – delivered from notes or memory
		contains features of spoken language, such as false starts, hesitation fillers and repetition
		uses incomplete phrases or clauses – signalled by pauses or micro-markers, e.g., *well, so, now, OK.*
		uses macro-markers to signpost lecture organization, but also to link to previous or future lectures
Purpose		subject content is the main focus – see list of purposes on page 219
Before listening		students can choose to read a textbook to prepare key vocabulary
		builds on previous input to develop understanding of key terms/ideas
While listening		only heard once (unless students record it) – although key ideas may be summarized several times
		visual aids support the lecture, showing structure and key terms or ideas
		students may take notes in order to do coursework or answer exam questions some time after listening

After listening		students can read the set text and attend follow up tutorials
		the content will be assessed in coursework or an exam

Listening material in an ELT classroom is rarely similar to academic lectures.[18] It is usually very short (less than ten minutes), and often scripted with few of the features of spoken language. Signalling language is only used to show when the speaker is moving to a new topic within the text; it does not refer outside the text to other lectures or reading material. Signalling language may also be overused and thus seem artificial over short stretches of discourse. Even at advanced levels of proficiency, the topics are not usually covered in great depth. Each listening passage is usually discrete with little connection to previous listening material or recycling of ideas and vocabulary to build on previous content knowledge.

The purpose of a listening lesson in a general English class is usually language acquisition. Although the comprehension tasks may focus on meaning, the aim is to provide comprehensible language input which requires the learners to collaborate in negotiating their understanding of the meaning, and to produce language output which can be understood by their peers. This comprehensible output in the form of discussion or writing does require students to have content knowledge, but it need only be superficial. This is very different from a lecture, where content and its application is the primary focus, and it is these aspects which will be assessed later on. Skills such as note-taking are valuable in lectures only if they enable students to retrieve content accurately and appropriately. They do not receive any credit for the quality of their note-taking and are free to choose other strategies to record and revise content.

Pre-listening activities can form the longest phase of a listening lesson. The teacher chooses tasks to set the context and activate students' knowledge of the topic, e.g., by predicting likely content. The teacher may also present key vocabulary items judged to be important for understanding meaning. In lectures, on the other hand, there is no pre-listening phase. The students come to the lecture with content and key vocabulary already in mind from previous lectures or textbooks, which they may have reviewed in tutorials or study groups.

In a typical ELT listening activity, students listen first for gist and then a second or third time for detail, and answer a set of questions to check their comprehension. In a lecture, students listen once and make their own decisions about what to pay attention to and what to record. The notion of attending first to gist, and then to detail in ELT listening activities, has been transferred from the teaching of reading skills. This is a useful reading strategy because it allows students to see the big picture in a text which they are then able to re-read. However, it is not very useful for listening to lectures because students cannot usually revisit the text. Instead, they need to develop their ability to hold a mental representation of new ideas in short-term memory, and integrate these with knowledge and experience in long-term memory as the lecture proceeds.[19]

Post-listening activities for ELT students usually involve giving their personal opinions, whereas students at university are required to engage with the subjects they are studying at a deeper level, through reading and tutorial discussion. Topics in ELT classes are rarely recycled, whereas the material in lectures must be supplemented and revised for exams.

Developing EAP students' listening competence

Listening skills activities in the EAP classroom can seem to simulate the target situation more authentically than an ELT listening lesson because EAP listening activities are often based on a lecture on an academic topic delivered by a native speaker. However, the format of the lesson often follows the ELT model, with the aim of making the content of this authentic material familiar through repeated listening at the same pace as the target performance. This renders the experience of listening highly inauthentic for students. The difficulties for NNS students arise because they do not have enough language, and cannot listen and take notes as fluently as they can in their first language. Lessons which prioritize the authenticity of the material and the pace of delivery do so at the expense of exploring effective listening strategies which enable students to listen beyond their current level of competence. There needs to be a trade-off between different types of authenticity, and this should be approached in a principled way.

A principled approach to authenticity

Authenticity can be considered in terms of goals, materials, interaction, processes and tasks.[20] The most authentic goal is the target performance, where students listen to a series of lectures, supported by readings, and use the content in coursework or exams. Teachers often feel they should aim to simulate this, but the constraints of the EAP classroom will usually make target performance a rare event. However, it is important to keep this ultimate goal in mind so that you can be aware how far listening activities depart from it.

Authenticity of materials is often achieved through live lectures, given by invited speakers, or recordings of these. It is tempting to assume that authenticity of materials simply involves academic topics delivered by native speaker lecturers. However, in many academic contexts, lecturers may not be native speakers, and there are other contributing factors which may limit the use of authentic lectures in the EAP classroom, such as duration, purpose, structure, style of delivery, and specificity of topic. In EAP classes with students from a range of disciplines, it will be necessary to compromise on authenticity of topic by using lectures on general academic topics which all students can understand. If the content has to be non-specific, it should not, therefore, be the main focus of a listening lesson or the basis for choosing listening material.

Authenticity of interaction between the lecturer and the students in a live lecture is absent in recorded lectures, although a recording can be paused after a question from the lecturer, to give students time to think about an answer. Published materials can be made more authentic in this respect by reducing the lecture to note form and delivering it yourself.[21] This adds elements of spontaneous spoken discourse with the option to repeat or summarize ideas.

Authenticity of process can be considered in terms of the strategies which contribute to the target performance. These include activating prior knowledge of the topic, predicting likely content, decoding the stream of speech, monitoring performance while listening, and developing a mental representation of ideas.[22] These strategies can be introduced in the listening lesson and explored systematically by reducing the authenticity of the target performance in terms of the pace of delivery. Students can listen in 'slow motion': working through the material with regular pauses to isolate and practise aspects of the process in a highly supported way. This reduces the number of simultaneous activities they have to perform, and hence the cognitive processing load. For example, before they listen, students can work on dictations of short extracts from the lecture which contain key vocabulary and ideas. This kind of support reduces the amount of bottom–up processing required, and introduces some ideas from the lecture into working memory. Students can then pay more attention to global aspects, such as organization and the links between ideas, and improve their ability to monitor these. The reduction in authenticity of the target performance is compensated for by increased process authenticity because slowing down the pace of delivery allows students to obtain a better mental representation of the content. This use of dictation prior to listening might seem surprising because it effectively gives students an understanding of the passage before they listen. However, it is only surprising if we consider a listening skills lesson to be a test of students' ability to achieve target listening performance. Understanding part of the material before listening to all of it is a better simulation of authentic performance than listening several times at authentic speed.

Authenticity of task concerns the appropriacy of the listening tasks used in the lesson. Comprehension questions often ask about specific details that students might be expected to catch from the stream of speech, and they tend not to check students' understanding of the main purpose, or the connection between ideas, both of which require more global understanding. Class time is used more effectively if some aspects of task complexity are controlled to enable others to be singled out for notice and practice.[23] For example, providing students in advance of the lecture with a complete set of notes which clearly indicate the structure and the main points reduces the amount of top–down processing they need to do and allows them to concentrate on decoding the stream of speech. If the notes are similar to lecture handouts, this also contributes to authenticity of process.

In a general English listening lesson, post-listening tasks tend to focus on negotiating meaning and producing comprehensible output, rather than on the exact recall of language used to achieve the meaning. However, for language acquisition to occur, students need to focus on form as well as meaning, so it is important to include tasks which help students notice language.[24] This also applies in EAP listening classes, where the focus on form can involve noticing characteristic features of lecture purpose and organization as well as the language used to achieve this. For example, students can work with a transcript to identify the purpose of a lecture and its organization, e.g., a narrative, an argument or a problem with solutions. They can then focus on the language which signposts that organization or indicates the functional relationships between ideas. This helps students to recognize language cues, which tell them how to view the content of the lecture, so they can concentrate on retrieving the meaning. These tasks develop their ability to listen on two levels: paying attention to content, and using strategies for monitoring, evaluating and checking their understanding.

EAP listening lessons should enable students to develop strategies for listening beyond their current level of competence by supporting performance, rather than testing it. Each type of authenticity can be controlled systematically to contribute to this overall goal. At the beginning of a course, extreme process and task inauthenticity allows for highly supported, slow motion performance in class. Support can be gradually withdrawn until students can decide for themselves how best to retrieve and record the meanings they need. It is also essential to link supported classroom activities explicitly to self-study, by making materials available outside class, and providing additional material and tasks on related topics which are closer to authentic listening.

Classroom materials 7.1 *Academic listening strategies* shows an activity for using experimental and control groups to evaluate pre-reading as an aid to understanding lectures.

When selecting materials and designing tasks for classroom activities, your main aim should be to enable students to listen beyond their current level of competence. This may involve quite inauthentic tasks and processes at first, but these can be given greater authenticity by creating an atmosphere of exploration and experiment in the classroom. For example, the class can be divided into groups which each try out different strategies, e.g., for accessing prior knowledge. Post-listening discussion then involves deciding which one was more effective.

Finding listening material

Task 5

- Where do you usually find listening material for your students?

- How authentic is it compared to the features of academic lectures in the table in Task 4?

Good approximations to authentic lectures are off-air recordings of quality television documentaries.[25] They often have clear functional links between ideas, e.g., comparing old and new situations, or explaining causes and effects. The choice of what to film and how to edit the sequence of pictures allows the film-maker to establish a clear stance towards the content.[26] They are an appropriate length and often include some form of unscripted dialogue or interaction. While the visual images may not signal structure in the same way as a Powerpoint™ or handout, they provide a better support to comprehension than purely audio material.

As well as inviting subject lecturers to give guest lectures, you can also simulate lectures by taking your students on guided visits (if you work in an English-speaking environment). In both these cases, the experience is enhanced if there is good liaison between the speaker and the teacher beforehand, to ensure appropriate and predictable content. If outside speakers are not available, a group of EAP teachers can each prepare a lecture and deliver it in rotation to a number of classes. This is useful for professional development, as it raises teachers' awareness of the features of long monologues and how they might support students' understanding of them. It also provides an opportunity for students to practise taking notes and checking understanding in a supportive environment. As well as lectures which present information, it is essential to include ones which present a viewpoint or evaluate ideas, in order to familiarize students with these knowledge transforming purposes.

It is essential to make a transcript of listening material you have recorded, as it is easier to see patterns of organization and functional or discourse-structuring language in a written text. It also helps you decide what to focus on during the listening tasks and how best to support students in understanding the content of the lecture. Creating a transcript requires an investment of time and effort although television documentaries sometimes provide transcripts on a website. Sharing materials with colleagues to build a bank of lectures and transcripts reduces the amount of time each teacher spends on materials development.

Below is a transcript of a short off-air recording. It was part of a Channel 4 series called 'Black Holes of Science'. This lecture is entitled 'Glue' and was delivered by Professor Richard Gregory. The speaker's delivery was quite fast and somewhat unclear. The transcript is laid out in paragraphs to show when the speaker moves to a new idea. Signals for these new ideas are underlined, asides are shown in round brackets, and the actions seen on the video are in italics in square brackets.

Task 6

Analyse this text using the following questions.

- What is the lecturer's purpose?
- How close is it to any of the purposes listed on page 219?
- What organization has been selected to achieve that purpose?
- What are the stages or moves through which this organization proceeds?
- What type of signpost language is used to indicate a move to the next stage?
- What are the main ideas in the lecture?
- How is the relationship between the ideas managed?
- What features of the delivery might cause difficulties for students?

Something that puzzles me is glue.
Why is it that one glue will stick to one thing; that thing will stick to something else but it won't stick to another substance or object? What is the relationship between glue and the surfaces of objects? Now when we're at school we learn a lot about Chemistry (I never learned a lot actually but one does, one's supposed to) of liquids and you find out about reactions between liquids. What we're actually interested in though, really, is objects and how they react to each other. Now I've got a non-stick frying pan here.

Why doesn't that stick to food and how does the non-stick surface stick to the pan?

Because obviously it does stick to a non-stick surface. And what happens if I take an ordinary glue (and this calls itself universal glue) and I've got a bit of wood and I'm going to put some glue on it. *[the speaker glues the piece of wood to the pan and holds it there]* This is an experiment. I don't know the answer to this myself. This is something I know nothing about. So I'm going to put it on the pan and hold it for a bit and see what happens.

Now it's clear, isn't it, that there are molecular, atomic perhaps, forces within an object, which hold the bits of it together, and when it's one object which sticks to another object with a glue, there are obviously complex forces at the atomic level, which we can't see and I gather that they're very difficult actually to measure, these forces, and I think Russian scientists recently have made advances in this. So I rather think, actually, that exactly how glue works is not really known very well in science. Whatever the case, I often think that, you know, questions... that exciting things that make us live in our heads, that make us have fun talking to each other and experimenting with objects.

So let's see what's happened in this little experiment. If I turn the pan upside down with the piece of wood on it, what happens? It's stuck. Now I wonder how actually stuck that is. I'm going to give it a bit... *[the speaker tries to move the piece of wood]* Oh that's stuck quite well... or has it? *[the piece of wood comes unstuck]* Well, I don't really know the answer now. How much stick has there got to be before we say that glue sticks. I don't think that's good enough for carpentry. Probably want to say that's not really stuck very well.

But what would be fun would be to get lots of glues, lots of different kinds of objects and see what sticks to what and then you'd get the sort of relationship between objects that stick and glue, and hopefully, after it, an explanation of what's going on at the atomic hidden level and the tiny minutiae of matter. Wouldn't that be fun?

The original purpose of this recording was to promote public understanding of science, and to demonstrate to a non-specialist audience how scientists carry out experiments. This matches some of the purposes on page 219, for example, engaging enthusiasm for the subject and demonstrating how theoretical principles can be used to explain phenomena or solve practical problems. Although the recording is very short, the purpose is reasonably authentic for an audience of undergraduate students, and the topic is accessible for a mixed discipline class of scientists and engineers.

The lecture is organized around the stages of an experiment, and the lecturer actually performs the experiment as he talks. Because the lecture is very brief and self-contained, it does not contain macro-markers which show how sections fit together, or link to other lectures. Instead, the lecturer uses the micro-markers *now, and, so, well* and *but* and cleft sentences (*what would be fun*) as signposts for new ideas. The relationship between ideas is managed through questions about the steps in the experimental process. Although not apparent from the transcript, the speaker's delivery was fast and unclear, with some faster and softer asides, causing difficulty even for native speakers.

Designing listening tasks

Task 7

- What tasks and activities would you suggest to accompany this material in order to work on listening strategies with a class of students who had just started a pre-sessional course?
  You could focus on the listening process and the organization of the lecture (rather than the topic) and think about the following questions:

- When would you let students use the transcript?

- How would you help students to cope with the delivery both before and while they listen?

- How would you encourage students to collaborate to take notes and share their understanding?

- What language would you direct the students to notice in the transcript?

- What follow-up would you suggest for self-study?

In EAP listening lessons, decisions about when and how often to listen and how much of the lecture to listen to at any time will depend on the strategies selected for practice. The following activities, based on the lecture about glue, involve listening only once but pausing several times and providing maximum support for the tasks. This slows down the listening process, and reduces the authenticity of performance considerably. General suggestions are given for withdrawing support and thus increasing performance authenticity.

Preparation and listening

The purpose and organization of this lecture are its most interesting aspects. Science and engineering students are likely to be familiar with the stages of an experiment, so these can be elicited and linked explicitly to the purpose of the lecture for the original audience. This values the students' prior experience, and also sets up a framework for a mental representation of the content.

In this lecture, students will need help to understand the fast, unclear delivery of the lecturer. This can be provided before they listen, using dictation of the first part of the lecture to the end of: 'What we're actually interested in though, really, is objects and how they react to each other'. This covers various aspects of delivery: there are two questions, the second a more academic reformulation of the first, and an aside, shown in brackets in the transcript. This part also contains key vocabulary, and establishes the main point of the lecture: investigating the reaction of substances to one another. The whole extract could be dictated slowly the first time, increasing the speed for each repetition, until it matches the pace of the lecture.[27] This type of support can be reduced in subsequent lessons, or for more proficient students, by decreasing the length of the extracts or introducing gaps. In this example, students could work with the first question, and the second, more academic, reformulation could be elicited or retrieved as they listen. For longer lectures, a summary of the main ideas can be prepared for dictation.

Since the content of this lecture is not particularly difficult for students, there is little to be gained from asking detailed questions to check comprehension. Instead, students can be given a task with a big picture question about the main point, which groups have to discuss and agree an answer. Questions for this lecture might be: 'Was the experiment successful?' or for advanced levels: 'What is the relationship between glue and the surfaces of objects?'

In order to develop strategies to support the listening process, Field[28] suggests modelling strategies that students might use in their own language. For example, native speakers do not always hear every word, so they make inferences from the context about content they have not heard clearly. Practice in such strategies can be devised for the lecture about glue by asking students to listen from the beginning (which is now familiar) up to the part where the professor sets up the experiment, which ends 'So I'm going to put it on the pan and hold it for a bit and see what happens'. Students focus on the unfamiliar part of the extract, and write down words they can pick out from the stream of speech, noting how sure they are about each one. They then try to reformulate this part of the lecture, using the words they noted, the visual context, and the mental representation set up from the first part of the lecture. They can then check their version by listening from the beginning again.[29]

Another way of providing a high level of support for the listening process is by giving students the lecture transcript. They can read it as they listen, and then put it away while they discuss their understanding of the main points. Each student can then choose whether to listen again (and whether to use the transcript again) in order to complete tasks which show their understanding.[30]

As students gain confidence, the challenge in these activities can be increased by selectively deleting sections of the transcript, e.g., where the lecturer paraphrases or summarizes ideas, and asking students to supply the ideas. Instead of the transcript, students can be given a summary which does not match the lecture monologue precisely. In the lecture about glue, the point at which the lecturer discusses the theory behind the experiment could be supported with the following summary. The underlined words are all used in the lecture and could be gapped to further reduce the support.

> The underlined words are all used in the lecture and could be gapped to further reduce the support.

The <u>relationship</u> between glue and the surfaces it <u>bonds</u> to is not well understood. Some recent <u>advances</u> have been made by Russian scientists, who have tried to <u>measure</u> the molecular <u>forces</u> acting between two objects <u>glued</u> to each other. These forces may be similar to the <u>bonds</u> which hold atoms and <u>molecules</u> together but they are likely to be much <u>weaker</u>.

For advanced proficiency levels, the video could be stopped at this point and the students asked to provide an oral summary themselves. If they are unable to do this, they could formulate questions they would like to ask. In real academic settings, lecturers sometimes open up spaces in a lecture for students to seek clarification, so this task simulates authenticity of process and interaction.

Once students have explored a variety of strategies through highly supported, slow motion listening lessons, they can be given more autonomy through peer support, with the listening material delivered at a more authentic pace. Students can experiment with jigsaw tasks to share the listening load: in pairs they can listen selectively[31] for different types of information, and then discuss what they heard to build a complete picture. This type of task can be used to focus attention on particular information or rhetorical functions, e.g., students can be directed to note either causes or effects, similarities or differences in a lecture. For example, in the lecture about glue, different students could be asked to listen for information about a particular stage of the experiment. Another way of sharing the listening load in pairs or groups is for one or more students to take notes while others simply concentrate on listening for the development of the ideas. After a short time, agreed in advance, they can exchange roles and then at the end discuss their notes and their understanding. This simulates the real-world coping strategy mentioned on page 221. It also enables students to explore their preferred learning style, e.g., holistic or analytic, and how this might inform their choice of listening strategy.

Note-taking can be practised in a supported way, using a variety of note formats, including graphs, tables or diagrams, to show the main points and organization of the lecture and, in particular, the functional relationships between ideas. These notes can be gapped selectively to provide different amounts of support for a range of proficiency levels at different stages of the course. For minimal support, the organization can be mapped with statements which label the sections of the lecture, and these can be presented in a different order from the lecture, for the students to reorder as they listen. For the example above, the stages of the lecture about glue are:

- a problem or puzzle
- some general questions to frame the problem
- some specific questions to aid experimental design
- theory and other research to help with an explanation
- results and the evaluation of them
- further questions which arise
- replication of the experiment

Individuals vary greatly in their preferred note-taking style, so care should be taken not to impose particular formats. Instead, students should be encouraged to explore a variety of formats, and also to reflect on and discuss the use of their first language in note-taking. Abbreviations should also be presented as a matter for personal choice.

Listening outcomes

Before students use the content of a lecture in discussion or writing, it is important to include tasks which focus on the organization and language which enabled them to understand the content. The transcript, or a summary of the lecture, can be used to highlight key functional and discourse-structuring language and features of spoken delivery. Often, the contrast between spoken and written language can be found within a lecture. Alternatively, a prepared summary can be compared with the transcript.

Training to improve students' ability to hold strings of sounds in working memory long enough to decode and process them can be developed both before and after the lecture. Students can be given dictoclips, short sections of the lecture (usually less than a minute), to listen to and transcribe accurately. The students, rather than the teacher, control the number and length of repetitions. This also works well as a regular self-access activity.

Post-listening discussion of the content should have a focused outcome. Students can be asked to compare the ideas with their previous knowledge and experience, or to preparatory texts they have read. They can also be encouraged to ask questions about what they have heard, e.g., *What if...? What next...?*[32] For this lecture, they might discuss whether experiments like this are carried out in their target discipline and describe some examples.

Listening skills improve with practice and familiarity with the topic, so students need to listen as much as possible outside the classroom. However, they need guidance and support from the teacher in order to learn how to listen by themselves. This may involve training in using self-access facilities, and initial monitoring of this use. Students can be required to keep a listening log, in which they comment on the usefulness of any strategies they practised, and say whether they think their listening has improved. Self-access is more effective if it is linked closely to classroom activities. Once the students have understood a lecture and worked on developing listening strategies in a highly supported way in class, they can listen to the lecture again in self-access, or to other lectures on related topics, to experience the target performance in a more authentic way. For full-length lectures, students can work on only the first part in class, then complete listening in self-access, and prepare for a class discussion in the next lesson. Alternatively, students can agree in advance to watch or listen to a news or factual programme on television, radio or the Internet and report back in class. This extensive listening is closer to listening at university, as it gives students an authentic purpose, and hands them the responsibility for managing their time outside class.

Conclusion

In order to help students to cope with the demands of retrieving information from lectures, EAP listening activities can be designed in a principled way based on the notion of authenticity. At the beginning of a course, teachers should focus on authenticity of process and task rather than authenticity of target performance. This means the performance effectively occurs in slow motion, enabling students to develop strategies for listening. The approach should be developmental, providing a high level of support at the beginning which is gradually withdrawn as the course proceeds. Close links should be made between activities inside and outside the classroom to encourage student autonomy.

Speaking in group discussions

Overseas students have a variety of communication needs in academic contexts. In addition to participating in discussions and making presentations on their degree courses, they need to communicate with administrative and academic staff, for example, to find accommodation or open a bank account, borrow library books, ask for help with an assignment, or request an extension to a deadline. In order to integrate socially and make friends, they need conversation skills. For all these situations, students need pragmatic competence: 'the ability to use language effectively in order to achieve a specific purpose and to understand language in context'.[33] Since it is beyond the scope of this book to address all these needs, this section will only consider those speaking skills students require for their degrees.

Many university courses include some form of group discussion to facilitate learning. On undergraduate courses, this may take the form of tutorials led by a lecturer or a postgraduate tutor, which usually have convergent tasks, i.e., problems or questions with precise answers. At postgraduate level, where students are expected to need less guidance, they may be asked to participate in seminars with divergent discussion tasks, i.e., with no specific answer. Preparation may involve reading several research papers or case studies. For courses with a strong vocational orientation, there is also an emphasis on developing communication skills which can be transferred to the workplace. In such courses, learning through group discussion can be formalized into a requirement for team working, with assessed tasks to which all team members must contribute. Once students are working on research projects, either for masters dissertations or doctoral theses, they will have supervision sessions, where they may be expected to take the lead in discussing their research activity.

International students often find academic speaking their most challenging task. They tend to see discussions as public places where they are required to perform in front of a possibly hostile audience of other students, who may laugh at their accent, their language mistakes, or the inadequacy of their ideas, as indicated in the following comments: [34]

- *Unless you are sure your contribution will be good, to save our face we will stay silent.*
- *We need time to get familiar with people to express our ideas.*
- *I'm afraid to be judged in public unless I have confidence.*
- *It's OK to speak if you have permission from another person – if they ask your opinion.*
- *It takes a lot to change; you just want to stay who you are and how you are.*

The conventions of group discussion

The conventions of group discussion are not usually made explicit to students and may be very different from their previous learning experiences. Students who are used to learning from lecturers rather than other students may not take group discussions seriously and, therefore, not prepare well for them.

Task 8

- What do you consider to be the main aims of discussion at university?

- How are discussions expected to facilitate learning?

- What are the unwritten conventions for participating in discussions?

- How is silence viewed?

The main aim of discussion is to reach a deeper level of understanding through analysis and negotiation of ideas. Students demonstrate understanding by being able to reformulate and summarize ideas and concepts, and apply them to new situations or problems. They can also learn from peers whose level of understanding is just above their own.[35] Discussion gives lecturers feedback, as it shows what has not been well understood and needs further explanation. As students move from undergraduate to postgraduate level they become members of the discourse community for their subject. Discussion shows them how this community evaluates research and incorporates it into its knowledge base. It also allows them to participate increasingly in these activities.

Discussions are sometimes likened to conversations in which participants are expected to work together to establish meaning. It is assumed that the power distance between lecturer and students is reduced, and the lecturer may adopt a more informal conversational style of speaking to facilitate this.[36] Nevertheless, talk is not as informal as a conversation because there is usually a specific topic to discuss, for example, a case study, and students are often expected to prepare in advance, even if they are not responsible for presenting the topic. This preparation may require quite a heavy reading load. There is an expectation that everyone will contribute, so silence denotes a lack of involvement.

EAP students often do not know these conventions. They do not always understand the different role a lecturer assumes to facilitate discussion, and they may not recognize that ideas are emergent and co-constructed, rather than presented already formed for inspection and disagreement. Students cite lack of confidence in their spoken skills and content knowledge as key factors which prevent them from participating actively.[37] However, there may be other complicating factors, as the following case study illustrates.

Case study B:
Working in teams

The context of this case study is a taught masters degree in Project Management in a department which specializes in applied and vocational degrees. The course attracts students from a wide range of cultures, who usually have some work experience, and may view postgraduate study as a route into management positions. Team-based working is a fundamental aspect of management by projects, so students are organized into teams of seven or eight at the beginning of the course, using a series of self-perception tests which attempt to assess the type of contribution each person is likely to make to the team. The aim is to achieve a balance in the teams. Students receive input on effective team working and managing conflict. Each team prepares a contract which specifies how the team will work together and share tasks. Lecturers make use of the teams during their lectures, often setting long and challenging discussion tasks which the team members work on together. Within the first five weeks, students are required to submit several team tasks for assessment. Part of each submission includes keeping a record of how the team carried out the tasks, and writing an assessment of how the team is functioning. In a separate task, each team member evaluates the contribution of the others and these evaluations are used to adjust each individual's mark for the task.

On one of the courses, a problem arose with some of the teams. Shortly after the due date for submission of the team tasks, the course director was approached by several students who were native speakers of English (NS) with a complaint about other members of their teams who were non-native speakers (NNS) from Arabic, Asian and Eastern European cultures. The students had drafted a list of the specific problems they were having, and the issues for them in continuing with team working. They highlighted:

- what they considered to be the low level of language proficiency of some NNS, which meant that they appeared not to understand the lectures or the requirements of tasks

- the reluctance (or inability) of NNS to contribute to discussion in class, which lowered the quality of the learning experience for the NS

- the need for the NS to become teachers, helping the NNS with those aspects of the course they had not understood, thus reducing their own time for reading and study

- the need for NS to take over responsibility for team tasks in order to ensure they were completed on time, even though the team contract specified that tasks should be shared

- the likelihood that some NNS were lowering the quality of the team assignments and hence the grades

Task 9

- How far do you think the problems involved language or team or cultural issues?

- Which cultural issues might have been involved?

- Do you have any comments about the attitude of the NS students who complained?

- What would you recommend the course leader do to deal with this situation?

- What could EAP teachers do to help NNS students to function in such settings?

The main problem in this case study was a lack of participation from some members of the team, which the NS students attributed to a low level of proficiency in English. Clearly, this would prevent students from keeping up with the pace of discussion, and making their own contribution. However, all the students had satisfied the requirement for language proficiency before being accepted onto the course. The course director identified some students who had the required language proficiency, but whose coursework results showed they were finding the content of the course challenging. They were possibly relying on the more able students for support. Another factor which may have contributed to the problem is that, in team working, there is always the potential for conflict, with some members being more committed to the team than others. In addition, the teams were rather large and this may have allowed shy members to remain passive.

It is possible that cultural factors may have been involved.[38] In cultures which are influenced by the Confucian tradition, children are taught to be modest and silent. They are encouraged to develop a strong sense of group co-operation and interdependency, and to be self-effacing. The education system reinforces these values. Teachers are viewed as authority figures who transmit knowledge. Students are not encouraged to express opinions publicly, unless they are given permission to do so. They can come to devalue their ideas, and expect to be laughed at if they make mistakes in front of their peers. It might be expected that team-working would be a natural extension of the ethos of group co-operation, but students from these cultures need a lengthy group-forming process before they feel comfortable working in groups with strangers.

It is also possible that the problems stemmed from the NS students' cultural values, where individual needs often take priority. They were concerned about their own grades in the team assignments which may have made them reluctant to allow the NNS to take responsibility for the team tasks. By giving more priority to team working, they could have gained valuable insights into other ways of seeing the world, and learned how to interact in international teams. Instead of resenting the intrusion into their own study time, they could have seen this as an opportunity to learn more deeply by trying to teach others.

In this particular case, the course director decided that the best way to deal with the complaint was to view the problems and issues as resulting from poor team communication, and to try to facilitate better commitment to team working on the part of all students in the team. A team facilitation session was held with all students on the course, in which the issues were aired, and everyone had an opportunity to respond. This enabled the students who had complained to see the effect of their actions. The class was then permitted to form new teams of their own choosing, with fewer members than before. The problem was not fully resolved, but it had been addressed sufficiently for it to be set aside.

Differences between seminar discussions and speaking skills lessons

It is not easy to find out what actually occurs during tutorials, seminars and supervision sessions because it is not easy to gain access to, or record, the activities in these sessions,[39] and it is likely that they vary widely. The findings from one study[40] of a small number of seminar discussions on an MBA programme at a British university provide useful insights, which you can verify in your own context, and use to inform discussion activities you prepare for your students.

Task 10

- What materials and tasks do you use to develop your students' discussion skills?

- How similar do you think these materials and tasks are to the purpose and content of authentic seminars?

  Make notes in the left-hand side of the following table.

	EAP/ELT speaking skills lesson	Seminars in a UK university
Discussion material		convergent tasks[41] with specific answers; related to lecture content
		divergent tasks with negotiated outcomes; related to lecture content
		articles or case studies to prepare in advance of the session
Purpose		to reach a deeper level of understanding through analysis / negotiation of ideas
Role of participants		Students are responsible for preparing and presenting material for discussion.
		The lecturer or tutor adopts a conversational style, encouraging participation.
		Turn-taking is managed non-verbally through eye contact, back channels (*hmm uh huh*) or overlap of utterances.
		Turns are quite long and complex; participants jointly construct meaning; ideas are not formed prior to discussion.
Language		Student talk proceeds via moves eliciting information or confirmation.
		Moves tend to be supported by justification and evidence from reading.
		Moves are usually prefaced with back references or titles to specify the topic or labels to make the intention explicit.
		Speakers indicate varying levels of commitment and politeness with their choice of question types.

Basturkmen[42] identified typical organizational patterns in the exchanges that occurred during MBA seminars and compared these findings with the descriptions and practice tasks in several EAP course books. She found that turns in the seminars could be quite long and complex with participants jointly constructing meaning, which allowed more in-depth ideas and opinions to emerge. EAP descriptions, on the other hand, tended to view discussion skills as the abilities of individual speakers to present ideas and opinions they had already formed prior to the discussion. Whereas student moves in the seminars proceeded through requests for information and confirmation, the guidance offered to EAP students usually took the form of functions such as agreeing, disagreeing and asking for clarification.

In looking closely at the language used in the MBA seminars, Basturkmen found that requests for information and confirmation were usually supported by justification and evidence. These supporting moves served to show that the speakers were informed about the topic but they also had a politeness function. Speakers showed weak commitment to the requests by formulating them using closed or alternative question types (*Did they...? Has it been...? Was it X or Y?*) and stronger commitment by using statements, negative questions or tag questions. Requests for confirmation could be a means of disagreeing with the speaker, e.g.,

'*You mentioned the possibility of a merger but did you consider the possibility of an alliance with other organizations?*'

When speakers brought up a previous topic they tended to orient listeners to it by giving a very brief summary or fronting the topic as a title for their turn, e.g.,

'*...your pan European policy then + has it been...?*'

Speakers also used prefacing devices to label moves in the discourse (*the point I'm making*) both to indicate their intention and make an interruption more polite. Disagreement was usually handled indirectly, perhaps by finding an aspect to agree with before raising a question about a previous speaker's point.

Basturkmen recommended that as well as a focus on functions such as agreeing, EAP course objectives should go beyond the requirement to present preformed ideas and include the ability to 'engage in extended exchanges until a satisfactory outcome is achieved.'[43] Students should be asked to prepare transcripts of short extracts from authentic seminar discussions in order to analyse features of spoken discourse and identify strategies used by experts in discussion.

Supporting students

The situations described in Basturkmen's research and in Case study B illustrate the complex and unpredictable nature of interaction in academic discussion and team work, and the potential for breakdown in communication. EAP teachers cannot control this situation or make it safer for students, but they can prepare them to understand the requirements of group discussion and to gain confidence to take risks in participating.

Awareness

The purpose of group discussion, and the type of learning it is thought to promote, should be made explicit. If students see how discussion skills transfer to work or other settings, they are more motivated to develop these skills. Individuals need time to feel confident in a group before they are willing to contribute. Nevertheless, it is often easier to contribute early on when the group is forming, and ideas are relatively unsophisticated. Students should understand that if they miss that first opportunity, they will probably never contribute.

Students benefit from experiencing real discussions. If possible, you should find out what types of group discussion take place in your institution, and video-record some of these for analysis in the EAP classroom. Alternatively, you can invite lecturers and students into EAP classrooms to talk about discussions, or arrange to have students sit in on tutorials and seminars. The unwritten rules of interaction and turn-taking in group discussion can be made explicit in this way, and compared with the rules in other cultures.

Approaches

Ideally, the topics and tasks for group discussion would be based on content from the students' academic fields. If this is not feasible, you should select topics which require preparation, and can be discussed with academic rigour. Students need to have something to say in discussion, and to base their contributions on evidence and ideas from their reading. Case studies are a good basis for discussion, and you can write these yourself to suit the interest and level of the class.[44] The more successful discussions have an outcome: either a list of criteria, or a decision, or an oral or written presentation of the main points that arose. If provided with a task, students are more likely to engage in discussion, although reticent students may need to be given explicit permission to speak.

Students can be encouraged to take a more realistic view of their own ability, and a positive approach to risk-taking by examining their beliefs using 'rational emotive therapy'.[45] This involves identifying an irrational belief, e.g., 'I must speak good English before I can contribute in group discussion', and then asking students to identify what evidence exists, from their own experience or from analysis of authentic discussions, for the falseness or the truth of this belief.

The EAP classroom environment should encourage talk, and allow students to interrupt politely and ask questions when they do not understand. You may have to open up spaces for student questions, and nominate individual students to speak until they feel comfortable interacting spontaneously in the group. Teachers can reduce their own prominence in the class by sitting down rather than standing, or removing themselves from group activities and avoiding eye contact. Small groups can be used to support individuals, so that ideas presented as held by the group are not the responsibility of one individual. Peer feedback, for example, is less threatening for the students if it is presented as a group rather than an individual evaluation.[46] Talk can be monitored in groups of three to encourage reflective practice, with two students interacting and one observing in turn. Students can be invited to discuss class issues, or comment on and evaluate your teaching aims and materials. If you can respond to students' requests, they learn that their views are important.

Activities

Jones[47] describes a communication game for cross-cultural understanding which can also be used to encourage students to take risks, and to contribute spontaneously to discussion. After reading a text, teams of students in turn ask each other questions about it. Points are awarded for each question and response, but also for appropriate follow-up questions and elaborations. However, no individual can speak for a second time, until each team member has contributed.

Participation in discussions on simple topics can be monitored using tokens, for example, matchsticks, which give permission to speak.[48] Each member of the discussion group has the same number of tokens, but must surrender one each time they speak. Once the active participants run out of tokens, they may not speak unless nominated to do so by another student who still has some tokens. However, the new speaker must end their turn by bringing another team member into the discussion. These activities encourage students to focus on both the content of discussion and the strategies for contributing. Once students are able to manage turn-taking and negotiation of ideas with simple discussion topics, more complex topics which require reading and preparation can be used.

Giving oral presentations

Oral presentation is a key skill in academic life. A great deal of academic knowledge and research is communicated in this way, within an institution in lectures and seminars, within a discourse community at conferences, and to an interested public audience through radio and television. Researchers establish a reputation, and a space for their research, by presenting it at conferences where it can be publicly scrutinized by an audience of peers. In research fields which are highly competitive, it is important to become known as the originator of an idea as quickly as possible before other research groups can claim it for themselves. Conference presentations serve to establish this ownership.

Because oral presentation is highly valued at university and in the workplace, time is devoted on degree programmes to developing this skill. At undergraduate level, students (especially those on vocational courses) may be asked to make group presentations, possibly to an outside audience, for example, from business or industry. At postgraduate masters level, students may be expected to present jointly or individually to initiate discussion in seminars. Once they begin doctoral research, students are usually required to present their research both informally to supervisors, and more formally in viva sessions. In most cases, they are also expected to make conference presentations, and many institutions set up postgraduate conferences to create a platform for this.

Task 11

- What concerns do your students express about giving presentations?

- How far do their concerns match the difficulties experienced by their audience?

The main concern that most students have about making a presentation is the feeling of anxiety about performing in public, although the main difficulty that audiences often have is the incomprehensibility of the presentation in terms of its content and structure, but most often in terms of its delivery. EAP courses can address these issues through graded presentation tasks which raise students' awareness of what constitutes good performance, and provide practice in a supportive environment.

Effective presentations

Effective presentations leave members of the audience feeling that they have had an entertaining conversation with the presenter, which has added to their understanding or changed their way of thinking about a topic. Edwards[49] suggests that the entertainment factor is often played down by academic presenters, but that 'it is impossible to communicate and persuade effectively without keeping your audience entertained', which he takes to mean interested and involved. Although it may seem paradoxical to describe a presentation in this way, many of the features of effective presentations also underpin good conversations, for example, a relaxed posture with some movement (but not too much), good eye contact with the audience, attention to their level of knowledge, and awareness of their needs.

Talking to an audience is not a particularly efficient means of giving them information. Most audiences lose concentration after about 20 minutes, and need a change of activity or pace to renew their attention.[50] An audience will forget much of the detail that a speaker presents unless this can be noted down or related to existing knowledge already held in long-term memory. Good presenters take these aspects into account when preparing their talks. They begin with a general statement of the purpose and rationale for the talk[51] in order to hook the attention of the audience. They pitch the talk at an appropriate level, by setting new information against a background of what they judge will be familiar, and they provide definitions or explanations for any items which they think might cause confusion. An audience needs to be oriented to each new section or point or slide in a talk with a general statement about the content before being given specific details. Good speakers understand that a talk is a very different genre from a written report, so they present their material as a narrative, or explicitly structure their talk using questions and answers.

Guidebooks often recommend the rule of three: tell them what you are going to say; say it; tell them what you said. However, good speakers may also give very brief summaries as the talk proceeds, to help the audience follow the thread. Rather than simply signalling structure, e.g., *Now I'm going to talk about...*, they will use functional signalling language to preface their summaries, e.g., *The reason for* [+ summary of previous point], *The difference between* [+ summary of two items], to make clear to the audience the relationship between ideas.

Academic audiences are usually well disposed towards speakers and want them to perform well, but good speakers do not see this as an excuse to relax. Students need to be reminded that a certain degree of nervousness is needed in order to give a good performance, although too much can be debilitating. A presentation is never effective if read aloud, as the conversational style and audience interaction are lost. For the same reason, it is also not effective if learned by rote and recited. Good speakers aim for a speaking style which seems spontaneous, with space for digressions or anecdotes, although these will be planned to avoid running out of time. The most effective delivery is slower and louder than normal speech. This requires presenters to open their mouths more, and can feel unnatural at first. Good speakers pay attention to achieving accurate word and sentence stress, and to varying pitch and intonation. It is not by accident that the word monotony comes from monotone.

At the end of the talk, the conversational aspect is more evident because an audience usually has a chance to ask questions. Guidebooks often give advice to speakers for responding to questions, but neglect to explain how to ask them effectively. Basturkmen's analysis of questions, mentioned above for seminars, applies also to questions after a talk. Questions are usually asked in order to request additional information or clarify a point. A request for confirmation can often be a polite way to disagree with a point or check if a speaker has considered an alternative explanation or perspective. Effective questions will follow the given-new structure, reminding the speaker of a specific part of the talk, and then asking for an expansion, e.g., *You mentioned*...[summary of speaker's point], but *you didn't say anything about*... [aspect which interests the questioner]. *Have you considered...?*

Supporting students

It is important to help students not to set themselves impossible standards for giving a talk. Awareness of oral presentations comes mainly though television or public speeches, which are usually delivered by very competent speakers who have spent years perfecting their style. Students need a supportive environment to allow them the possibility of performing badly at first, and getting feedback to improve their performance. They also need strategies for dealing with the main difficulties, which are likely to be choice of appropriate structure and content, anxiety about the performance, and problems with delivery.

Awareness

Most students will have experience of watching both good and bad presentations, so you can elicit from them the key features of effective ones. These can be used, together with advice from guidebooks or course books, to build a checklist of criteria for evaluating their own presentations.[52] You can also use this checklist to evaluate video presentations or lectures that have been used in listening classes. If your course incorporates oral presentations as part of student assessment, you can video-record some of these (with the permission of the presenters), and show them to students in subsequent years. Students' anxiety about giving a presentation is reduced when they can see the performance of peers, and when the assessment criteria are made explicit.

Students need a clear understanding of the differences between written and spoken communication. If their oral presentation is based on an essay or research report they have written, they will need help to find a different focus for the information, and an organization appropriate for their audience. For example, a research report in the field of actuarial mathematics which compared different pension schemes was made accessible for a student audience by presenting the findings as a checklist of what to look for in a pension scheme when applying for a job. References in a report, e.g., business trade names or acronyms or specific cultural practices, can cause difficulties for a multi-cultural audience unless they are explained in detail when they are first introduced. Students who have pronunciation difficulties need to be made aware of these, and consciously compensate for them, e.g., using visual aids to provide a supporting format for key terms.

Approaches

The overall aim is to build students' confidence in small steps through which they progress from giving short mini-presentations on familiar topics to longer presentations on topics related to their degree studies. The topics should always specify a purpose and audience, even in mini-presentations, so that thought has to go into the content, organization and links between ideas. Critical questioning at the end of a rehearsal helps students to approach the presentation task in an academic way. The content of several mini-presentations might build into the introduction for a longer presentation, e.g., by giving students practice in introducing themselves, their institution, and their degree subject or research interests. This would form an appropriate introduction for a postgraduate conference, where presenters are likely to come from different institutions.

Student anxiety about giving the talk can be reduced if the key content, vocabulary and pronunciation for the beginning of the talk have been rehearsed sufficiently to become automatic. This makes it easier for the student to begin the presentation, and get to the main part. You should try to avoid asking students to learn cumbersome fixed phrases to structure their talks, e.g., *I have divided my talk into … parts*. As the example lecture about glue shows, simple micro-markers and conversational phrases, e.g., *I'm going to talk about…, Now I'll look at…*, are better suited to a general audience.

In order to improve their performance, students need feedback, but the type of feedback and the order in which to give it are important. Feedback is less threatening if it begins with self-assessment followed by peer feedback, and then teacher feedback. Peer feedback can be based on checklists or assessment criteria previously discussed. It can also be given indirectly, e.g., listeners can be asked to reconstruct the main points, thus indicating how much of the information they obtained. Both these types of activity give the audience a purpose for listening. Teacher feedback should focus mainly on the organization and content: whether the speaker's purpose was clear, and the main points easy to understand; whether the content was academic, and the speaker provided sufficient evidence for the claims made. Feedback on surface features, such as grammatical accuracy or signalling language, should focus on just those aspects which reduce comprehensibility, and which the presenter will be able to improve in the time available, so as not to take the emphasis away from the main point of a presentation: saying something interesting for the audience. Teacher feedback can be given privately as it may not be relevant to the whole class. While the students discuss their feedback in groups, the teacher can discuss particular problems with each presenter.

Activities

Classroom materials 7.4 and 7.5 *Mini-presentation skills* and *Presentation titles* show examples of these activities.

The teacher can model the beginning of a presentation, and students can note the organization and main ideas before identifying the stress on particular words and phrases, or the changes in pitch and intonation. Students can be asked to prepare a mini-presentation on their degree studies or research interests, and the key noun phrases which describe these topics can be analysed for their required pronunciation and stress, and then practised using a communication game. The main part of the presentation can be built up by asking students to prepare one or two slides or other visuals, and present these to the class. If the presentation includes graphs or other non-verbal data, these can also form the basis for a mini-presentation.

Jordan[53] recommends the '4/3/2 technique' in which students practise giving their presentations in pairs but, for each repetition with a different student, the time is reduced by one minute. This can be updated to a form of 'speed presenting', which is based on the notion of speed dating.[54] Each student prepares a three-minute presentation, e.g., about their former university campus. The class is then divided, with half the students seated and the other half, the presenters, moving from one student to another, repeating their talk at intervals of three minutes. The audience and presenters then change roles and repeat the activity. At the end, there can be an evaluation task for whole class discussion, e.g., students can decide which campus sounded most attractive for an exchange visit. A more challenging version of this idea, the poster carousel,[55] involves students, in pairs, creating a conference poster, and then each one of the pair taking a turn to be questioned about it by the other students in the class.

Students may need individual work on their pronunciation, which could be a self-access activity, but practice exercises should be based around the key items they need for their presentation. Shadow reading, i.e., reading aloud in parallel with a recording, using the same pace, pronunciation, stress, pitch and intonation, can help students to improve this aspect of their performance.

Conclusion

Academic speaking presents considerable challenges to overseas students. Interaction in group discussion is complex and unpredictable, while individual presentations require unsupported public performance. EAP teachers can prepare students for these challenges by making the conventions clear, and by providing a supportive classroom environment which encourages risk-taking.

Further reading

Anderson, K., Maclean, J. and Lynch, T. (2004) *Study Speaking*. Cambridge: Cambridge University Press.

Furneaux, C. and Rignall, M. (1997) *English for Academic Study: Speaking*. London: Prentice Hall/Phoenix ELT.

Lebauer, R. (2000) *Learn to Listen; Listen to Learn*. 2nd edn. White Plains, NY: Longman, Pearson Education.

Lynch, T. (2004) *Study Listening*. Cambridge: Cambridge University Press.

Rost, M. (2002) *Teaching and Researching Listening*. Harlow: Longman Pearson.

Chapter 8: Critical thinking

This chapter will examine:

- what critical thinking means

- the main skills and sub skills involved

- three key considerations for delivering critical thinking in EAP

You will have the opportunity to:

- reflect on the critical thinking skills and sub skills your students need

- design your own critical thinking tasks to accompany a reading text

Critical thinking is a highly valued skill in academic study, and university course descriptors frequently refer to it. The development of thinking skills across the school curriculum is an explicit aim of the National Curriculum for England;[2] the Qualifications and Curriculum Authority even offers an A level in Critical Thinking.[2] To be successful at university, students need to understand and express critical thinking effectively through the medium of English. This raises two important questions for EAP teachers:

- What exactly does the term *critical thinking* mean?

- How do we enable students to demonstrate critical thinking in English?

Task 1

Complete this statement in as much detail as you can:

A student who thinks critically …

Task 2

List any activities you use with your students to encourage critical thinking.

You will be able to review this list and add to it as you read the chapter.

Critical thinking at university

Critical thinking is a term given to a wide range of thinking activities in university study, but it is difficult to find a definition that includes all of them. Although lecturers claim to value critical thinking highly, they tend to recognize it mainly by its absence. Here are some typical generalizations from UK lecturers about weak students, both native and non-native English speakers, in undergraduate and sometimes postgraduate courses:

- *They don't think for themselves.*
- *They never question what they read.*
- *They just regurgitate.*

However, when asked to explain exactly what they want, lecturers' responses tend to be too vague to indicate exactly how the EAP teacher can address critical thinking in the classroom. Typical recommendations are:

- *They should give their own opinions more.*
- *They should be more critical.*
- *They should be more original.*

Task 3

- How do the lecturers' recommendations compare with your description of a critical thinker in Task 1?

- Do your critical thinking activities in Task 2 reflect the lecturers' recommendations?

It is not easy to derive classroom activities from the lecturers' recommendations as they stand. Much of the familiar routine thinking that happens in an EAP classroom does not seem to reflect what the lecturers require.

Task 4

Look at the list of ten classroom activities below.

- Which do you consider involve critical thinking?
- In what ways is critical thinking involved?

1 identifying what is wrong in an argument

2 suggesting applications or examples from personal experience to clarify a concept

3 discussing possible reasons for a change in a trend

4 defining a concept from a set of examples

5 deciding how to group ideas for an essay

6 guessing what will happen next in a trend

7 giving another student some feedback on their writing, using a checklist

8 setting up and testing a research hypothesis

9 giving excuses for not doing a homework task

10 understanding a metaphor

You probably already include some of these activities in your teaching, but may not have analysed the thinking processes they involve. In fact, all ten of the above classroom activities require some form of critical thinking, and could be included in the list you began in Task 2. In order to justify these as critical thinking activities and, therefore, important preparation for academic study, the terminology in the lecturers' recommendations needs to be clarified.

Clarifying terms

The lecturers' recommendations for students contained three key words, *critical*, *opinions* and *original*. All are potentially problematic in EAP teaching.

- *They should give their own* **opinions** *more.*
- *They should be more* **critical**.
- *They should be more* **original**.

Task 5

- Write your definition of *opinion, critical* and *original.*
- If a student asked you what these words meant, what would you say?

Opinion

This word introduces a potential paradox to EAP teaching. The difficulty was neatly summed up by a student, who is clearly a critical thinker:

- *You tell me I can't say 'in my opinion', but you say you want my ideas!*

The reason for this paradox is that there are two conflicting meanings of *opinion*.

a   unsupported views: views adopted without supporting evidence
You have to distinguish facts from opinions.
That's just a matter of opinion.

b   views: thoughts, judgements
There are many different opinions on this issue.

Meaning a) is pejorative in the sense of being unsupported by evidence, whereas b) has a neutral meaning. Academic writers tend to avoid using *In my/ our opinion*.[3] EAP students who use the phrase in their writing tend to sound opinionated and non-academic. Unfortunately, we sometimes give students the wrong message, for example, writing tests which ask a candidate to *give your opinion* are inevitably prompting him or her to use the phrase *in my opinion* in their writing. Coffin examines how far one such test of academic English and the associated practice books encourage or measure proficiency in academic argument. In her concluding remarks she notes:

... research indicates that a less personally involved, analytical style of argumentation is generally favoured at tertiary level. Therefore it is somewhat surprising to find that candidates may be successful in terms of band score despite their approach to argumentation being more reminiscent of letters to the press than of academic prose.[4]

The answer to the dilemma of the student quoted above is that there is no need for a writer to explicitly state ownership of the views expressed in an academic text. We assume that the writer is presenting his or her own views, except when acknowledging the views of others. In other words, we assume as a default position that all the views expressed are the writer's until we see other sources mentioned. However, we expect the writer's view or stance to be supported in terms of explanation, examples, facts and evidence.[5] It is therefore quite legitimate for lecturers to say:

- *They should give their own opinions more.*

Classroom materials 8.1 Mystery graphs, 8.2 Good and bad examples and 8.10 Should teachers do your washing? are designed to encourage students to present and support ideas.

What they are asking for are the students' own ideas. However, they want these ideas to be expressed in an academic way, and with adequate support, i.e., as a supported stance. In Task 4, any activity in which students make suggestions or give reasons can be a way for the EAP teacher to develop this ability – even activity 9 is an opportunity to require a student to give good reasons for not doing the homework.

Critical

Critical has three main meanings relevant to EAP:

a   important or important to the point of causing a threshold to be crossed
Accurate calibration is critical for valid results.
Once the temperature drops below the critical value, growth ceases.

b   evaluative, making an assessment according to a set of criteria
He was asked to write a critical review of the research in this field.

c   finding fault / criticizing
He was highly critical of the research in this field.

Notice that the term *critical review* may mean *either evaluating or criticizing*. The lecturer's comment is similarly ambiguous: *students should be more critical* could either mean that they should evaluate more, or that they should criticize more. In Task 4, activities 1: evaluating an argument, 5: grouping ideas, 7: giving peer feedback, and 9: making an excuse, all involve evaluating using criteria. However, only two possibly require the student to be critical, in the sense of to criticize: 1: identifying what is wrong in an argument and 7: giving another student feedback on their writing – though, on the whole, EAP teachers would discourage negativity in peer feedback. Activity 9 could also involve criticizing if a student felt bold enough to excuse a lack of commitment to the homework by saying that it was

Classroom materials 8.2 *Good and bad examples*, 8.7 *What's wrong with these claims* and 8.8 *Critical analysis: evaluating dictionaries* involve critical evaluation.

boring or not useful. Criticizing has a role in critical thinking, but it is not central; it is simply one possible outcome of a process of evaluation according to clear criteria. It also needs to be expressed in suitable academic language.

Original

As used in *original thinking*, this word has a stronger and a weaker meaning.

a The stronger meaning is: *thinking that is totally new and has never been expressed before.*

b The weaker meaning is: *seeing new relationships. Originality* is sometimes explicitly used as a criterion for marking, e.g., in masters assignments in Logistics and Supply Chain Management, where it is explained as seeing 'links across the course and links to other courses'.[6]

Classroom materials 8.5 *It's in the genes* is an example of a task that asks students to assemble what they know and be ready to make connections with new information. **Classroom materials 8.6 *Seeing beyond the text*** helps students to discern connections that are not obvious. **Classroom materials 8.9 *EAP pills*** and **8.10 *Should teachers do your washing?*** involve making imaginative connections.

The first type of original thinking is quite rare and special. This type of original thought in any field will be a product of expertise in that field. It is unlikely to be found at undergraduate level, and not likely to be teachable in an EAP class. In Task 4, activity 8, setting up and testing a research hypothesis, might require this truly original thought as the first step in a piece of new research. Activity 4, defining a concept from a set of examples, might also require this special originality if the concept is an entirely new one in the field.

On the other hand, many of the activities in Task 4 involve students looking at things creatively, that is, seeing new relationships or making new connections. Finding new examples, grouping ideas, linking information to what they already know, and understanding a metaphor all involve seeing new relationships. There is a range of academic activities in which seeing new relationships is important, for example, Chapter 10: *Assessment* shows a critical thinking exam question, from a first-year Business Studies unit, requiring students to apply knowledge of the concept of money to tradable items such as bananas. This approach can clearly be developed in an EAP classroom.

Arriving at a definition

The lecturers' recommendations quoted above can now be re-presented.

- *They should express more of their own ideas, taking a stance, together with support for these views.*
- *They should evaluate, using clear criteria.*
- *They need to be flexible, make connections, apply knowledge to new situations, and look at things in new and different ways.*

These recommendations represent three important types of critical thinking as a key academic skill. Critical thinking for EAP students is:

- taking a stance – expressing their own considered, supported views
- evaluating – assessing what is, for example, good or bad according to clear criteria
- making connections – looking at things in new and different ways and applying knowledge

---

Task 6

Look at your list of critical thinking activities in the EAP classroom in Task 2.

- Can you classify the activities in terms of the three types of critical thinking?

In authentic academic activities such as research, argument and problem solving, these types of thinking work together. In an EAP syllabus, they have to be explored in meaningful contexts, and developed coherently as strategies through the syllabus content and delivery. The next two sections explain the *what* and the *how* of critical thinking in EAP.

Critical thinking content: what to include in an EAP syllabus and in the classroom

Unfortunately, most published EAP materials present a confusing picture of critical thinking. Explanations can involve very different views of what it is.[7] This lack of shape and definition makes critical thinking a difficult concept for the classroom EAP teacher to handle confidently as a teaching aim. A further difficulty is a tendency to present only higher order skills as critical thinking skills, such as arguing, analysing critically and identifying faulty reasoning[8]. Your description of a critical thinker in Task 1 probably includes these desirable higher order abilities. However, besides being advanced in terms of thinking, these higher order abilities tend to be expressed through complex content and language, which often means that exploration of critical thinking is delayed until the very end of a course, or is not attempted with students who have a lower-intermediate level of language. This view of critical thinking does not recognize the developmental steps needed to reach the higher levels of competence, nor how these steps can be supported and integrated with a student's emerging academic language and skills. An approach combining two simple ideas, thinking and questioning, can help EAP teachers to identify and exploit critical thinking opportunities with students at all levels.

Thinking

The first step is to move the focus away from the rather distracting and ambiguous word *critical*, in the phrase *critical thinking*, to the much more useful word *thinking*. This reveals a hierarchy of skills from very uncomplicated thinking skills, such as identifying the 'odd one out', to complex activities such as presenting an argument or testing a hypothesis.

The four tasks in the table below illustrate levels of complexity in critical thinking, and their relationship with the knowledge telling/knowledge transforming continuum.[9] They also illustrate how simpler levels of thinking underpin higher order critical thinking.

	Task	Critical thinking
Knowledge telling	1 Name the group that these items all belong to *car bus airplane bicycle train*	simple
	2 Find the odd one out *car bus airplane bicycle train*	simple
	3 Explain why bicycle is the odd one out	more complex
Knowledge transforming	4 Present an argument for the bicycle as a solution to the problem of climate change	most complex

Table 1: *Levels of complexity in four critical thinking tasks*

In the functional strand of an EAP syllabus, critical thinking skills and associated language become more important and more complex as the course takes students through the explaining and then the persuading functions. The persuading functions (argument, problem/solution and evidence/conclusion) involve the highest order critical thinking.

Task 7

Put the tasks below into three groups according to the complexity of thinking required: 1 for the simplest; 2 for the more complex; 3 for the most complex.

a   relate new knowledge to your existing knowledge

b   give your own examples of a category of things

c   identify what are not examples of a category of things

d   suggest reasons for an unexplained trend

e   apply knowledge to solve a problem

f   devise a set of criteria to evaluate something

g   apply a set of criteria to evaluate something

h   define a concept from a set of examples

i   decide how to group similar or different ideas

The simplest thinking tasks are probably i), c) and b). Grouping similar ideas, or separating different ones, is a common type of thinking in many familiar contexts, e.g., sorting clothes for washing. It is slightly more difficult to think of further examples of a category, b), because this involves going beyond what is given.

Tasks a) and d) represent a level of thinking which goes much further than what is given, and involves establishing a more complex set of connections, for example, between new knowledge and what has already been learned, or between a trend and its causes. Task g) requires the application of what has been learned (a set of criteria) to a new context.

Classroom materials tasks 8.2 *Good and bad examples*, 8.4 *Speculating why* and 8.9 *EAP pills* also reflect these three levels of complexity. The most difficult thinking tasks are f), h) and e) because they are essentially creative. Devising a set of criteria to evaluate something, f), is a much more complex and creative task than simply applying given criteria. Defining a concept from a set of examples, h), is similarly creative thinking. Task e), applying knowledge to solve a problem, involves a complex integration of thinking tasks. There has to be detailed analysis of the causes of the problem, or even of evidence that these are causes, as well as the creation and evaluation of solutions.

Task 8

Can you rank your activities from Task 2 into three levels of complexity?

Questioning

The second element in a classroom approach to teaching critical thinking is to use questions. Curiosity is a key characteristic of a critical thinker. You probably included a reference to asking questions in your description of a critical thinker in Task 1. Many experienced teachers see critical thinking as questioning a text, but this is only part of the picture. Questioning is an extremely versatile tool that enables the EAP teacher and students to shape learning and thinking. It can include questions[10] such as:

- Is this the same or different?
- What's next?
- Which group does this belong to?

Within a task, questioning can help students by breaking down complexity into manageable components – the sub-skills that make up critical thinking. Below is a sample of the critical thinking questions that can identify the components of an evaluation task:

- What is good or bad about this?
- How do you know?
- What criteria for evaluation can you use?
- Are some criteria more important than others?
- Can the criteria be grouped into different types?
- Can the same criteria be used to evaluate other cases?
- Do other writers use the same or different criteria?

Classroom materials 8.5 *It's in the genes* provides a typical task to assemble previous knowledge prior to reading.

Questions can give a framework that allows more complex thinking to be developed through simpler thinking tasks or sub-skills. This helps to build student confidence in dealing with complexity, as in the following set of critical thinking questions for a problem-solution task:

- What do I already know about this topic?
- How does my previous knowledge fit with this new information?
- How can I apply this information to this new situation?
- How can I apply this new knowledge to solve this problem?

Questions are also an essential strategy used by dominant readers (see Chapter 4: *Reading*). Critical thinking questions for understanding a text include:

- Who are the intended readers of this text?
- Why was this text written?
- Why am I reading it?

Classroom materials 8.3
What does the writer think?
provides a task which develops this type of questioning.

- What do I need to focus on in my reading?
- What does this writer think?
- Does the writer do enough to support this stance?
- What do I think?

A questioning approach makes learners more independent, but requires transparency from teachers, who also need to question themselves about what they are doing. Below are examples of critical thinking questions that help teachers and students to reflect on learning, in particular on their purposes:

- Why are we doing this?
- Why are we doing it this way and not that way?
- Why can't students copy from journal articles or Internet sources?
- Why do we have to reference everything?

This approach encourages the first steps in critical literacy, enabling students to evaluate, and perhaps even challenge, the conventions of their academic community. A prerequisite of this approach is that the EAP teachers and students are partners in the learning process, the steps in learning are explicit, and the teachers themselves are open to questioning of their own practice.[11]

The critical thinking approach in EAP, put at its simplest, is: Anything that makes students think has a place in the EAP classroom, and questioning is an excellent way to make students think. Focusing on thinking and questioning also provides a framework (Figure 1) that encompasses the professional concerns of academic disciplines at one extreme, and the sub-skills of critical thinking in the EAP classroom at the other.

What academics do

research, argue, solve problems (extreme knowledge transforming)

$\downarrow$

What these activities involve

higher order critical thinking skills, e.g., evaluating evidence,

synthesizing argument

$\downarrow$

Skills learners need to perform these activities

key critical thinking skills, e.g., taking a stance, evaluating, seeing new
relationships

$\downarrow$

Sub-skills learners need to deploy to interact critically

with materials in the EAP classroom

questioning: Is it relevant or not relevant? Is it good or not good?

How do you know? What are the criteria? What next? What if...?

Figure 1: *A suggested framework for analysing critical thinking in EAP*

Naming the many sub-skills involved in critical thinking is less helpful in the
classroom than the more practical approach of setting out the questions that
EAP teachers and students need to ask to interact with classroom materials.
For example:

Sub-skill	Question
identifying the relationships between acquired and new knowledge	*How does this relate to what I already know?*

Table 2 uses this framework to analyse the three main academic concerns into
key critical thinking skills, and then into critical thinking sub-skills questions
for the classroom.

Table 2: *Critical thinking skills analysed for the EAP classroom*

What academics do	Higher order critical thinking skills needed	Key critical thinking skills (receptive/productive) • take a stance/support claims • evaluate using criteria • see new relationships	Critical thinking sub-skills in terms of questions that students need to ask
Research	critically analyse a body of knowledge	identify the elements of a research project; understand the relationships between the elements	What do I already know about this? How does this relate to my own knowledge?
	select a research focus		What if . . .? Is this relevant? What are the criteria for relevance? Is the reasoning correct?
	construct and test a hypothesis against relevant evidence	draw inferences to support a stance (hypothesis)	What are the implications of the hypothesis? How was evidence collected? What are the criteria for evaluation? How are they applied?
		evaluate / justify evidence collected	
	deduce the status of the hypothesis on the basis of evidence	evaluate hypothesis in terms of evidence	Are there other reasons / explanations? Is the reasoning correct? What next?

What academics do	Higher order critical thinking skills needed	Key critical thinking skills (receptive/productive) • take a stance/support claims • evaluate using criteria • see new relationships	Critical thinking sub-skills in terms of questions that students need to ask
Argue a case	understand – critically analyse the components of an argument produce – synthesize the elements of an argument appropriately	identify the components of an argument identify/take a stance identify/make a claim evaluate the support for a claim (e.g., examples, reasons)/justify a claim (e.g. with appropriate examples, reasons) identify/concede or make counter-arguments evaluate/justify counter arguments rebut counter-arguments with support	Why was this text written? Who is the audience? What is my/the writer's view? What are the criteria for evaluation? How are they applied? Are there other reasons and examples? Is the reasoning correct? What do I already know about this? How does this relate to my own knowledge? Is this relevant? Are there any hidden meanings/assumptions? What are the implications?

What academics do	Higher order critical thinking skills needed	Key critical thinking skills (receptive/productive) • take a stance/support claims • evaluate using criteria • see new relationships	Critical thinking sub-skills in terms of questions that students need to ask
Solve problems	critically analyse the components of a problem	identify and describe a problem from a situation	What do I already know about this? How does this relate to my own knowledge? How do I know there is a problem?
		identify and evaluate solutions	What do I already know about these? How do these relate to my own knowledge? Are they relevant? What are the criteria for evaluating the solutions? How are they applied? Are there any other possible solutions?
	argue a case for one or more solutions	recommend solutions evaluate/justify counter arguments rebut counter-arguments with support	Is the reasoning correct? What are the implications? What is my/the writer's view/stance?

Task 9

Can you match some of your critical thinking activities from Task 2 to the key critical thinking skills and the questions that students need to ask in Table 2?

Critical thinking: delivery through an EAP syllabus and in the classroom

It is important to start from the position that EAP students already know how to exercise critical thinking in their everyday lives. On a day-to-day basis, they give opinions, evaluate, and see new relationships. However, the extent to which they are accustomed to using these skills in the context of learning will vary.[12] We do not have to teach them to think, but we do have to teach them:

- the contexts in which thinking skills are valued
- what kinds of thinking are relevant in academic study
- how to express these skills in English

Staging, stepping and scaffolding

Critical thinking skills are developed through repeated practice and staged and stepped tasks.[13] Staging refers to the process of developing higher order skills through the sequencing of the syllabus, ensuring at an early stage that students gain confidence in using the simpler level skills. Stepping involves breaking down a complex task into smaller steps, especially when first tackling higher order critical thinking tasks. Staging and stepping enable students to see the whole process, and how the sub-skills lead them through the elements of the task to successful completion. Another approach is to scaffold the task. Scaffolding means supporting students in completing a task, by inserting supporting hints or clues in the materials or through dialogue.[14] Questions in particular are useful strategies for scaffolding.

Integration

Critical thinking should not be delayed until the advanced parts of a course; it can, and should, have a role throughout any EAP course, but not as a separate component. It might be tempting to use critical thinking resources for native speakers of English[15] because they generally present a more comprehensive and detailed analysis of critical thinking than most current EAP resources.

Classroom materials 1.1
Rich Aunty – an introduction to writer's stance integrates the idea of writer's stance closely with the language used to express it.

However, they do not integrate critical thinking with language and other skills input. It is particularly important in EAP to reinforce the ways in which critical thinking is expressed in academic contexts. This calls for a sustained and thorough integration of critical thinking skills practice with EAP course content. Without such integration, the transfer of thinking skills into academic settings is likely to be weak. It is essential to teach critical thinking with and through the language and study skills of an EAP course. It is easy to see how critical thinking is a key feature of those parts of an EAP syllabus that deal with argument, research and problem solving but, by the time students reach this level, they need to have developed habits of critical thinking at a simpler level in the earlier parts of the syllabus. Critical thinking should become as familiar an aspect of the EAP lesson as review or pair work.

Task 10

Assess how often you include critical thinking in your classroom.

- How often do your lessons review earlier work?

- How often do they involve pair or group work?

- How often do students think critically (e.g., comment on the success or usefulness of tasks, or of the course content)?

Explicitness

Strategic awareness is essential if a student is to develop his or her own critical voice: each student needs to know what the skills are, and when to think critically, so as to take true ownership of the new skills and use them well. To achieve this awareness, it is important to be explicit for students when critical thinking is needed or is happening. Above all, critical thinking must be valued.

There are three important criteria for evaluating the delivery of critical thinking through an EAP syllabus:

- development from sub-skills to higher-order skills by staging over the EAP programme, and by stepping or scaffolding higher-order tasks in the classroom

- integration with the rest of the EAP syllabus

- explicitness in labelling and valuing critical thinking skills and tasks, both in the syllabus and in the classroom

Task 11

Do your syllabus and classroom activities (from Task 2) meet these three criteria for developing critical thinking?

Freedom to explore and enjoy critical thinking

There are more ways of stimulating critical thinking in EAP than it is possible to include in this chapter and the accompanying materials. The potential range of critical thinking activities is enormous. A critical thinker in the academic context has to be rigorous and disciplined but, at the same time, must be curious and creative, and this makes the EAP classroom an enjoyable and engaging place to be for both students and teachers.

Critical thinking activities provide contexts for real language use, and they also lend themselves to stimulating and engaging communicative activities such as problem solving, guessing games and puzzles. Knowing the solution to a puzzle, but having to struggle to express it in English, can lead to the kind of frustration that stimulates genuine language learning. As one student commented:

- *I always know when I am doing critical thinking because I can feel my brain working!*

By thinking and questioning, you and your students will be able to find new ways of practising critical thinking for yourselves. These can be very simple and obvious – for example, some teachers find thinking out loud is a good way of modelling critical thinking for students.[16]

It is not always necessary to focus closely on presenting the elements of a thinking process. At times, even when critical thinking might be quite new to students, it is useful to take a task-based approach[17] and present a complex thinking task for students to struggle with. Sometimes, students prove to be surprisingly capable, and to have real expertise in these situations. Simulations, such as Classroom materials 8.8 *Evaluating dictionaries*, 8.9 *Testing a manufacturer's claim for EAP pills* and 8.10 *Dealing with controversial arguments*, can be presented as task-based learning activities in which the teacher is an observer and language resource. Case studies, which are an important medium for learning in many academic disciplines, also demand critical thinking, and can be used in a task-based approach.[18] At the end of the activity, it is important for the teacher to elicit or present an analysis of the thinking which contributed, or did not contribute, to a successful outcome, together with the associated language. This helps to develop a metalanguage for critical thinking and makes the critical thinking skills explicit. As you work through any materials with your students, keep looking for opportunities to practise critical thinking.

The ten sets of classroom materials for critical thinking presented with this book illustrate the important features of critical thinking and its delivery, features which we have taken from lecturers' comments, our own experience, and published materials and articles. There are at least three kinds of complexity in a critical thinking task: complexity of the thinking task itself, complexity of the information load involved in performing the task, and complexity of the language needed to complete the task,[19] and all three interact. We have attempted to arrange the activities with the simpler thinking tasks earlier in the sequence, but this is not an exact science. The activities are ready for classroom use, but you should feel free to use the ideas behind them to improvise your own tasks to suit your own students, particularly in terms of content.

Task 12

Read the text 'Smoking twins' below and devise as many critical thinking activities as you can for this text. Give answers.

Try to design:

- a pre-reading task asking students to organize and reflect on their own relevant knowledge

- a task which asks students to give a reason in their own words

- a task to explain an unstated implication or assumption in the text

- a task to think of other possible reasons for the results

- a task to identify a problem with the evidence or source of information

Smoking twins

Doctors at a teaching hospital in London in the early 90s set out to investigate the health effects of different lifestyles, such as choosing to smoke or not to smoke, on skin, bones and joints. The best way to control for the effects of genetic difference is to use identical twins, because in this type the twins have exactly the same genes. The researchers gathered data from 25 pairs of identical twins who had agreed to take part in the survey. In each pair of twins there was one smoker and one non-smoker.

The twins underwent skin thickness tests using ultrasound. In addition, photographs were taken showing microscopic details of the skin surface. In the results the smokers had considerably thinner, drier and less supple or elastic skin than their non-smoking twins. The results demonstrated conclusively that smoking has an aging effect on the skin. The experts

If you need some ideas, look at **Classroom materials 8.4, 8.5, 8.6, 8.7** and **8.9. Classroom materials 8.11** *Smoking twins* includes our suggestions for activities for this text.

who carried out the research believe that chemicals released in the body when a person smokes break down skin tissue. The blood supply to the skin is also known to be affected by smoking and the reduced blood supply leads to the destruction of tissue in the top layer of skin.

The effect of these changes on the appearance of the skin can be a noticeably more aged look with more obvious wrinkles. In the UK where male smoking is in decline but female smoking is still increasing, this new finding could have implications for future government anti-smoking campaigns.

(250 words)

Conclusion

Now that you have reflected on many aspects of critical thinking, and worked through some example materials, look again at Task 1, in which you described a critical thinker, and Task 2, in which you listed critical thinking activities that you can use in your classroom. How have your views changed?

Although critical thinking is identified as a crucial skill for academic study, current EAP resources do not explain its content, or how to deliver it sufficiently clearly. Teachers need an approach that will give them confidence to develop it in their programmes. Three main types of critical thinking are: taking a supported stance; evaluating by means of criteria; seeing new relationships between ideas. An approach that sees critical thinking as principally thinking and questioning leads to a clearer understanding of the many sub-skills which underpin critical thinking, and of the diverse materials and tasks which require critical thinking. This approach enables teachers to begin to see for themselves how to exploit tasks and materials in their own practice.

There are three main issues of delivery: scaffolding, stepping and staging for developing student confidence and ability in critical thinking; integration with EAP content to ensure transfer of critical thinking skills; explicitness to enable students to develop their own critical voice. We hope that you feel confident enough to make critical thinking an enjoyable and regular feature of your EAP lessons. For teachers who wish to look further into critical thinking, there is some suggested reading.

Further reading

*EAP course books which have the development of critical thinking
as a stated aim*

Cox, C. and Hill, D. (2004) *EAP Now!: English for Academic Purposes.*
Frenchs Forest: Pearson Education Australia.

Gardner, P. S. (2005) *New Directions: Reading Writing and Critical Thinking.*
2nd edn. New York: Cambridge University Press.

Glendinning, E. H. and Holmstrom, B. (2004) *Study Reading.* 2nd edn.
Cambridge: Cambridge University Press.

Nukui, C. and Brooks, J. (2007) *Critical Thinking.* TASK Series. Reading:
Garnet.

Pallant, A. (2004) *English for Academic Study: Writing.* Reading: Garnet
Education.

Waters, M. and Waters, A. (1995) *Study Tasks in English.* Cambridge:
Cambridge University Press.

*Many EAP books practise critical thinking but without expressing
it as an explicit aim, for example:*

Haarman, L., Leech, P. and Murray, J. (1988) *Reading Skills for the Social
Sciences.* Oxford: Oxford University Press.

*Critical thinking books specifically designed for native English speakers
but a useful source of inspiration for EAP work*

Browne, N. M. and Keeley, S. M. (2004) *Asking the Right Questions: A Guide
to Critical Thinking.* 7th edn. New Jersey: Pearson Prentice Hall.

Cottrell, S. (2005) *Critical Thinking Skills: Developing Effective Analysis and
Argument.* Palgrave Study Guides. Basingstoke: Palgrave Macmillan.

Chapter 9: Student autonomy

This chapter will examine:

- the need for autonomous learning at university

- what autonomous learning means in an EAP context

- the role of the EAP teacher in the development of autonomous learning

You will have the opportunity to:

- identify the characteristics of autonomous and non-autonomous EAP students

- see how to design student autonomy into your EAP classroom activities

A high level of student autonomy is one of the clearest requirements for successful English-medium academic study, as this lecturer's comment illustrates:

- *My students are great – they work really hard – now I want them to work smart.*[1]

The members of his first-year undergraduate class of international students were well-motivated high-flyers with excellent high school exam results, and prepared to study long hours. Yet they lacked something he described as working smart. This chapter looks at the main component of working smart, student autonomy, and how this capacity can be developed in an EAP classroom. Autonomy is important not just for university degree subjects. It is vital for EAP students because they need to be language learners throughout their studies, yet their EAP class may be the last English class they will have.[2]

The importance of student autonomy as a teaching aim in EAP

EAP practice has to ensure continued learning beyond the lifespan and location of EAP instruction, whether classroom or self-access based. Penaflorida describes the development of learner autonomy as:

> a process that enables learners to recognise and address their own needs, to choose and apply their own learning strategies or styles eventually leading to the effective management of learning.[3]

Autonomy for an EAP student must involve self-direction, and the ability to see and use wisely opportunities for learning in the various situations in which an individual functions. For Field, it is not enough for students to be independent in the classroom, or even in the self-access centre, where we are in danger of creating 'instruction-dependent students'. Instead, he argues:

> We need to design programmes that both equip students for the world beyond the classroom and enable them to extract linguistic information from the resources which an L2-rich environment provides.[4]

EAP students have to be autonomous in two important respects: in learning about the content and approaches of their subject discipline, and also in learning its language. The chapter will analyse both aspects of autonomy in the context of EAP, and show ways to develop them through the whole range of EAP practice, from the way that the classroom and the course are managed to the most spontaneous teacher–student interactions.

Task 1

Imagine an EAP student who is highly teacher-dependent.

- List some of the characteristics of this student's behaviour. *A dependent student is someone who…*

You will have an opportunity to check your ideas later, in Task 4.

What autonomy means for an EAP student

At university, students have to become adept at finding and using sources of information by themselves, perhaps after a high school career in which teachers selected and processed information for them. They have to organize their study activities for themselves, when they may have previously worked within a highly structured framework that allowed very little free choice or free time. They have to work on collaborative projects with new colleagues, writing group reports and making joint presentations, when they may have experienced only individual work and assessment in school. These are challenges that are shared by all students when moving from high school to university. For EAP students, the challenge is often made greater by the move from the educational culture of one country to that of another.

A further challenge for a student studying as a non-native user of the language of instruction is the need to continue the *language* learning process beyond any EAP courses available. This is seldom explicitly addressed in published EAP materials. Without the help of a language teacher, a student has to take responsibility for learning how to communicate competently in his or her specialist field, i.e., how to function as a member of the appropriate discourse community. The development of this capacity to continue independently acquiring the language of the academic and professional community must be a key teaching aim in EAP. Each EAP student needs the underlying competence, including language awareness, reflective skills and confidence, to enable continued language acquisition through self-directed exploitation of texts, and through monitoring the interactions of the community.

Student autonomy, study competence and study skills

Although EAP practitioners tend to agree on the importance of producing autonomous learners, there is a lack of clarity about how to meet this challenge. A teacher recently commented that he was looking forward to the opening of his institution's new multi-media self-access centre, because the students could then 'start independent learning'. In fact, this teacher's classroom practice incorporated many excellent strategies for developing learner autonomy. However, he seemed to feel that student autonomy was best achieved through a self-access centre. As Benson observes, '... it is often assumed, without any strong justification for the assumption, that self-access work will automatically lead to autonomy'.[5]

Case study A:
EAP students in a self-access centre

Here is a typical scene in an imaginary self-access centre. Five students are watching DVDs of popular films. Two or three are listening to cassettes with graded readers. Quite a few are e-mailing, all in English. One student is on a website recommended by her teacher, working through a vocabulary exercise but, after five minutes, she switches to a listening task. A little later, she gets up, starts a conversation with another student, then watches a few minutes of the film he is watching. Several of the e-mailers consult electronic translating dictionaries. Another student comes in and, after searching the Internet for some information, starts word-processing his next English essay. He also consults a dictionary – a well-thumbed *Oxford Concise English Dictionary*.

It is difficult to know how far these students are 'working smart' without looking more closely at what they are doing, and asking them some searching questions. While there is no doubt that a well-designed and well-stocked self-access centre is a tremendous resource for developing autonomy, it is not sufficient. A student who has never learned how to use answer keys effectively in the classroom, for example, is unlikely to be able to use them effectively in an online learning activity. Student autonomy is a great deal more than the ability to keep busy in a self-access centre.[6]

The two aspects of autonomy in EAP – autonomy for academic study and autonomy for continued language acquisition – share an underlying competence. There have been several analyses of this concept,[7] with Waters and Waters[8] offering the most useful term, referring to a general, underlying capacity for study as *study competence.*

It is important to distinguish this deeper level study *competence* from the more surface level study *skills*, a range of techniques which students can be trained to use for effective study. Increasingly, modern EAP course books and EAP study skills books are acknowledging the need for the input of study skills for learning the content of a university subject. They include skills such as time management, proofreading, making notes, and the conventions of referencing. Most EAP teachers incorporate this type of work in their courses.

Task 2

Think about the following study skills needed at university: time management, proofreading, making notes and using correct referencing conventions in writing.

- Note in detail some activities you currently use to develop student autonomy in meeting these needs.

Study skills are a useful part of any student's repertoire, but they need to be acquired through explicit awareness of the underlying study competence. There has been a tendency in some published EAP materials to concentrate on the more mechanical and superficial aspects of study skills because these are easier to present as exercises in a course book unit or lesson.[9] In contrast, teachers using a study-competence approach apply three principles to ensure more effective learning. Firstly, they exploit study skills by analysing each skill in depth, and providing opportunities to experience and develop its underlying competence. Secondly, they keep activities as personally relevant as possible, i.e., relevant to the individual student or to the group in which the individual is working.[10] Thirdly, they integrate the autonomous aspects of study skills into all EAP classroom activities,[11] to ensure better transferability.

An example of a sometimes superficially taught study skill is time management, in particular when lessons are spent simply completing blank study timetables and discussing daily study routines. A much deeper and more thoroughly integrated approach than this is needed to develop the underlying competence for effective time management. The most successful time managers are not those who simply plan how to spend time, but those who recognize when time has been used effectively, and when it has not. Students need to assess regularly whether the time spent on learning activities was time well spent, and what this means for their next learning activity. For deeper and more transferable acquisition, time management also has to be made an important and highly visible feature of the course itself, for example, by regular negotiation and review of time limits on class activities and adherence to deadlines for essays. Rather than spend valuable class time on time management exercises, teachers can include a study timetable as part of a self-study induction pack, which is followed up on a tutorial basis. This sends the message that time management is a personal responsibility. In addition, by monitoring the class for individuals with serious time management problems, the teacher can focus help towards these students. Such students need scaffolding to review their time management, by thinking how successful each study activity was for them and why.

Classroom materials 9.1 *Correction code and error log* is a typical example of a framework to support proofreading.

Proofreading has to be personally relevant for students in order to be effective. When students do activities aimed to make them responsible for proofreading their own writing, it does not make much sense to have them find errors in a specially devised course book text. Most EAP teachers use correction codes to support students when redrafting their own work. This is excellent for making students take responsibility for improving their drafts. In addition, students can keep error logs to monitor their own proofreading, and to see how much their writing develops. There are many other ways of getting students to take responsibility for proofreading. They can proofread class-constructed texts, perhaps in teams, to see which team can find the most errors. They also need to proofread each other's texts – a collaborative sharing of responsibility which will be necessary in their future academic careers.[12]

Classroom materials 7.1 *Academic listening strategies* and **8.10 *Evaluating dictionaries*** are examples of the experiment and evaluate approach.

Writing notes is a very complex activity. It is important to take into account the purpose and context for making notes. For example, are the notes to help plan an essay or to acquire information from a book or lecture? Students need to experiment with, and reflect on, a wide range of formats and strategies for each context. An *experiment and evaluate* approach means that students can take personal ownership of how they study. At the same time, the approach encourages a widening of the repertoire of strategies they take away with them from the EAP course. Adult students have some degree of control over their individual learning styles, and can change their beliefs and preferences to learn more effectively if they are enabled to experience new approaches and reflect on these.[13]

A research approach is also useful in relation to referencing. Exercises to correct the details of artificially constructed and faulty referencing in a bibliography are among the most tedious ever invented by course book writers. The underlying reasons for referencing need to be clear to students. Perhaps the most important of these is to enable a reader to access the source of an idea, and referencing tasks can be devised to simulate this. Students need to find the conventions used in books and journals in their own disciplines, and use them in their EAP writing. If this is not feasible, they can learn to use a manual or a recognized website to check one of the more widely used types of referencing conventions, and apply this to their own (and each other's) writing. Many students use software packages to do the tedious, mechanical part of the referencing task for them. These are the resources a native speaker would use. Problems with plagiarism for EAP students lie much deeper than the conventions of referencing. Unfortunately, it is easy to waste time on the latter at the expense of helping students with the more difficult task of carefully incorporating the ideas of others into their own arguments.[14]

In addition to superficiality, a serious problem with some traditional EAP study skills activities is that they can be perceived as patronizing. This is particularly so where study skills are the topic of texts being used to teach study skills: the temptation to base the content of EAP classes on information about how people learn is powerful and understandable because it appears efficient. This approach superficially resembles a type of experiential learning known as 'loop input'.[15] Loop input requires the use of the techniques described in the content to deliver the teaching – 'show' as well as 'tell'. Unfortunately, in EAP study skills materials, the more valuable experiential element, the element that develops study competence most effectively, can become lost. Too many texts describing how we learn can become didactic and miss their mark. Turner quotes a student informant who felt patronized and bored with this kind of study skills input.

> They [such topics] may be alright for British students who don't know about studying but we already know all that.[16]

It is highly likely that such students do not in fact know everything, but we must not assume that they know nothing. Rather than holding discussions around how to get to class on time, have a healthy lifestyle or organize folders,[17] we need to gain students' confidence by acknowledging where they do have the required expertise, so that we can reveal and fill the more serious gaps in their study competence.

In line with the distinction between study skills and study competence, the term *training* suggests too superficial a level of teaching to reflect what underlies student autonomy and its development.[18] In this chapter, the term *development* is used in relation to learner autonomy to reflect an approach that fosters transferable strategies and, like critical thinking, operates at a deeper level of learning (i.e. the level of study competence) than the term *training* normally suggests. Training may be suitable for study skills, but autonomy can only come through a developmental process that enhances study competence. In summary, three principles for EAP practice in fostering student autonomy are:

- to develop the deep level of study competence that underpins independent learning, rather than simply train students in study skills
- to foster the development of study competence, by making any input as personally relevant to the students as possible
- to integrate the development of study competence into all aspects of EAP, rather than try to teach it in isolation in independent learning or study skills lessons or expect it to develop spontaneously in a self-access centre

The elements of study competence

In discussions about the features of a good language learner,[19] several elements emerge which are also important in study competence. A student with study competence is:

1 self-aware, or knows about self as a learner

2 willing to find out things

3 willing to tolerate uncertainty

4 able to self-evaluate

5 realistic in setting manageable goals

6 willing to experiment with new methods and materials

7 actively involved in the learning process

8 organized in terms of time and resources inside and outside the classroom

9 self-confident

10 able to monitor own learning

11 a critical thinker

The elements form into three clusters based on three core competencies: being active in learning, taking risks in learning, and reflecting on learning. These core competencies form three dimensions or clines of study competence:

passive   ⟶   active

risk-averse   ⟶   risk-comfortable

unreflective   ⟶   reflective

All three core competencies underlie good practice in language teaching. For example, in a general English teaching context, EFL teachers use methodologies, such as the communicative approach, to encourage students to be active learners who are ready to take risks in using the language – particularly outside the classroom. The reflective dimension, though, is particularly important in English for Academic Purposes.

Task 3

Categorize the 11 elements of study competence mentioned above by writing *active, risk taking or reflective* next to each element.

There is inevitably some overlap between dimensions when considering actual tasks, but generally the passive–active dimension involves willingness to discover, active participation and resource organization in and out of the classroom (2, 7 and 8); the risk-averse–risk-comfortable dimension involves tolerance of uncertainty, an experimental approach, and self-confidence (3, 6 and 9); the unreflective–reflective dimension involves self-awareness, self-evaluation, realistic goal setting, monitoring learning and critical thinking (1, 4, 5, 10 and 11). These dimensions help the teacher both to assess student need and to evaluate how well tasks promote autonomy, because both tasks and students can be located on the clines. Developing autonomy is seen when students move towards the autonomous end of the clines, becoming more active, risk comfortable and reflective. Tasks can also be designed to require increasing autonomy in terms of activity, risk-taking and reflection.

Task 4

In Task 1 you listed some characteristics of a dependent learner.

- Compare your list with the table below, which shows the characteristics of a student who is located towards the non-autonomous end of the three clines.

- Cover the right-hand column and assign the characteristics in the table to the three dimensions (P = passive, RA = risk-averse, U = unreflective).

- List the corresponding characteristics of a student who is located towards the desirable autonomous end of the three clines.

A student with low autonomy ...	Study competence dimension
moves from task to task without stopping to think	U
expects the teacher to choose suitable materials and activities	P
is reluctant to try new approaches / prefers to use very familiar approaches to learning	RA
dislikes ambiguity / not knowing the meaning of a word in a text; depends on translation	RA
will not give an answer to a question in class unless sure it is correct	RA
describes needs in very general terms	U
regards errors as failure	RA
does not analyse errors or self-correct	U
wants the teacher to correct all work	P
prefers working with the teacher rather than classmates	RA
tends to evaluate study in terms of quantity (time spent) rather than quality	U
does not seek out material or activity beyond the classroom	P
expects the teacher to assess student performance – usually as a grade compared with peers	P
wants the teacher to set goals for the student: 'tell me what to do to improve my speaking'	P
is happiest when busy on tasks with straightforward answers	U
is reluctant to make guesses	RA

Students have to move to the desirable end of the autonomy cline on all three dimensions, in acquiring both language and academic study skills. They have to become:

active

- finding for themselves suitable materials and activities beyond the classroom
- self-assessing and self-correcting
- setting their own goals

risk-comfortable

- trying new approaches
- tolerating ambiguity
- willing to guess and risk failure
- seeing errors as opportunities to learn
- seeing classmates as learning resources

reflective

- planning how to do a task and reflecting on it when completed
- identifying specific needs
- analysing errors in order to self-correct
- evaluating study in terms of effectiveness
- willing to engage with tasks which demand a thoughtful approach

To sum up, EAP students need to be:

- active in taking responsibility for their learning
- comfortable in taking risks in order to exploit their learning potential fully
- able to reflect deeply on their learning

The following constructed[20] case study illustrates how autonomous students function in their academic environment.

Case study B:
An informal study group working smart

Zhang Zhang, Fahad and Kirill are all studying for a masters degree in electronic engineering. None has English as a first language but, in their busy schedule, they do not have time to attend English classes. They have formed an informal study group to help each other to meet some of the challenges of studying in another language and culture.

They are attending a one-day conference and want to see three presentations that are scheduled at the same time. They agree on who will see which presentation, and arrange to meet to share information at lunchtime. Zhang Zhang has noticed that the lecturer in her presentation used one phrase several times: *on-the-fly*. She has written it down, but cannot find it in a dictionary. From the way it was used, it seems to mean *spontaneous, unplanned, in response to changing conditions*. She uses the phrase when she gives her report back to the others. Kirill notices and comments that Dr Bell used the same phrase in her lab session the other day, so it must be important.

The following week, Fahad is finding it difficult to get started on a coursework essay, and visits Kirill to see how he is doing. Fahad is amazed to find his friend gazing at a network of words and coloured symbols on his computer screen. Kirill says it is a *mind map* and explains how he is using it to plan his essay. It is *Freeware*[21] so Fahad goes back to his room, downloads the software, and spends an enjoyable afternoon transferring his essay notes from paper onto his new mind map and adding the little coloured icons. Eventually, he decides it is time to start writing the first draft of the essay. But, after half an hour struggling with the mind map, he retrieves his original notes and uses them instead. He has soon written more than half the essay. He decides he needs more time to get used to the mind map but thanks Kirill later, saying that playing with the mind map got his brain working again by showing that there were so many different ways to organize his points. Actually, he is not quite sure if this is true, but thinks he will try the mind map again for the next essay.

Task 5

What evidence is there in this case study of active, risk-comfortable, reflective learning in language acquisition and in academic study?

These students have taken a significant step in learner autonomy by making the choice to work collaboratively. Zhang Zhang shows autonomy in language learning. She is an active learner in noticing and recording the new phrase.[22] She is reflective in the way she works out the likely meaning of the phrase, specific to her discipline, and takes a risk by using it so soon in her feedback to the others, without having been able to find it in an 'authoritative' source. She clearly feels comfortable in taking this risk.

Fahad demonstrates both an active and risk-comfortable approach to academic study by trying a new note-making technique for writing an essay. He even invests an afternoon's work in the project. He evaluates (by reflection and critical thinking) the success of the technique, and judges that perhaps he has not given it an adequate trial.

Clearly, these students are working much more autonomously than the EAP students we met earlier in the self-access centre. How can students reach the stage where they can work like Zhang Zhang, Fahad and Kirill?

Task 6

Think of ways in which you promote learner autonomy in your EAP classroom.

- List ways of fostering autonomy in academic study generally.
- List ways of fostering autonomy in continued language learning in an academic discipline.

Keep referring to your list as you read on through this chapter.

Developing autonomy through EAP classroom practice

To develop student autonomy, an EAP teacher has to be aware, on a minute-by-minute basis, of her role in the classroom, the learning environment she is creating, and the extent to which she is asking students to reflect. Field suggests, 'the most effective teacher is one who provides for her/his own redundancy'.[23]

There may seem to be a paradox in the idea of *teaching* independence. However, realizing learner autonomy through classroom practice is not self-contradictory. Student autonomy is not something that can be taught in a specific lesson; it comes through changing the role of the teacher as responsibility for learning is gradually handed over to students.[25]

Changing the role of the teacher to develop student autonomy

At the very beginning of an EAP course, the teacher of the class usually has the role of expert and decision maker. The teacher:

- is an expert on features of the target language, and has considerable expertise in language learning and teaching
- is an expert on the EAP course – the aims, the components, what materials will be used, how and when it will be assessed, what is fixed and what can be adapted, perhaps even how successful the course has been in the past
- has control of decision-making by virtue of possessing all this knowledge, and also through the expectations of the class

At an initial stage, the students may seem to be very limited as experts and decision makers. However, they are clearly experts in their L1, and in many aspects of their L1 education culture. If they are already graduates or on a degree course, the students will also have expertise in specialist subjects. As far as decision-making is concerned, each student has been at least a party in the decision to undertake study, including the EAP course, and has the option to decide whether or not to continue, cooperate and do the work asked in the way asked.

By continuing to exercise control, the teacher denies students opportunities to be active, to take risks and to reflect on learning.[25] Responsibility for learning has to be handed over to the students, but it has to be done gradually by a principled sharing of control through sharing knowledge and decision-making. By the end of an EAP course, students have to make their own decisions, and have enough expertise to function autonomously in the university system, particularly as language learners.[26] EAP teaching therefore has to perform this transition – to transfer expertise and responsibility for decision-making. At the heart of the process is the move from teacher control to student control on the following cline.

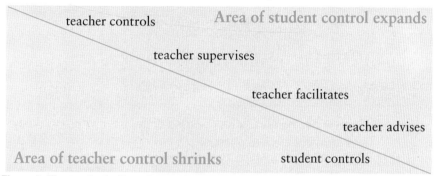

Figure 1: *The teacher's cline of control*

There are five phases in the transition, and in each phase the teacher's role shifts.[27] Initially, the teacher controls all aspects of learning, and knowledge passes exclusively in one direction – from teacher to students. At this stage, the teacher corrects all work and tells the students everything they need to know.

In the *supervising* phase, the teacher explicitly encourages more active engagement in learning, elicits input from the class, and starts to build in reflective processes, e.g., by handing out answer keys, but monitors closely what the students do. Limited choice might be offered to encourage individuals to make decisions (therefore, to start to experiment and take risks) about how they learn.

In the *facilitating* phase, there is an opening up of decision-making about how students interact and organize learning collaboratively, as a class. Some responsibility for monitoring passes to students themselves and to peers. Of course, this requires an accumulation of knowledge and expertise on the part of the students.

By the *advising* phase, students are partly or wholly driving the lessons, by feeding in materials, suggesting activities, negotiating in groups to determine aims and criteria for achieving them, running projects involving a whole series of complex tasks – all with the teacher as a consultant. Much of the learning can now take place outside the classroom, with the teacher only contacted when the students feel they need to. By the time the course is over, the students should be competent to take full responsibility for learning, supported by confidence in self and other students, by greater awareness of what is required in academic study, and by habitual reflection.

Teachers have to plan the journey down the cline, moving away from controlling towards handing over responsibility to students. However, they have to be flexible and responsive to what the students can do, as it is not a smooth transition. For different tasks and different students at different stages in their EAP learning, varying degrees of control and knowledge-sharing are required. Students may reach a facilitating phase for one type of task while needing more supervision for another in the same lesson.

Task 7

Consider these typical classroom scenarios.

- Identify, on the table below, approximately where the teacher is positioning herself on the cline of control by ranking the scenarios in terms of the five phases.

- Comment in the right-hand column on whose expertise is being used.

The first item has been done to demonstrate the task.

1 The teacher corrects all errors in a student's writing before returning it.

2 Students compare different meanings in their own dictionaries for a new word, and the teacher tries to elicit and then confirms which is the most relevant meaning for EAP.

3 At the beginning of the lesson, the teacher presents the lesson objectives on the board.

4 At the beginning of the lesson, the teacher presents the lesson objectives on the board, and asks the students what they would like to do first.

5 The teacher hands out examples of good writing from the class's last writing task, and elicits what is good about them.

6 As homework, the teacher asks students to identify five academic words in a text from their academic discipline, and prepare to explain their use to other students in the next lesson.

7 A student (N.B. not the teacher) is writing on the board at the front of the class a noun phrase in English together with its translation in her L1. She explains to the class and to the teacher the construction of the L1 translation.

8 In a lesson for postgraduates on giving presentations, the teacher starts by giving a handout of do's and don'ts for giving presentations.

9 The teacher tells the class that the next lesson, a review lesson, will include an hour of question and answers. She will spend the hour answering any questions they have about what they have been trying to learn on the course.

10 In a lesson for postgraduates on giving presentations, the teacher starts by asking students what worries them most about giving presentations.

11 In a listening lesson, the teacher allows students to choose whether to listen with or without the transcript.

TC = teacher controls   TS = teacher supervises   TF = teacher facilitates
TA = teacher advises   SC = student controls

Scenarios in order of position on the teacher's cline of control	Degree of control	Whose expertise is being used by the class?
1	TC	exclusively the teacher's expertise
	SC	mainly students' expertise

Teacher control, that uses predominantly teacher expertise, is demonstrated by scenarios 1 and 8. The students have no input or choice here. The supervision phase is beginning in scenario 3 because the teacher is sharing what the lesson is about (providing an opportunity to reflect back later to assess what was achieved). However, unless there is input from students, the expertise remains the teacher's. In 2, the teacher is still supervising, but has chosen a discovery activity that uses student knowledge and resources, as well as collaborative learning. However, scenario 2, arguably, is the beginning of the facilitating phase.

The facilitating phase also includes scenarios 5 and 6 which both involve active choice by students. Scenario 5 is still supervisory in that the teacher made the initial choices, but students are selecting from them and the teacher is valuing the expertise of class members. Scenario 6 requires students to select vocabulary from their subject speciality. Therefore, the teacher is facilitating by offering choices and by using some student expertise. (Will a student select a technical term that the teacher does not know? It does not matter as long as the class discusses its value to them as well as its value to the original student.) In scenario 4, the teacher is allowing students control (though in a limited way) in what is normally an area of teacher expertise, the way the lesson proceeds; this is facilitation. Its value lies in activating students by giving them a stake in lesson organization. Similarly, in scenario 11, the teacher is giving students choice in which listening strategy they will use, handing over responsibility for how they learn.

The advising phase starts with scenario 9; the teacher is handing over control of part of the lesson to the class. The teacher can do this because it is a review lesson, where students are the experts in knowing what they do not know, and the teacher's role will be to advise in response to their revelations. Scenario 10, in contrast to scenario 8, starts with student experience, which then drives the teacher's input to the lesson. Some postgraduates have a great deal of experience of giving presentations, others have little, and the teacher's input into the lesson might eventually prove identical to that in 8, but the point is that it is presented as advice in response to students' self-identified need.

The student control phase is clear in scenario 7, where, even though this may be a brief part of the lesson, a student controls the class and presents individual linguistic expertise.

Task 8

Consider your position on the teacher's cline of control when you give feedback on a writing or speaking activity in your classes.

- To what extent do you share your privileged knowledge (e.g., of assessment criteria) with students?

- To what extent do you use their expertise in the classroom?

The withdrawal of teacher control is a developmental process, requiring careful steps, a high level of sensitivity, and observant, reflective teaching. Moreover, loosening control is not always easy in what is, in most cultures, a somewhat controlling profession.

> A teacher who espouses the aim of learner autonomy and the development of critical reflection in students may be frustrated by results while being unaware of the dependency she engenders in students by passive teaching methods, mysterious assessment strategies and lack of feedback.[28]

One of the most difficult things for teachers is to keep silent when watching a group apparently failing to achieve a task – they feel the need to rush in when what may be needed is just a little more time. Teachers also fear being unprepared, and sometimes believe that opening up student choice might mean being asked for something they cannot deliver or do not know. However, honest attempts to meet student choices are usually well received, and often what at first seems undeliverable can, on reflection, be achieved. Not knowing something can lead the teacher on a fruitful joint investigation with the students, e.g., in concordancing a word or phrase to establish how it is used.[29]

Teachers have to allow learners to assert their autonomy.[30] However, in doing so, even when a teacher is committed to student autonomy, it can be difficult deliberately to risk the failure of a task, a student or lesson or, worse still, risk loss of face in front of a class. All three of the authors of this book have experienced these kinds of 'failures' in the classroom. Here is a flavour of our experience.

Case study C:
Three teachers' experiences of sharing responsibility

Olwyn Alexander
When I was working through the answers to a particularly dull exercise from the course book, a student stood up in the middle of the class and said, 'This is not what we want. What you are doing is not useful for us.' It was the worst moment of my teaching career to date, and 55 pairs of eyes fixed themselves on me to see what I would do next. I felt like bursting into tears and walking out of the classroom. I finished the lesson, found the course director and asked her to find another teacher for the class.

Jenifer Spencer
A student with a particularly negative attitude kept interrupting the class, and shouted at me that he never received any real teaching – I was just 'drowning him in paper'. Afterwards, the class complained to

---

the course leader about the student's disruptive behaviour. That night I could not sleep.

Sue Argent

I was asked to teach EAP writing to a large group of final year engineering undergraduates in a Chinese university. After only a week, the class monitor took me aside and asked me if I had ever taught English before. He said that I needed to make my lessons more interesting, by using topics such as 'western food' and 'culture in the UK', rather than engineering processes and cause and effect. I was devastated. Despite my years of teaching experience, I just wanted to give up and go back home to the UK.

All three episodes were, however, productive because they made us reflect, as teachers, about what we were doing. Here is what happened next.

Olwyn Alexander

Now, I wish that I had not given up and had, instead, stopped what I was doing, picked up a pad and a pen, sat down in a chair, in as casual a fashion as I could, and said to the whole class, 'What do you want?'

Jenifer Spencer

It began to dawn on me that there might be a grain of truth in his complaint. Although the rest of the class did not seem to have a problem with the amount of reading and self-study required for this postgraduate writing course, I wondered if I could present the materials in a more organized way, for example, by preparing my handouts into little packs that could be given out once a week, so that the students could see clearly what was coming, and could pre-prepare or make up for work they missed. I do this as a routine, now. I have learnt that sometimes the complaints of unsatisfactory or unreasonable students pick up weaknesses in my teaching methods or content that more polite and more motivated students will just accept as something they can't change.

Sue Argent

During a sleepless night, it occurred to me that I could teach EAP through 'western food' – at least for a couple of lessons! My photographs of places in the UK could be the basis for tasks on describing and comparing locations. It would also do no harm to have an occasional 'fun' lesson, or invent some competitive EAP vocabulary games.

Failures are most painful when they occur in the early stages of a course – a good reason for initial clarity in the shared agenda, and for checking expectations. Later, when trust has been established, such events become surprises rather than failures, and are not only less painful but often enlightening, as in Case study D, an authentic example.

Case study D:
A dependent learner

In order to promote reflection, a teacher had succeeded in getting most students in the EAP class routinely to predict scores on self-test tasks before they completed them and checked the answers. Student D consistently avoided doing this for a while and when pressed gently, just refused to do it, shaking his head in genuine distress and repeating 'I can't!' and 'How do I know?', and asking the teacher to set him a target score. Even his classmates tried to get him to make a prediction: 'Just guess! It doesn't matter what it is!'

D was otherwise a model student, doing everything asked of him, quite happy to work in groups and pairs, and very pleasant to have in the class. He was much older than his classmates, had successfully managed a company in his home country, and now wished to study for a masters degree.

The teacher was perplexed. She had met resistance before, but had always worn it down – reluctant students always co-operated simply for a quiet life: they would write down a score to keep the teacher happy. This was not working here. The teacher did not even have a point from which to get D to start self-evaluating. D would not even say on previewing a task whether he thought it might be easy or difficult.

Task 9

Reflect on the following questions:

- D was at the dependent end of which of the three dimensions of study competence?

- Why do you think D was so resistant?

- What could the EAP teacher do in the short term, and in the longer term, to help D?

- What, if any, are the implications of not complying for D's future studies?

D seemed to display teacher-dependent behaviour on all three dimensions of study competence. He appeared unwilling to evaluate (reflect on) the difficulty of the task he faced, wishing to rely passively on his teacher to do this for him.

He would certainly not take the risk of guessing a score. There could be various reasons for this reluctance, including D's experience of, and therefore perception of, the power relationship between teacher and student: he may have thought that it was the teacher's responsibility to evaluate the difficulty of tasks or any student's performance. Such perceptions often underlie dependent behaviour. It is likely that the teacher had placed him in a cultural dilemma: it might be face-losing to predict a low score, or immodest to predict a high score. On the other hand, D really did seem to find it impossible to estimate the difficulty of the task. Perhaps he had never consciously applied his reflective ability to language learning or inside a language classroom. Benson points out that many learners have been autonomous in learning a range of complex skills in their lives, and it is the teacher's role to transfer this autonomy to the academic context.[31]

The teacher could do as D wished and suggest a score, but deliberately set it too low. She could then invite D to modify this prediction either before or after completing the task. This would reduce the autonomy challenge that D faced, but would still be a teacher-initiated solution.

In fact, there was an interesting resolution. The problem was solved by D's sympathetic classmate, who suggested, 'Can I predict your score?' D was happy with this and thereafter his self-evaluation proceeded this way, with D soliciting peer prediction, and afterwards comparing his actual score with his partner's prediction. This compromise meant D was able to move forward, just a little, in terms of reflecting on his learning. Such collaborative solutions between students are an important way to promote autonomy.

Ultimately, D and students like D have to make choices based on some kind of self-evaluation, e.g., in choosing module options on a masters course, or a dissertation topic. In the course of postgraduate study, detailed day-to-day decisions which depend on how well a student is doing are not necessarily made by subject lecturers or research supervisors.

This case study illustrates three important considerations in promoting learner autonomy:

- the same student can be completely autonomous in life skills, but appear highly teacher-dependent as a learner
- a teacher cannot expect autonomy on demand from students, i.e., by simply telling students to take control of their own learning
- student-to-student dependence can be a way for a teacher to relinquish control, as a step towards student autonomy[32] and the formation of collaborative student groups.

Collaborative work is now a requirement in almost all degree programmes, to promote team working.[33] It is regarded as useful both in itself (as shown in Case study B, the informal study group), and as preparation for the work place. Group learners were also found to be more effective than individual learners in a self-access centre. For all these reasons, it should be used as much as possible in EAP practice.

The withdrawal of teacher control makes students engage more actively in the learning process, and familiarizes them with increasing responsibility and therefore with the risks that come with making changes and choices. Increasing student responsibility has to go hand in hand with the development of reflective habits that enable students to engage effectively in learning and make wise choices – to work smart. The EAP teacher has to create a context for the student that closely simulates the academic environment in which they will need to function independently and, at the same time, help the students to think through what is happening and how they respond.

Creating a context for the development of autonomy

In order to develop autonomy, students need to be in a context where it is required, and in which it is explicitly encouraged and valued. An EAP course can provide this context by creating an academic ethos – by simulating the expectations and activities that students will find on an academic course of study in a university. The students need to know that this is happening, and so the agenda has to be shared with them. Through this ethos, their expectations of academic study can be addressed, and aligned with what they are likely to experience on their university course.

As discussed in Chapter 3: *Course design*, many teachers work in non-university settings or in departments that have an EFL ethos. For EAP students, this ethos needs to be modified, by simulating the expectations of a higher education institution. This creates an environment in which students are not just *told* about academic expectations in university, they *experience* them[35] – but without risking the serious consequences of a failed university course. Students can be expected to submit coursework to deadlines, and risk a grade penalty for lateness and for under- or over-length work. An individual may even be deemed to have failed a group assessment by failing to contact or work with the rest of the group.[36] Access to teachers can be strictly in office hours (timetabled) or by appointment, rather than on a *see me anytime* basis. EAP departments often try to establish links with subject departments in order to find out what happens on degree programmes, and apply these standards to their courses as far as possible. It is valuable to go to university open days or presentations with students, prepared to ask questions that will reveal the context in which the students will be studying. Inviting in students who are currently studying on academic courses is also very useful, especially if they have previously been on the EAP course, because they give first-hand evidence of its value.

Another way of introducing an academic atmosphere to EAP lessons is for the teacher and the students to carry out research together into different ways of learning. As with the informal study group in Case study B, trying different study strategies is an important aspect of becoming an autonomous learner. Such an approach does not simply make *how to learn* the topic of lessons. Firstly, it is genuine loop input, in that it asks students to experience the approaches being considered. Secondly, such lessons simulate an important academic activity (research). The approach is also less controlling than if, for example, a particular note-taking format is imposed. Additionally, by setting out with the class to research these issues, the teacher can make the risk-taking (trying an unfamiliar note-taking format) safe. Such in-class research projects demand a great deal of personally relevant reflection and critical thinking.

Classroom materials 7.1 *Academic listening strategies* shows an activity, using experimental and control groups, to evaluate pre-reading as an aid to understanding lectures.

Autonomy in learners does not happen overnight, nor does it necessarily happen in a special class devoted to independent learning or study skills. It touches all aspects of academic study and language learning. Like critical thinking, and for the same reasons, it has to be an explicit aim, and integrated into the curriculum.[37] From day one lesson one in an EAP course, it is crucial to be absolutely clear with students about the autonomy agenda – that they will be expected to become autonomous learners and why. One of the most important things to ask students is:

- *Who will be your next English teacher?*

The answer is that there will probably be no one. This should help them to see the importance of thinking about how they will learn by themselves.

As well as providing this type of learning environment, it is necessary to monitor sensitively how students interact with it. The best way to deal with any problems individual students have is through tutorials. Problems which are common in the class can be given class time for discussion – an opportunity for students to share best practice. However, it is counter-productive to impose on the whole class a tedious analysis of difficulties which most of them do not share; the journey towards autonomy is a very personal one. On our three clines of activity, risk-taking and reflection, an individual can display a wide range of positions in different contexts.

As part of sharing the agenda, teacher and student expectations have to be made explicit, and examined pro-actively rather than dealt with re-actively (although this will sometimes be necessary). A good way to start the process is to ask students to state their expectations of their teacher, themselves, and of each other, by asking them to complete, in as many ways as possible, statements such as *A good EAP teacher...* and *A good EAP student...* The resulting lists can then be compared with the teacher's lists. This comparison can set up a tension that has to be resolved by both sides negotiating as the course proceeds. The main benefits of sharing expectations are:

- Student awareness of the learning environment is raised.
- Teacher awareness of the starting point for the class, and for individuals within the class, is raised.

The combination of relinquishing control and critical reflection on the part of the teacher requires that both parties to the negotiation be flexible and capable of change. In developing student autonomy, a teacher should expect to be challenged. For example, the university-style practices advocated above may seem rigid to other staff or students, and might be challenged. In such a situation, a teacher has to be prepared to justify the approach, but might have to make principled adaptations.

Classroom materials 9.2 *Self-access quiz* is an example of a quiz to encourage reflection on strategies for studying in a self-access centre.

Introducing students to the idea of learner autonomy is best done in the classroom. In some circumstances, however (for example, in a distance-learning or self-study context), it may not be possible to share expectations in a classroom setting. In this situation, a magazine-style quiz can be used to develop strategic awareness. Students each gain a score showing how independent they are, and the answers are a good basis for tutorial discussion. There are many such checklists in study skills course books. However, it is important not to generate too many tick-box type activities that might be completed mechanically. Such exercises can be useful for structuring student reflection, but are not a substitute for dialogue with a teacher. Paradoxically, promoting autonomy needs an initial investment of skilfully managed one-to-one teacher–student interaction. The process is reminiscent of the Socratic method, in which an individual is led into reflection and understanding by the teacher's questioning. This kind of interaction is essential for student autonomy.

Developing reflection as a key component of autonomy

Good teaching practice in general English emphasizes two of the dimensions of autonomy, active participation in learning and the need to be a risk taker, while the third requirement of autonomy, reflection, is not given as much prominence. However, reflection is particularly important in academic work.

Careful analysis of activities by both teacher and learner is required to enable students to go deeper than the level of superficial study skills to achieve study competence. Earlier in this chapter, the point was made that effective time management depends on knowing when time spent on a particular study activity has been successful or not and understanding why. Self-evaluation of this type is a key element of autonomy, and takes place through the *plan–do–review* cycle (below) familiar in all sectors of education and training.

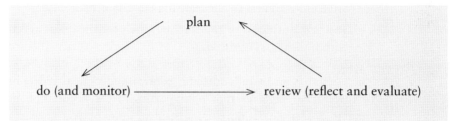

Figure 2: *The plan–do–review cycle*

The plan–do–review cycle is a useful principle to apply to any study activity in order to develop autonomy. Teacher training encourages teachers to reflect on lessons they have taught, and feed their insights into planning the next lesson. In the same way, autonomous students monitor their performance in a task, and evaluate this in order to plan the next activity. However, *plan–do–review* is shorthand for a very complex procedure. Among other things, a student has to know:

- what to pay attention to when monitoring performance
- how to evaluate performance as good enough
- how to choose from the possible options for planning the next step

Making sure that this cycle becomes a regular, explicit and valued feature of student activity in lessons establishes an environment in which student autonomy can develop. Applying such protocols to self-access material is particularly important for effective learning, and difficulty in applying them lies at the heart of many problems with both traditional self-access centres and with effective use of distance and online self-study programmes.[38]

The plan–do–review cycle is an example of *single-loop* learning.[39] Single-loop learning involves the constant refinement (review) of learning by means of experience and input. It is important in academic study, but it only enables students to improve what they already know how to do. In order to change behaviour and strategies more fundamentally, *double-loop* learning is required. Double-loop learning occurs when the learner moves out of, or is jolted out of, the context of the single-loop into a realization that a whole new frame of reference applies.[40] Such learning can involve shifts in cultural and personal perspectives. One postgraduate in an EAP class described his new understanding that critical thinking was about evaluating rather than criticizing as 'turning on a light in my head'. A class of pre-university students became much more committed to redrafting their writing when their teacher showed them the plan and two drafts she had written of a model answer. They suddenly realized that she was not asking them to redraft simply as another English exercise, but she wanted them to do what she did herself when writing. For teachers, double-loop learning can happen when teaching in a completely different country, or working with an innovative colleague or set of materials, or even when attending a particularly good conference.

Although a programme, a unit of work, or a lesson can be planned to promote reflection, deep, and therefore autonomous, learning is most likely to result from minute-by-minute interactions in the classroom. Brockbank and McGill describe such interaction as *reflective dialogue*:

> The learner, by engaging in an active process with the teacher through reflective dialogue begins the journey to greater agency, autonomy and independence rather than remaining dependent and passive.[41]

Most teachers instinctively use reflective dialogue in their teaching. Here is an extract from a student text on the problem of bird flu in which the teacher has indicated a difficulty with cohesion.

> *The better idea is that government to buy and store large quantities of vaccine against flu. It can control bird flu in a short time but not in a long time.*

The following reflective dialogue helped the student not only to improve the cohesion of the text, but also to clarify her own voice as a writer.

Teacher	Student
Is there anything you don't understand?	This one, 'it' ... I'm not sure why...
What does 'it' mean? In the sentence before?	'Government' ... no, 'vaccine'... Could be 'idea'.
Try each one at the beginning of sentence 2 – which do you mean?	'Idea to get a lot of vaccine...' is best, I think, a whole sentence.
Too long ... How could you make this shorter?	'This idea...'
Good. Can you think of a better word for 'idea'? Look at your problem–solution reference page.[42]	'This solution', 'This approach/method/measure'

Task 10

Think about the last time you had this kind of interaction with a student.

- Write down your comments and questions and the student's responses.
- How effective was the interaction in making the student think more deeply?
- How could you have made the interaction more effective?

A teacher and a student are discussing an end-of-unit vocabulary self-test which the student has completed and marked herself in class. She recorded the scores on the test paper as shown:

estimated score 7/20   actual score 7/20

Task 11

Cover the teacher's side of the dialogue below and try to reconstruct it from the student's responses.

Teacher	Student
What does this score show about your learning?	I'm learning the words, but not enough deeply.
What can you do about this?	Review the unit again.
What will you do differently?	More concentrated on word.
In what way?	Maybe check how a word is in the text.
How will you do that? What will you pay attention to?	See what words are around it.
How will you remember?	Write some examples sentences and learn them.

It is particularly important to allow time for reflective dialogue: time within a planned lesson, and time in terms of waiting a little longer for student comment. Language teachers tend to be afraid of pauses, particularly silent ones, but they are often necessary to give students space to think.

Although reflective dialogue is an important part of classroom activity, it can also take place when discussing learner diaries in tutorials. Here, the time factor is less of a problem. In fact, using learner diaries or logs as the basis for reflective dialogue is an excellent way to use tutorial time. Information and communications technology (ICT)[43] offers opportunities to develop reflective dialogue with students through e-mail, or synchronous or asynchronous discussion spaces (e.g., discussion boards).

Task 12

Look back at Case study A.

• If you were the tutor in this self-access centre, what questions could you ask the students to start reflective dialogue and encourage autonomy?

There are some generally applicable questions that can form the basis of tutorials or a generalized self-access user document. They structure a plan–do–review approach:

> Why did you choose this task? What did you want to learn from it? How easy/difficult was it? Was it successful? How do you know? What did you learn? What will you do next? Why?

For the students watching films:

> Why did you choose this film? Did you enjoy it? What was good about it? In what ways? Is there an outcome – will you write about it or tell someone else about it in English? Did you learn any English from it? How useful will this language be? Where and when do you think you will use this English?

For the students listening to graded readers, the questions will be the same as for those watching films, plus:

> Did you choose according to level or topic? Why? What is the difference between doing this and just listening or just reading? What are the advantages of listening and reading together?

For the e-mailers and users of dictionaries:

> What do you learn from e-mailing in English? What do you usually e-mail about? Why do you like this dictionary? Have you tried any other dictionaries in the centre, e.g., online English–English dictionaries, learners' dictionaries? Have you ever compared dictionaries when you are trying to find out about a particular word, to see which one is best?

For the essay writer:

> What information did you find for your essay? Do you have a way of checking if a source is good/reliable? How do you avoid just copying into your essay from the source? What other online resources do you use when you are writing an essay?

An issue for the student doing the online vocabulary and listening exercises is whether he/she is using answer keys or the tape script effectively.

> When do you look at the key – before, during or after doing a task? Why? How carefully do you check your answers? Do you need to use *Hints*? What does it mean if most of your answers are wrong? What does it mean if most of your answers are correct? What should you do next? Do you listen with or without the tape script? Why? Do you read the tape script first, ever?

Classroom materials 8.2 *Good and bad examples* has a hint type two-stage key.

This student keeps switching tasks, and is an interesting case because she probably feels that she is a 'good' student. Lai and Hamp-Lyons call this strategy 'flip-flop' learning behaviour in their study of self-access learners. One of their interviewees comments:

> I don't mean that I read a book, watch a video and use a CD ROM all at the same time, but spend some time here and there. This makes sense to me. And I'm working.[44]

Such learners need to think about the coherence of their strategy, and there are two ways they can be helped to do this. Firstly, they can keep a log or diary of their activities, and apply the general questions for plan–do–review (above) to each task they choose. Secondly, they can use their log or diary to discuss their choices with a tutor. As Lai and Hamp-Lyons conclude,[45] tutor guidance is likely to be the best solution for students who have this problem. Benson also stresses the need for this kind of teacher input:

> However innovative the self-access system, it is unlikely to be effective unless it is backed up by structures for counselling or classroom support in which learners have the opportunity to discuss and refine their goals and plans.[46]

In addition, the skill of reflection is assessed through such logs and diaries as part of coursework in many university disciplines, and so such tutorials also provide an opportunity to introduce students to this specific type of coursework.

This type of reflective review of tasks is also important in a classroom setting. How far a teacher is in control of what is actually learned in a lesson is a debateable issue. It is important to remember that 'teaching does not cause learning'[47] and that 'we cannot control what students learn, in what order they will learn and how fast they will learn.'[48] It is essential therefore that teachers, and especially students, make themselves as aware as possible of what is learned. As a matter of regular classroom practice, teachers need to stop to review the success of a task, and analyse what contributed to the success or lack of it. This review does not have to be elaborate or time-consuming, just a familiar activity in the lesson so that students become habitually reflective as part of their activities.

The final case study in this chapter examines how student autonomy can be developed in an EAP lesson.

Case study E:
A lesson observation

A colleague (Eve) wants you to observe one of her lessons and give feedback on the development of student autonomy in her class. Here is an outline of the key features of the lesson you observed.

Lesson phase 1: Eve starts the lesson by putting up the answers to the homework questions on the board. Students silently check the answers to their homework from this key. Eve asks if there were any answers that they did not understand. Two students volunteer items, and Eve explains each one. One of the questions is whether you can 'arrive at' a conclusion as well as 'come to' a conclusion, and Eve says 'Yes'. Eve collects their homework when they have marked it.

Lesson phase 2: The main part of the lesson is to introduce the features of academic style. Eve gives a brief presentation, and hands out a list of the features to each student. Eve puts students in groups of three or four, and gives each group the same four short texts to study. When they have had time, as a group, to read and discuss them, and to check any unknown words, Eve asks them to work together to identify examples of academic style in their material, and to agree a rank order for the texts from most to least academic. Eve spends a few minutes with each group to help to resolve any disagreements they have. As there is not much time with each group, she answers their questions quickly.

Plenary: Eve elicits some answers which she knows will be correct from each group, and then hands out an answer key to each student.

Lesson phase 3: Eve asks each group to take the least academic text and rewrite it in a more academic style as a group onto a visual. She visits each group while they are working to check their progress and answer any queries.

She collects these to present for review in the next lesson.

Homework: Eve asks the students to select and learn five words from the most academic text, and prepare to present an explanation of these in the next lesson.

Task 13

Prepare feedback for Eve on what was good and what might be improved by:

- identifying Eve's position on the cline of control
- commenting on the dimension(s) of study competence she is developing in her class
- suggesting activities for the next lesson

Generally, Eve is still supervising learning, but beginning to facilitate independence, particularly through collaborative learning. Eve could do more to develop reflection in students, and could model risk-taking herself by being slightly less of an expert and more of a facilitator.

Phase 1: Eve shared the answer key with the students, giving them the responsibility for checking and identifying the need for any further input from her. However, Eve missed an opportunity for students to discuss (therefore reflect on) their answers. It is a good idea routinely to require students to compare answers, and discuss discrepancies with a partner before checking a key or referring to the teacher.

The question about collocations with *conclusion* is one that a teacher should be reluctant to answer without checking first. It is good for students to realize that the EAP teacher does not know everything, and sometimes needs to refer to her resources. In this case, a dictionary would probably not help, and Eve would need to concordance *conclusion*.[49] The resulting concordance lines could be used in the next lesson (tidied up if the students are new to this approach)[50] to get students to do the research themselves to answer the question.

Phase 2: Eve is using collaborative learning to foster student responsibility for completing tasks and negotiating an outcome. It would have been much better to elicit what students think are the features of academic style (using their knowledge) so that Eve could edit and draw up a list generated from what they already know – and also provide an opportunity for reflective dialogue. Eve could consider not trying to support groups unless they request help. Students need to resolve disagreements for themselves. She seemed pressed for time and so it might be more profitable to monitor rather than join discussions, and use what she observes as insights to offer in the plenary.

Plenary: Eve endorses the collaborative work of the groups by eliciting correct answers. She could have added value to the plenary by exploring any difficulties that groups had, using reflective dialogue with the class or groups.

Phase 3: Writing a text is another good collaborative task. The proposal to review these in the next lesson is also good because it widens collaboration, and offers more opportunity for reflective dialogue. Again, monitoring, and only supporting when requested, is a more productive strategy in general – Eve seems to be doing this here, but not quite unobtrusively enough; her visits might disrupt the work of the group. It would also be useful to build into lessons some reflective review: how was that task? easy? difficult? what were the problems? what helped?

Homework: Eve relinquishes some control by offering choice, and giving students the responsibility for preparing input into the next lesson (valuing their expertise). A useful further step would be to ask students to bring in a page of academic text (from their academic discipline if possible) for similar analysis next lesson. Again, this promotes activity on the part of students and further values their expertise. It also has the added value of bringing in some authentic texts.

Of course, this sort of teacher-to-teacher feedback is itself best undertaken through reflective dialogue.

Task 14

Look back now to your response to Task 6.

- Do you think you do enough to promote autonomy in language learning?

- Do you think you do enough to promote autonomy in academic skills?

- Will you change any aspects of your teaching or include new strategies to promote student autonomy?

- If so, what will you do?

Conclusion

Student autonomy is a crucial requirement for successful English-medium academic study, and it is important in EAP practice to develop student autonomy as fully as possible. Two student needs have to be addressed: the need to continue autonomous language acquisition beyond the life of the EAP course, and the need to learn the content and approaches of the academic disciplines that the students enter. Students do not become autonomous simply by acquiring a set of study skills – in fact, an over-emphasis on presenting, rather than experiencing, good study skills in EAP can be counter-productive. Autonomy lies in the successful application of the study competence that underpins both language learning and academic study. This study competence has three dimensions; autonomy can be improved by helping students to be more active, more ready to take risks, and more reflective. This principle needs to be an open and shared agenda, it has to be made personally relevant to the students, and it informs all aspects of teaching and learning in EAP – it cannot be relegated to a study skills class.

The teacher's role has to change through the lifetime of an EAP course by moving down the cline of control, from controlling to advising, as students increasingly take responsibility for their learning, and as expertise and knowledge are shared. The teacher also needs to create an academic context, to simulate as far as possible the academic experiences that students will encounter. However, the most important role for an EAP teacher is in developing reflective capacity, in both herself and her students, through reflective dialogue.

Further reading

Benson, P. (2001) *Teaching and Researching Autonomy in Language Learning.* Hounslow: Pearson Education.

Gardner, P. S. (2005) *New Directions: Reading, Writing, and Critical Thinking.* 2nd edn. New York: Cambridge University Press.

Waters, M. and Waters, A. (1995) *Study Tasks in English.* Cambridge: Cambridge University Press.

Swales, J. M. and Feak, C. (2004) *Academic Writing for Graduate Students: Essential Tasks and Skills.* 2nd edn. Ann Arbor: University of Michigan Press.

Chapter 10: Assessment

This chapter will examine:

  the nature and purposes of assessment in academic contexts

  the principles for ensuring quality in assessment

You will have the opportunity to:

  evaluate test items, using a model of test usefulness

  use assessment criteria to evaluate student writing

Assessment lies at the heart of teaching and learning, even on courses which do not prepare students to sit formal examinations. It involves making judgements about students' current or future abilities.

Task 1

Think about a class you have taught recently.

● In what ways did you assess your students' knowledge and abilities?

● What evidence did you have for making these assessments?

Assessment in EAP might happen formally at the end of a course, perhaps using an external exam, but it also happens informally all the time in the classroom. Here are some typical judgements which teachers make to support student learning:

1 *He still reads very slowly.*

2 *She'd be happier in a lower level class.*

3 *He's not really a very good language learner.*

4 *She makes typical [insert first language] mistakes.*

5 *They'll probably find it difficult to cope at university.*

These are subjective comments based on intuitions drawn from classroom observation or interaction. In EAP, even such informal assessment can have quite serious consequences, if it is made public, because it indicates to students whether they are ready for university study or should spend more time on an EAP course. Therefore, as with formal assessment, these informal comments between teachers in staff rooms need to be as objective as possible, and supported with sound evidence. Teachers starting out in EAP often report feeling uncomfortable with aspects of assessment practice. Here are some typical comments:

- *It's very difficult to understand the standard required for EAP compared to ELT exams.*
- *I'm not confident using marking criteria and applying them to student coursework.*
- *How can you assess a student you've only taught for a few hours a week over four weeks?*
- *This student is motivated and has worked hard in my class; how can I give him a low grade?*

This chapter looks at the principles of language assessment in academic contexts in order to show how teachers can support the kinds of informal judgements listed above, and feel more confident with formal assessment. There is not space here to give a detailed account of statistical procedures used to ensure quality in large-scale testing – indeed, it is questionable how useful such procedures are for classroom practice.[1] It is also beyond the scope of this chapter to describe the process of test development, but this is dealt with in detail in other publications.[2] Instead, the assumptions underlying test design and evaluation will be explained and illustrated, to demonstrate how to ensure quality when testing students and interpreting test results.

The purpose of assessment

All types of language assessment make claims about students' knowledge and ability based on measurements of their performance under controlled conditions. These claims must be supported with evidence that the students were given the best chance to show what they could do, and that the means of assessment were as appropriate as possible for the purpose.[3] It is, therefore, important to be clear about the different purposes of assessment. These purposes can be classified as shown in the following diagram.

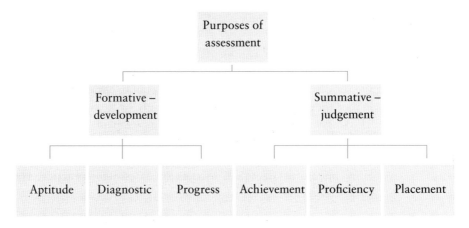

The first level in this classification distinguishes between formative and summative assessment. Formative assessment is developmental, and is intended to give feedback to improve students' understanding and performance. Summative assessment, on the other hand, is judgemental, and is concerned with permission to proceed to the next stage:[4] this might be into university, into the next level of study, or out into the world of work. Both these types of assessment are used to evaluate what has been learned or to make predictions about future performance.

Task 2

Look back to the typical judgements (above) that teachers make about students.

- What purposes do you think the teachers had in making these assessments?

- Identify which categories in the diagram these comments illustrate?

Formative assessment

Formative assessment provides students with ongoing informal feedback which is intended to shape and change their learning. Because it is shared and negotiated between teachers and students, it requires a climate of trust in which students are prepared to take risks, make mistakes and learn from these, knowing that they will not be disadvantaged. Teachers are able to give more support to a performance without worrying that the work is not then entirely the student's own. It should carry no consequences for their final grades and, indeed, some writers argue that it should not even be given a grade[5] because that changes the way students respond. However, grades are important to students, and it is only by assigning grades to their own or their classmates' work that they learn what constitutes acceptable performance. The possibility of increasing their grade can be used to encourage students to engage with feedback, and use it to improve their work. Formative assessment also provides ongoing informal feedback to the teacher on the appropriateness of course design and the effectiveness of teaching.

Formative assessment can be carried out formally with aptitude, diagnostic and progress tests, or informally, based on homework tasks or teachers' observations, and interactions with students in class. Comment 3 above, about not being a good language learner, describes aptitude, and could form the basis for guiding a student towards choosing a degree subject that does not make a high demand on language competence. Comments 1 and 4, about reading and typical mistakes, are likely to be diagnostic or about progress. Diagnostic assessment evaluates what a student can or cannot do at a particular point, e.g., the beginning of a course, whereas statements about progress involve commenting on students' process of learning, how they have developed over the duration of a course, and whether they are moving in the right direction. Although aptitude, diagnostic and progress tests are usually targeted specifically at the needs of students on a particular course or programme, they share some of the features of summative tests.

Summative assessment

Summative assessment is usually carried out formally, using achievement, proficiency or placement tests, often with large cohorts of students. This is a necessary part of learning and, although teachers may wish otherwise, it is usually the most important focus for students. Achievement tests are given at the end of a course, and relate directly back to the content and skills that have been taught. They are designed to measure how well the students have achieved the objectives of the course, so both the course content and the assessment tasks must be aligned closely with the course objectives to provide meaningful results. Once EAP students have gained entry to university, most of their summative assessment will be concerned with achievement.

Unlike achievement tests, proficiency tests do not look back to a pre-set body of knowledge and skills which has been presented during a course. The purpose of these tests is to make predictions about language performance in the future, either for a specific work or study purpose, or in general terms. Therefore, they are based on specifications of the target language used in specific situations, or the general standards that a student can be expected to achieve in understanding and using language. One such set of standards is the Common European Framework of Reference for Languages[6] to which, for example, the UK Trinity College and University of Cambridge ESOL suites of proficiency tests are linked. Whereas achievement tests can measure short-term gains over a term or semester, and also indicate aptitude for learning, proficiency tests attempt to measure a characteristic, proficiency level, which is relatively stable over that period.[7] Comment 5 above, about coping at university, is a comment about proficiency and, indeed, the main purpose of proficiency testing in EAP is to select students for university entrance.

Placement testing is used to decide in which language class or level a student should study. There are usually no serious consequences to this because students placed initially in a class inappropriate for their level are normally able to move. Comment 2 above, about the best class for a student, is a comment about placement. Placement tests are often similar to proficiency tests in that a set of tasks for the test is obtained by sampling the entire language. Both tests aim to discriminate between different levels of ability in order to rank students. One way placement tests do this is to include more items than it is normally possible to complete in the time allowed for the test. This means that lower level students do not manage to complete as much of the test as higher level students, and this results in a wide range of marks.

In practice, it is not as easy as this classification suggests to separate the functions of tests – formative or summative – or the types of tests from one another. For example, a summative achievement test for the final year of an undergraduate degree might also provide formative feedback on aptitude for further study in the subject at postgraduate level. A language proficiency test might give diagnostic information. However, in choosing to administer a particular type of test, it is important to be clear about the uses to which the test and its results will be put, and how appropriate the test is for those purposes.

Tests are often used inappropriately because they are available, and are well known for one purpose, and therefore assumed to be equally useful for other purposes. For example, achievement or progress on a short, intensive pre-sessional EAP course will not be measured fairly by using a proficiency test[8] because there has not been enough time for students' overall level of proficiency to improve. A study[9] of IELTS candidates on such short courses showed that those who entered with a writing band score of 5 or 6 made almost no gains in this score on courses lasting less than seven weeks. However, these students are likely to have gained useful information, and improved their skills for studying at university, aspects which proficiency tests are not able to measure. Progress on pre-sessional courses is more appropriately tested with a project which integrates reading and writing, and requires students to demonstrate that they can use study and research skills in authentic ways.

The impact of assessment

Even the most carefully constructed tests can be used in ways that are not foreseen by the test designers. Global proficiency exams such as TOEFL (Test of English as a Foreign Language)[10] or IELTS (International English Language Testing System)[11] are routinely used to predict whether students are likely to have a level of language sufficient for university study. These are referred to as *high stakes* tests because the consequences for a student are crucial for gaining entry to university programmes. There is a cut-off point in the range of test scores above which students are accepted and below which they are rejected. Both testing agencies emphasize that language proficiency should not be the only criterion for entry or exclusion, but should be considered together with academic qualifications and the language requirements of particular courses.[12] In practice, other very different factors can influence the decision by an institution to accept or reject students. Indeed, this can sometimes simply depend on whether quotas for numbers on courses have been met, with cut-off scores being set high for popular courses and low for less popular ones.

Naturally, students and their teachers tend to adjust their learning and teaching to accommodate preparation for these global exams, and the publishers of teaching materials accommodate this focus.[13] For example, there are many more textbooks available to provide students with strategies to handle the tasks in these exams than there are to teach the language and skills needed for university study. This impact of a test on learning and teaching – referred to as *washback* – can have negative consequences, which will be examined later in more detail.

A number of studies[14] have compared the task types and the assessment criteria used in high stakes proficiency tests with those used in university assessment. The tasks for large-scale proficiency tests are necessarily less diverse and complex than assessment tasks at university, and the assessment criteria, e.g., for writing and speaking, focus mainly on language, while university assessment criteria are more concerned with content, critical analysis, and logical development of ideas and argument. This means that the construct for the proficiency test, i.e., the underlying assumptions about language and skills on which measurements are based, leaves out important aspects. A university preparation course which focuses mainly on proficiency test preparation risks under-preparing students for the language and assessment demands of their university courses.[15] Increasingly, university language centres in the UK which run pre-sessional courses use a wider range of assessment types, and the relatively small number of students on such courses enables these centres to provide detailed reports on each student for admissions tutors in their institutions. These are thought to give a more accurate indication of students' aptitude for university study than a one-off external proficiency test designed for large numbers of test-takers world-wide.

There are important considerations in the design and reporting of EAP assessments if they are to give accurate predictions about students' ability to cope with university study using the medium of English. Tests need to simulate authentic academic study and assessment tasks, and require students to use language in ways that reflect these authentic tasks.[16] The preceding chapters outlined the kinds of reading, writing, listening and speaking abilities that are expected of students at university. However, it is also important to investigate university assessment practices in order to match EAP assessment to these.

Assessment at university

University assessment practices are changing in response to wider access, a focus on lifelong learning, and new course structures. In the last 30 years, which have seen rapid social and technological change, universities in industrialized countries have been encouraged to admit larger numbers of students from a wider range of backgrounds, and to educate and train them for new types of employment.[17] Although governments do not have direct control over university curricula, they can have an indirect influence through decisions to fund particular types of courses, e.g., science and engineering. Degrees are also sometimes linked to professional qualifications, which do have a direct influence on course design and assessment. There has been a shift from a focus on what is taught to a focus on what is to be learned, with greater emphasis generally on the development of professional skills transferable to work.[18] Students are now expected to be able to understand not only the subject matter of a course but also how and when to apply this knowledge in practice.[19] Course content is specified in terms of learning outcomes, i.e., not what is in a syllabus but what students should be able to understand and do. The learning process has been made more explicit to enable students to continue learning once they leave university and begin work. At the same time, university courses have been restructured into smaller units or modules. The ultimate aim is to try to harmonize standards across the huge variety of degrees and disciplines, and facilitate student transfer between institutions. In practice, however, modular structures have sometimes led to increased assessment loads and a reduction in the coherence of courses.

Task 3

Think back to your experience of undergraduate university study.

- What types of assessment were you given?

- What was being tested in these assessments?

- What was your attitude to these assessments?

- Did you consider that they gave a fair indication of your knowledge and abilities?

- Did you think they were a useful way to prepare you for working life?

Prior to the changes of the last 30 years, assessment at university undergraduate level in the UK typically took the form of coursework and exams, with the latter providing most of the evidence of achievement for final grades. Coursework consisted of essays (for humanities and social sciences) and reports of practical laboratory sessions or field trips (for science and engineering). Although there is now a much wider range of assessment types, these traditional forms are still common. Lecturers see essays as 'more open-ended, less structured' with 'an argument of some sort', giving students an opportunity to show 'evidence of independent thought'.[20] Reports have a more conventional structure with the aim of presenting information accurately. Both these types of assessment are intended only for an academic audience, and would not be appropriate in the workplace, where, for example, reports are usually brief and are less likely to contain citations.

Examinations

Assessment through examinations is supposed to ensure that all students receive the same type of assessment, and the possibility for cheating is minimized – an administrative rather than an educational purpose. Exams are most suitable for determining students' knowledge and understanding of core content, and their ability to use familiar problem-solving strategies. It is claimed they also test an ability to structure thinking and write quickly under pressure. While this may be the case, writing to display knowledge does not simulate any time-constrained performance in the real world. Even academics and professionals who have succeeded at university report feelings of panic and inadequacy before exams, and frustration that this could prevent them from displaying what they had learned.[21] Exam revision was thought to encourage students to develop an overall picture of their learning. In reality, it is more likely to encourage rote memorization, and a strategic approach through question-spotting.[22] The main problem with exams is that they are snapshot assessments, and thus highly dependent on how the candidate is feeling and performing on the day.

Coursework

Assessed coursework was introduced to give a more rounded picture of student ability, and to reduce the threatening nature of assessment, by allowing students more time and resources to complete their tasks. It was also seen as more authentic in relation to professional tasks. There is now an enormous variety of assessment types,[23] both oral and written, within institutions, and a greater emphasis on reflective writing, in which students evaluate their own performance and learning. Open-book or take-home exams have been introduced, providing an opportunity to assess learning at the level of analysis and application. Oral and practice assessments are common, especially on courses linked to professional qualifications. Students are often involved as agents in assessment processes rather than being just the recipients of grades. In portfolio assessments, they prepare a range of assignments in a variety of formats, and choose what to include for assessment, and, in team assignments, individuals assess the contribution of team members. There is also a greater awareness that, in order to transfer their learning to work, students need practice-based assessments which require them to write professional genres, for example, case reports in nursing, medicine and law, or site investigation reports in engineering.[24]

Two approaches to assessment at university

As learning and teaching approaches and assessment practices change, the way that grades are determined and reported has also changed. Rather than comparing and ranking students so that the most able can be identified, as in *norm-referenced assessment* (NRA), student performance is now compared to benchmark statements which indicate a specified standard of achievement, termed *criterion-referenced assessment* (CRA).[25]

When marks are *norm-referenced*, they are expressed against a statistical average, or norm, for all the students taking a particular test diet. Tests are designed so that student scores spread out across a range of marks.[26] This range is then divided into bands or grades, with fixed proportions of students for each grade. Although such statistical measures may seem objective, precise and consistent, in fact they can be elastic and arbitrary. They assume that every cohort of students at a certain level has a similar range of abilities, so that any differences in the numbers of students achieving high or low marks from one year to the next will be a consequence of differences in the composition of each test or the way it is marked. This allows the marks to be adjusted so that the same proportion of students achieves a grade A or B or C every year. As a consequence, if a particular cohort happens to contain a high number of academically advanced students, some will be disadvantaged as there is only a fixed percentage of A grades available to the group.

In contrast, when assessment is *criterion-referenced*, students pass or fail depending on whether they meet specified criteria. This is the way people learn in real life, e.g., to swim or drive a car. For each of these performances, the criteria or standards that define success are clear in advance. There is also the possibility of learning at different rates, and trying the assessment several times until the standard has been achieved. If the criteria for each level of performance are clearly described, the assessment can be objective, precise and consistent. The proportion of students passing or failing can be expected to vary from year to year. Criterion-referenced assessment requires teaching and learning to be closely aligned to assessment. This makes strategic use of students' natural focus on assessment, creating washback that is more positive. An example of this type of assessment is seen at postgraduate level when assessing dissertations and theses. Judgements are made about the quality of the research, the methods used, and the review of background literature against expected standards for each of these elements.

Criterion-referenced assessment requires the criteria for success to be clearly specified in advance, as these give a transparent basis for grading performance. If students can study the criteria, they understand what constitutes success. However, marking practices at university have not always been transparent, as illustrated in the following case study.

Case study A:

In the mid-1990s (when I was new to EAP teaching), I was asked to help a group of mature students who were studying a single module from a degree in community education as part of their workplace professional development. They were struggling to write an essay examining an aspect of their practice in the light of the theoretical concepts they had been studying on the module. The lecturer gave me the essay questions that the students could choose from, and we had the following exchange:

EAP teacher: What do you expect students to write in this essay?

Lecturer: I won't know until they've written it.

Task 4

- How do you imagine the lecturer was going to assess the students' essays?

- How helpful do you think this response was for the students and for the EAP teacher?

The lecturer was probably going to assess the essays globally or holistically, from a general impression of their overall quality rather than by awarding marks for different aspects such as content, argument, organization and language. (I assume that if he had a set of specified criteria against which to mark the essays, he would have given them to me.) As an experienced lecturer who had previously seen a large number of essays on similar topics, he might have had a general idea of what the students would produce. However, his response suggests that he was also open to the possibility that the students might produce something original, and he did not want to preclude this by specifying criteria in advance. Of course, it is also possible that he had set the essay topics without giving much thought to what the students might write or how he might help them, and had called in an EAP teacher when he realized they were going to struggle.

His response was not at all helpful for the students or the EAP teacher, neither of whom had any idea how to approach this particular essay. The students had written many workplace reports which detailed their daily practice, but did not know how these might be incorporated into the essay. As a new EAP teacher, I had a generic concept of an essay as an answer to a question which required reference to a variety of different viewpoints, but I did not know how this was similar or different to the lecturer's view of this genre within his field of community education. I discovered later (from colleagues who had studied the full course) that this particular degree was underpinned by a hidden discourse of critical literacy which the students would have been expected to use as a theoretical framework. If the lecturer had made this information explicit to the students, it would have helped them enormously, and it is likely they would have written better essays as a result.

Alignment in the curriculum

This case study is an example of the hidden curriculum, where students have to guess what is required in their assessments.[27] It was common in norm-referenced assessment practice because it could be used to identify the academically able students,[28] and may still be prevalent in some universities. However, advocates of criterion-referenced assessment[29] suggest that, in order to engage students from a variety of different backgrounds in the learning process, there needs to be a close alignment between learning outcomes, teaching, and learning methods and assessment. The criteria for assessment must be specified, and the standards required to achieve different levels of performance for each criterion clearly described and linked to particular grades. These standards should be made explicit to students before they attempt the tasks. The documents which specify criteria, describe standards, and link them to grades are called descriptors. Students interact with the descriptors by applying the criteria and standards they describe to essays written by former students, and discussing the suggested grades with the teacher. This interaction ensures that students understand how to do a task and, in the process, they learn to assess their own performance. Students' ability to continue learning and evaluating their performance once they leave university can be enhanced if they are also involved in designing some assessment tasks, and negotiating descriptors to apply to their own and their peers' work.

Students also need formative feedback on their work linked explicitly to the assessment descriptors, and a chance to discuss this individually with a teacher. Conscientious teachers expend considerable efforts in providing useful feedback which students do not always put to good use by redrafting their work.[30] They need encouragement in the form of exercises based on model answers. These can help them engage actively with feedback, and use it to improve their work. Feedback should highlight positive aspects of the work as well as negative, comment on only a few areas which are directly relevant to the purpose of the assignment, and help students identify patterns of problems which they can try to avoid in the next assignment.[31]

Universities are moving towards a model of good practice which requires that both summative and formative assessment be appropriate for its purpose, and closely aligned with learning outcomes and course content. The process is made transparent by providing clear assessment goals and criteria which students can use to evaluate their own work. This good practice in assessment at university is followed in many EAP courses which are accredited by their institutions, or by professional organizations such as the British Association of Lecturers of EAP (BALEAP).[32]

Quality assurance in university assessment

University summative assessment is supported by quality assurance procedures such as the requirements for exams to be checked, and exam scripts to be marked *blind*, so the markers do not know the identity of the students. These procedures are overseen by external examiners from other universities, who attend examination boards to check consistency and fairness in the awarding of grades. In EAP teaching centres situated within universities, this good practice is also followed because teaching, learning and assessment, e.g., on foundation courses, are also subject to the university's quality assurance procedures. In this case, EAP courses can match their learning outcomes and assessment to the requirements of particular degree programmes, and students who do not quite make the grade can, nevertheless, be admitted to a programme with a recommendation to study on in-sessional EAP courses. However, these options are not usually available in centres outside a university context. Students preparing for academic study in these centres have to demonstrate that they have the appropriate language proficiency to be successful at university by taking one of the global proficiency exams, for example, IELTS and TOEFL. In the next section, these exams are considered within a framework designed to evaluate the usefulness of a test for its specified purpose.

Evaluating the usefulness of a test

It is important to remember that all language tests make compromises. Communicative language ability is an abstract concept which cannot be measured directly, so it is necessary to specify tasks which elicit language behaviour that can be measured. These tasks cannot measure language behaviour in an authentic situation, but in a test situation. An assumption is made that the two situations and the tasks are sufficiently similar to allow inferences to be drawn from students' scores in the test about their ability to use language in a real situation. Evaluating the quality of any test involves asking questions about these underlying assumptions, and the usefulness of the test for a particular purpose.

Bachman and Palmer[33] developed a model for evaluating the usefulness of a test for its specified purpose. Their model (modified slightly by Douglas[34]) contains the following test qualities, which interact in combinations that vary with each test situation:

- *Validity* concerns the evidence that is provided to justify interpretations of test performance, and is derived from the *test construct*, i.e., the underlying assumptions about language and skills on which measurements for a particular test are based. It is important to be sure that the test measures what it claims to measure, and that it is appropriate to measure this for the particular test purpose.

- *Reliability* involves the consistency of measurement in different situations, and is influenced by factors such as the setting, the different forms of a test, and the different raters who score the test. It is important to be sure that students are not disadvantaged by taking one form of the test rather than another or being rated by different people.

- *Authenticity* concerns the degree to which tasks in the test are representative of tasks in the target language situation, and to what extent they engage the test takers communicative language ability, background knowledge and strategic competence.

- *Impact* considers what happens as a result of using tests for particular purposes, both in terms of the way society views or uses a test and the way it affects individuals. The notion of washback is part of the impact of a test.

- *Practicality* is the availability of resources required to develop and deliver the test, and how costly the test is in terms of these resources.

Validity and reliability are often discussed together in the literature on testing because changes in one tend to affect the other for a particular test purpose. Their relationship can be illustrated simply by using the example of a driving test carried out on a computer simulator rather than on the road. The design of the computer simulation for the test is based on a *construct* of driving which describes measurable performance on which to base test tasks. The construct could be very narrow, resulting in a limited set of tasks, e.g., each driver sees a road moving past him on the computer screen and, by operating the controls, he is able to stay on the correct side of the road and turn a corner or stop when so instructed. If each driver saw the same road with the same sequence of corners and stops, this performance could be measured very reliably by simply counting the number of times each driver drifted to the wrong side or failed to turn a corner or stop. However, this construct *under-represents* the complexity of authentic driving performance and reduces validity. These test results could not be used with confidence to make predictions about a driver's safety on the real road.

More complexity could be added to the computer simulation to widen the construct, and make it a better representation of the authentic driving situation, by including random pedestrians, traffic controls or other potential hazards. Validity would be improved because predictions on the basis of the test results could be made with more confidence. However, this new complexity would make it more difficult to ensure that if the same driver was tested on two different days, he would achieve the same result. Drivers with different skills profiles would perform better on different parts of the test. Thus, the reliability of the test would be reduced. The more closely the construct matches the complexity of the authentic situation, the more confidence there can be in predicting a driver's safety on the road, but the less reliable the measurement is likely to be. This is also the case for language testing.

Applying the model of test usefulness to global exams

TOEFL and IELTS are large-scale high stakes tests used worldwide by over 6,000 agencies and institutions in the case of TOEFL, and close to 5,000 institutions and 700,000 students for IELTS. Their stated purposes are very similar.

- IELTS 'measures ability to communicate in English across all four language skills – listening, reading, writing and speaking – for people who intend to study or work where English is the language of communication'.
- TOEFL 'measures the ability of non-native speakers of English to use and understand English as it is spoken, written, and heard in college and university settings'.[35]

In aiming to maximize usefulness, designers of these large-scale high stakes tests try to achieve a balance among all five qualities, so that one of them does not drive the test at the expense of the others. The way this is done can be illustrated by considering example tasks from TOEFL and IELTS. There is not space to evaluate all aspects of these tests in detail, so only tasks designed to test academic writing are considered.

Task 5

The four test items below were all designed to test writing ability for university.

- For each of the test qualities outlined above, Validity, Reliability, Authenticity, Impact and Practicality, decide if this item would be high or low [in the case of impact, decide if it would be positive or negative].

- Which item do you think achieves the best balance between the five qualities?

Item 1 Multiple choice
Choose the best answer to fill the gap from the four listed below it. [constructed example]
Writing is a complex activity which _____ a variety of skills.
    1 requires
    2 is required
    3 required
    4 is requiring
	V =
	
	R =
	
	A =
	
	I =
	
	P =

Item 2 Essay prompt Do you agree or disagree with the following statement? *Always telling the truth is the most important consideration in any relationship.* Use specific reasons and examples to support your answer.[36]	V = R = A = I = P =
Item 3 Essay prompt Write about the following topic. *It is inevitable that as technology develops so traditional cultures must be lost. Technology and tradition are incompatible – you cannot have both together. To what extent do you agree or disagree?* Give reasons for your answer and include any relevant examples from your own knowledge or experience.[37]	V = R = A = I = P =
Item 4 Integrated skills prompt Test takers are given time to read a passage and take notes. They then listen to a lecture on the same topic, but with a different point of view to that in the reading passage. The reading passage is then presented again together with the following prompt: Summarize the points made in the lecture you just heard, explaining how they cast doubt on points made in the reading.[38]	V = R = A = I = P =

The first multiple-choice item focuses on knowledge of discrete grammar points, and is derived from a fairly narrow construct which assumes that testing knowledge of grammar is sufficient to indicate writing ability. This was similar to the question type for the TOEFL before it was substantially revised. Validity and authenticity would be low as this is not a direct test of real performance. However, reliability and practicality would be high because such tests are easy to mark and administer, especially in computerized form. Impact, in terms of washback, is likely to be negative because students might prepare for the test by practising multiple-choice items rather than by trying to use correct grammar in their writing. The teacher might focus more on grammar knowledge rather than writing performance.

Essay prompts 2 and 3 are examples from the current TOEFL and IELTS tests. They aim to assess writing directly through tasks which elicit performance. In comparison with item 1, they are based on a much wider construct of communicative language ability, which includes not just knowledge about language, but knowledge about when and how to use language. Student writing for these items is scored using descriptors which give a single holistic score based on an overall impression of the text – in the case of TOEFL – or specify different levels of performance for task response, coherence and cohesion, lexical resource, and grammatical range and accuracy – in the case of IELTS. Reliability is ensured by training raters, and statistically comparing their judgements on samples of student writing. For TOEFL, all scripts are double marked, whereas, for IELTS, only a sample of scripts are marked by two raters. Thus validity is likely to be higher than item 1 but reliability and practicality would be lower as the responses are more complex and require human judgement.

These test items make compromises in terms of the authenticity of the task, and the students' interaction with it. Neither of the essay prompts simulates real-life academic writing tasks, which are usually much longer, are based not on personal opinion but on ideas from source materials such as lectures or textbooks and, except in exams, are not written under time constraints. These items either do not specify an audience or refer in general terms to 'a university lecturer', whereas academic essays are usually written for a particular tutor who is relatively well known to the student writers and who will grade the writing mainly on content rather than language.[39] In addition, the essay prompts in items 2 and 3 can encourage formulaic responses in students with low proficiency, or a classroom focus that over-emphasizes a personal viewpoint. However, this impact is likely to be less negative than for item 1.

TOEFL has recently undergone substantial redevelopment. Designers have sought to improve the measurement of writing ability, increase the authenticity of the writing response, and create positive washback by introducing an integrated skills writing task,[40] as illustrated in item 4. Reliability in marking is likely to be about the same as items 2 and 3 as it is also scored holistically using descriptors, but validity should be higher as the construct for this item integrates reading and writing. The integrated skills task is closer to the authentic type of writing expected at university, so it should also encourage positive washback in teaching and learning. The new format of the test is based on research into common types of texts and interactions, using a corpus of university texts containing 2.7 million words.[41] This item probably achieves the best balance between the qualities in the model of test usefulness.

However, the quality of authenticity in the test usefulness model includes the extent to which tasks engage the test takers' communicative language ability and background knowledge, suggesting an interaction between these. The effect of background knowledge on test scores in the IELTS reading sub-test was investigated in a detailed study[42] which found that postgraduate students achieved higher scores on a reading test related to their degree subject if the text topic was specific enough. There was no significant effect for undergraduate students, and there seemed to be a threshold of language proficiency below which students were not able to make use of background knowledge. Studies have also demonstrated the influence of background knowledge in writing.[43] These findings suggest that students with an intermediate proficiency level (e.g., IELTS 5.5) could use their knowledge of a subject in reading and writing tasks at university to compensate for a lack of language proficiency.[44] However, this important interaction between language knowledge and subject knowledge is not tested in either IELTS or TOEFL. Instead, test designers try to reduce the effects of background knowledge in order to avoid introducing cultural bias so that the test can be used with students from a wide range of backgrounds.

The impact of global exams

The evaluation of these test items illustrates the kinds of compromises that are made to try to balance the five test qualities in the test usefulness model when designing and delivering large-scale, high stakes tests for a diverse population of students. The constraints of administering global tests of the size of IELTS and TOEFL mean that the quality of *practicality* predominates requiring a narrower test construct and reduced task complexity. This means that these global tests are likely to be less suitable for specific groups of students than tests developed locally and adapted to their specific context, provided these are carefully designed.[45] However, it is often not possible for teachers to develop their own local tests, so it is important to try to ensure that the impact of global tests on teaching and learning is positive.

Task 6

> Think about your experience of preparing students for any high stakes test you are familiar with.
>
> - What were your feelings about the test? Did you expect it would be a fair test of your students' language ability?
>
> - Did you change the materials you used in class, or your style of teaching, because your students were going to sit this test?
>
> - If you did change your materials or teaching style, was this your own decision or as a result of pressure, e.g., from students or your institution?
>
> - Were you happy about any changes you made to your materials or teaching style?

Spratt reviewed 11 empirical studies of washback conducted in a variety of teaching and learning contexts in Hong Kong, New Zealand, Canada, Sri-Lanka and Japan.[46] Findings from these studies suggest that the beliefs and attitudes of teachers towards an exam are key factors in determining whether, and to what extent, they will change their teaching approaches when preparing students for that exam. Some teachers do not change their materials or teaching style, but find creative ways of bringing test preparation into the classroom, while others become 'textbook slaves' and overtly teach to the test, with less interaction or laughter in their classes and more teacher talk. This is more likely to happen if teachers do not like the test or do not understand its role in the educational system. If they perceive that the test does not align with their course aims or teaching content, they may not see it as a fair assessment of their students' abilities. Teachers sometimes say that they like exam classes because the aims are clear and the students work in a more focused way, but that pressure from students forces them to spend more time on exam strategies and exam practice. However, in a survey of 108 students from mainland China studying on university preparation courses in the UK with IELTS or non-IELTS exit exams,[47] Green found that students on both types of course arrived with very similar expectations of what they would learn about writing, although they went on to have very different experiences in terms of the content of their courses. The classes which did not use IELTS focused on university writing tasks and the conventions of referencing. In contrast, the classes which used IELTS had a more narrow focus on question 1 of the academic writing test, the description of graphs and diagrams. This may be because the teachers themselves found this type of writing difficult, and assumed their students would also.[48] The study concluded that the students in IELTS classes may not have received sufficient instruction to prepare them for university writing.

Spratt concludes her review by suggesting that 'washback is not inevitable ... [and] is largely in the teacher's control'.[49] Inexperienced or unmotivated teachers may feel more comfortable relying on an exam preparation course book, but their students may be disadvantaged as a result. There is currently no evidence that coaching for an EAP exam produces better results, and it certainly does not contribute to long-term quality learning. When preparing students for exams, Spratt recommends using authentic texts and tasks drawn from the target academic context, setting clear goals which take students beyond the gate-keeping exam, but including activities, e.g., short, time-constrained writing tasks, which will also be useful for the exam. Students need to interact with the exam marking criteria and apply these to their own performance in writing or speaking. They also need regular feedback from the teacher and their peers which clearly shows them how they can improve. The next section looks at ways to create a classroom ethos which encourages positive washback.

Encouraging learning through classroom assessment

The EAP classroom is a rich and complex social space which allows for more authentic performance and interaction in assessment than is possible in a high stakes exam. Whereas global exams tend to prioritize the qualities of reliability and practicality in the model of test usefulness above, classroom assessment can focus on validity, authenticity and impact.[50] For example, in addition to timed exams, it is possible to use extended pieces of coursework for writing assessment, which enable students to research and write about their degree subject, to work through the writing process, and to produce better quality work as a result of feedback from their teacher and classmates.[51] Reliability and practicality are still important to ensure consistency in giving grades, and efficiency in time spent on providing formative feedback, but they need not be the main focus.

Ensuring validity

In terms of validity, EAP classroom assessment tasks can be based on a construct of communicative language ability which is more complex than those underlying global language exams. This includes knowledge of when and how to use language in specified contexts for particular purposes and audiences. Most classroom assessment, both oral and written, can be performance-based[52] and integrated. For example, students can work on an assignment over several weeks, with classroom support for activities such as understanding essay questions, in the case of undergraduates, or defining their own research question for postgraduates. Language and skills can be integrated in purposeful tasks, such as selecting and reading relevant sources to summarize or quote from directly, using appropriate referencing conventions. Assessment of listening and speaking skills can be managed through presentation and discussion of essay content or research findings, suitably modified for the peer group audience. The university context can be simulated by setting deadlines for submitting drafts, and students can gain familiarity with assessment criteria by applying them to drafts written by their classmates in discussion with the teacher. Students improve their ability to formulate evidence-based reasoning in discussions by justifying their evaluation of their own and their classmates' work against the assessment criteria.

Validity is also enhanced by having a variety of assessment tasks of different types and lengths to demonstrate both development and achievement. This can be formalized in portfolio assessment, where students select a range of performances for different purposes and audiences. Some of these might be authentic samples written for content courses, or multiple drafts to show the process of revision in response to peer or teacher feedback. The collection is usually accompanied by a reflective essay in which the student introduces the contents, explains why they were chosen, and how they demonstrate strengths and progress. This requirement to document thought and practice as they evolve enables students to become aware of their metacognitive development.[53] An essential feature of portfolios is delayed evaluation, giving students a chance to improve their work before receiving a final grade. Assessment is based on descriptors which evaluate individual items, as well as the overall coherence of the portfolio and the writer's capacity for self-awareness and reflection.[54] Portfolios are good instruments for aligning learning outcomes with assessment because students need to know in advance how their work will be assessed in order to be able to choose the contents appropriately.

In addition to longer assignments such as those described above, the variety of assessment can include quick checks on learning. For example, at the beginning of a lesson, you can conduct an informal review by asking students to report what they remember from the previous lesson or what the point of it was. This tests whether students can remember information and re-present it in their own words. It can be done in a slightly more formal way by constructing an *oral paragraph*. Each student in turn is required to add more detail to a general statement responding to a question about the content and learning in a previous lesson, with prompting from the teacher if necessary. An example for part of a review of the listening lesson in Classroom materials 7.1 *Academic listening strategies* might be as follows:

T   What did we do in the last lesson?

S1 We watched a video.

S2 We did some reading before we watched the video.

S3 Not all of us read. Only one group had the reading and then we all watched the video.

T   Can you remember the names we used for the two groups?

S4 The control group. They didn't read but the experimental group read before the class.

T   Why did we do it this way?

S5 To find out if reading helps when we are listening.

S6 We compared the groups so we could see if the reading group could understand better.

For exam preparation classes targeting either global or local exams, the first five minutes of a lesson can be used for practising timed writing based on a prompt in the form of a functional diagram such as a comparison and contrast table, a cause and effect chain, or a classification diagram. This helps students to practise thinking and writing quickly for exams, it recycles functional vocabulary, and it also shows the advantage of making an outline plan based on the function specified in an exam prompt before starting to write. These writing prompts can be recycled as end-of-unit writing questions, with the timed writing then acting as revision. Quick-fire exam strategies, such as reading quickly to answer a Big Picture question, can also be tested at the beginning of a lesson.

You can design short tests, e.g., to check vocabulary knowledge, but you should warn students to expect these regularly, and negotiate with them what form the tests should take, how often they should occur, and the best way to prepare for them. Generally, tasks should test vocabulary in context, as described in Chapter 4, using a meaningful piece of text, perhaps a summary of a class reading, rather than a set of decontextualized sentences. Tasks might range from retrieval and matching tasks, e.g., finding collocates or matching words to definitions, to production tasks, such as completing gapped texts or using new vocabulary in writing. Traditional gap-fills can be revitalized by presenting them as crossword grids with a variety of clues, e.g., definitions or collocations. Reference pages can be gapped, and a text containing the functional language provided for support if required. Students can also create their own gap-fill tests, using the Academic Word Highlighter, or paper versions of a text and some White-out™. The topics for the oral paragraph and timed writing tasks described above can be chosen to provide further opportunities to revise vocabulary.

These short tests are ideal for moving students down the cline of control mentioned in Chapter 9 in order to help them become autonomous and develop the capacity for reflection and self-evaluation. For example, before doing a timed writing task, students could choose whether they want to revise a functional reference page for a few minutes or have it to support them as they write. In addition to negotiating the timing and type of vocabulary tests, students can take responsibility for predicting their scores on the tests, marking them using a key, and keeping a record of the difference between their predicted and actual scores. These records are the responsibility of the students, and only need to be shown to the teacher during tutorials when reviewing vocabulary learning strategies. The same tests can be used to diagnose gaps in students' vocabulary knowledge, and then presented later in the course to discover what students have learned. If students protest that they have already seen the test and will remember the answers, you can point out that this is an appropriate outcome.

If you administer a diagnostic writing test at the beginning of a course, this can also be used to demonstrate to students what they have learned. The same writing prompt can be given again towards the end of the course for students to compare their first and second attempts. If they have learned to apply marking criteria to sample essays during the course, they can apply these to an unmarked copy of their diagnostic writing, and then reflect on the progress they have made in the course.[55]

Ensuring authenticity

Authenticity concerns the target language situation and students' ability to interact with tasks required in that situation. Whereas the global language exams attempt to remove contextual references to ensure fairness to students going into a broad range of disciplines, classroom assessment can make full use of students' background knowledge. Especially for mixed EAP classes, where the content of lessons has to be more general to be appropriate to all the students, individual coursework can be tied to the specific subjects they will be studying. For example, if they are following a functional syllabus, students can be asked to define a concept or discuss a problem in their field in a way that makes it clear to educated non-specialists (their teacher and classmates). Authenticity in assessment requires an analysis of the target situation[56] but, in these types of assessment tasks, the analysis is effectively carried out by the students, who already have some background knowledge and can add to this through their reading for the task. Teacher and classmates provide an authentic audience who are likely to know less about the topic than the writers, encouraging them to produce an appropriate amount of description and explanation which will demonstrate their knowledge.

University language centres which are not obliged to use global exams to assess their students usually design exams to test performance on integrated tasks, enabling students to demonstrate a range of reading, writing and language skills tied to the content and outcomes of the course. The following format is an example taken from the exams for the Academic English for Business Studies course designed by the authors, and offered through the External Programmes at Heriot-Watt University. Other texts are used to test knowledge of vocabulary and grammar in context.

Stage	Timed tasks
Reading text: *The important features of money*	Big picture: choose the writer's purpose in a multiple choice question.[57]
	Critical thinking: think about an item, e.g., bananas, and say which of their features make them suitable or unsuitable as money.
	Focused note-taking: take notes from the text in order to answer a specific essay question, e.g., *To what extent are fish, salt or gold suitable or unsuitable as forms of money?*
Writing	Writing task (200–300 words): the critical thinking question is reworded slightly. Students should explain which of the three items would be the best one to consider as a form of money, and say what is wrong with the other two. The students are thus provided with the content for the writing task, but have to interact critically with this content and transform it in their writing.

Creating positive impact

In order for the impact of assessment on classroom activities to be positive, it must be aligned with course learning outcomes and course content. In particular, students applying for university who need to take a global language exam should be given clear explanations of how preparation for this exam fits into the wider learning goals, e.g., for academic research and referencing, and any other assessments on the course. EAP centres will normally have a student handbook which provides details of the course outcomes, content and assessment, but the EAP teacher needs to understand how these fit together in order to explain this clearly to students. As a general rule, students should see a plan of work each week which links the classroom activities to the syllabus for the course. They should be clear about the aims of each lesson and be able to see explicit links between the materials and activities in the lesson, and the texts and tasks they will meet both in assessment, and in their degree studies following the EAP course. This enables teachers to justify time spent on classroom activities.

Formal formative testing should be a regular aspect of EAP classroom routine as it gives students a sense of purpose in their learning, and provides feedback to teachers for fine-tuning the course. For example, students should have a short piece of writing at the end of each unit, typically once a week on a pre-sessional course with small class sizes, with an opportunity to redraft their work in response to feedback. Spoken performance can be tested with regular seminar discussions in which students evaluate each other's contributions. Moss[58] argues against giving grades for formative assessment, suggesting that it takes time to develop appropriate descriptors for each formative task and to assign grades. She also warns that, instead of using writing tutorials to learn how to improve their work, students might waste time arguing why their grade should be higher.

Task 7

- Do you consider it appropriate to give grades for formative assessment?

- How can teachers deal with students' obsession with grades?

Case study B:

A teacher working in a university language centre in the Middle East[59] reported that, when students received their grades at the end of a course, they would compare these with other students, and then request an interview with their teacher to discuss their grades with a view to improving them. The teacher found the interviews uncomfortable and frustrating, and they took up a lot of time. The reasons students gave usually had little to do with the quality of their coursework, and more to do with the consequences of receiving a low grade, e.g., disapproval from their families.

The teacher decided to involve the students in their final assessment. She gave out a self-evaluation sheet which described the performance, skills and knowledge they were expected to improve, but also asked about effort, motivation and participation. The teacher was apprehensive about the students' reaction, but in fact they took the task very seriously, and she was surprised by their accurate judgement of their work. They had a very clear idea of what they had done and still needed to work on. After this, the number of requests for grade improvements fell dramatically, and the teacher continued to encourage students to self-assess their work at the course end and at mid-term.

Teachers are sometimes afraid to share knowledge of their assessment practices with students, but it made this teacher's life easier. This transparency had a calming effect on the students, and made them less critical of the teacher's assessment and more focused. Students also need tasks which help them to engage with the criteria, e.g., applying them to a model answer or to their peers' assignments. Comparing their work with that of others helps students to assess their own performance. As well as applying assessment criteria, students can be involved in negotiating specific criteria, e.g., to define task achievement for an assignment.

Classroom
materials
10.1 *Applying
assessment
criteria* shows
how EAP students
can be encouraged
to interact with
assessment
criteria.

Students can be encouraged to take a critical view of assessment. Having attempted an assignment or timed writing activity, they can critically deconstruct the task, identifying features which caused difficulty, and suggesting how to deal with these in the next task or how the task prompt should be reworded. The teacher can present aspects of performance that were unsuccessful in some scripts and successful in others for whole class discussion. Students can examine model answers to understand how these achieve the purpose and are addressed appropriately to the audience specified in the task. This is important as it reminds students that, in addition to analysing features such as task achievement, language and organization, they should evaluate how the whole text makes an impact on the reader.

Ensuring reliability

Global language exams have had a beneficial effect on classroom assessment practices in terms of reliability because they have introduced assessment criteria to ensure consistency in grading between one student script and the next or between different raters. For large-scale exams, consistency in applying criteria and standards is checked statistically after the exams have been marked. These statistical measures are required because of the large number of test takers and their anonymity for those marking the test. In contrast, in the language classroom, the teacher comes to know the students well through regular informal measurement of their performance. Reliability in assessment is ensured through discussion with colleagues in moderation meetings, where each student's performance in a range of assessments can be considered. Assessment criteria are used as a framework to inform this discussion by providing statements of evidence to support evaluations of student work.[60]

Designing assessment criteria and standards

The criteria for assessing the construct to be measured must be specified, and the standards required to achieve different levels of performance for each criterion must be clearly described and linked to particular grades. The documents which specify criteria, describe standards and link them to grades are called descriptors. The descriptors might be holistic, in which case a single score is given, based on an overall impression of the text, and there is only one summary describing several criteria at each level. The TOEFL writing test uses this type of descriptor.[61] It can be quick and reliable to use but its main disadvantage is that it is difficult to apply to scripts which are weak in some criteria but strong in others. A better alternative for classroom use are *analytic* descriptors which describe levels for separate criteria such as task response, organization, cohesion, lexical and grammatical range, and accuracy. Marks or grades relating to the standard achieved for each criterion can be aggregated to give an overall score, or reported separately for diagnostic purposes. The IELTS writing and speaking tests use these kinds of descriptors, with a priority or weighting towards language rather than content. An alternative type of descriptor for classroom use is described by Upshur and Turner.[62] This is developed from an actual sample of student speaking or writing and 'requires the rater to make a series of binary choices about student performance that define boundaries between score levels'.

Analytic descriptors for classroom assessment can be modified to suit each assignment, and weighted to prioritize content and organization in the same way as university assessment.[63] Decisions about how to specify criteria have to be made on the basis of the construct for the assessment, e.g., whether cohesion is considered to be an aspect of organization or of language. It is difficult to define assessment criteria and standards unambiguously, and this is not in fact desirable.[64] If they are specified too closely, there is a danger that they will be applied mechanically. For example, if the descriptors used to assess writing explicitly specify the use of linking devices, then the absence of them could be wrongly interpreted as a weakness.[65] A text such as *Groups and group formation* in Chapter 2 is coherent because the ideas flow logically from one sentence to the next, even though this coherence is not signalled directly with linking devices. Such a text would receive a low mark if the criterion applied was the number of linking devices. However, there does need to be consistency in the description of standards between one level and the next, while also specifying a clear difference in level. This is often achieved by the use of lexical scales across the descriptors, e.g., complete–extensive–moderate–limited–none[66] or fully–generally–adequately–inadequately–rarely. An example set of analytic assessment descriptors designed for a classification task is shown on the following pages.

Table 1: *Example assessment criteria for writing a classification*

	A+ A A−	B+ B B−	C+ C C−	D+ D D−	E
Task achievement This concerns the main issues to be discussed, as well as the ability to establish a clear focus on the question.	• It fully answers all aspects of the task in sufficient depth. • The classification is set in an appropriate context, and the purpose explained. • The categories are clearly distinguished and explained.	• It answers the task in sufficient depth to cover the main points. • The classification is set in context, although the purpose may be unclear. • The categories are explained, but the classification may be unbalanced with one category dominating.	• The main points are covered, but there may be some unnecessary or irrelevant ideas. • The context and purpose may not be explained clearly. • There is some attempt to explain categories, but it may not be clear that the text is a classification.	• Not all aspects of the task are covered, or not in enough depth. • The context and purpose are not explained. • The text may be a description rather than a classification and fail to distinguish different categories.	• It misses the topic entirely or is much shorter than the required length. • The writer clearly does not understand the concept of classification.

	A+ A A−	B+ B B−	C+ C C−	D+ D D−	E
Structure and organization This relates to the overall structure of the writing, and the presence of an introduction and conclusion, as well as the division and linking of paragraphs.	• There is a suitable introduction and conclusion. • The sequence of paragraphs enhances understanding of the points being made. • Paragraphs follow a general to specific structure. • Understanding of the text is enhanced by the use of sentence linking devices, including summarizing noun phrases.	• There is an introduction and conclusion. • The sequence of paragraphs contributes to understanding of the points being made. • Most paragraphs follow a general to specific structure. • The use of sentence linking devices, including summarizing noun phrases, largely helps the reader to understand the text.	• There is an introduction and conclusion although they may be rather brief. • The sequence of paragraphs may show some weaknesses. • Some paragraphs follow a general to specific structure. • Sentence linking devices, including summarizing noun phrases, are sometimes used incorrectly, leading to misunderstanding.	• There may not be a suitable introduction or conclusion. • Attempts to sequence the paragraphs are evident but insufficient. • There is a general lack of structure in paragraphs. • Sentence linking devices, including summarizing noun phrases, are incorrectly or rarely used, making it difficult for the reader to follow the ideas or understand the text.	• The essay is unstructured or structured in such a way that prevents understanding. • Very few sentence linking devices appear and these are usually used incorrectly.

Language	A+ A A–	B+ B B–	C+ C C–	D+ D D–	E
Language This relates to the use of functional language and accuracy, and range in grammar and vocabulary.	• Mistakes are not significant. • A wide range of functional language is used which is appropriate for the essay question. • Vocabulary is appropriate throughout. • Appropriate academic style is used.	• Occasional mistakes occur, which do not prevent understanding. • A good range of functional language is used, which is appropriate for the question. • Vocabulary is mostly appropriate throughout. • Academic style is used for most of the essay.	• Repeated mistakes occur, which sometimes prevent understanding. • Some functional language is used. • Vocabulary is not always appropriate. • The style is sometimes not academic.	• There are a large number of serious mistakes. Meaning is often unclear. • There is only limited use of functional language. • Vocabulary and style are frequently inappropriate.	• The student has very little control over grammar and vocabulary, and is unable to make the meaning clear to a reader.

The descriptors illustrated were used for an assessed piece of coursework given to postgraduate students on an EAP course, in which they were asked to classify a concept or process in their field of study in around 300 words. They could use their own knowledge or investigate the topic through reading, but were not required to reference any sources because this was a consolidation task for a unit focusing on the organization and language for definition and classification. The prompt specified that their text should include an introduction to the field of study which also set the context and purpose for the classification; a definition of the concept or process; an explanation of the categories on which the classification was based; and examples which illustrated the categories clearly for a non-specialist reader.

Task 8

Below is a text written by a student in response to the prompt above.

- Apply the assessment criteria to this text to give it a grade. If possible, you should do this exercise with a colleague and discuss your assessment of the text.

- Note how you applied the criteria and if you had any problems using them to assess this student text.

Human resource management

Human resource management (HRM) is generally broken down into three or more functions. The first one of these is recruitment such as selecting application and interviewing candidate. Training is essential function to HRM including on-job-training (OJT) and off-job-training form. The third one, performance assessment (PA), is one of the most important elements for company's management. HRM is multi-function approach supporting system for members and organization's development and benefit.

Recruitment is a process of hiring right people for suitable position. The first step is that job vacancy should be analyzed and discovers core properties belonged to the position. According to the analyses, HRM employs different channels to notify and attract people. Next stage, HRM arranges interviews for qualified applicants who were selected form the job applications by assessments. Since demand departments and HRM both agree with the candidate, the recruitment is concluded.

The second category of HRM functions is training. Employee training separates into OJT and off-job-training. The difference between the two forms is training surroundings which are on or off company. OJT holds during working hours and focuses on the connection between practice and training. Off-job-training make employees pay more attention on the content of training because the training location is independent of company. The design of training activities bases on a company's business strategy. Discovering and understanding company and employees' sufficiency in the future, training supports and fulfils the task.

Probably the most important element of HRM function is PA. PA includes object formulating and assessment. The object formulating shall base on company's plan and be distributed responsibility to employees who is in charge. Recent performance of employees were compared with the object formulating and assessed. Consequently, the outcome of assessment connects with promotion and bonus given. Through PA, management becomes object approach. Not only dose a company manages employee easily, but also the employee is treated fair.

This student's teacher (T1) had some difficulties deciding what grade to give this particular script and asked her colleagues (T2 and T3) to discuss the grading with her.

Task 9

Below are some extracts from their discussion about task achievement together with their final decision.

- Did they discuss some of the problems you had with this text?

- Do you agree with their assessment?

- What do you notice about the way they used the criteria to arrive at the grade?

- T1 *I'll start with task achievement. I'm a little bit uncertain here because he hasn't really defined HRM but, on the other hand, he does have this sentence at the end of paragraph 1, so this is really a context.*

- T2 *It does look like a definition, doesn't it? But it's in the wrong place.*

- T3 *Yes, it would be better coming earlier but I don't think it's enough of a context either [reads the student's text]; a development and benefit of what?*

- T2 *No, and I can't see a purpose for the classification. One thing I'd say about this piece is I'm not even totally sure it's a classification. It feels more like a description to me, but I'm not sure because I don't have a business background.*

- T3 *Do you mean you think it would have to have more than one layer to be a classification? He's really saying HRM consists of these three things.*

- T2 *Consists of. Yes, he's just describing the parts.*

- T1 *Well, I actually feel OK about that because he uses the word functions and not everyone recognizes that's a business word. That means actual departmental responsibilities.*

- T3 *Yes, he's classifying on the basis of function. If he's got three things that are sorted out on the basis of something, then it's a classification.*

- T1 *Once he gets into the classification then I like it. For training, he actually sub-classifies: on-the-job training, and off-the-job. In the last paragraph, he says [reads the student's text] the most important element, so he's setting up a bit of a hierarchy.*

- T2 *Well, yes, you're right [refers to the criteria]: he's got an explanation of categories on which the classification is based. So are we up around B+ for task achievement?*

- T1 *It feels like it. Part of me wants to penalize him because he doesn't have a clear definition or a context, but what follows is so clear. [refers to the criteria] It says for B the classification is unbalanced with one category dominating. In this case, it's unbalanced with not enough about the context.*

- T3 *Yes, for me the classification is very good; the only thing wrong is the problem setting up the context.*

The teachers decided that, in terms of organization, the order of paragraphs one and three could be improved by moving the last sentence earlier in both cases, but that the logical development using summarizing noun phrases, e.g., *the second category, the most important element*, showed promise. However, they thought the text was weak at the sentence level, with errors in vocabulary choice, word class and sentence structure, impeding understanding at some points.

- T2 *OK, so we're going to give him B+, C+ and C, which will probably bring him out around B–. Is that OK?*

- T1 *It's perhaps a bit high.*

- T3 *I think so, too. We could penalize his language. He's got it in some places, but that last sentence in paragraph 3 is almost incomprehensible.*

- T2 *It's an early assignment so should we give more weighting to language not content?*

- T1 *Yes, and he should understand how to use simple functional language like since and according to, because we did work on those in class. I'd be happier with a C+ overall.*

The main problem these teachers had in assessing this text was reconciling what they viewed as good content and organization with poor use of language at sentence level. To arrive at a score, they followed a three-stage process[67] in which they formed an overall impression of the text, assigned a grade to each category in turn, referring to the assessment descriptors, and then reviewed the overall grade. Assessment descriptors can never adequately capture the complexity of texts,[68] so there will always be cases, such as this one, which are difficult to interpret in terms of the criteria. The teachers commented on the inadequacy of the descriptors in capturing the unbalanced nature of the text, and discussed their own understandings of the construct for classification, in general and in a business context, to reach an agreement about the evaluation of content. The descriptors gave no specific information about the weighting of the three categories, but a decision was made to prioritize language, and this was justified with reference to the position of the assignment in the course. These teachers were not constrained by the assessment descriptors, but decided for themselves what to pay attention to, and used the descriptors for evidence to justify their decisions.[69] They also drew on each other's knowledge and experience in their negotiations, in particular T1's knowledge of the business context. Assessments of oral performance would be negotiated and supported in a similar way.

Teachers will have their own construct of what constitutes good writing or speaking which they can use to form holistic judgements of student performance.[70] However, because of their variety of beliefs, attitudes and experience, teachers will not necessarily share the same construct, and will give different weighting to different aspects. In order to ensure consistency in grading student production, and hence validity and reliability for their assessments, teachers need to conduct moderation sessions in which they compare and discuss their decisions about grades. These sessions are important to reach common understandings on how to deal with problem texts, and to evaluate the robustness of assessment descriptors, which can be modified accordingly. They are also the place where new teachers learn about local assessment practices, and check their developing construct of academic language against those of experienced colleagues.

Case study C:

A colleague (Mary) teaches an IELTS exam preparation class. She has asked you to observe one of her lessons and give feedback on how she might increase the involvement of her students in formative assessment. Here is an outline of the key features of the lesson you observed.

Lesson phase 1: Mary starts the lesson by explaining her lesson objectives, using a visual. The main aim of the lesson is to prepare for and practise timed writing for question 1 of the IELTS written paper, describing graphs and diagrams. Several students arrive late, and she has to repeat her explanation or part of it twice. Some students seem surprised and quietly ask classmates if they knew there would be exam practice.

Lesson phase 2: Mary elicits from the class the important aspects to consider when describing graphs, in particular the importance of providing a general statement of the overall picture or trend, rather than describing every detail. She reminds them of the requirement in IELTS not to attempt to account for or explain the data, but just to describe it. She contrasts this with the purpose of writing about graphs at university which also requires a general comment on the data, but some explanation as well.

Mary then asks the class if they would like to study their language reference pages[71] for describing data and trends before they begin. Several students nod their heads and begin looking for the appropriate sheet in their folders. A few students do not have their reference pages, and Mary asks them to share with another student.

Lesson phase 3: Mary shows a visual of a question prompt, taken from an exam practice book, and tells the students they will have 20 minutes to answer it. While they are writing, she takes out some scripts from another class, and uses a set of assessment criteria to mark the writing.

Lesson phase 4: After 20 minutes, Mary tells the students to finish writing, and asks them to give their written answer to a partner, and choose one aspect they like and one that could be improved in the writing. The students then discuss these aspects with their partner. Several students ask Mary what kinds of things they should look for, and she reminds the whole class of the earlier discussion about the key aspects in a description of graphs.

Mary collects the scripts to take away for marking. She tells the students they worked hard so she won't give them any homework.

Task 10

- In your view how much active involvement did the students have in their assessment?

  too much   enough   not enough   none

- How could Mary involve her students more?

  Write your feedback in two parts: what was good in her formative assessment practice, and what could be improved to encourage students to become more actively engaged. Finally, suggest what she could do in the next lesson.

The students were quite actively involved in terms of formative assessment, but not always aware of the level of their involvement. For example, in phase 2, Mary elicited from them the task achievement criterion for this question, and in phase 4 the students assessed their peers' writing. However, they did not seem to realize that they had been given assessment criteria to use in the peer review because Mary's instruction for it was too general.

Positive aspects of this lesson include Mary's explanation of the lesson objectives, and the way she showed that practice for the exam fits into the wider context of writing at university. Mary's contrast between the requirements of the exam and the requirements of university writing helps the students to look beyond the entrance exam. She oriented the students to the writing task by discussing an important aspect of their answer, and also allowed them time to refer to their language reference pages before writing.

Mary could involve her students more by making sure they know in advance when they will be doing exam practice, and what form it will take. This should ensure that they come to class on time, and also have with them the appropriate reference page to review before they start writing. However, if some students habitually come late to class, rather than waste time repeating herself, Mary could routinely designate the first ten minutes for advice on exam strategies. This effectively makes it the students' responsibility to arrive on time because latecomers do not disrupt her planned lesson, but do lose out on the exam input.

The peer review immediately following the writing was a good idea as the students still had the task in mind, and could make specific comments about what their partner had written. Mary could have framed the preparation as establishing the criteria for a good exam answer more explicitly, using a question to focus this – *What will the examiner want to see?* – and showing the criteria she used for marking writing.

Mary effectively left the class while the students were writing because she was marking scripts written by another class. Instead, she could have used that time to answer the exam question herself, perhaps writing directly onto a visual. Her answer would not have been perfect because it was written under the same time constraints as the student answers. However, it would have provided her with a model answer that she could have used to model peer review. Before they saw each other's texts, the students could have used the assessment descriptors to give her writing a grade, and suggest how it could be improved. Mary could have introduced an element of humour if she gave her writing a B grade or even a C. It is very motivating for students to see a teacher's process of writing, and realize that she struggles to write in the same way that they do.

Mary 'rewarded' her students' hard work by not giving any homework but, in exam classes, students need to be encouraged to study independently. She could have asked the students to try the writing again in the light of the feedback they had received, using the same time limit. In the next lesson, they could have checked their second attempt against her feedback on their first attempt to see what improvements they had been able to make. She could also share with the class some common problems she had noticed, and get the class to suggest solutions and strategies to overcome them. She could encourage students to seek clarification on her feedback, and negotiate the time and nature of the next formative assessment.

Conclusion

Assessment lies at the heart of teaching and learning and is very important for EAP students, both prior to and during their degree studies. All test results are claims about students' underlying knowledge and ability based on measurements of their performance. These claims must be supported with evidence that the means of assessment were appropriate, and the performances were graded fairly and consistently. The model of test usefulness can be used to evaluate the quality of both global and local assessment practices. In the rich and complex social environment that constitutes a classroom, assessment can be based on authentic integrated performance which links language, skills and background knowledge. Students should understand how assessment descriptors are used to evaluate their work, and be involved in applying these to give feedback to peers. To ensure reliability, students' results should be discussed in moderation sessions, with the assessment descriptors providing a framework for negotiation. In order to ensure positive washback, learning outcomes, course content and assessment should be closely aligned.

Further reading

Bachman, L. F. and Palmer, A. S. (1996) *Language Testing in Practice: Designing and Developing Useful Language Tests*. Oxford: Oxford University Press.

Biggs, J. (2003) *Teaching for Quality Learning at University*. Maidenhead, UK: The Society for Research into Higher Education and Open University Press.

Douglas, D. (2000) *Assessing Language for Specific Purposes*. Cambridge: Cambridge University Press.

Fulcher, G. and Davidson, F. (2007) *Language Testing and Assessment*. London: Routledge.

Hughes, A. (2003) *Testing for Language Teachers*. 2nd edn. Cambridge: Cambridge University Press.

Notes

Chapter 1

1   See Chapter 10: *Assessment*.

2   More information on these important aspects of texts can be found in Chapter 2: *Text analysis*.

3   Hart (1961)

4   Becher (1989)

5   Laurillard (2002) page 81

6   See Beard and Wilson (2002). Chapter 3: *Course design* refers to this principle again.

7   Both Chapter 3: *Course design* and Chapter 9: *Student autonomy* emphasize the importance of this kind of dialogue.

8   Adapted from Marchant (2007)

9   Sharpling (2002) page 86, quoting Brookes and Grundy (1990)

10 Thorp (1991) page 109, quoting Philips (1983), refers to this kind of expectation as the 'invisible culture of the classroom'.

11 Charlene Constable, lecturer in Arabic, Heriot-Watt University, personal communication

12 This book explores these concepts fully in Chapters 2: *Text Analysis*, 6: *Writing*, 8: *Critical thinking* and 9: *Autonomy*.

13 Sharpling (2002) pages 86–87

14 Williams (2007), for example, discusses the problems of attempted plagiarism in an editorial in the academic journal which he edits.

15 Jin (1992) page 335

16 Ballard and Clanchy (1997) quoted in Biggs (2003) page 129

17 Cortazzi and Jin (1997) pages 78–79

18 Olwyn Alexander gives an account of this experience in Lynch (2004) pages 136–137.

19 Thanks are due to Charlene Constable, lecturer in Arabic at Heriot-Watt University for advice in composing this case study.

20 Chapter 4: *Reading* explores this and many other aspects of reading.

21 Chapter 7: *Listening and speaking* explores more fully the purposes of lectures.

22 Chapter 9: *Student autonomy* looks at the importance of informal study groups.

23 Salter-Dvorak (2007)

24 From a survey carried out (2005) at Heriot-Watt University.

25 Biggs (2003) page125

26 Biggs (2003) page 130 cites several studies which demonstrate the high degree of adaptability of students from Confucian traditions.

27 Biggs (2003) pages 120–139

28 Biggs (2003) page 129. This point is also made strongly in Chapter 3: *Course design* and Chapter 10: *Assessment*.

29 See the discussion on plagiarism between Sowden and Liu: Sowden (2005).

30 Chapter 9: *Student autonomy* suggests ways of making students more actively engaged in their learning and Chapter 7: *Listening and speaking* looks at the factors affecting group collaboration.

31 Biggs (2003) Chapter 7

32 Ding, Jones and King (2004) found a feeling of being de-skilled in their survey of pre-sessional teachers.

33 Chapter 9: *Student autonomy* examines how such processes underpin effective study skills.

34 Hitchcock (2007)

35 Cortazzi and Jin (1997) page 85

36 This type of dialogue has been referred to as 'collaborative conversation' (Laurillard: 2002), discussed in Chapter 3: *Course design*, and as 'reflective dialogue' (Brockbank and McGill: 1998), discussed in Chapter 9: *Student autonomy*.

37 See Chapter 9: *Student autonomy*, and Chapter 8: *Critical thinking*.

38 Chapter 3: *Course design* looks at how these needs for a specific student group are used to draw up a syllabus.

39 Chapter 2: *Text Analysis* explains all these terms and their implications for EAP practice.

40 Alexander (2007) reviews the research and the main findings are summarized here.

41 These concerns are themes which are explored throughout the book.

42 The classic 'self-fulfilling prophecy' effect of teacher expectations of students is described in Rosenthal and Jacobson (1968). There is likely to be a similar effect of teacher expectations of materials.

43 Clough (2007) compares these two models.

44 The foundation programme of CELE, Nottingham University and University of Nottingham Ningbo Campus, China. This course is part of a case study in Chapter 3: *Course design*.

45 The Heriot-Watt Management Programme Academic English for Business Course.

46 Chapter 7: *Listening and speaking* and Chapter 4: *Reading* both examine the issue of authenticity.

47 Chapter 3: *Course design* further examines the issue of EAP for students with lower levels of language ability.

48 See Chapter 4: *Reading*.

49 See Chapter 9: *Autonomy*.

50 See Chapter 2: *Text analysis* and Chapter 6: *Writing*.

51 See Chapter 2: on register analysis.

52 See Chapter 4: *Reading*.

53 Philip Warwick, personal communication

54 For example, in Chapter 3: *Course design* two texts with very different treatments of the same topic *Twin Lives* and *Consumption and Identity* are compared.

55 Marchant (2007) MSc in Logistics and Supply Chain Management: An Introductory Guide to Teaching and Learning at Heriot-Watt University (Student course material)

56 Chapter 7: *Writing* expands on this concept.

57 See Chapter 10: *Assessment*.

58 See Chapter 2: *Text analysis*.

59 Hyland (2006)

60 Academic journals are amongst the institutions that can and do claim such authority, some appearing to wield it with a lighter hand than others: Kirkpatrick (2007)

61 These advantages are discussed in Chapter 3: *Course design*.

62 See, for example, Bowler and Harrison (2007).

63 Hyland (2005) page 63 and Turner (2004)

64 Benson (2001) pages 160–162

65 Auerbach (1995) quoted in Benson (2001)

66 Pennycook (1997) cited in Benson (2001)

67 Chapter 9: *Student autonomy* discusses this further.

68 Yang, J., lecturer in Electrical Engineering, personal communication

69   Argent (2001). Chapter 6: *Writing* explores further what is expected in exam questions.

70   Philip Warwick (School of Management), personal communication. More on this quiet revolution in academic practice is described in more detail in Chapter 3: *Course design*.

71   Hyland (2006) page 58 explains this approach, and in this book, Chapter 2: *Text Analysis* and Chapter 5: *Vocabulary* explain its use in the EAP classroom.

Chapter 2

1   Alexander (2007)

2   Zhang and Austin (2005)

3   Halliday and Hasan (1976) page 22. *Field, tenor* and *mode* are the technical names given to these concepts in register analysis. They are not used here but are necessary for further reading.

4   *Hilgard's Introduction to Psychology*, 12th edition by Atkinson. 1996, page 71

5   *New Scientist* no 2127 28 March 1998

6   Wright, J. V. 1993. *UK Political System*. Ayrshire: Pulse Publications

7   Proposal for a research project written by a Chinese student on a Foundation English course

8   Skelton (1988)

9   Swales (1990) page 58

10   Johns (2002) page 3

11   Flowerdew (2002) pages 91–92; Swales (2004) pages 72–73

12   A great deal of research on genres has been published since the term was first applied to academic texts in the early 1980s and these research findings have now been incorporated into a number of course books and teacher resource books, e.g., Weissburg and Buker (1990); Swales and Feak (2004); Paltridge (2001); Johns, A. ed. (2002).

13   North and Hort (2002)

14   Hyland (2004) page 67

15   Martin (1992)

16   Paltridge (2001) pages 10–12; Paltridge (2006) page 84–85; Johns (2002) pages 3–13 explore definitions of genre.

17   Miller (1984)

18   Flowerdew (2002) pages 91–92 and Swales (2004) 72–73 explore the differences in these two approaches.

19   Hyland (2006) page 49

20   See Chapter 4: *Reading*.

21   Chapter 6: *Writing* develops the use of genre analysis to help EAP students with writing.

22   Swales and Feak (2004) page 244 provides a model for the analysis of introductions to research papers which is illustrated below on page 54.

23   These terms were first used in Bereiter and Scardamalia (1987)

24   Trimble (1985) contains a fuller discussion of rhetorical functions.

25   See Jordan (1997) or Hamp Lyons and Heasley (2006) for examples of writing course books which use functional syllabuses.

26   See Johns (2002); Bruce (2005); Hyland (2006) for a detailed discussion.

27   Alexander (1999)

28   Swales and Feak (2004) page 244

29   Halliday and Hasan (1976) page 10

30 There is no space to list these resources in detail but see McCarthy (1991) for a good summary.

31 Note: 'busying' here is shortened from 'which busied' so it is analysed as a conjunction.

32 Pinker (1994) page 209

33 Adjuncts are typically adverbs or prepositional phrases which give background information about the event in the main clause.

34 Halliday 3rd edition revised by Matthiessen (2004) pages 64ff and 579ff

35 Butt, Spinks and Yallop (2000) provide a detailed exploration of thematic analysis.

36 Vande Koppel (1996) gives practical suggestions for exercises to work on thematic development with students.

37 Flowerdew (2003)

38 Hill and Lewis (2000) page 101

39 Sinclair (1991)

40 Martin and Rose (2003) pages 175–190

41 Martin and Rose (2003) page 179

42 Martin and Rose (2003) page 186

Chapter 3

1 The Heriot-Watt University EAP Teacher Development Course: questions gathered in workshops on course design.

2 See Basturkmen (2003) for definitions and a thorough comparison.

3 Mavor and Trayner (2001) page 345 describe their teaching context in Portugal as ESAP/FL.

4 Hyland (2006) page 82

5 Hyland (2006) page 282

6 See Chapters 8: *Critical thinking* and 9: *Student autonomy*

7 Alexander (2007)

8 The British Association of Lecturers in English for Academic Purposes, available online at http://www.baleap.org.uk/

9 For example, Hyland (2006) page 74; Feez (2002) page 38; Finney (2002) page 75

10 Holliday and Cook, 1982, cited in Hyland (2006) page 75

11 The Heriot-Watt University EAP Teacher Development Course: reported teacher needs

12 A narrow-angled approach, for example, see Hyland (2006) and Basturkmen (2003) page 48.

13 A wide-angled course – see Bruce (2005) page 240.

14 Flowerdew (2005) page 139

15 Chapter 6: *Writing* emphasizes the diversity of genres even within different specialities of a subject group.

16 See Swales et al. (2001) page 455.

17 For the differences between EAP and general ELT, see Chapter 1: *The context of EAP.*

18 As in the case study of Anna in Kiely (2001) pages 255–257

19 Chapter 8: *Critical thinking* and Chapter 9: *Student autonomy* argue the case for integration of these two key skills throughout the EAP course.

20 Beard and Wilson (2002)

21 Feez (1998) pages 13–18 gives a clear and accessible account of syllabus types for language teaching generally, whilst Richards and Rodgers (2001) give a more detailed comparative overview.

22 See, for example, Ho and Wong (2004) page 455; Jin and Cortazzi (2004) pages 121–122.

23 These ideas are explored in detail in Chapter 5: *Vocabulary*.

24 Long-lived examples are: Sellen (1982), a uniquely comprehensive EAP course for its time, and writing courses such as Glendinning and Mantell (1983), Jordan (1980) and Hamp-Lyons and Heasley (1987).

25 See Chapter 2: *Text analysis*.

26 See Chapter 2: *Text analysis* for an introduction to the concept of genres.

27 See Chapter 6: *Writing*.

28 Bruce (2005) page 243

29 See also Chapter 6: *Writing*.

30 See Chapter 4: *Reading* for an exploration of criteria for selecting academic texts.

31 See Chapter 10: *Assessment*.

32 In Chapter 1: *The context of EAP*, these authentic activities were described as 'site visits'.

33 See Chapter 1: *The context of EAP*.

34 Turner (2004) page 98

35 Crewe (1990) discusses the poor analysis of connectors, for example.

36 Hyland (2005) page 59

37 Task-Based Learning and Teaching (TBLT) contributes a great deal to EAP methodology, as will be seen later in this chapter. For further information, see Richards and Rodgers (2001) pages 223–243; Feez (2002) page 17.

38 Robinson, Strong, Whittle and Nobe (2001)

39 Johnson (1981) page 34 cited in Hedge (2000) page 345

40 The authors are very grateful to Stevenson College, Edinburgh, for permission to reproduce this scenario and outline course design (Read to Write EAP, unpublished).

41 Heriot-Watt University, Edinburgh – the authors' own scenario and course design.

42 The authors are very grateful to Rebecca Hughes (director), John Hall and Ann Smith (course designers), Centre for English Language Education, University of Nottingham, for permission to reproduce this scenario and outline course design.

43 Jin, L. and Cortazzi, M. (2004) page 125

44 The authors are grateful to Philip Warwick and Bill Soden, University of York, for permission to include this scenario and outline course design from information published by Warwick (2006).

45 *Guidelines for writing flexible learning materials*, Carol Tweedie, Stevenson College (unpublished)

46 See Chapter 4: *Reading*.

47 Seitz (2002). This book was first used for theme-based EAP input at Northumbria, see Garner and Borg (2005).

48 Warwick (2006)

49 Warwick (2006) page 2

50 Warwick (2006) page 3

51 Ho and Wong (2004) page 455, and many, anonymous EAP teachers by personal communication

52 Cunningham and Moor (1998) page 37

53 Heriot-Watt University Management Programme

54 See Chapter 5: *Vocabulary*.

55 Classroom materials 8.5, Task 1b, shows this pre-reading task in detail.

56   Watson Todd (2003) page 150

57   Basturkmen (2006) pages 113–131

58   Dudley-Evans and St. John (1998) page 190

59   Feez (1998); Hammond et al. (1992)

60   Willis (1996)

61   Times Higher Education Supplement 19.01.2001

62   Flowerdew (2000) page 370

63   Hammond et al. (1992) page 17, cited in Paltridge, (2001) page 31; Feez (1998) page 28

64   Van den Branden (2006) page 8

65   Charles (1996)

66   Van den Branden (2006); Edwards and Willis (2005)

67   Skehan (1998) page 127

68   Hyland (2006) page 90

69   Wenger (1999)

70   Lave and Wenger (1991)

71   Vygotsky (1978)

72   Laurillard (2002)

73   Laurillard (2002) page 88

74   Chappelle (2001) page 2

75   Littlejohn and Higgison (2003)

76   Schrooten (2006) page 129

77   Biggs (2003) page 221

78   Clarke (2004) page 16

79   Benson (2001) page 140

80   Prensky (2001)

81   Prensky (2001)

82   Nicol (2007); www.reap.ac.uk

83   Warschauer (2002) page 55

84   ibid page 47

85   ibid page 48

86   ibid page 50

87   The use of concordance software is discussed in Chapter 4: *Vocabulary*.

88   Forms of web publishing which allow users to collaborate in the creation of web pages

89   Salmon (2004)

Chapter 4

1   Nuttall (1996) pages 56–58

2   Weir, Yang and Jin (2000) page 1

3   Dudley–Evans and St John (1998) page 96 and Nuttall (2000) page 54

4   The definitions used in this chapter follow Urquhart and Weir (1998) pages 96–109 (see above).

5   Marchant, C., and Torres-Sanchez, C., Heriot-Watt University (2007) Personal communication

6   See Chapter 2: *Text analysis* where the distinction between functions which involve knowledge telling and knowledge transforming is explained.

7   Heriot-Watt University School of Management and Languages, 2006 Dissertation Guide (unpublished)

8   Swales (2005) pages 7–8

9   Urquhart and Weir (1998) pages 96–100

10   Urquhart and Weir (1998) pages 103–104

11   Hyland (2006) page 43

12   Lewis (2001) page 47

13   Morton (1999)

14   Slaght (2004) and Glendinning and Holmstrom (2004)

15   Slaght (2004) pages 7–9

16   Holme and Chalauisaeng (2006) pages 411–413

17   Weir, Yang and Jin (2000) page 20

18   Running words refer to the total number of words in the text – repeats of the same word (e.g., *and* or *the*) are counted every time they occur.

19   Nation (2005) page 23

20   Nuttall (2000) pages 54–61

21   See Chapter 6: *Writing.*

22   Kwok, Fox, and Meila (2003)

23   See Chapter 2: *Text analysis.*

Chapter 5

1   Jordan (2002) page 149; Evans and Green (2007)

2   Kwok, Fox and Meila (2003)

3   Dudley Evans and St John (1998) pages 80–87; Coxhead and Nation (2001) discuss ways of classifying technical language. The term *semi-technical vocabulary* is sometimes used to label general academic vocabulary but, in this chapter, it is used for words having restricted meanings in specific subjects.

4   Nation (2001) page 12

5   Ward (2007) explores the role of this type of noun phrase collocation in technical texts, and suggests approaches to incorporating it into the EAP classroom.

6   West (1953)

7   For the principles on which this list was based, see Coxhead (2000). The AWL can be accessed on the Massey University website http://language.massey.ac.nz/staff/awl/mostfreq1.shtml

8   Coxhead (2000) gives this example of a word family: *indicate, indicates, indicating, indication, indications, indicative, indicator* and *indicators.*

9   There are four other adjectives which have a more subject-specific meaning, and may reflect the bias of the original corpus: *constitutional, economic, financial and legal.*

10   See Haywood (2003). The AWL Highlighter can be accessed at http://www.nottingham. ac.uk/~alzsh3/acvocab/awlhighlighter.htm

11   Biber, Conrad and Cortes (2004) page 400

12   See Gillett (2005) for a list showing each complete word family from the AWL and the most frequent word in each family.

13   The AWL represents about twenty per cent of the words in the Particle filters text used in this chapter.

14   Lewis (1993) page 80

15 Lewis (1998) page 215

16 Pilcher (2005) has identified a range of words from the first 2,000 of the GSL which were more frequent in a corpus of academic texts from Heriot-Watt University courses than in a general corpus. These were mainly words which express rhetorical functions, and some were identified as not known by students in the study.

17 Partington (1998) found that *if* was almost twice as common in an academic corpus as in a corpus of newspaper texts.

18 Flowerdew (2003) pages 329–346

19 See Dudley Evans and St John (1998); Coxhead and Nation (2001); Ward (2007).

20 Jordan (2002) page 46

21 Lewis (2001) page 50

22 LDOCE online accessed 06/04/2007

23 Lakoff and Johnson (1980) provide a classic account of this metaphorical aspect of English.

24 See Lewis (1993) page 92; Partington (1998) pages 79–87.

25 Lewis (1993) pages 133–4 and 171–2

26 Gavioli and Aston (2001)

27 Scott (2001) describes the use of this software package.

28 *The Compleat Lexical Tutor* can be accessed at http://132.208.224.131/

29 Information is available at http://www.natcorp.ox.ac.uk/

30 Information about this online corpus query system can be found at http://www.sketchengine.co.uk/

31 Guidance on using concordances and language data for teaching and research can be found in Woolard (2000); Partington (1998); Ghadessy *et al*, (2001); Bowker and Pearson (2001).

32 Nation (2001) pages 74–81

33 Lewis (2000) page 177

34 McCarthy (2000) pages 34–48

35 All but four of the AWL words which occur in this text appear in this grid on the basis of their problem-solution function. The four were *computational, resources, estimation* and *thereby.*

36 *Macmillan English Dictionary for Advanced Learners* (2002)

37 Thurston and Candlin (1998); Woolard (2000)

Chapter 6

1 Chapter 2: *Text analysis* explores the role these aspects play in fluent writing.

2 See Chapter 4: *Reading.*

3 For example, Chinese students. See Jin and Cortazzi (2004) pages 119–134.

4 Personal research. Gillett and Hammond (2006), page 10, also found a wide variety of assessment tasks used in university courses. In Chapter 10: *Assessment* there is further discussion of assessment genres.

5 Jackson, Meyer and Parkinson (2006) page 274

6 ibid. page 267

7 Paltridge (2001) pages 24–25

8 Thaiss and Zawacki (2006) page 63

9 Lillis (2001) pages 63–68

10   Dudley-Evans (2002) pages 225–226

11   Hamp-Lyons and Heasley (2006) show how students can do this.

12   Chapter 4: *Reading*

13   Paltridge (2001) pages 26–30 and Swales (2004) pages 100–101 discuss this process.

14   Lecturers in different disciplines at Heriot-Watt University (2007)

15   Chapter 2, Task 3, analyses academic style.

16   Thaiss and Zawacki (2006) pages 58–94

17   In Chapter 8: *Critical thinking*, there is an analysis of the term *critical* as it is used by lecturers to describe what they expect in students' reading and writing.

18   Thaiss and Zawacki (2006) page 137

19   Silva *et al.* (2003) pages 93–113

20   ibid. page 99

21   Connor (2003) pages 232–339

22   Thaiss and Zawacki (2006) pages 95–135

23   Silva *et al.* (2003) page 96

24   Silva *et al.* (2003) pages 103–104

25   Thaiss and Zawacki (2006) page 116

26   Thaiss and Zawacki (2006) pages 95–135

27   Silva *et al.* (2003) pages 93–113

28   Perry (2004) page 7

29   Hyland (1999) pages 341–367 gives a very full discussion based on citation practices in several different disciplines.

30   Swales (2005) page 149

31   Thaiss and Zawacki (2006) pages 112–115

32   Swales and Feak (2004) pages 117–120 provide exercises to do this.

33   Chapter 4: *Reading* shows how expert writers are in control of their sources.

34   Appropriate self-study practice exercises in both the mechanical aspects of citation and writing citation summaries can be found on Gillett (2008) *Using English for Academic Purposes.*

35   Chapter 3, Case study C, showed an example of a writing lesson on data commentary.

36   Swales and Feak (2004) pages 85–90

37   Hyland (2004) pages 7–8 discusses these two approaches and the role each plays in teaching academic writing.

38   Hyland (2004) page 3

39   Swales (2005) pages 220–221

40   Swales (2004) pages 100–101

41   Swales and Feak (2004) and McCormack and Slaght (2005) are course books using this approach.

42   Pallant (2006) uses this approach as the basis for a course book in Academic Writing.

43   Chapter 5: *Vocabulary* shows how students can collect functional vocabulary over a series of reading tasks, and record it in reference pages.

44   Assessment for grading and progression purposes is dealt with in Chapter 10: *Assessment*.

45   See Chapter 9: *Student autonomy* and Chapter 10: *Assessment*.

46   See Chapter 9: *Student autonomy*, Case study D.

47   Hyland and Hyland (2006) page 6

48   Alexander (1999) pages 121–134 presents a reader response protocol for feedback on writing.

49 See Chapter 1 for a brief discussion of this issue.

50 This same text is used in Chapter 10: *Assessment*, Tasks 7 and 8, applying assessment criteria to grade student writing.

51 For an extended explanation of the *given to new* pattern of information structure and its importance, refer back to Chapter 2 in the sections entitled *Cohesion*, and the following section *What to put first in a sentence*.

52 Jordan (1997) pages 174–176 explains this technique.

Chapter 7

1   Myers (2000) page 180

2   Flowerdew and Miller (1997)

3   Rost (2002) page 162

4   See Myers (2000) for a discussion of lectures as a changing genre.

5   See Brown and Atkins (1988) for a discussion of the organization and delivery of lectures.

6   Flowerdew and Miller (1996)

7   Flowerdew and Miller (1992)

8   Sutherland, Badger and White (2002)

9   For a discussion of listening processes, see Rost (2002).

10 Strodt-Lopez (1991)

11 Flowerdew and Miller (1996) page 134

12 Scollon and Scollon (1991)

13 King (1994)

14 Chaudron, Loschky and Cook (1994); Rost (1994); Sutherland, Badger and White (2002)

15 Rost (1994) page 112

16 King (1992)

17 Jordan (1997)

18 Flowerdew and Miller (1997); MacDonald, Badger and White (2000)

19 Rost (1994) page 96

20 See MacDonald, Badger and White (2000) pages 253–255 for a review of the concept of authenticity within ELT and EAP.

21 Flowerdew and Miller (1997)

22 See Rost (2002) pages 154–7 for a discussion of listening strategies and Lebauer (2000); Lynch (2004) and Phillips (2005) for examples of course books which are organized around the development of listening strategies.

23 Anderson and Lynch (1988) pages 80–96

24 Richards (2005)

25 MacDonald, Badger and White (2000)

26 Laurillard (2002) page 99

27 Cauldwell (2003) provides practice in this type of bottom-up processing.

28 Field (1998)

29 This process is similar to grammar dictation; see Wajnryb (1988). However, the focus here is on meaning retrieval rather than grammatical accuracy.

30 If available, lectures which are subtitled can also be used. Recording these off-air requires special equipment but they are available in DVD format for private use.

31 Rost (2002) page 140

32 See Chapter 8 for ideas to introduce critical thinking into EAP tasks.

33 Thomas (1983) page 91

34 Focus group with Chinese, Arabic and Farsi speakers conducted at Heriot-Watt University 16.2.07

35 See Tan Bee Tin (2003) for a summary of the research into the role of talk in learning.

36 Jones (1999)

37 Focus group 16.2.07

38 Flowerdew (1998); Focus group 16.2.07

39 Nesi (2003) pages 1–3

40 Basturkmen (1999)

41 See Tan Bee Tin (2003) for a description of convergent and divergent discussion tasks.

42 Basturkmen (1999)

43 Basturkmen (2002) page 240

44 Smith (2007); see also Chapter 4 for the process of writing a case study.

45 Foss and Reitzel (1991) cited in Liu and Littlewood (1997)

46 Flowerdew (1998)

47 Jones (1999)

48 With thanks to Ann Smith for this idea.

49 Edwards (2004)

50 Brown and Atkins (1990) page 10

51 Kurtz (2006)

52 Anderson, Maclean and Lynch (2004) or Furneaux and Rignall (1997) contain examples of such checklists.

53 Jordan (1997) page 202

54 With thanks to Jane Bell for this idea.

55 Lynch and Maclean (2000) page 226

Chapter 8

1 QCA

2 QCA (2007)

3 In the Heriot-Watt University Management Corpus (of written texts) of nearly 1 million words the phrase is only used by auditors signing off accounts.

4 Coffin (2004) page 243

5 See Chapters 4: *Reading* and 6: *Writing*.

6 Marchant (2006)

7 For example, see the explanations of critical thinking in the introductions to the respective students' books of Pallant (2004) page 9. Cox and Hill (2004) page v. The former relates critical thinking to problem solving and the latter to power relationships. Pallant (2004) gives a fuller explanation in the Teacher's Book, pages 1–2, but still differing from Cox and Hill.

8 These examples are from Gardner (2005) Introduction, page vii.

9 See Chapter 2: *Text analysis*.

10 Cottrell (2005) Chapter 2

11 Cardew (2006) page 4

12 Biggs (2003) Chapter 7, Hitchcock (2007)

13 Richards (2000) page 95 and Pallant (2000) page 106

14 Hyland (2006) page 91

15 Cottrell (2005); Browne and Keeley (2004)

16 Richards (2000) page 99

17 See Chapter 3: *Course design* for an explanation of task based learning.

18 Smith (2006)

19 Richards (2000) page 93

Chapter 9

1 A UK History and Politics lecturer, personal communication

2 Jordan (1997) page 116 and Field (2007) pages 30–38 are among several authors who stress the need for EAP students to continue language learning after leaving language instruction.

3 Penaflorida in Richards and Renandya (2002) page 346

4 Field (2007) page 30

5 Benson (2001) page 9

6 Benson (2001) explores the issues around self-access centres more fully, citing Sturtridge (1992), for example, in distinguishing between a centre for *practising* and a centre for *learning*, page 123.

7 See Waters and Waters (1995), O'Malley and Chamot (1990) and Ellis and Sinclair (1989) for useful discussions.

8 Waters and Waters (1995) pages 1–2

9 There are notable exceptions, e.g., Swales and Feak (2004).

10 Holec (1985), cited in Benson (2001) page 158, stresses that it is important in developing autonomy for all aspects of teaching and learning to be relevant to the learner.

11 Benson (2001) page 143, and citing McDonough (1999) page 144, emphasizes the need for the development of autonomy to be integrated with rather than separate from language learning.

12 Chapter 6: *Writing* explores this issue in greater detail.

13 Little and Singleton (1990) cited in Benson (2001) page 74

14 Chapter 6: *Writing* explores this issue in greater detail.

15 Woodward (2003) page 301

16 Turner (2004) page 103

17 All three of these activities were found in published course books. While we are not suggesting that they are unimportant, we are suggesting they are bringing to the classroom issues which might be better addressed on an individual basis.

18 Richards (2000) page 98; Sheerin (1997) cited in Benson (2001)

19 Waters and Waters (1995); O'Malley and Chamot (1990); Ellis and Sinclair (1989)

20 As in other constructed case studies in this book, the key characteristics presented here have all been observed in real students.

21 Such freeware can be found easily on the Internet by putting *mindmap* into an Internet search engine. The advantages they have over paper mind maps include potentially infinite space (using expandable nodes).

22 See Chapter 5: *Vocabulary*.

23 Field (2007) page 38

24   Voller (1997), cited in Benson (2001) page 15, suggests that autonomy requires the negotiated and carefully monitored transfer of control from teacher to student.

25   Allwright (1975), cited in Benson (2001), goes so far as to describe such controlling behaviour as 'irresponsible'.

26   Students on academic courses may get support in their study skills from their subject tutors. Support for continued language learning, however, depends on two factors: the availability of good, in-sessional EAP provision, and how much time the student can spare.

27   Assinder (1991) and Voller (1997), both cited in Benson (2001) pages 154 and 170, respectively also identify the need for changing roles for a teacher promoting autonomy.

28   Brockbank and McGill (1998) page 2

29   See Chapter 5 *Vocabulary*.

30   Breen and Mann (1997) cited in Benson (2001) page 173

31   Benson (2001) page 53. This aspect of a teacher's role is also discussed in Chapter 1: *The context of EAP*, where the idea of contextual difference rather than cultural difference is presented.

32   Benson (2001) page 14 points out that 'independence' is not the opposite of 'interdependence'.

33   See Chapter 3: *Course design* and Case study C in Chapter 7: *Listening and speaking*.

34   Lai and Hamp-Lyons (2001) page 77

35   This is genuine 'loop input', Woodward (2003).

36   This is a first-year undergraduate problem reported fairly frequently by subject lecturers.

37   Oxford (2002) page 126 cites integrating learner training with language learning activities in the classroom as one of the major factors for success. Crabbe (1993), cited in Benson (2001) page 163, argues for the development of student autonomy to be fully integrated into the curriculum rather than presented as occasional learning input.

38   Oxford (2002) page 126, in reviewing research on strategies employed by language learners, notes that weak language learners tend to use strategies, but at random and unreflectively, rather like the behaviour of the last student in the self-access centre case study at the beginning of this chapter.

39   Agyris and Schon (1974) and Kolb (1984), quoted in Brockbank and McGill (1998) pages 43–44. Note this is not the same as *loop input*, Woodward (2003), a type of experiential learning described earlier.

40   Brockbank and McGill (1998) pages 43–44

41   Ibid. page 54

42   A reference page is a student's record of key vocabulary for a rhetorical function such as problem–solution, see Chapter 5: *Vocabulary*. The earliest use of such reference pages that I can find is Sellen (1982).

43   See Chapter 3: *Course design*.

44   Lai and Hamp-Lyons (2001) pages 73–74

45   Lai and Hamp-Lyons (2001) page 77

46   Benson (2001) page 121

47   Larsen-Freeman (1977) quoted in Lewis (2000) page 11

48   Lewis (2000) page 11

49   In the Heriot-Watt University Corpus of nearly one million words *come to a conclusion* is much more frequent than *arrive at a conclusion*.

50   See Chapter 5: *Vocabulary*.

Chapter 10

1   Smith (2003) cited in Fulcher and Davidson (2007) page 30

2   Bachman and Palmer (1996); Douglas (2000); Hughes (2003); Weir (1993)

3   Douglas (2000) page 258

4   Brown et al. (1997) page 9

5   Moss (2003) cited in Fulcher and Davidson (2007) page 201; Rust (2002) page 155

6   Council of Europe (2001)

7   Alderson (2000) page 21

8   Alderson (2000) page 22; Bachman and Palmer (1996) page 4

9   Green (2005)

10 Designed and administered by Educational Testing Service http://www.ets.org/

11 Jointly managed by British Council, IDP: IELTS Australia and the University of Cambridge ESOL Examinations (Cambridge ESOL) http://www.ielts.org/default.aspx

12 Brindley and Ross (2001) page 150

13 Spratt (2005)

14 Reviewed in Banerjee and Wall (2006) page 54

15 Green (2005) page 58 and (2006) page 131

16 Douglas (2000) page 90

17 Brindley (1998) page 45; Boud (2000) page 154

18 Rust (2002) page 146

19 Biggs (2003) page 42

20 Comments reported in Nesi and Gardner (2006)

21 Race (1995)

22 Biggs (2003) page 114; Brown *et al.* (1997) page 14

23 Harthill (2000); Gillett and Hammond (2006)

24 Nesi and Gardner (2006)

25 Biggs (2003) page 144

26 Fulcher and Davidson (2006) page 370

27 Boud (2000) page 155

28 Biggs (2003) page 150

29 Boud (2000); Rust (2002); Biggs (2003)

30 Rust (2002) page 153

31 Stern and Solomon (2006) pages 25–6

32 www.baleap.org.uk

33 Bachman and Palmer (1996) page 38

34 Douglas (2000) page 114

35 Information taken from ETS website http://www.ets.org/ and IELTS website http://www.ielts.org/

36 Sample TOEFL task prompt available online at http://www.ets.org/

37 Sample IELTS writing task 2 available online at http://www.ielts.org/candidates/findoutmore/freesamples/article330.aspx

38 Sample TOEFL task prompt available online at http://www.ets.org/

39 Weigle (2002) page 52

40 Cumming *et al.* (2005) page 6

41   Biber *et al.* (2004) page 111

42   Clapham (1996) reviewed in Douglas (2000) page 30–33

43   Cumming *et al.* (2005) page 11

44   Brindley and Ross (2001) page 150

45   See Qian (2007) for a comparison of IELTS with a locally developed English language exit test.

46   Spratt (2005)

47   Green (2006)

48   Chapter 6: *Writing* contains a detailed section on writing from data with several classroom materials.

49   Spratt (2005) page 23–4

50   Weigle (2002) page 175

51   McCormack and Slaght (2006) is an example of a course book to support extended writing.

52   Fulcher and Davidson (2007) page 29

53   Klenowski (2002)

54   Weigle (2002) page 219

55   With thanks to Fiona Cotton of the ADFA at the University of NSW for this suggestion.

56   Douglas (2000)

57   Refer to Chapter 4: *Reading* for examples.

58   Moss (2003) cited in Fulcher and Davidson (2007) page 201

59   With thanks to Ralitza Vass for this case study.

60   Davison (2004)

61   Weigle (2002) page 113

62   Upshur and Turner (1995)

63   Weigle (2002) pages 188–9

64   Davison (2004) page 309

65   Lumley (2002) page 266

66   Bachman and Palmer (1996) page 214

67   Lumley (2002) page 255

68   Lumley (2002) page 268

69   Lumley (2002) page 267

70   Davison (2004) page 310

71   See Chapter 5: *Vocabulary*.

Bibliography

Alderson, J. C. (2000) Testing in EAP: progress? achievement? proficiency? In Blue *et al.* (eds.)(2000) pages 21–47.

Alderson, J. C., Clapham, C. and Wall, D. (1995) *Language Test Construction and Evaluation.* Cambridge: Cambridge University Press.

Alexander, O. (1999) Raising audience awareness in ESL writers using reader-response protocols. In Thompson, P. (ed.)(1999) *Issues in EAP Writing Research and Instruction.* Reading: CALS, University of Reading.

Alexander, O. (2007) Groping in the dark or turning on the light: routes into teaching English for Academic Purposes. In Lynch, T. and Northcott, J. (eds.) (2007) *Teacher Education in Teaching EAP.* Edinburgh: IALS, Edinburgh University.

Alexander, O. (ed.)(2007) *New Approaches to Materials Development for Language Learning.* Oxford: Peter Lang.

Anderson, A. and Lynch, T. (1988) *Listening.* Oxford: Oxford University Press.

Anderson, K., Maclean, J. and Lynch, T. (2004) *Study Speaking.* Cambridge: Cambridge University Press.

Argent, S. (2001) *EAP for Business Studies: English Language Modules for the New Induction Programme.* Edinburgh: Internal Report, Heriot-Watt University.

Bachman, L. F. and Palmer, A. S. (1996) *Language Testing in Practice: Designing and Developing Useful Language Tests.* Oxford: Oxford University Press.

Banerjee, J. and Wall, D. (2006) Assessing and reporting performances on pre-sessional EAP courses: developing a final assessment checklist and investigating its validity. *Journal of English for Academic Purposes,* 5/1, pages 50–69.

Basturkmen, H. (1999) Discourse in MBA seminars: towards a description for pedagogical purposes. *English for Specific Purposes,* 18/1, pages 63–80.

Basturkmen, H. (2002) Negotiating meaning in seminar-type discussion and EAP. *English for Specific Purposes,* 21/3, pages 233–242.

Basturkmen, H. (2003) Specificity and EAP course design. *RELC Journal,* 34/1, pages 48–63.

Basturkmen, H. (2006) *Ideas and Options in English for Specific Purposes.* Mahwah, New Jersey: Lawrence Erlbaum Associates.

Beard, C. and Wilson, J. P. (2002) *The Power of Experiential Learning: a Handbook for Trainers and Educators.* London: Kogan Page.

Becher, T. (1989) *Academic Tribes and Territories: Intellectual Inquiry and the Cultures of Disciplines.* Milton Keynes: Society for Research in Higher Education and Open University Press.

Benson, P. (2001) *Teaching and Researching Autonomy in Language Learning.* Harlow, Essex: Longman.

Bereiter, C. and Scardamalia, M. (1987) *The Psychology of Written Composition.* New Jersey: Hillsdale.

Biber, D., Conrad, S. and Cortes, V. (2004) 'In fact if you look at'... lexical bundles in university teaching and textbooks. *Applied Linguistics* 25/3, pages 371–405.

Biber, D., Conrad, S. M., Reppen, R. et al. (2004) Representing language use in the university: analysis of the TOEFL 2000 spoken and written academic language corpus. Educational Testing Service, TOEFL Monograph Series MS-25. http://www.ets.org/Media/Research/pdf/RM-04-03.pdf Retrieved 10/12/07.

Biggs, J. (2003) *Teaching for Quality Learning at University.* Maidenhead, UK: The Society for Research into Higher Education and Open University Press.

Blue, G. M., Milton, J. and Saville, J. (eds.)(2000) *Assessing English for Academic Purposes.* Oxford: Peter Lang.

Boud, D. (2000) Sustainable assessment: rethinking assessment in the learning society. *Studies in Continuing Education*, 22/2, pages 151–167.

Bowker, L. and Pearson, J. (2002) *Working with Specialized Language: A Practical Guide to Using Corpora.* Oxford: Routledge.

Bowler, B. and Harrison, R. (2007) Skills all round. *English Teaching Professional*, 49, pages 55–57.

Brindley, G. (1998) Outcomes-based assessment and reporting in language learning programmes: a review of the issues. *Language Testing*, 15/1, pages 45–85.

Brindley, G. and Ross, S. (2001) EAP assessment: issues, models and outcomes. In Flowerdew, J. and Peacock, M. (eds.)(2001) pages 148–166.

Brockbank, A. and McGill, I. (1998) *Facilitating Reflective Learning in Higher Education.* Buckingham, UK: Open University Press.

Brookes, A. and Grundy, P. (1990) *Writing for Study Purposes.* Cambridge: Cambridge University Press.

Brown, G. and Atkins, M. (1988) *Effective Teaching in Higher Education.* London: Routledge.

Brown, G. with Bull, J. and Pendlebury, M. (1997) *Assessing Student Learning in Higher Education.* London: Routledge.

Brown, S. (2004) Assessment for learning. *Learning and Teaching in Higher Education*, 1, pages 81–89.

Browne, N. M. and Keeley, S. M. (2004) *Asking the Right Questions: a Guide to Critical Thinking*. 7th edn. New Jersey: Pearson Prentice Hall.

Bruce, I. (2005) Syllabus design for general EAP writing courses: a cognitive approach. *Journal of English for Academic Purposes* 4/3, pages 239–256.

Butt, D., Spinks, S. and Yallop, C. (2000) *Using Functional Grammar: an Explorer's Guide*. Sydney: NCELTR, Macquarie University.

Cardew, S. (2007) Critical thinking about cultural and academic identity. In Alexander, O. (ed.)(2007) pages 17–26.

Cauldwell, R. (2003) *Streaming Speech*. Birmingham: Speech in Action.

Chappelle, C. (2001) *Computer Applications in Second Language Acquisition*. Cambridge: Cambridge University Press.

Charles, M. (1996) Practice or performance? In Hewings, M. and Dudley-Evans, T. (eds.)(1996) *Evaluation and Course Design in EAP*. Hertfordshire: Prentice Hall Macmillan in association with the British Council.

Chaudron, C., Loschky, L. and Cook, J. (1994) L2 listening comprehension and note-taking. In Flowerdew, J. (ed.)(1994).

Clarke, A. (2004) *E-learning Skills*. Basingstoke: Palgrave Macmillan.

Clough, G. (2007) Content based EAP support for the Arts: two approaches compared. BALEAP Conference (2007). *EAP in a Globalising World: an Academic Lingua Franca*, University of Durham.

Coffin, C. (2004) Arguing about how the world is or how the world should be: the role of argument in IELTS tests. *Journal of English for Academic Purposes* 3/3, pages 229–246.

Collins Cobuild English Grammar. 2nd edn. (2005) London: HarperCollins.

Compleat Lexical Tutor, The (no date) http://132.208.224.131/ Retrieved 30/03/07.

Connor, U. (2003) Changing currents in contrastive rhetoric: implications for teaching and research. In Kroll, B. (ed.)(2003) pages 218–241.

Cortazzi, M. and Jin, L. (1997) Communication for learning across cultures. In McNamara, D. and Harris R. (eds.)(1997) *Overseas Students in Higher Education*, pages 76–90. London: Routledge.

Cottrell, S. (2005) Critical thinking skills: developing effective analysis and argument. *Palgrave Study Guides*. Basingstoke: Palgrave Macmillan.

Council of Europe (2001) *Common European Framework of Reference for Languages: Learning, Teaching, Assessment.* http://www.coe.int/t/dg4/linguistic/CADRE_EN.asp Retrieved 02/10/07.

Cox, C. and Hill, D. (2004) *EAP Now! English for Academic Purposes.* Frenchs Forest: Pearson Education Australia.

Coxhead, A. (2000) A new academic word list. *TESOL Quarterly*, 34/2, pages 213–238.

Coxhead, A. (2006) *Essentials of Teaching Academic Vocabulary.* Massachusetts: Houghton Mifflin.

Coxhead, A. and Nation, I. S. P. (2001) The specialised vocabulary of English for academic purposes. In Flowerdew, J. and Peacock, M. (eds.)(2001) pages 252–267.

Cumming, A., Kantor, R., Baba, K., Erdosy, U., Eouanzoui, K. and James, M. (2005) Differences in written discourse in independent and integrated prototype tasks for next generation TOEFL. *Assessing Writing*, 10, pages 5–43.

Cunningham, S. and Moor, P. (1998) *Cutting Edge Intermediate Students' Book.* Harlow: Addison Wesley Longman.

Davison, C. (2004) The contradictory culture of teacher-based assessment: ESL teacher assessment practices in Australia and Hong Kong secondary schools. *Language Testing*, 21/3, pages 305–334.

Ding, A., Jones, M., and King, J. (2004) Perfect match? Meeting EAP teachers' needs and expectations in training. BALEAP Professional Issues Meeting, *Teacher Training in EAP*: University of Essex.

Douglas, D. (2000) *Assessing Language for Specific Purposes.* Cambridge: Cambridge University Press.

Dudley-Evans, T. (2002) The teaching of the academic essay; is a genre approach possible? In Johns, A. (ed.)(2002) pages 225–236.

Dudley-Evans, T. and St. John, M. (1998) *Developments in English for Specific Purposes.* Cambridge: Cambridge University Press.

Edwards, C. and Willis, J. (2005) *Teachers Exploring Tasks in English Language Teaching.* Basingstoke: Palgrave Macmillan.

Ellis, G. and Sinclair, B. (1989) *Learning to Learn English: Teacher's Book.* Cambridge: Cambridge University Press.

Ellis, R. (2005) *Instructed Second Language Acquisition: a Literature Review.* Wellington: Ministry of Education, New Zealand. http://www.educationcounts.edcentre.govt.nz/publications/downloads/instructed-second-language.pdf Retrieved 20/07/07.

Evans, S. and Green, C. (2007) Why EAP is necessary: a survey of Hong Kong tertiary students. *Journal of English for Academic Purposes*, 6/1, pages 3–17.

Feez, S. (1998) *Text-based Syllabus Design*. Sydney, NSW: AMES.

Field, J. (1998) Skills and strategies: towards a new methodology for listening. *ELT Journal*, 52/2, pages 110–118.

Field, J. (2007) Looking outwards, not inwards. *ELT Journal*, 61/1, pages 30–38.

Finney, D. (2002) The ELT curriculum: a flexible model for a changing world. In Richards, J. C. and Reynandya, W. A. (eds.)(2002) *Methodology in Language Teaching: an Anthology of Current Practice*. Cambridge: Cambridge University Press.

Flowerdew, J. (ed.)(1994) *Academic Listening: Research Perspectives*. Cambridge: Cambridge University Press.

Flowerdew, J. (2002) Genre in the classroom: a linguistic approach. In Johns, A. M. (ed.)(2002).

Flowerdew, J. (2003) Signalling nouns in discourse. *English for Specific Purposes*, 22/4, pages 329–346.

Flowerdew, J. and Miller, L. (1992) Student perceptions, problems and strategies in second language lecture comprehension. *RELC Journal*, 23/2, pages 60–80.

Flowerdew, J. and Miller, L. (1996) Lectures in a second language: notes towards a cultural grammar. *English for Specific Purposes*, 15/2, pages 121–140.

Flowerdew, J. and Miller, L. (1997) The teaching of academic listening comprehension and the question of authenticity. *English for Specific Purposes*, 16/1, pages 27–46.

Flowerdew, J. and Peacock, M. (eds.)(2001) *Research Perspectives on English for Academic Purposes*. Cambridge: Cambridge University Press.

Flowerdew, L. (1998) A cultural perspective on group work. *ELT Journal*, 52/4, pages 323–329.

Flowerdew, L. (2000) Using a genre-based framework to teach organisational structure in academic writing. *ELT Journal*, 54/4, pages 369–378.

Fulcher, G. and Davidson, F. (2007) *Language Testing and Assessment*. London: Routledge.

Furneaux, C. and Rignall, M. (1997) *English for Academic Study: Speaking*. London: Prentice Hall/Phoenix ELT.

Gardner, P. S. (2005) *New Directions: Reading Writing and Critical Thinking.* 2nd edn. New York: Cambridge University Press.

Gardner, S. (2007) *Conclusions in the introduction?* Posting to the BALEAP discussion list, baleap@jiscmail.ac.uk sent 29/06/07.

Garner, M. and Borg, E. (2005) An ecological perspective on content-based instruction. *Journal of English for Academic Purposes*, 4/2, pages 119–134.

Gavioli, L. and Aston, G. (2001) Enriching reality: language corpora in language pedagogy. *ELT Journal* 55/3, pages 238–246.

Ghadessy, M., Henry A. and Roseberry, R.L. (eds.)(2001). *Small Corpus Studies in ELT: Theory and Practice.* Amsterdam: John Benjamins.

Gillett, A. J. (n.d.) Using English for Academic Purposes: A Guide for Students in Higher Education. Academic Writing. School of Combined Studies University of Hertfordshire. http://www.uefap.com/writing/writfram.htm Retrieved 08/11/07.

Gillet, A. J. (last updated 2005) *Vocabulary in EAP.* http://www.uefap.co.uk/vocab/vocfram.htm Retrieved 10/04/07.

Gillett, A. J. and Hammond, A. (2008 in press) Mapping the maze of assessment: an investigation into practice. Forthcoming in *Active Learning in Higher Education.*

Glendinning, E. H. and Holmstrom, B. (2004) *Study Reading.* 2nd edn. Cambridge: Cambridge University Press.

Glendinning, E. and Mantell, H. (1983) *Write Ideas.* Harlow: Longman.

Granger, S. and Tyson, S. (1996) The use of connectors in the English essay writing of native and non-native students. *World Englishes* 15/1, pages 17–27.

Green, A. (2005) EAP study recommendations and score gains on the IELTS academic writing test. *Assessing Writing*, 10, pages 44–60.

Green, A. (2006) Washback to the learner: learner and teacher perspectives on IELTS preparation course expectations and outcomes. *Assessing Writing*, 11, pages 113–134.

Haarman, L., Leech, P. and Murray, J. (1988) *Reading Skills for the Social Sciences.* Oxford: Oxford University Press.

Halliday, M. A. K. revised by Matthiessen, Christian M. I. M. (2004) *An Introduction to Functional Grammar.* 3rd edn. London: Arnold.

Halliday, M. A. K. and Hasan, R. (1976) *Cohesion in English.* London: Longman.

Hamp-Lyons, L. and Heasley, B. (2006) *Study Writing.* 2nd edn. Cambridge: Cambridge University Press.

Hart, I. B. (1961) *The World of Leonardo da Vinci*. London: MacDonald.

Harthill, J. (2000) Assessing postgraduates in the real world. In Blue *et al.* (eds.)(2000) pages 117–130.

Haywood, S. (2003) Making effective use of the AWL. BALEAP Professional Issues Meeting, *Academic Vocabulary*. http://www.baleap.org.uk/pimreports/2003/warwick/abstracts.htm Retrieved 10/04/07.

Hedge, T. (2000) *Teaching and Learning in the Language Classroom*. Oxford: Oxford University Press.

Hill, J. and Lewis, M. (2000) Classroom strategies, activities and exercises. In Lewis, M. (ed.)(2000).

Hitchcock, R. (2007) Evolving academic identities: expectation and understandings affecting transition from the home (Chinese) to a UK EAP setting. BALEAP Conference (2007) *EAP in a Globalising World: an Academic Lingua Franca*.

Ho, W. K. and Wong, R. Y. L. (2004) Epilogue. In Ho, W. K. and Wong, R. Y. L. (eds.)(2004) pages 455–465.

Ho, W. K. and Wong, R. Y. L. (eds.)(2004) *English Language Teaching in East Asia Today: Changing Policies and Practices*. Singapore: Eastern Universities Press by Marshall Cavendish.

Holme, R. and Chalauisaeng, B. (2006) The Learner as needs analyst: the use of participatory appraisal in the EAP reading classroom. *English for Specific Purposes*, 28/4, pages 403–419.

Hughes, A. (2003) *Testing for Language Teachers*. 2nd edn. Cambridge: Cambridge University Press.

Hyland, K. (1999) Academic attribution: citation and the construction of disciplinary knowledge. *Journal of Applied Linguistics*, 20/3, pages 341–367.

Hyland, K. (2004) *Genre and Second Language Writing*. Ann Arbor: University of Michigan Press.

Hyland, K. (2004) *Disciplinary Discourses: Social Interactions in Academic Writing*. 2nd edn. Ann Arbor: University of Michigan Press.

Hyland, K. (2006) *English for Academic Purposes: an Advanced Resource Book*. Abingdon, UK: Routledge.

Hyland, K. and Hyland, F. (2006) *Feedback in Second Language Writing*. Cambridge: Cambridge University Press.

Jackson, L., Meyer, W. and Parkinson, J. (2006) A study of the writing tasks and reading assigned to undergraduate science students at a South African University. *English for Specific Purposes*, 25/3, pages 260–281.

Jin, L. (1992) Academic Cultural Expectations and Second Language use: Chinese Postgraduate Students in the UK – A Cultural Synergy Model. Unpublished PhD Thesis, University of Leicester.

Jin, L. and Cortazzi, M. (2004) English Language Teaching in China: a bridge to the future. In Ho, W. K. and Wong, R. Y. L. (eds.)(2004) pages 119–134.

Johns, A. M. (1997) Text, *Role and Context: Developing Academic Literacies*. Cambridge: Cambridge University Press.

Johns, A. M. (2002) *Genre in the Classroom: Multiple Perspectives*. Mahwah, NJ: Lawrence Erlbaum Associates.

Jones, J. F. (1999) From silence to talk: cross-cultural ideas on students' participation in academic group discussion. *English for Specific Purposes*, 18/3, pages 243–259.

Jordan, R. R. (1997) *Academic Writing*. 2nd edn. London: Longman.

Jordan, R. R. (1997) *English for Academic Purposes: a Guide and Resource Book for Teachers*. Cambridge: Cambridge University Press.

Jordan, R. R. (2002) The growth of EAP in Britain. *Journal of English for Academic Purposes*, 1/1, pages 69–78.

Kiely, R. (2001) Classroom evaluation – values, interests and teacher development. *Language Teaching Research*, 5/3, pages 241–261.

King, A. (1992) Comparison of self-questioning, summarizing, and notetaking-review as strategies for learning from lectures. *American Educational Research Journal*, 29/2, pages 303–323.

King, P. (1994) Visuals and verbal messages in the engineering lecture: note-taking by postgraduate L2 students. In Flowerdew, J. (ed.)(1994) pages 219–238.

Kirkpatrick, A. (2007) EAP in a globalising world: English as an academic lingua franca. BALEAP Conference (2007) *EAP in a Globalising World: an Academic Lingua Franca*.

Klenowski, V. (2002) *Developing Portfolios for Learning and Assessment*. London: Routledge.

Krashen, S. (2005) Free voluntary reading: new research, applications and controversies. In Poedjosoedarmo, G. (ed.)(2005) *Innovative Approaches to Reading and Writing Instruction*. Singapore: SEAMO Regional Language Centre.

Kroll, B. (ed.)(2003) *Exploring the Dynamics of Second Language Writing*. Cambridge: Cambridge University Press.

Kurtz, D. W. (2006) Advice on giving a scientific talk. *Aspects of Variable Stars ASP Conference Series*, vol. 349. http://www.phys.au.dk/bachelor/studieordning/advice.pdf. Retrieved 26/02/07.

Kwok, C., Fox, D. and Meila, M. Adaptive real-time particle filters for robot localization *Robotics and Automation* (2003) Proceedings ICRA '03, IEEE International Conference. http://www.lasmea.univ-bpclermont.fr/ftp/pub/trassou/SLAM/biblioHorsNorme/slam%20icra%202003/2836.pdf Retrieved 10/10/07.

Lai, L. K. and Hamp-Lyons, L. (2001) Different learning patterns in self-access. *RELC Journal*, 32/2, pages 63–79

Lakoff, G. and Johnson M. (1980) *Metaphors We Live By*. Chicago: University of Chicago Press.

Laurillard, D. (2002) *Rethinking University Teaching: a Framework for the Effective Use of Learning Technologies*. London: Routledge Falmer.

Lave, J. and Wenger, E. (1991) *Situated Learning: Legitimate Peripheral Participation*. Cambridge: Cambridge University Press.

Lebauer, R. (2000) *Learn to Listen; Listen to Learn*. 2nd edn. White Plains, NY: Longman, Pearson Education.

Lewis, M. (1993) *The Lexical Approach: The State of ELT and a Way Forward*. Hove, UK: Language Teaching Publications.

Lewis, M. (ed.)(2000) *Teaching Collocation: Further Developments in the Lexical Approach*. Hove: Language Teaching Publications.

Lewis, M. (2000) There is nothing as practical as a good theory in Lewis, M. (ed.)(2000) pages 155–185.

Lewis, M. (2001) Lexis in the Syllabus. In Hall, D. and Hewings A. (eds.) (2001) *Innovations in English Language Teaching*, pages 46–54. Abingdon, UK: Routledge.

Lillis, T. M. (2001) *Student Writing: Access, Regulation, Desire*. London: Routledge.

Littlejohn, A. and Higgison, C. (2003) E-learning series no. 3: a guide for teachers. Learning and Teaching Support Network Generic Centre. http://ltsn.ac.uk/generic centre. Retrieved 12/06/03.

Liu, D. (2005) Plagiarism in ESOL students: is cultural conditioning truly the major culprit? *Point and counterpoint, ELT Journal*, 59/3, pages 234–241.

Liu, Ngar-Fun and Littlewood, W. (1997) Why do many students appear reluctant to participate in classroom learning discourse? System, 25/3, pages 371–384.

Longman Dictionary of Contemporary English (2004) Harlow: Longman.

Lumley, T. (2002) Assessment criteria in a large-scale writing test: what do they really mean to the raters? *Language Testing*, 19/3, pages 246–276.

Lynch, T. (2004) *Study Listening*. 2nd edn. Cambridge: Cambridge University Press.

Lynch, T. and Maclean, J. Exploring the benefits of task repetition and recycling for classroom language learning. *Language Teaching Research*, 4/3, pages 221–250.

McCarthy, M. (1991) *Discourse Analysis for Language Teachers*. Cambridge: Cambridge University Press.

McCarthy, M. (2000) *Vocabulary*. Oxford: Oxford University Press.

McCormack, J. and Slaght, J. (2006) *English for Academic Study: Extended Writing and Research Skills*. Reading: Garnet Education.

MacDonald, M., Badger, R. and White, G. (2000) The real thing?: authenticity and academic listening. *English for Specific Purposes*, 19/3, pages 253–267.

Macmillan Advanced Learner's Dictionary (2002) Oxford: Macmillan.

Marchant, C. (2006) Marking criteria for Masters assignments in Logistics and Supply Chain Management. Edinburgh: Unpublished internal report, Heriot-Watt University.

Marchant, C. (2007) *MSc in Logistics and Supply Chain Management: An Introductory Guide to Teaching and Learning at Heriot-Watt University*. Edinburgh: Unpublished course material, Heriot-Watt University.

Martin, J. (1992) *English Text: System and Structure*. Amsterdam: John Benjamins.

Martin, J. R. and Rose, D. (2003) *Working with Discourse: Meaning Beyond the Clause*. London: Continuum.

Massey University, School of Language Studies (updated November 2006) *Academic Word List*. http://language.massey.ac.nz/staff/awl/mostfreq1.shtml Retrieved 17/12/07.

Mavor, S. and Traynor, B. (2001) Aligning genre and practice with learning in Higher Education: an interdisciplinary perspective for course design and teaching. *English for Specific Purposes*, 20/4, pages 345–366.

Miller, C. R. (1984) Genre as social action. *Quarterly Journal of Speech*, 70, pages 151–167.

Morton, R. (1999) Abstracts as authentic material for EAP classes. *ELT Journal*, 53/3, pages 177–182.

Myers, G. (2000) Powerpoints: technology, lectures and changing genres. In Trosborg, A. (ed.)(2000) *Analysing Professional Genres*, pages 177–191. Amsterdam: John Benjamins.

Nation, I. S. P. (2001) *Learning Vocabulary in Another Language*. Cambridge: Cambridge University Press.

Nesi, H. (2003) Editorial. *Journal of English for Academic Purposes*, 2/1, pages 1–3.

Nesi, H. and Gardner, S. (2006) Variation in disciplinary culture: university tutors' views on assessed writing tasks. http://www2.warwick.ac.uk/fac/soc/celte/research/bawe/papers/ Retrieved 6/05/07.

Nicol, D. (in press 2008) Assessment for learner self-regulation: enhancing achievement in the first year using learning technologies. Assessment and Evaluation in Higher Education. Abstract available online at http://www.reap.ac.uk/ Retrieved 9/12/07.

North, R. and Hort, L. (2002) Cross-cultural influences on employee commitment in the hotel industry: some preliminary thoughts. *Research and Practice in Human Resource Management*, 10/1, pages 22–34.

Nukui, C. and Brooks, J. (2007) *Critical thinking*. TASK Series. Reading: Garnet Education.

Nuttall, C. (1996) *Teaching Reading Skills*. Oxford: Macmillan Education.

O'Malley, J. M. and Chamot, A. U. (1990) *Learning Strategies in Second Language Acquisition*. Cambridge Applied Linguistics. Cambridge: Cambridge University Press.

Oxford, R. L. (2002) Language learning strategies in a nutshell: update and ESL suggestions. In Richards, J. C. and Renandya, W. A. (eds.)(2002) pages 124–132.

Pallant, A. (2000) Developing critical thinking in writing. In Thompson, P. (ed.)(2000) pages 103–116.

Pallant, A. (2004) *English for Academic Study: Writing*. Reading: Garnet Education.

Paltridge, B. (2001) *Genre and the Language Learning Classroom*. Ann Arbor: University of Michigan Press.

Paltridge, B. (2006) *Discourse Analysis*. London: Continuum.

Partington, A. (1998) *Patterns and Meanings: Using Corpora for English Language Research and Teaching*. Amsterdam: John Benjamins.

Penaflorida, A. H. (2002) Nontraditional forms of assessment and response to student writing: a step toward learner autonomy. In Richards, J. C. and Renandya, W. A. (eds.)(2002) pages 344–353.

Perry, C. (2004) Addressing the needs of students from diverse cultural backgrounds with respect to academic writing. Unpublished proceedings of the Plagiarism: Prevention, Practice and Policy Conference. http://www.jiscpas.ac.uk/conference2006/documents/papers/2004papers19.pdf Retrieved 17/12/07.

Phillips, T. (2005) *Skills in English: Listening.* Level 3. Reading: Garnet Education.

Pilcher, J. (2005) *A Corpus Analysis.* Unpublished MSc dissertation, University of Edinburgh.

Pinker, S. (1994) *The Language Instinct.* London: Penguin Books.

Prensky, M. (2001) Digital Natives, Digital Immigrants. On the Horizon: NCB University Press, 9/5. http://www.marcprensky.com/writing/Prensky%20-%20Digital%20Natives,%20Digital%20Immigrants%20-%20Part1.pdf Retrieved 1/08/07.

Qualifications and Curriculum Authority National Curriculum Online. Learning across the curriculum: thinking skiiis. http://www.nc.uk.net/webdav/harmonise?Page/@id=6011andSession/@id=D_jcJsz93rfiWla537Ylqq Retrieved 13.10.07.

Qualifications and Curriculum Authority (updated 12/09/07), Curriculum 6th Form Schools. http://www.qca.org.uk/14-19/6th-form-schools/68_1871.htm Retrieved 13/10/07.

Qian, D. D. (2007) Assessing university students: searching for an English language exit test. *RELC Journal*, 38/1, pages 18–37.

Race, P. (1995) What has assessment done for us – and to us? In Knight, P. (ed.) (1995) *Assessment for Learning in Higher Education*, pages 61–74. London: Kogan Page.

Richards, J. C. (2005) Second thoughts on teaching listening. *RELC Journal*, 36/1, pages 85–92.

Richards, J. C. and Renandya, W. A. (eds.)(2002) *Methodology in Language Teaching: an Anthology of Current Practice.* Cambridge: Cambridge University Press.

Richards, J. C. and Rodgers, T. S. (2001) *Approaches and Methods in Language Teaching.* 2nd edn. Cambridge: Cambridge University Press.

Richards, R. (2000) How does the development of critical thinking relate to the demands of academic writing in Higher Education? In Thompson, P. (ed.) (2000) pages 88–102.

Robinson, P., Strong, G., Whittle, J. and Nobe, S. (2001) The development of EAP oral discussion ability. In Flowerdew, J. and Peacock, M. (eds.)(2001) pages 347–359.

Rosenthal, R. and Jacobson, L. (1968) *Pygmalion in the Classroom: Teacher Expectation and Pupils' Intellectual Development*. New York: Rinehart and Winston.

Rost, M. (1994) Online summaries as representations of lecture understanding. In Flowerdew, J. (ed.)(1994) pages 93–127.

Rost, M. (2002) *Teaching and Researching Listening*. Harlow: Longman Pearson.

Rust, C. (2002) The impact of assessment on student learning. *Active Learning in Higher Education, 3/2*, pages 145–148.

Salmon, G. (2004) *E-moderating: the Key to Teaching and Learning Online*. 2nd edn. London: Routledge Falmer.

Salter-Dvorak, H. (2007) Academic tourism or a truly multicultural community? Why international students need pragmatic training for British Higher Education. In Alexander, O. (ed.)(2007) pages 37–48.

Schrooten, W. (2006) Task-based language teaching and ICT: developing and assessing interactive multimedia for task-based language teaching. In Van den Branden, K. (ed.)(2006) pages 129–150.

Scollon, R. and Scollon, S. W. (1991) Topic confusion in English-Asian discourse. *In World Englishes, 10/2*, pages 113–125.

Scott, M. (2001) Comparing Corpora and identifying key words, collocations, frequency distributions through the WordSmith Tools suite of computer programmes. In Ghadessy, M., Henry, A. and Roseberry, R. L. (eds.)(2001) *Small Corpus Studies in ELT*. Amsterdam: John Benjamins.

Seitz, J. L. (2002) *Global Issues: an Introduction*. Oxford: Blackwell.

Sellen, D. (1982) *Skills in Action*. London: Hodder and Stoughton.

Sharpling, G. P. (2002) Learning to teach English for Academic Purposes. *ELTD, 6*, pages 82–94.

Silva, T., Reichelt, M., Chikuma, Y., Duval-Couetil, N., Mo, T.J., Velez-Renden, G. and Wood, S. (2003) Second language writing up close and personal: some success stories. In Kroll, B. (ed.)(2003) pages 93–114.

Sinclair, J. (1991) *Corpus, Concordance, Collocation*. Oxford: Oxford University Press.

Skehan, P. (1998) *A Cognitive Approach to Language Learning*. Oxford: Oxford University Press.

Skelton, J. (1988) The care and maintenance of hedges. *ELT Journal*, 42, pages 37–44.

Slaght, J. (2004) *English for Academic Study: Reading Source Book*. Reading: Garnet Education.

Smith, A. (2007) Developing critical awareness through case-based teaching. In Alexander, O. (ed.)pages 149–157.

Sowden, C. (2005) Plagiarism and the culture of multilingual students in higher education abroad. Point and counterpoint, *ELT Journal*, 59/3, pages 226–233 and 242–243.

Spratt, M. (2005) Washback and the classroom: the implications for teaching and learning of studies of washback from exams. *Language Teaching Research*, 9/1, pages 5–9.

Stern, L. A. and Solomon, A. (2006) Effective faculty feedback: the road less travelled. *Assessing Writing*, 11, pages 22–41.

Strodt-Lopez, B. (1991) Tying it all in: asides in university lectures. *Applied Linguistics*, 12/2. pages 117–140.

Sutherland, P., Badger, R. and White, G. (2002) How new students take notes at lectures. *Journal of Further and Higher Education*, 26/4, pages 377– 388.

Swales, J. (1990) *Genre Analysis*. Cambridge: Cambridge University Press.

Swales, J. (2004) *Research Genres: Exploration and Analysis*. Cambridge: Cambridge University Press.

Swales, J. M., Barks, D., Ostermann, A. C. and Simpson, R. C. (2001) Between critique and accommodation on an EAP course for Masters of Architecture students. *English for Specific Purposes*, 20, pages 439–458.

Swales, J. and Feak, C. (2004) *Academic Writing for Graduate Students*. 2nd edn. Ann Arbor: University of Michigan Press.

Tan Bee Tin (2003) Does talking with peers help learning? The role of expertise and talk in convergent group discussion tasks. *Journal of English for Academic Purposes*, 2/1, pages 53–66.

Thaiss, C. and Zawacki, T. M. (2006) *Engaged Writers Dynamic Disciplines*. Portsmouth, New Hampshire: Boynton/Cook Heinemann.

Thomas, J. (1983) Cross Cultural Pragmatic Failure. *Applied Linguistics* 4/2, pages 91–112.

Thompson, P. (ed.)(2000) *Patterns and Perspectives: Insights into EAP Writing Practice*. Reading: CALS, University of Reading.

Thurstun, J. and Candlin C. N. (1998) *Exploring Academic English: a Workbook for Student Essay Writing*. Sydney: NCELTR, Macquarie University.

Trimble, L. (1985) *English for Science and Technology: a Discourse Approach*. Cambridge: Cambridge University Press.

Turner, J. (2004) Language as academic purpose. *Journal of English for Academic Purposes* 3/2, pages 95–109

Upshur, J. A. and Turner, C. E. (1995) Constructing rating scales for second language tests. *ELT Journal*, 49/1, pages 3–12.

Urquhart, A. H. and Weir, C. J. (1998) *Reading in a Second Language*. London: Longman.

Vande Kopple, W. J. (1996) Using the concepts of given and new information in classes on the English language. *The Journal of TESOL France*, 3, 53–68. Reprinted in Tom Miller (ed.) *Functional Approaches to Written Text: Classroom Applications*. Washington, DC: United States Information Agency.

Van den Branden, K. (ed.)(2006) *Task-Based Language Education: From Theory to Practice*. Cambridge: Cambridge University Press.

Vygotsky, L. S. (1978) *Mind in Society*. Cambridge, MA: Harvard University Press.

Wajnryb, R. (1988) *Grammar Dictation*. Oxford: Oxford University Press.

Ward, J. (2007) Collocation and technicality in EAP engineering. *Journal of English for Academic Purposes*, 6/1, pages 18–35.

Warschauer, M. (2002) Networking into academic discourse. *Journal of English for Academic Purposes*, 1/1, pages 45–58.

Warwick, P. (2006) Well meaning but misguided: an initiative to provide targeted language support to Management Studies students. *Higher Education Academy*. http://www.heacademy.ac.uk/assets/York/documents/resources/resourcedatabase/id613_well_meaning_but_misguided.doc Retrieved 10/10/07.

Waters, M. and Waters, A. (1995) *Study Tasks in English*. Cambridge: Cambridge University Press.

Watson Todd, R. (2003) EAP or TEAP? *Journal of English for Academic Purposes*, 2/2, pages 147–156.

Weigle, S. C. (2002) *Assessing Writing*. Cambridge: Cambridge University Press.

Weir, C. (1993) *Understanding and Developing Language Tests*. Hemel Hempstead, UK: Prentice Hall.

Weir, C. J., Yang, H. and Jin, Y. (2000) *An Empirical Investigation of the Componentiality of L2 Reading for English for Academic Purposes.* Cambridge: Cambridge University Press.

Weissburg, R. and Buker, S. (1990) *Writing up Research.* Englewood, NJ: Prentice-Hall.

Wenger, E. (1999) *Communities of Practice: Learning, Meaning and Identity.* Cambridge: Cambridge University Press.

West, M. (1953) *A General Service List of English Words.* London: Longman, Green.

Williams, D. (2007) Editorial. *Biomaterials,* 28/16, page 2535.

Willis, J. (1996) *A Framework for Task-Based Learning.* Essex: Longman.

Woodward, T. (2003) Loop input. *ELT Journal.* 57/3, pages 301–304.

Woolard, G. (2000) Collocation: encouraging learner independence. In Lewis, M. (ed.)(2000) pages 28–46.

Zhang X-Y and Austin, B. (2005) Haemolysins in *Vibrio* Species. *Journal of Applied Microbiology,* 98, pages 1011–1019.

Index

cultural differences 10, 11–12, 17, 155, 220, 239

curriculum 81, 81f

Davidson , F. 326

deep-end performance 110–11

diagnostic tests 305–6, 324

dictionaries 162, 165, 174–5, 179, 297

discourse grammar 76–7, 92, 141

'discuss' 28

discussion and brainstorming 205–7; *see also* group discussions

discussion boards 114, 297

discussion forums 117

dissertations 125, 134

distributed learning 114

documented essays 182

double-loop learning 294–5

Douglas, D. 315

e-learning 17, 113–17
  advantages 114, 117
  assessment 115
  disadvantages 114–15
  rationale for use 115–16

e-mail 12, 114, 117, 210, 297

Edwards (2004) 245–6

ellipsis 57, 59

English as an international language 25–6

English for Academic Purposes (EAP) 6
  key features 3–5, 3–5t, 18–19
  types of courses 81

English Language Teaching (ELT) 2, 3–5t

essays 182, 202, 297–8, 309–10, 322

examinations, global proficiency *see* language tests

examinations, university 27–8, 183–4, 310, 314

experiential learning 87

Feak, C. 54

feedback 180, 209, 210–13, 248–9, 313–14; *see also* formative assessment; peer assessment; self–assessment

Feez, S. 343n21

field 37

Field, J. 232, 272

Flowerdew, J. 70

focus on form 111, 227

formative assessment 305–6, 307, 326–7, 336–8

Fulcher, G. 326

functions *see* rhetorical functions

General Service Word List (GSL) 158, 160, 347n16

genre 35, 43–8
  in academic writing 181–4
  definitions 37, 53
  functions–genre relationship 53–7
  moves 45–6, 54, 56
  questions for students 47–8
  syllabus design 91
  text selection 133, 135
  views of genre 47
  writing in the EAP classroom 146, 191, 199–200, 201–4

genre chains/systems 184

gist 77

global reading 120, 145

grammar 35, 76–7, 89–90, 92, 141, 164–5

graphs 198

Green, A. 320

group discussions 236–44, 250
  activities 244
  approaches 243–4
  awareness 243
  conventions of group discussion 236–40
  difficulties for EAP students 236, 237–40
  peer feedback 244
  supporting students 243–4
  vs. speaking skills lessons 240–2

Sharpling, G. P. 9
sheltered EAP model 20
signalling nouns 58, 59, 70, 220, 224
Silva, T. et al. 187–8(n19), 192
Sinclair, J. 72
single-loop learning 294
skimming 130, 143
speaking
    classroom assessment 322, 326
    difficulties for EAP students 216, 236
    students' needs 235–6
    see also group discussions; oral
    presentations
Spratt, M. 320–1
student autonomy: development through
    classroom practice 282–302
    creating a context 291–3
    developing reflection 293–301
    and e-learning 114
    plan–do–review cycle 294, 294f, 297
    role of the teacher 282–91, 283f, 293
    student collaboration 290–1
student autonomy as teaching aim
    271–81
    challenges for EAP students 272–3
    definition 271
    self-access centres 273–4
    study competence 274–81
    study skills 175, 274–7
    see also student autonomy: development
    through classroom practice
student expectations 10–16
student needs 84–5, 86, 88–9, 94–8,
    235–6
study competence 274–81
study groups 221
study skills 16, 26, 175, 274–7
substitution 57, 59
summarizing 173, 195, 221, 233
summative assessment 305, 306–7
Swales, J. 54
Swales (2005) 127, 201
syllabus design 83–105
    academic skills 93

building the framework 88–98
content and topics 92, 99–105
course goals and aims 86
design process 83f, 94
discourse grammar 92
experiential learning 87
genres and texts 91
integration 87
needs 86, 88–9, 94–8
organizing principles 86–8
progression 87
recycling 87
rhetorical functions 90–1, 96
role of the classroom teacher 98–105
role of the syllabus 82–3
sentence grammar 89–90
tasks 93
transfer of learning 87–8
types of syllabus 88, 343n21
vocabulary 90
see also critical thinking in the EAP
    classroom

task-based learning and teaching 106,
    110–11, 137, 145–6, 267–9
tasks 21, 93, 227, 231–5
teacher expectations 16–17, 20, 341n42
teacher-training needs 105
teacher's role 282–91, 283f, 293
    advising 283, 286
    controlling 282–3, 285, 287
    facilitating 283, 286
    supervising 283, 285–6
    in syllabus design 98–105
teacher–student relationship 7, 11–12,
    14, 217, 220, 237, 293
teaching and learning at university 7–9
    activities and skills 7–8, 8t
    methods 7
    student expectations 10–16
    teacher expectations 16–17
    see also learning; teaching and learning
    in EAP

vocabulary in the EAP classroom
157–77
  activities 171–4
  concordances 165–7, 166f, 175
  context-based approach 159
  corpora 167–8
  exploring vocabulary 174–6
  frequency 157–9
  function 159–60, 161, 174
  gap-fill activities 172–3, 175
  knowledge about words 161–8
  language reference pages 170, 295,
    352n42
  learning strategies 174–275
  lexical approach 159, 165
  noticing and recording 168–71
  recording formats 170–1
  researching language 165–8
  selection criteria 146, 152–3, 161
  subject-related vocabulary 160, 198,
    213
  summary writing 173
  tests 323–4
  vocabulary selection 157–61
  writing tasks 173–4

Warschauer, M. 115
Warwick, P. 98(n48)
Waters, A. 274
Waters, M. 274
Williams, D. 340n14
writing at university 178–98, 214
  academic style 186
  academic writers 187–9
  assessment 181–2
  concerns of EAP students 178–9
  developing academic writers 189–98
  examination answers 183–4
  fluency 189
  genres 181–4
  lecturers' expectations 22–5, 27,
    184–7
  questions for students 77
  reading as foundation for writing 188

  texts 181–4
writing in the EAP classroom 136,
  189–214
  concerns of EAP teachers 179–80
  diagnostic tests 324
  discussion and brainstorming 205–7
  errors 210
  feedback 180, 207–13
  formative testing 326
  genre 146, 191, 199–200, 201–4
  individual conferencing 210–13
  marking 213, 255
  peer-assessment 207–8
  planning and drafting 206–7
  process approach 199, 200–1, 204–13
  purpose and audience 190–2
  reformulation 213
  scaffolding 202
  self-assessment 207–9, 210
  teacher-assessment 209
  timed writing 323
  writing from data 106–8, 195–8
  writing from sources 192–5
  see also writing at university
writing texts for the classroom 134–6

Zawacki, T. M. 182, 186–7, 188,
  192, 194